changing the way the world learns℠

To get extra value from this book for no additional cost, go to:

http://www.thomson.com/wadsworth.html

thomson.com is the World Wide Web site for Wadsworth/ITP and is your direct source to dozens of on-line resources. *thomson.com* helps you find out about supplements, experiment with demonstration software, search for a job, and send e-mail to many of our authors. You can even preview new publications and exciting new technologies.

thomson.com: *It's where you'll find us in the future.*

Dedication

Captain Steven Simmons
Minneapolis Police Department
1943–1995

As this text was nearing completion, the authors lost a colleague and friend. In December 1995 Steve Simmons died after a five-year battle with cancer. At the time of his death, Steve held the rank of captain with the Minneapolis Police Department. He had been a faculty member of the law enforcement department at Normandale Community College (Bloomington, Minnesota) and at Minneapolis Community College. Steve was, in every sense of the word, a legal scholar.

Steve had a bachelor of science degree in sociology with specialization in criminal justice studies from the University of Minnesota. He also attended the University of Minnesota Graduate School, the Minnesota Management Academy and the Police Executive Research Forum, Senior Management Institute for Police.

Steve began his career in law enforcement as a Minneapolis patrol officer from 1966 to 1973, serving in the patrol division, the special operations division and the planning and research unit. He was promoted to lieutenant in 1973 and served as an investigator in homicide, family violence and burglary, as well as an administrative assistant to the chief, a training director and a shift commander. In 1992 he was promoted to captain. He balanced his life through his passion for family and sailing.

Steve Simmons lived the law and upheld the United States Constitution through his work as a police officer and educator. But more importantly, Steve was a friend. He embodied every attribute of the professional law enforcement officer, and he will be sorely missed by the community he served, his students, his friends and his family. It was our intention to present this dedication to him in person. We are sorry that we were not able to do so.

"May you always have blue skies, a pleasant breeze and good sailing."

Constitutional Law for Criminal Justice Professionals

J. Scott Harr, JD
Kären M. Hess, PhD

West/Wadsworth
I⊤P® an International Thomson Publishing Company

Belmont, CA ■ Albany, NY ■ Bonn ■ Boston ■ Cincinnati ■ Detroit ■ Johannesburg
London ■ Los Angeles ■ Madrid ■ Melbourne ■ Mexico City ■ New York ■ Paris
Singapore ■ Tokyo ■ Toronto ■ Washington

Criminal Justice Editor:
Sabra Horne

Assistant Editor:
Claire Masson

Editorial Assistant:
Kate Barrett

Marketing Manager:
Mike Dew

Senior Project Editor:
Debby Kramer

Print Buyer:
Karen Hunt

Production:
Clarinda Company

Designer:
David J. Farr,
ImageSmythe

Copy Editor:
Trish Finley

Cover:
Ross Carron

Compositor:
Clarinda Company

Printer:
West Publishing Company

Indexer:
Christine M. H. Orthmann

COPYRIGHT © 1998 by Wadsworth
Publishing Company A Division of
International Thomson Publishing Inc.
I(T)P® The ITP logo is a registered
trademark under license.

Printed in the United States of America
3 4 5 6 7 8 9 10

For more information, contact Wadsworth
Publishing Company, 10 Davis Drive,
Belmont, CA 94002, or electronically at
http://www.thomson.com/wadsworth.html

International Thomson Publishing Europe
Berkshire House 168-173
High Holborn
London, WC1V7AA, England

Thomas Nelson Australia
102 Dodds Street
South Melbourne 3205
Victoria, Australia

Nelson Canada
1120 Birchmount Road
Scarborough, Ontario
Canada M1K 5G4

International Thomson Publishing GmbH
Königswinterer Strasse 418
53227 Bonn, Germany

International Thomson Editores
Campos Eliseos 385, Piso 7
Col. Polanco
11560 México D.F. México

International Thomson Publishing Asia
221 Henderson Road
#05-10 Henderson Building
Singapore 0315

International Thomson Publishing Japan
Hirakawacho Kyowa Building, 3F
2-2-1 Hirakawacho
Chiyoda-ku, Tokyo 102, Japan

International Thomson Publishing
  Southern Africa
Building 18, Constantia Park
240 Old Pretoria Road
Halfway House, 1685 South Africa

**Library of Congress
Cataloging-in-Publication Data**

Harr, J. Scott.
    Constitutional law for criminal justice
        professionals / J. Scott Harr,
        Kären M. Hess.
        p.   cm.
    Includes bibliographical references
        and index.
    ISBN 0-314-20414-8 (hardcover : alk.
        paper)
    1. Criminal procedure—United States.
        2. Criminal investigation—
United States.   3. Civil rights—
    United States.   I. Hess,
        Kären M.   II. Title.
KF9619.3.H36   1997
345.73′05—dc21   96-50481

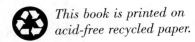 *This book is printed on
acid-free recycled paper.*

Brief Contents

Contents

5 **Knowing Where to Find the Law**   72

Section Three **The Guarantees of the Constitution to Citizens: Civil Rights and Civil Liberties**   86

6 **Equal Protection under the Law: Balancing Individual, State and Federal Rights**   88

List of Illustrations

List of Tables

List of Cases

About the Authors

Scott Harr's interest in the law stems from having worked in a variety of legal jobs for more than 20 years. He is presently the public safety director in one of Minneapolis' fastest growing suburbs and has been a police officer for two other cities as well, serving as both a patrol officer and police/school liaison officer. He attended William Mitchell College of Law in St. Paul, Minnesota, where he received the Warren E. Burger Award. He completed his law degree at Cambridge University, England. As a member of the United States Supreme Court bar, Scott is among the attorneys permitted to practice before the Court. Scott is a licensed attorney, police officer and private investigator in Minnesota. He founded Scott Harr Legal Investigations. In addition to *Constitutional Law for Criminal Justice Professionals,* he coauthored *Criminal Procedure* and *Seeking Employment in Criminal Justice and Related Fields,* and contributed to numerous other titles. He has taught college-level courses in constitutional law, criminal procedure, juvenile justice, introduction to law enforcement, report writing and private security.

Kären Hess holds a PhD in English from the University of Minnesota and a PhD in criminal justice from Pacific Western University. She has been developing instructional programs for 30 years. Kären coauthored *Community Policing: Theory and Practice, Criminal Investigation, Criminal Procedure, Introduction to Law Enforcement and Criminal Justice, Juvenile Justice, Police Operations* and *Seeking Employment in Criminal Justice and Related Fields.*

Foreword

Jim Ramstad, R, Minnesota
Member of the United States House
of Representatives

More than 200 years ago, our nation's founders wrote a remarkable document—our Constitution. It is just as relevant now as it was in 1787. To this day, newly freed peoples across the world refer to it when crafting their own constitutions.

The drafters of this great text were artists. While you can read the Constitution in a matter of minutes, you will not appreciate its wonders until you examine each word, phrase and clause.

Like a work of fine art, one person's interpretation of the Constitution will differ from another's. So, too, does one generation's interpretation differ from another's.

That is why the study of constitutional law is a never-ending process, and for good reason. The America of today differs markedly from the America of 1787 and will no doubt change profoundly again in the next 200 years. The challenges and issues we face today simply didn't exist in earlier times.

As a lawmaker and former constitutional law professor at American University, I revere our Constitution and greatly enjoy studying its relationship to our lives today.

I highly commend Scott Harr and Kären Hess for writing this outstanding text on constitutional law. I'm confident the reader will soon gain our enthusiasm for the Constitution and the field of constitutional law.

Preface

Constitutional law—no other subject affects our daily lives as does the Constitution of the United States. Each of us can go about our lives in a fairly predictable, safe way because of the guarantees and freedoms assured by our Constitution.

What we, the authors of this text, have had personally reinforced as we have written this book is how wonderfully "simply complex" the United States Constitution is. It is brief and to the point, but serves as the cornerstone of the most fair and workable legal system to ever exist in any culture.

When you walk into any law library, the sheer volume of material is overwhelming. Yet to remain law, every one of these books must balance ever so delicately on that one other, much smaller, document—the United States Constitution. This is a heavy burden for the Constitution to bear, yet it has done so admirably for over two centuries.

Perhaps it is the very essence of the Constitution that makes it such a difficult, yet fascinating, work to study. When the document was drafted in 1787, it was never meant to be an all-inclusive compendium of legal answers. It was intended as a basic framework within which all other law must remain.

As proof that the law being discussed is indeed real and exists, we are honored to include photos of original manuscripts generously provided by Mr. David Karpeles, founder and director of the Karpeles Manuscript Libraries. Imagine the privilege of being able to view the actual signature of Abraham Lincoln or to view the same document provided to Benjamin Franklin! History is *not* just a concept—it is real. Mr. Karpeles collects handwritten drafts, letters and documents to provide the original reference sources from which to learn. Through his generosity the public may view his many, many documents free of charge by visiting his libraries located in California, New York, Washington, Florida, Minnesota and South Carolina.

Those drafting the Constitution had a timeless vision. They knew society would change, as would its needs. They realized they could never foresee all the issues their country would confront (and what issues there are!). But what the framers of our Constitution successfully accomplished was to develop the charters that established our uniquely *American* legal system. The basic organizational structure is created so no one person, royalty or dictator, shall ever have total rule, and so that a handful of precious basic rights are assured. *This* is what the United States Constitution is about. It is really quite simple.

So why does a course in constitutional law strike fear into the hearts of students everywhere? The answer is because anything that has worked so well for so many, for so long, *must* have some built-in complexity. And it does—*interpretation.*

The Constitution works because those who wrote it more than 200 years ago provided only basic tenets, leaving the challenge of interpreting them as they relate to *current* issues. For example, free speech issues are decidedly different today than two centuries ago—but the basic idea remains. The First and Fourth Amendments still guide government investigations, but such matters as the use of very sophisticated electronic eavesdropping and computer equipment now become an issue.

So it is how people *interpret* the Constitution that can cause confusion. For all who are certain how the Constitution should be read (in their favor, of course), others are just as sure it should be interpreted differently. And today's issues of abortion, gun control and the environment *beg* for interpretation, flip-flopping back and forth, up and down, through our legal system, always searching for a final interpretation. Most often, the United States Supreme Court, as the final arbiter of law, tells us what the interpretation is—until the Court makes a change itself. Or until another case with a slightly different twist than previous cases is decided differently.

Little wonder that when you begin your study of constitutional law frustration looms. "It just does not make sense," you say. But wait. The Constitution *does* make sense. What *is* confusing are the interpretations and arguments people develop to try and make the Constitution work for them. It is more accurate to say it is the *people* who are confusing, and confused, rather than the document itself. Sometimes, with enough effort, persistence and good legal argument, a decision is reached, and thus law is made that does not always *seem* to make sense. But when you return to the basic tenets of the Constitution itself, recalling the purpose for which it was drafted, the very sensible basics are there.

No arguments or legal philosophies will be presented in this text. Rather, the text will set out basic constitutional law. This text, along with your effort at learning, will provide you with a basic understanding of how the Constitution works, and why.

Don't get frustrated. If something does not seem to make sense, stop and reexamine it from a different perspective. This is how people successfully argue their points. Do not take everything at face value, and do not take it too seriously. Work with it, think about it, challenge yourself. Develop your understanding of the Constitution a bit at a time. It is far too large a pool of knowledge to leap into without learning the basics first. *Ease* into it. To do so any other way will result in unnecessary frustration. Soon enough you will find yourself immersed in the subject and as fascinated with it as others are.

This text is unlike most traditional legal works and was prepared this way intentionally. Our teaching experience and feedback from students and educators alike gave us the resounding message that there was a desire for something other than a traditional casebook approach to learning "con law." While there is certainly a place for traditional texts, people with whom we consulted wanted a text that fell between basic civics books and law school-level casebooks. Our text was written in response to what many told us they wanted. It is different, however, and this paradigm shift has not been embraced by the entire academic community. But for those who want an easy, painless journey through the fascinating study of American constitutional law, this text was written for you.

This approach to the study of constitutional law was welcomed by a reviewer of the manuscript who wrote:

> To clarify my attitude about this text I am going to start off this review with a point from my past. Some years ago I was in the midst of a civil trial in Denver. During a break I went down to the courthouse law library to check on a point of law. While standing in all my pin-striped splendor reading a casebook, a young, obviously poor woman, dragging a small child, approached me. She asked, "Are you a lawyer?" I responded, "Yes." She then asked, "Can you show me the book that has my rights in it?" I looked around at all the thousands of books in the rather large library and had an awakening. I realized that I could not even begin to explain where to look. I gave her some vague advice about legal aid and hurried from the room. Within a year I quit my city job and started the road to finding how I could teach the law to other-than-driven law students and those who were already sure they knew it. I wish at the time there had been a book like *Constitutional Law for Criminal Justice Professionals* to refer to that woman.

We have written the text to make the learning as enjoyable and productive as possible. It was written with you, the student, in mind. We have developed a natural progression to help you build your knowledge. Even the layout was done in a way that will make the learning less tedious. You will notice lots of white space to make the reading easier, with enough space to make notes or references as you proceed. Plain language is preferred to *legalese*. The traditional casebook approach to teaching constitutional law has been abandoned here because it is simply too difficult a way to learn legal basics.

Finally, be aware that mastering the basic concepts of constitutional law is only the beginning. American law is unique in that it can, and does, change to meet the changing needs of the society it serves. A part of the knowledge you will acquire is how to keep current with this changing, constantly evolving area of law.

We are excited for you as you begin this educational journey. American constitutional law is not a stagnant, boring subject. It is a vital, stimulating topic that is arguably the duty of every American to know . . . and to appreciate.

The authors would like to thank the reviewers of this text for their insightful comments and suggestions: Robert Chaires, University of Nevada, Reno; Michael Hughes, Scottsdale Community College; Ed Lee, Wallace State College, Alabama; Barbara May; Eric Moore, Texas A & M University, Corpus Christi; Michael Murray, attorney; Steven Murray, Community College of Rhode Island; William Schulman, Middle Tennessee State University; Kevin Weakley, Seward Community College, Kansas; Thomas Whitt, Fresno City College. Thank you also to Pamela Reierson, Normandale Community College, for her assistance in locating materials and references. A special thank you to Christine Hess Orthmann for proofreading and indexing and for preparing the Instructor's Manual. We would also like to thank our editors at West Publishing Company, Robert Jucha and Jana Otto Hiller, for their support, encouragement and advice and our production editor at Clarinda Company, Trish Finley, for her patience and skillful guidance of this manuscript through production.

Scott would like to acknowledge the influence of the following people in encouraging him to get to this point: Chief William Bernhjelm; Mayor Don Chmiel; Sergeant Dennis Conroy, PhD; Carol Dunsmore; Steve Gawron, Esq.; Reed and Barbara Harr; Hank Imm; Richard and Marie Lacy; Sergeant David Lindman; Richard Obershaw; Mrs. Yoonju Park; Lieutenant S. Schwartz; Sergeant Ray Weegman; Henry Wrobleski and Deputy Director Bob Zydowsky.

Scott would also like to acknowledge Major Choi, Sun Chang of the South Korean Air Force, and his wife, Park, Lipia, an educator in Seoul, Korea, for their contributions to this text. They helped him to better understand our Constitution by encouraging him to contemplate the world in which it works and by discussing law and society in a much more global manner than he could have done alone. Their friendship and profoundly positive influence on his family has been one of those unanticipated blessings that make life so grand! For all of this, he thanks them both. *Kahm sah hahm ni dah.*

Finally, Scott has a special thank you for his dearest wife, Diane Lacy Harr, daughter Kelsey and son Ricky with whom he has always shared his dreams. And from Kären, a special thank you to husband and best friend Sheldon, and to Christine and Tim—a family whose support and encouragement has been invaluable.

J. Scott Harr
Kären M. Hess

A Historical Overview

Section One

Study the Past—What Is Past Is Prologue. National Archives Building, Washington, D.C.

BEFORE YOU LOOK ahead, it is important to take time to reflect on the past. History seems to be an accurate predictor of the future, as it has a unique way of repeating itself.

As discussed in the introduction of this text, the topic of *constitutional law* can become complicated. This complexity prevents many students from taking time to learn about this area of law until they are *forced* to . . . and then it becomes drudgery. It does not have to be that way.

Any endeavor becomes easier if a firm base is established on which to build. For this reason a review of the historical evolution of the Constitution is important in developing not only a basic working knowledge of it, but also in learning to critically review how the Constitution plays into modern society and how it will shape our future. This section presents a discussion of the events leading up to the drafting of the United States Constitution (Chapter 1) and a broad overview of the Constitution and the Bill of Rights (Chapter 2).

Chapter 1   Events Leading up to the Constitution

Give me liberty, or give me death!

—PATRICK HENRY

The United States Capitol.

DO YOU KNOW . . .

What pluralism is and why it contributes so much to our society?

What empires were vying for control over territories in North America that lead to bloody confrontations?

What the Stamp Act was?

Why American colonists rebelled at Great Britain's taxes?

What the Quartering Act was?

What was symbolized by the Boston Tea Party?

What resulted from the First Continental Congress?

What resulted from the Second Continental Congress?

What the Declaration of Independence is?

What the Articles of Confederation were?

CAN YOU DEFINE THESE TERMS?

Loyalists
Minutemen
Patriots
Pluralism

INTRODUCTION

It has been said that the best way to know where you are going is to look where you have been. This chapter begins with a discussion of the roots of our Constitution and contributions from the past. This is followed by an examination of how the United States of America developed, including the convening of the First Continental Congress. Next the Revolution itself is described, including the convening of the Second Continental Congress, which resulted in the Declaration of Independence. The chapter concludes with an explanation of the Articles of Confederation, which established the first model for the United States government and the move toward the Constitution.

WHERE IT ALL BEGAN

The American Constitution (always written with a capital "C") is a relatively youthful work. But the history that influenced it can be traced back to when people first began to form groups. In an important way, every culture that has made its way to America has influenced our Constitution. Rules, which eventually become laws, are a part of *any* society. One reason American law is so unique is that many societies brought their laws with them when they came here, and these laws have helped form our laws.

The land that now comprises North America has always held an attraction. As long ago as 30,000 B.C. people began traversing the continent to seek something that held the promise of more than they had. And whether the motivations for these incredible journeys were as basic as food or as complicated as a search for political and religious freedoms, people came hoping for something better. This basic desire to seek out something more is the essence of the individuals who have contributed to the society that now exists. Figure 1–1 highlights important events in the United States and elsewhere.

CONTRIBUTIONS FROM THE PAST

Compared to the series of events that have contributed to and led up to the drafting of the Constitution itself, American law is very young. But the history cannot be ignored as this is the base on which our law has been constructed.

The earliest visitors to North America left their mark, which archaeologists can work with to better understand societal and cultural development. Similarly, by studying the events that have led to our present laws, we are better able to understand both how and why we have the laws we do.

Figure 1–1

Timeline of events in the Americas and elsewhere.

Source: Adapted from Richard C. Brown and Herbert J. Bass. *One Flag, One Land.* Morristown, NJ: Silver Burdett & Ginn, 1990, p. 21.

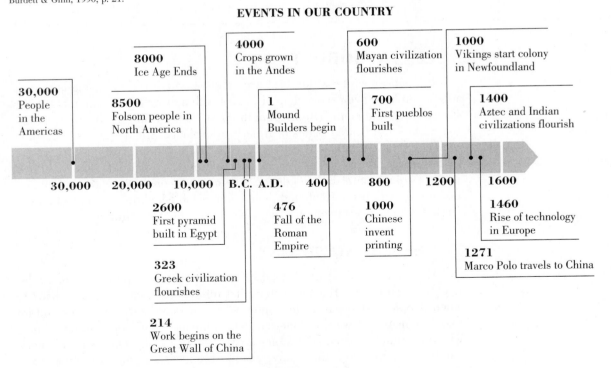

EVENTS IN OUR COUNTRY

30,000 People in the Americas

8000 Ice Age Ends

8500 Folsom people in North America

4000 Crops grown in the Andes

1 Mound Builders begin

600 Mayan civilization flourishes

700 First pueblos built

1000 Vikings start colony in Newfoundland

1400 Aztec and Indian civilizations flourish

30,000   20,000   10,000   B.C. A.D.   400   800   1200   1600

2600 First pyramid built in Egypt

323 Greek civilization flourishes

214 Work begins on the Great Wall of China

476 Fall of the Roman Empire

1000 Chinese invent printing

1460 Rise of technology in Europe

1271 Marco Polo travels to China

EVENTS ELSEWHERE

Representatives from every culture that have come to America, regardless of when they arrived or from where they came, share in the historical development of our country and legal system. It is the common thread that binds all who have come here—the desire for something better—that makes American law so unique in serving the society that created it.

Armento, et al. (1991, pp. 49–50) describe the concept of **pluralism** as a nation in which many ethnic, religious or cultural groups live together with the benefit that citizens of all such groups have a voice in the decision-making process of government.

> ⟫⟫ Pluralism refers to a society in which numerous distinct ethnic, religious or cultural groups coexist within one nation.

Before the colonization of the United States, the Native American tribes had their distinct territories, languages and cultures. Pluralism existed long before the colonists "discovered" America. When the colonists arrived and began taking over the land occupied by the Native Americans, the Native Americans began to band together in self-defense.

The colonists came from various countries and were of varied religions and cultures. Initially they settled in specific areas and maintained their original culture, for example, the Pennsylvania Dutch. They, too, represented pluralism.

A pluralistic society challenged the colonists to exercise tolerance and respect for the opinions, customs, traditions and lifestyles of others. Their diversity enriched early American life and strengthened the emerging nation. Often the distinct culture within a given colony influenced other colonies. For example, in 1682 William Penn, a Quaker and founder of Pennsylvania, set forth the "Great Law of Pennsylvania," abolishing corporal punishment, introducing fines and founding the first penetentiary—"dedicated to God." Penn's great law significantly influenced the development of corrections in America.

As more and more individuals inhabited North America, they were forced by necessity to interact. Established Native American cultures interacted with very foreign ways of life, and people became aware that there were different ways of developing a system for their lives. According to Armento, et al. (1991, p. 49), the ethnic population in the United States in 1775 was, by percentage:

48.7 English
20.0 African
 7.8 Scots-Irish
 6.9 German
 6.6 Scottish
 2.7 Dutch
 1.4 French
 0.6 Swedish
 5.3 Other

This illustrates that cultural and ethnic diversity has always been an attribute of America, with a rich blend in the 1700s. Interestingly, the Native Americans are absent from this chart as they were not considered part of the colonies. Also of interest is the 20% African population. This figure represents the slaves brought to this country to labor on southern plantations. While Native Americans and individuals of African ancestry are not always given the recognition they are due, they, too, have played a very important part in the development of America. Coexisting in the United States in 1775 were three large groups: the Native Americans, the African slaves and the colonists. The history of the United States, however, has generally focused on only the colonists.

Over time, interaction and, eventually, assimilation occurred among the colonists, commonly referred to as a "melting pot" because several different nationalities combined into what was known as "the American colonist." Such assimilation was encouraged by the vast, apparently unlimited resources available, as well as by the struggle for survival. Faced by the threat of foreign countries wishing to control them, as well as the dangers posed by the Native Americans they were displacing, it was natural that the colonists should band together. As noted by Miller and Hess (1994, pp. 117–118):

> The "melting pot" was accomplished relatively painlessly because of the many similarities among the cultures: they looked quite similar physically, they valued religion and "morality," most valued hard work, and, perhaps most important, there was plenty of land for everyone. The "homogenization" of the United States was fairly well accomplished . . . with the formerly distinct cultures blended into what became known as an American culture. . . .

These colonists, white male property holders, were sometimes referred to as a "seaboard aristocracy." They created the basic structure of our country as it still exists heading into the twenty-first century.

DEVELOPMENT OF THE UNITED STATES OF AMERICA

America was an attractive area for expansion of the world powers.

In addition to others, Spain, France and England saw great importance in adding the "New World" to their growing empires.

This desire for existing nations to make America a part of their government planted the tiny seed of what was to grow into independence. Just as Native Americans had seen their freedom threatened by the colonists, now the colonists realized that their freedom was in jeopardy from abroad.

An understanding of *why* and *how* the Constitution came about requires a review of events leading up to the American Revolution. The independence of the colonists in America, particularly at that time, established an identity that has made America a world leader. *Never* have Americans been willing to sit idly by while those asserting power attempted to coerce them into submission. When the colonies were confronted with attempts, primarily by Great Britain and France, to consume and control the New World, resistance grew, exemplifying the spirit associated with the United States of America.

Colonial Dissension Grows

As the population of the colonies began to grow, so did serious differences between those who saw themselves as free, independent colonies and those who wanted a foreign flag to fly over them. An ominous cloud was forming over North America. As existing empires positioned themselves both politically and militaristically to expand their boundaries into the New World, conflict was inevitable.

In 1750 French troops began arriving from Canada, building forts and laying claim to land that American Indians were occupying and that England was eyeing. Divine, et al. (1991, pp. 135–136) explain the showdown that eventually occurred in 1754 between the British and the French when British leaders ordered the governor of Virginia to use force to repel the French. George Washington and about 150 colonists marched against the French. By 1763, after the French and Indian War (1755–1763), French resistance was defeated, and the Treaty of Paris resulted in France losing most of the land it had claimed in America. But British problems were far from resolved.

Great Britain, according to Divine, et al. (1991, p. 42), was forced to confront two significant problems. One large problem was continued westward settlement by the colonists. This was a problem for Great Britain because the Indians fought to protect their land from the colonists, and the British army was not able to protect the isolated frontier settlements. As noted by Divine, et al. (p. 142): "Nearly 2,000 colonial men, women, and children died during what has become known as Pontiac's Rebellion. In December 1763 British and colonial troops finally crushed the Indians' defense of their territory."

When King George III learned of the fighting, he issued the Proclamation of 1763, which closed the western frontier to colonial settlement and placed it under military rule. Settlers already there were ordered to leave.

The second major problem facing Great Britain was the huge debt resulting from English military action to expand the empire. They felt the colonists should share this debt.

The colonies resisted the restrictions to westward settlement and to paying for Great Britain's war debts. Significant leaders had begun emerging, including George Washington, Benjamin Franklin, Paul Revere and Thomas Jefferson. These leaders had found strength in cooperating to resist the French. But now the resistance was redirected toward the British Parliament's obvious efforts to control America.

Because Parliament thought it only fair that the American colonies share in the expenses incurred, they passed acts to collect monies from the colonists.

> In 1765 Parliament passed the *Stamp Act,* requiring stamps to be purchased and placed on such items as legal documents and commodities.

Stamps attached by the British government to goods sold in the American colonies. (Provided by Corbis-Bettmann.)

The Stamp Act required that colonists buy special stamps to validate certain documents such as marriage licenses and wills. Stamps were also required on several commodities, including playing cards, dice, newspapers and calendars.

     ❧ The colonists resisted increased taxes because they felt it was taxation without representation.

The Quartering Act that Parliament passed in 1765 enraged the colonists even more.

     ❧ The *Quartering Act* required that the colonists feed and shelter British troops in America.

The colonists found abhorrent the demands on them to shelter and feed the 10,000 British troops in America. Protests against the increasing British attempts to rule the colonies intensified, and demands that Parliament repeal these laws were rejected.

In 1766 the Stamp Act was repealed, but was replaced by other taxes on commodities the colonists still needed to import from England. New York was resisting the Quartering Act, and Parliament again found itself in the position of trying to rule from abroad. It was not working. Dissension increased, as did the tensions between the colonists and those British soldiers sent to enforce Parliament's demands.

The Boston Tea Party. (Provided by Corbis-Bettmann.)

Finally, in 1770, after 4,000 armed British troops had come to Boston from Nova Scotia and Ireland, colonists began taunting British soldiers and throwing snowballs and ice at them. The soldiers fired on the taunting colonists in what was to be called the Boston Massacre.

Attempting to quell the volatile situation, Parliament eventually repealed most of the taxes and duties, except those on tea. For both sides, this remaining tax served as a symbol of British rule over the colonies. In December 1773, disguised as Native Americans, colonists boarded three ships carrying tea in Boston Harbor and dumped the tea into the harbor.

The Boston Tea Party, where colonists boarded British ships and threw their cargos of tea in the harbor, represented the colonists' unwillingness to pay taxes without representation.

As a result of the tea dumping, Parliament passed several laws in retaliation for such an open act of defiance, including the following:

❖ Town meetings were restricted to one a year.
❖ The king was required to appoint people to the governmental court rather than have them elected.
❖ The Quartering Act was expanded, requiring soldiers to be housed in private homes and buildings (which seemed like spying to the colonists).
❖ British officials accused of crimes in the colonies were permitted to be tried in England, away from angry people in America.

Again the colonists were not complacent. They met to address the situation together.

The First Continental Congress

In September of 1774, 55 delegates from the 12 colonies met in Philadelphia to address their mounting complaints against Great Britain. At this First Continental Congress, such leaders as Samuel Adams and Patrick Henry met and resolved to resist British rule.

~ The First Continental Congress resulted in the first written agreement among the colonies to stand together in resistance.

The Congress agreed on three important expedients.

First, they adopted a set of resolutions defining the rights, liberties and immunities of the colonists and listing actions of the British government which violated these rights.

Second, they drew up an address to King George III and another to the citizens of British America, presenting American grievances and calling for a restoration of American rights.

Third, they called for a boycott of British goods into the colonies until their demands were met. Each community was to establish a boycott committee to prevent colonists from buying British goods. In general, those who bought British goods were branded **Loyalists** or Tories. Those who supported the boycott were called **Patriots** or rebels.

The Tension Mounts

By the beginning of 1775 the colonies were actively preparing for what many now saw would be an inevitable confrontation with the British. **Minutemen,** the name given to the colonial soldiers, were drilled and equipped to respond at a moment's notice to protect American lives, American property and American rights. In March 1775 Patrick Henry delivered his famous plea for freedom:

> Sir, we have done everything that could be done to avert the storm which is now coming on. We have petitioned; we have remonstrated; we have supplicated; we have prostrated ourselves before the throne and have implored its interposition to arrest the tyrannical hands of the Ministry and Parliament. Our petitions have been slighted; our remonstrances have produced additional violence and insult; our supplications have been disregarded; and we have been spurned, with contempt, from the foot of the throne. In vain, after these things, may we indulge the fond hope of peace and reconciliation.
>
> There is no longer any room for hope. If we wish to be free; if we mean to preserve inviolate those inestimable privileges for which we have been so long contending; if we mean, not basely to abandon the noble struggle in which we have been so long engaged, and which we have pledged ourselves never to abandon, until the glorious object of our contest shall be obtained; we must fight! I repeat it, sir, we might fight!! An appeal to arms and to the God of hosts is all that is left to us! . . . It is vain, sir, to extenuate the matter. Gentlemen may cry, peace, peace; but there is no peace. The war is actually begun! The next gale that sweeps from the north will bring

to our ears the clash of resounding arms! Our brethren are already in the field! Why stand we here idle? What is it that gentlemen wish? What would they have? Is life so dear or peace so sweet as to be purchased at the price of chains and slavery?

Forbid it, Almighty God—I know not what course others may take, but as for me, give me liberty, or give me death! (Brown and Bass, 1990, p. 140)

THE REVOLUTION BEGINS

With tensions at their flash point, minutemen in Lexington and Concord were alerted that the British soldiers were coming by William Dawes, although Paul Revere is generally credited with spreading the alert.

On April 19, 1775, the waiting minutemen in Lexington saw the British redcoats approaching. Shots were exchanged, and eight Americans were killed by the British that morning. The British moved on to Concord, where they were fired upon by the minutemen. This battle was later immortalized by poet Ralph Waldo Emerson's "Concord Hymn,"

By the rude bridge that arched the flood,
Their flag to April's breeze unfurled,
Here once the embattled farmers stood
And fired the shot heard round the world.

In a mere 25 years, the colonists had come a long way in their march toward independence, as illustrated in Figure 1–2. The battles at Lexington and Concord strengthened the colonists' resolve and also prompted them to meet again to determine how to proceed.

The Battle of Lexington. (Provided by Corbis-Bettmann.)

Figure 1-2

**Timeline showing
events leading up to
the Revolution.**

Source: Robert A. Divine, et al.
*America: The People and the
Dream.* Glenview, IL.: Scott,
Foresman and Company, 1991,
p. 132. Reprinted by permission. All rights reserved.

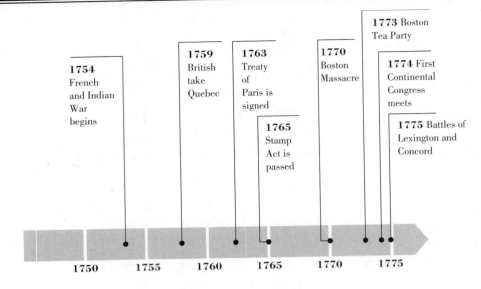

THE SECOND CONTINENTAL CONGRESS

In 1775 the Second Continental Congress was convened in Philadelphia.

> The Second Continental Congress established the
Continental Army and named George Washington as its
commander.

The Congress also made plans to raise money and buy supplies for the new army and to seek support from other countries by opening diplomatic relations with them. The colonists were now prepared for all-out war with the British.

George III denounced the American leaders as "rebels" and ordered the British military to suppress the disobedience and punish the authors of the "treacherous" resolves. The ensuing battles of Ticonderoga, Bunker Hill, Trenton and Saratoga, among others, showed the commitment of the American people to fight for what they held so dear—their independence. As the war continued, prospects for a reconciliation with Great Britain dimmed.

In May the Congress instructed each colony to form a government of its own, assuming the powers of independent states. The movement for a break with Great Britain spread upward from the colonies to the Continental Congress with the desire for independence now firmly resolved.

THE DECLARATION OF INDEPENDENCE

In July 1776, after arduous debate, delegates of the Second Continental Congress unanimously voted in favor of American independence. Thomas Jefferson was selected to coordinate the writing of the formal announcement, which came to be known as the Declaration of Independence. It listed the complaints the people had against Britain and justification for declaring independence.

Signing of the Declaration of Independence. (Provided by Corbis-Bettmann.)

On the 4th of July, 1776, the President of the Congress signed the American Declaration of Independence, which formally severed ties with Great Britain.

This historic work consisted of six important sections.

First, the opening paragraph explained why the Declaration was issued, that is, the compelling necessity for the colonists to break their political ties with Great Britain.

> When in the course of human events it becomes necessary for one people to dissolve the political bands which have connected them with another, and to assume among the powers of the earth the separate and equal station to which the laws of nature and of nature's God entitle them, a decent respect to the opinions of mankind requires that they should declare the causes which impel them to the separation.

The second paragraph was the crucial statement of the purposes of government, declaring all men to be equal and to have equal claims to "life, liberty, and the pursuit of happiness."

> We hold these truths to be self-evident, that all men are created equal, that they are endowed by their Creator with certain unalienable rights, that among these are life, liberty, and the pursuit of happiness.

No government can deny its people these rights.

According to Divine, et al. (1991, p. 164): "The document also stated for the first time in history that a government's right to rule is based on the 'consent of the governed.'"

> That to secure these rights, governments are instituted among men, deriving their just powers from the consent of the governed. That whenever any form of government becomes destructive to these ends, it is the right of the people to alter or to abolish it, and to institute new government, laying its foundation on such principles and organizing its powers in such form as to them shall seem most likely to effect their safety and happiness.

Third, charges against the British king were reviewed in a long list of ways in which the king's government had denied the American colonists their rights. Fourth, the Declaration described their attempts to obtain justice and the lack of response by the British. Fifth, the last paragraph proclaimed independence.

> We, therefore, the representatives of the United States of America, do, in the name, and by authority of the good people of these colonies, solemnly publish and declare, that these United colonies are, and of right ought to be free and independent states; that they are absolved from all Allegiance to the British Crown, and that all political connection between them and the State of Great Britain is, and ought to be totally dissolved. . . .

The final paragraph also listed actions the new United States of America could do as a country. Finally, the last sentence asserted the signers' resolve to pledge their lives and everything they owned to support the cause of independence. The entire text of the Declaration of Independence is contained in Appendix A.

THE ARTICLES OF CONFEDERATION

The Second Continental Congress not only acted to declare independence for America, but also set about to determine how government should be developed. Richard Henry Lee, the delegate who made the resolution for America to be independent, encouraged a confederation of independent states.

In 1777 the delegates to the Second Continental Congress agreed, and the Articles of Confederation created a governmental model for this new country. The 13 states were cherishing their independence and resisted agreeing to a single government of any kind. The tension over whether to secede from Great Britain in the first place, both for fear of the Crown's power and fear of the unknown, was replaced with a new tension. Once the break was made, might not a new government be even worse? Might they create a monster? Could any single government meet their needs? The colonists' solution was a confederation of independent states.

> The Articles of Confederation formally pledged the states to "a firm league of friendship," and "a perpetual union" created for "their common defense, the security of their liberties" and their "mutual and general welfare."

These Articles were important in that once approved in 1781, the duties of government were divided among the states and the government. During the eight years that America operated under them, great strides were made toward unifying a group of states that had, by their own desire, become separate. And while the inadequacies of this document eventually led to the Constitution itself, the Articles of Confederation were an important stepping-stone.

The Articles established a congress to conduct the necessary tasks of a central government, including:

❖ Wage war and make peace.
❖ Control trade with the Indians.
❖ Organize a mail service.
❖ Borrow money.

When you reflect on the reasons for the events that lead up to this point, you can easily understand that this preliminary attempt to establish a federal government left Congress with much weaker powers than would eventually be established. Congress was not empowered to do any of the following:

❖ Regulate trade—internally or externally.
❖ Levy taxes. They could ask, but could not compel.
❖ Draft soldiers. Again, they could ask, but could not compel.
❖ Establish a court system.
❖ Regulate money.

Nevertheless, Benjamin Franklin commented: "Americans are on the right road to improvement [with the Articles of Confederation], for we are making experiments." George Washington, however, cautioned that the Articles did not have the necessary strength to run a new country, and as the Confederation stood, it was "little more than the 'shadow without the substance'" (Armento, et al., 1991, p. 99).

The colonists were faced with the formidable task of governing themselves and holding together their agreed-upon union. As noted by Beard and Beard (1968, p. 123):

> No longer could disputes within and between colonies be carried to London for settlement. No longer did loyalty to the British King or the need for common action in the war against him constitute a unifying principle for Americans.

Loyalists who had opposed the Revolution called for reestablishing a monarchy for America. Others called for a military dictatorship. The need for some sort of strong leadership became more apparent as complaints against state governments grew in number and strength. In some states, such as Massachusetts, the right to vote was restricted to property owners and taxpayers. Creditors could sue debtors and take property away from farmers who could not pay what they owed. In 1786 a band of debt-burdened farmers in Massachusetts were led by Captain Daniel Shays in an attempt to shut down the courts through armed force. According to Beard and Beard (p. 125):

It was only with difficulty and some bloodshed that the state government put down "Shays' Rebellion." Even then popular sympathies with the uprising remained so strong that the state officials did not dare to execute Shays or any of his followers. Whatever the merits of this popular revolt, it increased the fears of property owners and conservatives in general, inciting them to work harder than ever for a powerful national government.

THE MOVE TOWARD THE CONSTITUTION

In 1787 the Constitutional Convention was convened in Philadelphia. Bearing in mind the combined difficulties of communication and travel, the willingness and persistence of the delegates who gathered to shape what was to become the Constitution speaks directly to their *need* for such a tool. For without it, even the most revered and capable politicians and leaders of the time would have been doomed to failure. Instead, the most incredible chapter of the history of the United States was slowly being opened. . . .

Summary

The United States Constitution was written to serve the needs of a pluralistic society. Pluralism refers to a society in which numerous distinct ethnic, religious or cultural groups coexist within one nation. The most important events leading up to the Constitution were the Declaration of Independence and the colonists' winning of the Revolutionary War.

The history of our Constitution is rooted in the colonists' desire for freedom from foreign rule. In addition to others, Spain, France and Great Britain saw great importance in adding the "New World" to their growing empires. Most threatening was Great Britain. In 1765 the British Parliament passed the Stamp Act, requiring stamps to be purchased and placed on such items as legal documents and certain commodities. This act was resisted because it was viewed as taxation without representation. That same year Parliament passed the Quartering Act, requiring that the colonists feed and shelter British troops in America.

Tensions between the colonists and the British army mounted, and in 1770 fighting broke out. This conflict became known as the Boston Massacre. In an attempt to lessen the conflict, Parliament repealed most of the taxes, but kept the tax on tea. In 1773 colonists boarded British ships in Boston Harbor and threw the ships' cargo of tea into the harbor. This event, the Boston Tea Party, represented the colonists' unwillingness to pay taxes without representation.

As tension between the British and the colonists increased, the First Continental Congress was called. This Congress resulted in the first written agreement among the colonies to stand together in resistance to Great Britain. The British retaliated by sending more troops to quell the "rebels." In 1775 the Second Continental Congress established the Continental Army and named George Washington as its commander. On July 4, 1776, the President of the Congress signed the American Declaration of Independence, which formally severed ties with Great Britain.

The Congress also drafted the Articles of Confederation. The Articles of Confederation formally pledged the states to "a firm league of friendship," and "a perpetual union" created for "their common defense, the security of their liberties" and their "mutual and general welfare." This loose governmental structure proved unsatisfactory and resulted in the colonists seeking a stronger central government—one established by our Constitution.

Discussion Questions

1. Why have people taken perilous risks to make America their home?

2. When *hasn't* history repeated itself? Can you think of incidents in world history that have *no* similarities?

3. Few people could live together and not have laws. Why?

4. Are there any negative aspects of pluralism? Why have some fought so hard against the concept here?

5. Why did the colonists tolerate so much from France and Great Britain before resisting?

6. Do demonstrations such as the Boston Tea Party have any effect? Are they positive or negative?

7. Is there any way that British rule of America could have worked? Why?

8. What reasons make it simply amazing that any organization among the colonies was successful?

9. Were the Articles of Confederation a waste of effort or were they needed? Why or why not?

10. Would a dictatorship for this new country have been significantly easier and more productive than the system that was developed? Couldn't someone like George Washington have successfully run the new country by himself?

References

Armento, Beverly J., Gary B. Nash, Christopher L. Salter and Karen K. Wixson. *A More Perfect Union.* Boston: Houghton Mifflin Company, 1991.

Beard, Charles A. and Mary R. Beard. *The Beards' New Basic History of the United States.* Garden City, NY: Doubleday & Company, Inc., 1968.

Brown, Richard C. and Herbert J. Bass. *One Flag, One Land.* Morristown, NJ: Silver Burdett & Ginn, 1990.

Divine, Robert A., T. H. Breen, George M. Fredrickson and R. Hal Williams. *America: The People and the Dream.* Glenview, IL: Scott, Foresman and Company, 1991.

Miller, Linda S. and Kären M. Hess. *Community Policing.* St. Paul: West Publishing Company, 1994.

Chapter 2

If men were angels, no government would be necessary. If angels were to govern men, neither external nor internal controls on government would be necessary. In framing a government which is to be administered by men over men, the great difficulty lies in this: you must first enable the government to control the governed; and in the next place oblige it to control itself. A dependence on the people is, no doubt, the primary control on the government; but experience has taught mankind the necessity of auxiliary precautions.

—JAMES MADISON, *The Federalist, No. 51*

The Constitution of the United States

The United States Constitution—featuring the preamble and Article I. (Provided by Corbis-Bettmann.)

DO YOU KNOW . . .

What the Magna Carta is?

What important role the Magna Carta played in framing the United States Constitution?

What the primary purpose of the Constitution is? How it is achieved?

What the first three articles of the Constitution accomplished?

What the supremacy clause established?

When and where the Constitution was signed?

Who were the Federalists? The Anti-Federalists?

Why some states were reluctant to accept the Constitution?

What the Bill of Rights is and how it was included with the Constitution?

What serious omission occurred in the Bill of Rights?

Where the Constitution and the Bill of Rights are housed?

CAN YOU DEFINE THESE TERMS?

Amendments
Anti-Federalists
Constitutionalism
Federalists
Great Compromise
Ratify

INTRODUCTION

As a preface to this chapter on the Constitution of the United States, a bit more history will explain both how and why our Constitution developed as it did. Our Constitution has important ties to what is perhaps the most important instrument of English government—the *Magna Carta*. This document, which King John was forced to sign on June 12, 1215, ensured feudal rights and guaranteed that the king could not put himself above the law.

〰️ The Magna Carta established the supremacy of the law over the ruler and guaranteed English feudal barons individual rights and "due process of law," including trial by jury.

The British, to this day, have never operated their government under a centralized "constitution." Rather, they work under *tradition,* and at the heart of that tradition is the historic Magna Carta, guaranteeing, among other things, basic due process.

The Magna Carta.

The British government established a tripartite balance of power between Sovereign, Lords and Commons. This tripartite balance was praised by French historian and philosopher Charles Louis de Secondat, Baron de laBrede et de Montesquieu (1689–1755). Montesquieu's most influential work, *The Spirit of the Laws* (1748), was a scientific study that compared various forms of government. Montesquieu wrote that the British subjects' sense of liberty, their feelings of safety and security, sprang from separating governmental powers into three parts with the king holding only executive power, Parliament alone being able to make laws and the judiciary functioning independently of them both. This tripartite division of power and Montesquieu's theory of checks and balances found their way into the United States Constitution.

In addition to the British Magna Carta, several other documents were developed over some 20 years in response to an evergrowing desire by the people for fairer treatment by their government.

This chapter looks at the development of the Constitution, the debates that occurred, the ratification process and the addition of the Bill of Rights. It concludes with a brief discussion of the current archiving of the Constitution and Bill of Rights.

AFTER THE REVOLUTIONARY WAR IS WON

Those who came to America in 1620 and their descendants, through the American Revolution, ultimately rejected rule under the British Crown and what it had come to symbolize. Nonetheless, even present American law has deep roots in what Great Britain had established as a legal system. This explains the importance of *continuity of law.* Consistency must run through all law to develop predictability. The framers of our Constitution sought to develop such a format that would guarantee the continuation of basic rights as specific law developed.

> ✎ Americans continued to believe in the principles contained in the Magna Carta, which was a precedent for democratic government and individual rights and the foundation for requiring rulers to uphold the law. It greatly influenced the writers of the United States Constitution.

Human nature holds secure things from the past. At least *some* stability in life is assured by holding onto our past. And although the colonists rejected British rule, they recognized that a document such as the Magna Carta provided a stable framework from which to start.

First, the Magna Carta was a step away from total rule by a single individual. Second, it had a fairly long history of success by the time the New World began to receive visitors from abroad seeking to colonize here. And finally, it provided some security in that not *everything* needed to start from scratch.

THE CHARGE OF THE 1787 CONVENTION OF DELEGATES

The Articles of Confederation had established "a firm league of friendship" between the states. However, they were inadequate as the foundation for effective government because they lacked a balance of power between the states and the central government. Therefore, in 1787, the Congress of the Confederation called for a convention of delegates from the original states to meet in Philadelphia to revise the Articles of Confederation.

During the convention, what might be considered a political revolution occurred, changing the form of government created in the violence of the break with England to a true union. It was a long, arduous process with much conflict and debate. One primary debate was between those who favored holding on to tradition and those who advocated a complete break with the past.

George Mason, who wrote the Virginia Declaration of Rights, recognized the importance of basing the new American government on tradition. Mason expressed his position by saying that there would be much difficulty in organizing a government on this great scale and at the same time reserving to the state legislatures a sufficient portion of power for promoting and securing the prosperity and happiness of their respective citizens (Atherton and Barlow, no date, p. 2).

Mason sought to lean upon the traditions established by the Magna Carta because of the fundamental rights that should not be threatened regardless of what government or governments would come and go in the United States. He advocated using the Magna Carta as a single stabilizing force in the growth of this country: ". . . no free government, or the blessings of liberty, can be preserved to any people, but . . . by frequent recurrence to fundamental principles" (Atherton and Barlow, no date, p. 2).

George Mason and James Madison, both delegates from Virginia, had significant roles in shaping the direction the new Constitution would take. Their views combined an anchor for stability from the past encouraged by Mason with a vision of the future provided by Madison. Clearly evident, even in the yearning this country had to be new and independent, was the fact that connections with the past cannot be discounted (Atherton and Barlow, no date, pp. 2–7). Again, continuity and predictability provided security, and security was what our ancestors were thirsting for.

THE CONCEPT OF A CONSTITUTION GROWS

In May 1787 delegates to the Constitutional Convention met at Independence Hall in Philadelphia. George Washington was elected to preside over the meetings. The public was not permitted in the meetings so the delegates could speak more freely. Arduous debate occurred during this Constitutional Convention. The summer of 1787 was one of record heat, and because of the standard dress of the day, the framers worked for only a few hours in the

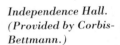

Independence Hall. (Provided by Corbis-Bettmann.)

mornings. Afternoons were filled with much camaraderie and imbibing of favorite beverages.

The delegates decided how many votes each state would have and that a new document was preferable to merely amending the Articles of Confederation. The challenge of drafting the Constitution began.

> ❧ The purpose of the Constitution was to establish a central government authorized to deal directly with individuals rather than states and to incorporate a system of checks and balances that would preserve the fundamental concepts contained in the Magna Carta.

The Constitution Takes Shape

It can be difficult to grasp all that lies behind the Constitution unless you keep in mind the underlying reason *for* the Constitution, that is, to provide a system of government that would prevent one *individual* from having complete power. Understandably, such a system would, of necessity, have complexities built in to achieve such a lofty goal, but the basic reasoning is simple.

Issues that became prominent were the structure and powers of Congress, of the executive branch and of the judicial system. What was sought was an array of checks and balances that would allow the system to work, while achieving the primary goal of limiting power to any individual or section of the government.

A unique element of our Constitution is that it was developed by people sharing the desires of common folk, undertaking a most challenging act. The delegates at the Constitutional Convention, who came from varied backgrounds, rose to the challenge. Individual power was never their objective, but rather societal cohesiveness and democratic power to achieve . . . "one nation, with liberty and justice for all." The delegates who would help make the Constitution came that year with differing views, but all were advocates of **constitutionalism.** That is, they believed in a government in which power is distributed and limited by a system of laws that must be obeyed by those who rule. According to that principle, constitutions are a system of fundamental laws and principles that prescribe the nature, functions and limits of a government or other body. Constitutions are distinguished from ordinary acts of legislation in that they are drafted by special assemblages and ratified by special conventions chosen by the people. A constitution is supreme law, not to be annulled by legislation. Constitutionalism is one of the most original, distinctive contributions of the American system of government.

Like those who wrote the Articles of Confederation, the framers of the Constitution recognized that *the people are the power.* The delegates to the First Continental Congress in Philadelphia had been selected by the people of the colonies, not by existing colonial governments. Likewise, the delegates to the Constitutional Convention represented the people.

All states except Rhode Island were represented at the Constitutional Convention, which met at the State House in Philadelphia from May 25 to September 15. The 55 delegates included many of the most influential men in the country. Eight had signed the Declaration of Independence, seven were governors of their states and 39 were Congressmen. More than half were college graduates, and at least one third were lawyers. Most held prominent positions in the Revolutionary War, and all were highly respected property owners of substance.

Although unanimously elected president, George Washington took a limited but effective role in the deliberations. Of greatest influence were Governor Morris and James Wilson of Pennsylvania, James Madison of Virginia, and Roger Sherman of Connecticut, each speaking more than 100 times.

Despite some talk of the larger states getting more votes than the smaller states, the Convention followed the procedures used to develop the Articles of Confederation, giving each state one vote, with seven states constituting a quorum. Any vote could be reconsidered, as many were during the convention. The convention was also governed by a rule of secrecy, requiring that nothing said during the deliberations be printed, published or otherwise communicated without permission. Such secrecy was vital to unbiased discussion and to prevent rumors and misconceptions. The official journal was closed until 1819.

The Convention first debated the Virginia resolution, calling for a national government with a bicameral legislature, an executive and a judiciary branch. The smaller states, however, backed the New Jersey Plan, calling for only modest revisions in the Articles of Confederation. In addition, the larger states supported representation proportional to a state's population, while the smaller states wanted one or two votes per state.

A threatened deadlock was averted by the **Great Compromise,** which gave each state an equal vote in the Senate and a proportionate vote in the House.

After lengthy debate, the delegates also decided to strengthen the central government, but to clearly define federal powers. All other powers were entrusted to the individual states and to the people. Specifically, the country was to be governed by a president, to be chosen by electors in each state, a national judiciary and a two-chamber legislature. The House of Representatives was to be popularly elected. The Senate, however, which shared certain executive powers with the president, was to be chosen by individual state legislatures. Under the Great Compromise between the large and small states, representation in the House was to be proportional to a state's population; in the Senate each state was to have two votes. The national plan for government agreed to by the Convention delegates clearly separated the powers of the three branches of government and created a system of checks and balances among these three branches, as well as between the federal and state governments and the people both were to serve. James Madison explained the delicate relationship between the federal and state governments and the division of power within the system *(The Federalist):*

> In the compound republic of America, the power surrendered by the people is first divided between two distinct governments, and then the portion allotted to each subdivided among distinct and separate departments. Hence a double security arises to the rights of people. The different governments will control each other at the same time that each will be controlled by itself.

After all issues had been debated and agreement reached, a committee was then to draft the Constitution based on the agreements reached.

On Tuesday, August 7, 1787, a draft Constitution was ready for a clause-by-clause review (Armento, et al., p. 140). After four months, what had developed is nothing short of amazing. The material was old, connected back to the Magna Carta, but it was new—with some rather brilliant concepts. It was the brainchild of a relatively select few, but if it was to work it would need to be accepted by all. The task was monumental. As noted by Mitchell (1986, pp. 1–2):

> In the Constitution that emerged from these deliberations, the concept of government by consent of the governed formed the basic principle; accountability was the watchword. The rights of the people were to be protected by diffusing power among rival interests.

The final document was put before the Convention on September 17. Following are the provisions of the articles contained in this final draft of the Constitution.

THE CONSTITUTION OF THE UNITED STATES: AN OVERVIEW

Descriptions of the debates that forged the Constitution during the summer of 1787 in Philadelphia are fascinating, and this is certainly worthwhile reading for those who wish to pursue it further. The following condensation describes the results of those debates—the articles contained in the final draft of our Constitution (Lieberman, 1976, pp. 33–41).

The Constitution is both a structure for government and a set of principles, a method for making law and a law itself. Of all the principles in this seven-thousand-word document, the single most important principle is that the government has been delegated its powers by the people. The government is not superior to them; its powers come only from them.

> The first three articles of the Constitution establish the legislative, executive and judicial branches of government and our system of checks and balances.

Article 1—The Legislative Branch

Article 1 establishes the legislature: "All legislative Powers herein granted shall be vested in a Congress of the United States." This legislature may pass laws, but it has no power to enforce them or to interpret them. This article contains the Great Compromise. Congress has two chambers, a Senate and House of Representatives, each acting as a check against the other. Senators are chosen by each state's legislature, with each state having two senators, and each senator having one vote. (Senators are no longer chosen by state legislatures.)

Membership in the House is based on state populations. The House has the "Power of Impeachment," the Senate the "sole Power to try all Impeachments." The House and Senate determine their own rules of procedure and conduct. They publish a journal, the *Congressional Record*, containing discussion, debate and a record of the members' votes.

Laws of the United States—in the form of bills—may originate in either house. The sole exception is that only the House of Representatives may first consider "bills for raising revenue." The cry "no taxation without representation" was still strong. Only the popular body, the house representing the people, was given the power to initiate taxes.

All bills must clear three hurdles before they can become laws. They first must pass each house in identical form and then meet the approval of the president. The president has the power to veto, but Congress in turn can override that veto if each house, by a two-thirds vote, chooses to do so.

Section 8 of Article 1 grants specific powers to Congress, in addition to coining money and establishing post offices, including the power to:

❖ Lay and collect taxes.
❖ Borrow money on the credit of the United States.
❖ Regulate international and interstate commerce.
❖ Naturalize foreign-born citizens.
❖ Raise and govern the military forces.
❖ Declare war.

In what has come to be known as the "elastic clause," Congress also was given the power "to make all Laws which shall be necessary and proper for carrying into effect the foregoing Powers, and all other Powers vested by this Constitution in the Government of the United States, or in any Department or Officer thereof."

In other words, Congress was granted an enormous potential reserve of power to do what was "necessary and proper" to pass laws for the nation. For the first time, the new Congress could do what the old Congress could not: enact laws that directly affected the people.

The Supreme Court addressed the necessary and proper clause in *McCulloch v. Maryland* (1819), establishing the authority of the federal government to address national issues. Historically, the clause caused considerable debate because of concern that it was too open-ended and could lead to excessive federal authority. However, the need to permit Congress to make necessary laws and carry out their enumerated powers was acknowledged in *McCulloch v. Maryland*. This need to allow Congress to pass necessary and proper laws was reinforced more recently in *Kinsella v. United States* (1960). In this case the clause was not considered a grant of federal power, but a declaration that Congress does possess the means needed to carry out its authority as set forth in the Constitution to run the country by enacting laws that are—necessary and proper.

Article 2—The Executive Branch

The office of president was created to carry out the law; to provide a commander in chief of the military forces; to carry out the nation's foreign policy, including entering into treaties with other nations and appointing the ambassadors, judges and officials needed for the government to function.

The president is chosen through a complex system using "electors," who are selected by procedures that vary from state to state. The number of electors equals each states' number of senators and representatives in Congress. Therefore, it is possible for a president to be elected without receiving a majority of the popular votes. Whether an electoral college is needed is a continuing controversy.

As a check against the president's power, many of the president's most significant actions must be approved by the Senate. Treaties require a two-thirds vote. Judges and appointed executive officials need a majority vote to be confirmed. In addition, the president must report periodically to Congress on the state of the Union and may recommend laws Congress should enact. The president's most important duty is phrased, characteristically, in very general language requiring that the president "shall take care that the laws be faithfully executed."

Article 3—The Judicial Branch

The third article completes the national government structure, vesting judicial power in the United States Supreme Court. Congress is also empowered to create lower courts. Federal court judges are appointed by the president and hold office for life.

As a check against judicial power, Congress is authorized to regulate the courts' dockets by deciding what kinds of cases the Supreme Court may hear on appeal. This power of Congress to regulate the courts' jurisdiction further illustrates how each branch of government is given significant power to affect the others. Congress enacts laws, but the president may veto them, and the courts may interpret them.

Article 4—Other Provisions

Article 4 contains a variety of provisions, some taken over from the Articles of Confederation, further describing the creation of the federal union. The article also deals with criminal extradition, formation of new states and Congress' power to govern in territorial lands not yet states.

Article 5—The Amendment Process

Article 5 dictates how the Constitution itself may be amended. An amendment must first be approved by a two-thirds vote in each house of Congress. It is then submitted to the states for ratification, requiring the approval of three fourths of the states to pass the amendment. The people may also begin the amendment process if the legislatures of two thirds of the states call for a constitutional convention. This article was extremely important in allowing our Bill of Rights to be added to the Constitution, as discussed shortly.

Article 6—The Constitution As the Supreme Law

The second section of Article 6 contains the famous *supremacy clause:*

> The Constitution and the Laws of the United States which shall be made in Pursuance thereof; and all Treaties made, or which shall be made, under the Authority of the United States, shall be the supreme Law of the Land; and the Judges in every state shall be bound thereby, anything in the Constitution or Laws of any state to the Contrary notwithstanding.

Here, in a stroke, was the solution to the problem of dual sovereignty of the federal and state governments. It was denied. In matters over which the Constitution grants the federal government authority, the states must concede.

 In the supremacy clause, the Constitution declared itself the supreme law of the land.

This clause establishing the supremacy of federal law was to do something else momentous: it permitted the Supreme Court to become the ultimate decision maker in whether laws and actions of the government circumvent the Constitution and to invalidate them if they do so. This article also requires the allegiance of every federal *and* state official to the Constitution.

THE SIGNING OF THE CONSTITUTION

Once the overall format was agreed upon, the next step was to seek approval of the document by the delegates. After hearing the debate over the final version of the Constitution, Benjamin Franklin, on Saturday, September 15, 1787, eloquently urged the Convention to respect the spirit of compromise, stating (Lieberman, 1987, p. 47):

> I confess that there are several parts of this Constitution which I do not at present approve. But I am not sure I shall ever approve them. For having lived long, I have experienced many instances of being obliged by better information or fuller consideration, to change opinions even on important subjects, which I once thought right, but found to be otherwise. . . . I consent, Sir, to this Constitution because I expect no better and because I am not sure that it is not the best.

Franklin urged: "[E]very member of the Convention who may still have objections to it [the Constitution], would, with me, on this occasion doubt a little of his own infallibility, and . . . put his name to this instrument." He moved that the Constitution be approved unanimously and signed by those states present. The delegates voted to accept the Constitution, and the following Monday, September 17, it was ready to be signed.

 The United States Constitution was signed in Philadelphia on September 17, 1787.

Forty-two of the 55 delegates were present on September 17 to sign the Constitution, with only three members refusing to sign, including George

Signing of the United States Constitution. (Provided by Corbis-Bettmann.)

Mason, who cited the lack of a bill of rights as a remaining concern. He proposed adding a bill of rights, but other delegates argued that the individual states' declarations of rights would sufficiently protect individual liberties. They voted against adding a bill of rights. James Madison was quoted *(The Records of the Federal Convention of 1787):*

> Whilst the last members were signing it, Doctor Franklin looking towards the President's chair, at the back of which a rising sun happened to be painted, observed to a few members near him, that painters had found it difficult to distinguish in their art a rising from a setting sun. I have, said he, often in the course of the session . . . looked at that [sun] behind the President without being able to tell whether it was rising or setting. But now at length I have the happiness to know that it is a rising and not a setting sun (Armento, et al., 1991, p. 133).

The delegates agreed that the Constitution should next be submitted to special conventions of the states for ratification.

RATIFICATION

While the delegates to the Constitutional Convention had agreed to the makeup of the Constitution, it was necessary for each state to approve or **ratify** it. Delaware was the first state to do so. New Hampshire cast the decisive vote, but ratification was not a sure thing. Many people had grave reservations. While they were all supportive of the Constitution, the dispute tended to be more about how strong or weak the central government should be.

The **Federalists** favored a strong central government. They were strongly challenged by the **Anti-Federalists** who favored a weaker central government.

Political leaders such as Alexander Hamilton, James Madison and John Jay wrote powerful essays in a newspaper called *The Federalist Papers,* which encouraged the ratification of the Constitution and the formation of a strong national government.

The Anti-Federalists, however, feared such a strong federal government—what would assure this country that this attempt would not fail, too? Further, they were reluctant to ratify the Constitution without a bill of rights to guarantee individual liberties.

The Anti-Federalists were not successful in blocking the final ratification of the Constitution, but they did raise awareness regarding the need for a bill of rights. Because the Constitution primarily addressed formation of a government with limited and distributed powers, a bill of rights to protect individuals was not considered necessary.

> Some states opposed the Constitution because it did not contain a bill of rights.

After the Philadelphia convention, most of those who drafted the Constitution could not understand why a bill of rights was such an issue for many states. They believed the Constitution could stand on its own. Nonetheless, most Federalists were willing to compromise on this issue to ratify the Con-

Figure 2–1

Timeline of events in America and elsewhere.

Source: Adapted from Richard C. Brown and Herbert J. Bass. *One Flag, One Land.* Morristown, NJ: Silver Burdett & Ginn, 1990, p. 175.

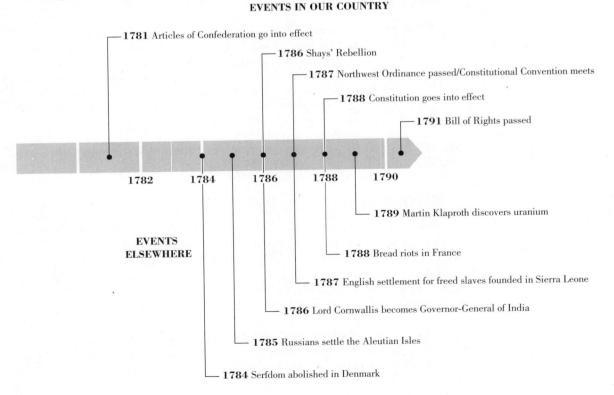

EVENTS IN OUR COUNTRY

1781 Articles of Confederation go into effect

1786 Shays' Rebellion

1787 Northwest Ordinance passed/Constitutional Convention meets

1788 Constitution goes into effect

1791 Bill of Rights passed

1782   1784   1786   1788   1790

EVENTS ELSEWHERE

1789 Martin Klaproth discovers uranium

1788 Bread riots in France

1787 English settlement for freed slaves founded in Sierra Leone

1786 Lord Cornwallis becomes Governor-General of India

1785 Russians settle the Aleutian Isles

1784 Serfdom abolished in Denmark

stitution establishing a new government. Fearing defeat in the Massachusetts ratifying convention, Federalist leaders sought support by drafting a list of **amendments,** additions to improve the Constitution. They enlisted John Hancock, the most popular man in Massachusetts, to present these amendments to the state convention. The proposed amendments made the Constitution acceptable to many who had opposed ratification.

The compromising strategy of the Massachusetts Federalists turned the tide of ratification. As other states debated ratification, they also insisted on amendments that would guarantee a person's rights.

The Bill of Rights was added to the Constitution in 1791 by the addition of 10 amendments designed to ensure that the national government would not interfere with individual liberties. By December 15, 1791, the states had ratified 10 out of the 12 proposed amendments to the Constitution and the United States had a bill of rights.

A BALANCE IS STRUCK

As stated by Armento, et al. (1991, p. 125):

> The framers of the Constitution had worked hard to create a system that balanced the powers of the three branches of government—legislative, executive, and judicial. The amendments proposed by the state ratifying conventions were aimed at another kind of balance: balancing the rights of the states and of individual citizens against the powers of the central government.

In December 1791 the 13 states had passed the 10 amendments that comprise the Bill of Rights. Proof of how well the Constitution would work was seen by the fact that it could, as a single document, embrace additions those it was drafted to serve determined necessary. Thomas Jefferson's comment on this process "The example of changing a Constitution by assembling the wise men of the State instead of assembling armies" was of great significance.

> In 1791, 10 amendments, known as the Bill of Rights, were added to the Constitution to ensure the individual rights of American citizens.

Had the Constitution been ratified without a bill of rights, it would have taken several years for those protections to be passed. By taking the form of amendments, these provisions became an integral part of the Constitution that many had argued be included originally. As noted by the Honorable Warren E. Burger during the Constitution's bicentennial (Armento, et al., 1991, p. 26):

> The Founders, conscious of the risks of abuse of power, created a system of liberty with order and placed the Bill of Rights as a harness on government to protect people from misuse of the powers. The evils of tyranny even today fall on most of the world's people and remind us of what life would be like without our respect for human dignity and freedom. We must never forget what our strength was meant to serve and what made that strength possible—the Constitution and the Bill of Rights as they stand today.

The Bill of Rights.

THE BILL OF RIGHTS

The remainder of this text focuses on the Bill of Rights as well as additional amendments made to the Constitution. The following brief introduction to each of the first 10 amendments provides an overview upon which later discussions can be based.

The First Amendment lists important individual liberties, including freedom of thought, belief and speech.

> *Congress shall make no law respecting an establishment of religion, or prohibiting the free exercise thereof; or abridging the freedom of speech, or of the press, or the right of the people peaceably to assemble, and to petition the Government for a redress of grievances.*

These freedoms are so basic to the American way of life that they are sometimes referred to as "First Amendment rights."

The Second Amendment preserves the right of the people "to keep and bear arms."

> *A well-regulated militia being necessary to the security of a free state, the right to the people to keep and bear arms shall not be infringed.*

The courts have ruled that this is not an absolute right. Laws prohibiting private paramilitary associations and carrying concealed weapons have been upheld.

The Third Amendment prohibits the government from housing soldiers in private homes in peacetime without the owner's consent.

No soldier shall, in time of peace, be quartered in any house without the consent of the owner, nor in time of war but in a manner to be prescribed by the law.

This is the only amendment that the government has never tried to violate (Lieberman, 1976, p. 46).

The Fourth Amendment is concerned with the right to privacy and security.

The right of the people to be secure in their persons, houses, papers, and effects, against unreasonable searches and seizures, shall not be violated, and no warrants shall issue but upon probable cause, supported by oath or affirmation, and particularly describing the place to be searched, and the persons or things to be seized.

The Fourth Amendment forbids the government or its agents from searching individuals, their homes or their personal possessions or from seizing them unless the government has "probable cause" to believe that a crime has been committed. If such probable cause exists, a search warrant describing in detail what (or who) is to be seized should be obtained. (This capsule description is necessarily loose: the police need not obtain warrants for every arrest or for every search. The past 15 years have seen an enormous volume of litigation over the precise limits of this amendment.)

The Fifth Amendment sets forth several restrictions on how the government may treat a person suspected of a crime.

No person shall be held to answer for a capital or otherwise infamous crime unless on a presentment or indictment of a grand jury, except in cases arising in the land or naval forces, or in the militia, when in actual service, in time of war or public danger; nor shall any person be subject for the same offense to be twice put in jeopardy of life or limb; nor shall be compelled in any criminal case to be a witness against himself; nor be deprived of life, liberty, or property, without due process of law; nor shall private property be taken for public use without just compensation.

The Fifth Amendment establishes the need for a grand jury indictment for felony cases. It prohibits double jeopardy, meaning a person acquitted by a jury of a crime may not be retried for the same offense. It prohibits the government from forcing a person to testify against himself, hence the expression "pleading the Fifth." It also contains the famous due process clause: "nor shall any person . . . be deprived of life, liberty, or property without due process of law."

The Sixth Amendment describes the requirements for a fair trial.

In all criminal prosecutions, the accused shall enjoy the right to a speedy and public trial, by an impartial jury of the state and district wherein the crime shall have been committed, which districts shall have been previously ascertained by law, and to be informed of the nature and cause of the accusation; to be confronted with the witnesses against him; to have compulsory process for obtaining witnesses in his favor, and to have the assistance of counsel for his defense.

The trial must be convened speedily and must be public. The accused is entitled to an impartial jury in the community where the crime occurred and must be advised of the crimes being charged. Accused individuals must also be allowed to cross-examine witnesses who testify against them. In addition, they can compel witnesses who will testify in their favor to come to court. Finally, they have the right to be represented by a lawyer.

The Seventh Amendment preserves the right to trial by jury in common law cases "where the value in controversy shall exceed twenty dollars."

In Suits at common law, where the value in controversy shall exceed twenty dollars, the right of trial by a jury shall be otherwise re-examined in any Court of the United States, than according to the rules of the common law.

This is one of the few clauses in the Constitution that includes a figure that has lost meaning over the years. By law today, federal courts cannot hear cases where the contested value is less than ten thousand dollars unless a federal law is involved. The amendment also forbids courts to reexamine facts found by juries, except as the common law permits.

The Eighth Amendment prohibits excessive bail, excessive fines and cruel and unusual punishment.

Excessive bail shall not be required, nor excessive fines imposed, nor cruel and unusual punishments inflicted.

It is this amendment that opponents of capital punishment most frequently cite.

The Ninth Amendment answered the objections of those who thought that naming some rights but not all might result in the government's claiming more power than was intended.

The enumeration in the Constitution of certain rights shall not be construed to deny or disparage others retained by the people.

The Tenth Amendment further underscores the intent of the framers to reserve certain powers to the states and to the people.

The powers not delegated to the United States by the Constitution, nor prohibited by it to the States, are reserved to the States respectively, or to the people.

This amendment establishes no rights, nor takes any away. It is a reminder that the government is for the people, not the reverse.

A LIVING LAW

The inclusion of the Bill of Rights stands as an example of how our American Constitution lives. It is not unchangeable, nor unresponsive. It is not merely a piece of paper locked away in a vault in Washington, DC. It was designed to grow, develop and be redefined if necessary to best serve the needs of the people it serves. A point of discussion is whether a lengthy and complicated document could achieve such a purpose. As you study the amendments and how they have been interpreted since their inception, it will become obvious that our Constitution is a *living* document that grows with the citizens it was written to protect.

A NEAR TIMELESS DOCUMENT

The final draft of the Constitution established a broad framework for the new American government. For 200 years the Constitution has been flexible enough to meet the nation's changing needs without extensive formal revision. Although the framers of the Constitution would find many modern governmental practices quite foreign, the basic system continues to operate as they planned. Recognizing the importance of assuring in practice the division of power, Madison suggested this could best be done "by so contriving the interior structure of the government as that its several constituent parts may, by their mutual relations, be the means of keeping each other in their proper places."

A Recent Example

A 1990s' example of the checks and balances at work is the stalemate over the budget that shut down the federal government in November of 1995. According to an article in the *Washington Post* ("Stalemate Wouldn't Surprise Founders," 1995, p. A18):

> The Founding Fathers might have been astonished at the scope of today's federal government and appalled at the size of the national debt, but in many ways the stalemate that led to last week's government shutdown would not have surprised them greatly.
>
> In fact, it is their system of checks and balances that produced the standoff.

Recall that the framers of the Constitution wanted to guard against taxation without representation, so they gave the critical "power of the purse"—that is the power to raise and spend money—to the legislature. But to keep this power in check, they gave the president the power to veto congressional spending authority. When budget talks turned into a stalemate, President Clinton ordered certain segments of the federal government to shut down immediately. As noted by the *Washington Post*:

> While both sides are crying foul—Congress that President Clinton is trying to undermine its budget-making authority, and Clinton that Congress is forcing him into a corner by attempting to enact policy along with an extension of the debt ceiling—

legal experts say the two branches are simply exploiting their constitutional authority to the fullest.

Legal experts also note that tacking policy items onto budget legislation would probably be viewed negatively by the founding fathers, but legislation was done that way during the Civil War to accommodate President Abraham Lincoln and has been used that way ever since. This longstanding practice has been engaged in by both political parties and has been criticized by many presidents. Practices such as this have formed the basis of the recent bipartisan effort to enact a line-item veto. The line-item veto has been requested by several presidents from both parties.

Lieberman (1976, p. 49) notes: "The Constitution has the distinction of being an almost timeless document but for one grievous flaw. It did not abolish slavery."

◅◅ The Constitution and Bill of Rights failed to abolish slavery.

Lieberman goes on:

> Those who detested slavery reconciled themselves to this grievous and glaring flaw that contradicted the Declaration of Independence at its most solemn point—that all men are created equal—by assuming that slavery would in time vanish naturally. But it would not go away so easily. The compromise that saved the Union could not be peacefully eliminated, and the amendments that would make the Constitution true to itself could come about only after the bloodiest war in American history.

The United States Constitution and Declaration of Independence at the National Archives. (Photo by Anthony Hayward. Provided by Reuters/Corbis-Bettmann.)

WHERE THE DECLARATION OF INDEPENDENCE AND CONSTITUTION ARE TODAY

The Declaration of Independence, which established the United States as an independent nation, and the Constitution, which established its form of government, have been carefully preserved.

≋ The Declaration of Independence and the United States Constitution are housed in the Rotunda of the National Archives in Washington, DC.

These valuable documents are contained in helium-filled bronze cases housed in a vault below the Exhibition Hall floor. The vault is 7½ feet long, 5 feet wide, 6 feet high and weighs 55 tons. The walls are of reinforced concrete and steel.

Summary

Our Constitution was greatly influenced by the Magna Carta, which established the supremacy of the law over the ruler and guaranteed English feudal barons individual rights and "due process of law," including trial by jury. Americans continued to believe in the principles contained in the Magna Carta, which was a precedent for democratic government and individual rights and the foundation for requiring rulers to uphold the law. It greatly influenced the writers of the United States Constitution.

The purpose of the Constitution was to provide a system of government that would prevent one individual from having complete power. The first three articles of the Constitution establish the legislative, executive and judicial branches of government and our system of checks and balances. The United States Constitution was signed in Philadelphia on September 17, 1787. The next step was for the individual states to ratify it.

The Federalists favored a strong central government. They were strongly challenged by the Anti-Federalists, who favored a weaker central government. Some states opposed the Constitution because it did not contain a bill of rights. In an important compromise, in 1791, 10 amendments, known as the Bill of Rights, were added to the Constitution to ensure the individual rights of American citizens. The Constitution and Bill of Rights had one serious shortcoming: they failed to abolish slavery.

The Declaration of Independence and the United States Constitution are housed in the Rotunda of the National Archives in Washington, DC.

Discussion Questions

1. Wouldn't it have been better to disregard the Magna Carta altogether when debating the Constitution?

2. What do you think about the Constitutional Convention being closed to the public? Was this a necessity?

3. How can the United States Constitution be such a *small* document, but do so much?

4. Discuss how the Constitution can be called a *living* document. Give examples.

5. Could the United States operate solely on the basis of tradition without a written Constitution, as Great Britain has for centuries? Why or why not?

6. What do you think the Anti-Federalists were really afraid of?

7. Why shouldn't the Bill of Rights have been left up to each state to develop on its own?

8. Why couldn't a president be given supreme powers and still make the American system work, without a separation of powers?

9. Do you think the Constitution would have been ratified without discussion of a bill of rights?

10. If the United States Constitution works so well, why don't all countries adopt it?

References

Armento, Beverly J., Gary B. Nash, Christopher L. Salter and Karen K. Wixson. *A More Perfect Union.* Boston: Houghton Mifflin Company, 1991.

Atherton, Herbert M. and J. Jackson Barlow, eds. *The Bill of Rights and Beyond.* Washington: Commission on the Bicentennial of the United States (no date).

Lieberman, Jethro K. *The Enduring Constitution: A Bicentennial Perspective.* St. Paul: West Publishing Company, 1987.

Lieberman, Jethro K. *Milestones!* St. Paul: West Publishing Company, 1976.

Mitchell, Ralph. *CQ's Guide to the U.S. Constitution: History, Text, Glossary, Index.* Washington: Congressional Quarterly, Inc., 1986.

"Stalemate Wouldn't Surprise Founders." *Washington Post,* as reported in the *Star Tribune* (Minneapolis/St. Paul), November 19, 1995, p. A18.

Cases Cited

Kinsella v. United States, 361 U.S. 234, 80 S.Ct. 297, 4 L.Ed.2d 268 (1960).

McCulloch v. Maryland, 17 U.S. (4 Wheat.) 316, 4 L.Ed. 579 (1819).

The Constitution at Work

The Korean War Memorial, Washington, D.C.

SECTION ONE TRACED the development of the United States of America, its Revolutionary War for independence, the interim Articles of Confederation, the initial basis of government and ultimately the Constitution, which was drafted to govern this new country. This section describes in detail the judicial branch of government and how it was designed to function and has functioned for more than 200 years.

The section begins with a discussion of our legal system (Chapter 3), including the system as it exists at both the state and federal level. This is followed by an up-close look at the Supreme Court—the highest court in the land (Chapter 4). The section concludes with an explanation of where the law can be found, that is, how it can be researched (Chapter 5). The remainder of the text focuses on the amendments making up the Bill of Rights and how they have evolved during the past two centuries.

Chapter 3 An Overview of Our Legal System

The law must be stable, but it must not stand still.

—ROSCOE POUND,
Introduction to the Philosophy of Law

Thurgood Marshall Building, Washington, D.C.

DO YOU KNOW . . .

What the basic purpose of the American legal system is?

What the scales of justice symbolize in law?

How the law serves society?

What common law is?

What stare decisis is?

Why American law is said to be a living law?

What statutory law is?

The difference between a crime and a tort?

What two main functions are served by courts?

On what two levels our judicial system operates?

Who are officers of the court?

CAN YOU DEFINE THESE TERMS?

Adversarial judicial system
Appellate jurisdiction
Codified law
Common law
Concurrent jurisdiction
Crimes
Exclusive jurisdiction
General jurisdiction
Jurisdiction
Law
Limited jurisdiction
Ordinances
Original jurisdiction
Penal codes
Petition for certiorari
Promulgate
Stare decisis
Statutory law
Torts
Venue

INTRODUCTION

This chapter describes how the American legal system operates. Through this awareness you can then understand the critical role that the Constitution of the United States plays in ensuring a truly workable and fair system.

This chapter begins with a discussion of the purpose of our legal system and a description of law and how it has developed throughout the centuries, including the extremely important development of common law and the concept of stare decisis. This is followed by a description of categories of law, often overlapping, found in the United States legal system. Next the dynamic nature of our "living law" is discussed, followed by a discussion of the components of our legal system and the officers of the court. The chapter concludes with an explanation of the adversarial nature of our legal system.

When examining the overall legal system, you may find it, like the Constitution itself, to be overwhelming and complex. As you proceed through this text, keep in mind the basic purpose of our legal system.

THE BASIC PURPOSE OF OUR LEGAL SYSTEM

Chapter 2 discussed the challenge facing the framers of the Constitution *to balance the rights of individuals against the rights of society.* Recollections of the tyranny of British rulers prompted the framers of the Constitution to build in many safeguards against any such tyranny in the United States. Nonetheless, to avoid anarchy, a country of laws had to be established.

> ≋ The basic purpose of our legal system is to ensure *fairness* in balancing individual and societal rights and needs.

Achieving a workable system that balances the rights and needs of individuals as well as those of the society being served is no small task. In fact, many have died here, and continue to die in other countries, fighting for a system of government that provides the freedoms that American citizens now enjoy.

> ≋ The scales of justice represent keeping individual and societal needs in balance.

Some argue that in striving to balance individual and societal rights and needs, the system itself has become so complicated that justice is compromised. While the Constitution appears complex, actually it is the many laws that have been added that create the huge amount of law in which "loopholes" occur. Because the Constitution is meant to be basic, it is, by itself, easy to begin to understand. Students of the Constitution need to grasp the "big picture" before looking at the developments that have occurred in the past 200 years. Details can get in the way of understanding the system and how it works.

THE LAW

Simply put, a **law** is a rule. Laws are in place to serve the perceived needs of the society by ensuring values of that particular group. In a broader sense, the laws a society adopts reflect that society and speak to what its people hold important.

As the group becomes larger and more complex, so do the rules and the ways the rules are enforced. Ross and Ross (1981, pp. 1–2) state:

> Law consists of the rules of community living; it is a structure of rules, regulations, and accumulated decisions of the courts [based on] the recorded experiences of society and the community. . . . Laws are rules established by a governing power to maintain peace, secure justice for its members, define the legal rights of the individual and the community, and to punish offenders for legal wrongs.

> ≋ Law responds to the perceived needs of the society it serves by defining unacceptable behavior and establishing consequences.

DEVELOPMENT OF THE LAW

The development of societal rules began the first time people congregated. When people are together, a norm must be established so individuals know what is expected of them in relation to the group as a whole. Laws generally have evolved through four phases:

1. People come together seeking collective security, to collectively gather food and to satisfy other mutual needs.
2. They discover that they need rules to maintain order and their sense of security.
3. Inevitably some individuals break the rules.
4. Punishments are established for breaking the rules.

A rule established for the good of society with a punishment attached for violating the rule is a law.

Of great influence on the American legal system was early Roman law, dealing with basic rules related to economic, religious and family life contained in the Twelve Tables, written about 450 B.C. These rules were based on tradition and a quest for fairness. Another important period in Roman history was the rule of Emperor Justinian I (527–565 A.D.). His Justinian Code distinguished public and private laws and influenced legal thought throughout the Middle Ages.

Perhaps of greatest influence on the development of our legal system was the common law consisting of a body of unwritten legal precedents that developed during the Middle Ages in England. As royal judges traveled their appointed territories and heard cases, they began to replace local custom with a national law followed in courts throughout the country. In essence, the law was "common" to the entire nation. These unwritten legal precedents were based on the customs of the day and supported by court decisions.

> ⮿ **Common law** was early English judge-made law based on custom and tradition.

Offenses that once were considered personal wrongs, such as murder, rape and burglary, were redefined by English judges, making them subject to state control and punishment, that is, making them into crimes against the state. Common law depended heavily upon precedent and upon the concept of stare decisis.

Stare Decisis

American common law has developed by building upon itself. Courts continue to rely on prior cases, directly, by implication or conceptually, to maintain continuity. This continuity will not only result in the case before a court being decided in a way that has a relation to existing law, but also provides another element to our system of law development that provides a stronger basis on which future cases will be determined. This concept is termed **stare decisis,** meaning that previous rules set forth in other cases shall be used to decide future cases.

While this doctrine has its roots in early English law, the court in *Moore v. City of Albany* (1885) set forth ". . . [T]hat when [a] court has once laid down a principle of law as applicable to a certain state of facts, it will adhere to that principle and apply it to all future cases where facts are substantially the same." The idea behind this approach is to permit people to arrange their lives in accordance with the rules of society that can be best understood by knowing existing and past matters with the understanding that future matters will adhere to these concepts. Previous legal decisions provide an example, or the authority, for similar cases coming afterwards.

> Stare decisis is a common law doctrine that requires that precedent set in one case shall be followed in all cases having the same or similar circumstances, thus assuring consistency in the law.

Stare decisis is a Latin term that literally means "let the decision stand." When a legal principle has been determined by a higher court, lower courts must apply it to all later cases containing the same or similar facts. Of course, one side will say the facts are the same, and so stare decisis dictates that a certain ruling prevail. The other side will assert that the facts are not the same, and so a different result should be reached. Nonetheless, the doctrine of stare decisis is firmly entrenched as a basis of our law development and continues to be relied on as cases are reviewed by courts at all levels. It does not, however, prevent the law from growing or changing, or even reconsidering itself in matters in which undesirable law resulted. Facts can and will be interpreted by those involved in a manner that will best suit society.

AMERICAN LAW LIVES

Because the perceived needs of any group change as that group changes, effective law should be flexible enough to respond to those needs. Human nature dictates that different needs are perceived at different times. For example, laws against witchcraft in colonial America are no longer perceived as needed. Similarly, laws pertaining to the use of drugs have changed as societal norms have changed, as evidenced by laws dealing with certain marijuana situations or drunken driving laws becoming stricter. The constitutional amendments dealing with prohibition provide a concrete example of how our law can advance and retreat as our needs and expectations change.

American law has the ability to change with the needs of society. It is referred to as a *living law* because it is not stagnant. Rather, it grows along with society. It can be changed, expanded or rescinded to serve the overall system.

> American law is considered a living law because it can change along with society.

As you develop an understanding of what it is and how it developed from the needs of the earliest gatherings of people, it becomes obvious why modern law has reached the level of complexity it has. With over 258 million people in the United States and with the importance we place on pluralism, our needs are varied. A legal system that responds to such diversity, out of necessity, becomes complex. One of the complexities is that various categories of law exist, often overlapping.

CATEGORIES OF LAW

One of the easiest ways to grasp the law is to use the following classifications (Harr and Hess, 1990, p. 38):

❖ By type: written and common law.
❖ By source: constitutional, statutory and case law; ecclesiastical or cannon law.
❖ By the parties involved: public and private law.
❖ By substance: civil and criminal law.

Type

Written law is made by the legislative body having the judicial authority to **promulgate**—publish or announce officially—such rules that have legal consequences. These may be constitutions, by-laws, treaties, statutes or ordinances. These laws do not refer to specific cases. *Common law,* as you have seen, is unwritten early English judge-made law based on custom and tradition. Earlier cases serve as a basis on which to decide subsequent cases. It is the basis for our present day case law involving specific court decisions.

Source

The source of a law might be a specific case (case law), a state or federal statute or a constitution. Classification refers to constitutional, statutory and case law.

Case law relies upon past cases with similar circumstances, or precedents on which to build a defense or prosecution. *Statutory law* does not involve specific cases, but rather describes laws passed by governing bodies.

    🍃 **Statutory law** is set forth by legislatures or governing bodies.

Statutory law can also be referred to as **codified law** because it is set forth in organized, structured codes such as the United States criminal code or the criminal code of a specific state. Local jurisdictions, such as at the county or municipal level, may also enact their own specific codes, usually referred to as **ordinances.** Of critical importance is the fact that no statutory law, regardless of the level of jurisdiction, can violate the Constitution.

Constitutional law, as the name implies, is found within the constitutions of each state and within the Constitution. Constitutional law is at a higher level than statutory law, which is at a higher level than case law, as shown in Figure 3–1. Constitutional law is the focus of this text, but it is important to understand where it fits within the total legal system.

Each state has a constitution that not only reinforces the United States Constitution, but sets forth the basic legal and philosophical ideals that a particular state holds as important to its own identity.

Of ultimate importance is the United States Constitution because it is this basic legal framework that all other laws, at all jurisdictional levels, must

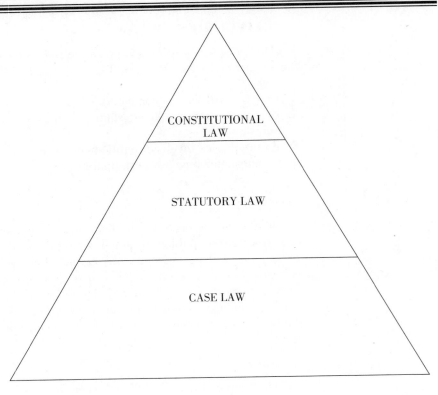

Figure 3–1
The hierarchy of
authority of laws.

abide. No treaty, state or local rule, or court decision can conflict with the Constitution, or that law is simply invalid.

Parties Involved

The public/private classification describes the scope of the law. As the name implies, public laws have a broad, general application, including such areas as traffic and crimes, as well as laws dealing with the relation of citizens to the government. Private laws have a much more limited scope, dealing with a few individuals, including such areas as contracts, negligence, wills and, in some states, divorce.

Substance

The civil/criminal classification describes the "wronged" party or individual victim. A civil wrong is called a *tort*. *Black's Law Dictionary* defines civil law as "laws concerned with civil or private rights and remedies, as contrasted with criminal laws." Civil laws deal with personal matters and with wrongs against individuals. The individual who has been wronged, the victim, seeks restitution or compensation, usually in the form of money.

Criminal laws, in contrast, deal with wrongs against society. *Black's Law Dictionary* defines criminal law as "that law which for the purpose of preventing harm to society, (a) declares what conduct is criminal, and (b) prescribes the punishment to be imposed for such conduct." Society, then, is the victim as a whole. Although, obviously, an individual has been hurt, it is the welfare of all society that has been violated. Criminal laws are found in the states' **penal codes.**

> Civil laws deal with personal matters and wrongs against individuals—called **torts.** Criminal laws deal with wrongs against society—called **crimes.** An act may be both a tort and a crime.

However, each act that constitutes both a tort and a crime must be dealt with separately; the crime through prosecution in the criminal courts, and the tort through redress the victim (or plaintiff) may seek to receive by filing a civil action against the wrongdoer. Torts are associated with liability; crimes are associated with innocence or guilt.

If one person assaults another person, that assault can be charged as a tort and the assailant sued in civil court. If found guilty, the person can be ordered to make *restitution* by paying the victim a specified amount of money. In addition, the assailant can be charged with a crime and tried in criminal court. If found guilty, the person can be sentenced to prison or some other appropriate *punishment.*

In the case of O. J. Simpson, although he was found not guilty of the crime of murder, as this text goes to press the victims' parents are suing him in civil court for the wrongful deaths of their children.

THE COMPONENTS OF OUR LEGAL SYSTEM

This chapter provides a starting point for studying the Constitution by helping you understand the system that permits the law to serve our society. Just like a complicated recipe made of many individual ingredients, our legal system has many components that must work together to produce the desired result.

Recall that Article 3 of the United States Constitution established our federal judicial system: "The judicial Power of the United States shall be vested in one Supreme Court, and in such inferior courts as the Congress may from time to time ordain and establish." In addition, the congresses of the individual states have established state supreme courts and inferior courts.

> The courts' two main functions are to settle controversies between parties and to decide the rules of law that apply in the specific case.

What kinds of cases a court can hear depends on its **jurisdiction.** The term *jurisdiction* refers either to:

❖ The authority of a legislative body to establish a law or a court to hear a case.
❖ The authority a law has over a specific group of people.

Three levels of jurisdiction exist: federal, state and local. In addition, jurisdiction can be original or appellate. **Original jurisdiction** describes a court authorized to hear cases first, try them and render decisions. Such courts are often called *trial courts*. **Appellate jurisdiction** describes a court authorized to review cases and to either affirm or reverse the actions of a lower court.

Courts may also have general or limited jurisdiction. As the names imply, courts with **general jurisdiction** may hear a wide range of cases; those of **limited jurisdiction** hear a much narrower range of cases. Further, courts may have exclusive or concurrent jurisdiction. **Exclusive jurisdiction** only applies to courts that can hear specific cases. **Concurrent jurisdiction** refers to two or more courts authorized to hear a specific type of case.

Finally, the term *jurisdiction* may refer to a geographical area. A more precise term to describe the geographical area in which a case may be heard is venue. **Venue** refers to the place a specific case may come to trial and the area from which the jury is selected.

With the terminology describing the authority of specific courts understood, look next at the court system of the United States, beginning with the lowest level and continuing to the highest—the United States Supreme Court.

THE COURT SYSTEM

Just as the United States Constitution established the federal court system, state constitutions establish their own court system with many variations from state to state.

Figure 3–2
The levels in the state and federal court systems.

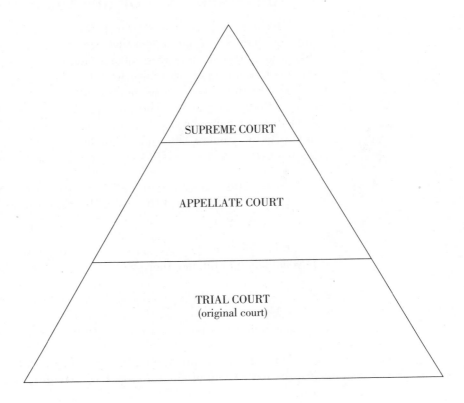

SUPREME COURT

APPELLATE COURT

TRIAL COURT
(original court)

    The United States judicial system is two-tiered, consisting of state and federal court systems. Each includes specific levels of courts.

At either tier function three levels of courts: a lower level or trial court, an appellate court and a court of last resort, or Supreme Court, as illustrated in Figure 3–2.

Our legal system was designed to provide individuals with a fair and just trial conducted under fair rules of procedure in an atmosphere of objectivity. These levels exist to assure that if either side feels procedural rules were violated, they can appeal the case to a higher court. This appellate court can uphold the lower court's finding, order a new trial or overturn/reverse/dismiss the charge.

THE STATE COURT SYSTEM

Individual states establish a variety of lower courts with a variety of names. Figure 3–3 illustrates the state court system.

Lower Courts

Lower courts include municipal courts, inferior courts of limited jurisdiction and county courts.

Municipal courts hear ordinance violations, minor criminal cases, traffic cases and sometimes more major cases. Their authority is usually limited to the city or county in which the court is located.

Inferior courts of limited jurisdiction include probate courts, family courts, police courts, justice of the peace courts and traffic courts. A few states still have police courts, courts that try misdemeanor offenses and conduct preliminary examinations to decide if evidence is sufficient to bring the case to trial in a higher level court. Some states have established these inferior courts of limited jurisdiction to eliminate the expense and inconvenience of having to travel to a county or district court.

County courts often have exclusive jurisdiction over misdemeanor cases and civil cases involving a limited amount of money. In some states, county courts also are probate courts and juvenile courts. Some states have combined various courts under the umbrella of the county courts.

Superior courts are the highest trial courts with general jurisdiction. More than 3,000 such courts exist in the United States. This is where most felony cases enter the system. Some states call them district courts, circuit courts or courts of common plea. These courts may have an appellate department to hear and decide appeals from the municipal courts.

Intermediate Appellate Courts

These courts were created in several states to reduce the case loads of the state supreme courts. Appealed cases generally go to the intermediate appellate court first.

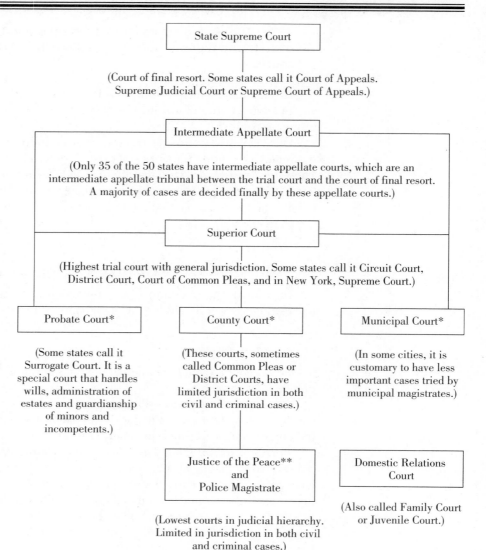

Figure 3–3

State judicial system.

*Courts of special jurisdiction such as probate, family or juvenile courts, and the so-called inferior courts such as common pleas or municipal courts may be separate courts or part of the trial court of general jurisdiction.
**Justices of the peace do not exist in all states. Where they do exist, their jurisdictions vary greatly from state to state. Note: In California all justice courts are now municipal courts.
Source: American Bar Association. *Law and the Courts* Chicago: American Bar Association, 1974, p. 20. Updated information provided by West Publishing Company, St Paul, Minnesota (Senna and Siegel, 7th ed., 1996, p. 387). Reprinted by permission. All rights reserved.

State Supreme Courts

State supreme courts are the highest courts in a state and are generally called supreme courts, although some states call them courts of appeals. These courts are given their power by the individual state constitutions. They generally oversee the intermediate appellate courts and have very few areas of original jurisdiction. If someone petitions the supreme court to review the decision of an appeals court, this is called a **petition for certiorari.** A lower court must abide by the decision of a higher court.

THE FEDERAL COURT SYSTEM

The federal court system consists of a number of specialized courts, a number of district courts with general jurisdiction, 12 circuit courts of appeals and the United States Supreme Court. See Figure 3–4.

Figure 3–4
Federal judicial system.

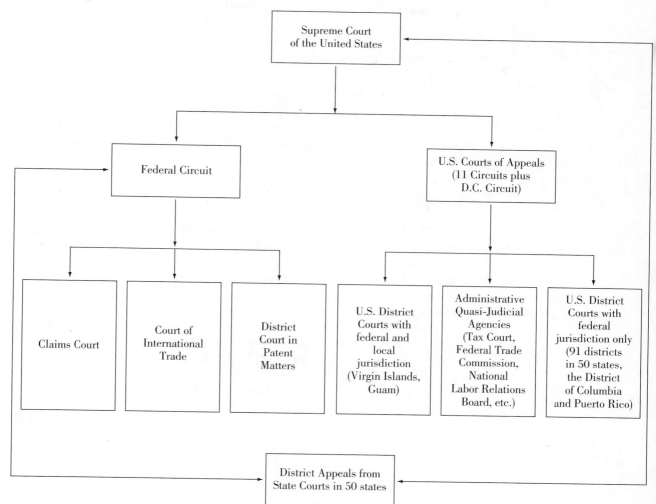

Special United States Courts

Congress has created several specialized courts with which you will probably never have any dealings. They include the Court of Military Appeals, the Court of Claims, the Court of Customs and Patent Appeals, the Customs Court and the Tax Court.

United States District Courts

The district courts are trial courts with general, original, *federal* jurisdiction. They try both civil and criminal cases. In civil cases, however, the plaintiff and defendant must be from different states, and the amount of the lawsuit must be over $10,000. The federal district courts try a very limited number of criminal cases.

Each state has at least one district court. Some large states have four. The total number of district courts is 94 (92 in the states, one in the District of Columbia and one in Puerto Rico).

United States Courts of Appeals

Like the intermediate appellate courts at the state level, the United States Courts of Appeals were created to ease the caseload of the Supreme Court. Each state is assigned to one of 11 districts or circuits. The District of Columbia has its own circuit and court. These courts have jurisdiction over final decisions of federal district courts. They are the court of last resort in most federal cases.

The United States Supreme Court

The United States Supreme Court is the ultimate court of appeal. Its chief function is as an appellate court. It receives petitions for certiorari for 2,000 to 4,000 cases a year, but usually accepts only 10% for review. More than a third of the cases received are from state supreme courts. The Supreme Court is restricted by act of Congress to hear only certain types of appeals from federal appeals courts and state supreme courts. Basically, the cases must involve a federal or state statute alleged to be unconstitutional. There is no right to have a case heard by the Supreme Court. It hears only cases of extreme national importance to set important policy.

The Supreme Court has dealt with such controversial issues as abortion, busing and school prayer. Bills have been introduced in Congress to prevent the Supreme Court from ruling on such "moral" issues, leaving it up to the individual states. The Supreme Court is the only court empowered to handle lawsuits between two states. Because of its extreme importance in shaping our laws, the next chapter is devoted to the Supreme Court.

OFFICERS OF THE COURT

Our judicial system does not consist simply of buildings. Within the courthouses are individuals charged with carrying out the administration of justice.

> The officers of the court are judges, lawyers, clerks of court, sheriffs, marshals and bailiffs.

Judges, sometimes called justices or magistrates, are elected in some states and appointed in other states. Judges preside over trials and hearings and render decisions. They also oversee the selection of juries and instruct them during jury cases.

Lawyers represent one side or the other. In a civil case, the plaintiff's lawyer represents the party bringing suit. In a criminal case, the prosecutor represents the state. The lawyer representing the other party is the defense attorney. They prepare and present their clients' cases to a judge and sometimes to a jury.

Clerks of court schedule the cases and officially record all business conducted by the court. Clerks also receive and file all official documents related to a case, for example, summons and complaints.

Sheriffs and *marshals,* as officers of the court, serve summons and other court documents and enforce court orders. Sheriffs function at the state level and marshals at the federal level.

Bailiffs are responsible for keeping the courtroom proceedings orderly and dignified and for protecting everyone in the courtroom.

OUR ADVERSARIAL JUDICIAL SYSTEM

Once a person is charged with an offense, civil or criminal, sides are drawn. The accusing side has the burden of proof to establish guilt. The defendant is presumed innocent until this has been accomplished.

The legal system established in the United States is termed an **adversarial judicial system** because only in an actual conflict will a judicial body hear the case. Theoretically, courts will not entertain "what if" questions. Actual people must have reached an impasse and require a binding decision by a court. In practice, however, as noted by Schulman (1995), the Court has frequently relaxed this barrier, has found exceptions to it and has applied it inconsistently. The abortion case *Roe v. Wade* (1973), for example, was decided long after the petitioner's pregnancy had terminated and the controversy ended.

As designed, however, the system places one side against the other, whether the government and a private party or individual against individual. While the system encourages problems to be settled out of court, the system is prepared to be accessed when necessary.

The overall legal system is organized to provide parties to a case the most accessible tribunal. For example, a matter involving a local building code dispute is best taken up by a municipal board of adjustments and appeals or the city council. The violation of a state statute, on the other hand, is best dealt with by a state court.

All levels of jurisdiction have avenues of appeals, so that the matter may be heard by another body of decision makers. This system provides a degree of checks and balances and removes the element of personal involvement sometimes questioned at the local level.

Summary

The basic purpose of our legal system is to ensure *fairness* in *balancing individual and societal rights and needs.* This balance between individual and societal rights and needs is represented by the scales of justice. The American legal system rests squarely upon a foundation of law. Law responds to the perceived needs of the society it serves by defining unacceptable behavior and establishing consequences for those engaging in unacceptable behavior.

Our legal system has its roots in the common law of England, the early English judge-made law based on custom and tradition. Inherent in the common law was the principle of stare decisis. Stare decisis requires that precedents set in one case be followed in all cases having similar circumstances, thus assuring consistency in the law. And although the law, in fairness, must be consistent, it is also flexible. American law is considered a living law because it can change along with society.

In addition to common law, our legal system also relies upon case law, statutory law—that is, law passed by legislature or governing bodies—and constitutional law. Our legal system categorizes offenses into two specific areas: civil and criminal. Civil laws deal with personal matters and wrongs against individuals—called *torts*. Criminal laws deal with wrongs against society—called *crimes*. An act may be both a tort and a crime.

When civil or criminal laws are broken, the courts' two main functions are to settle controversies between parties and to decide the rules of law that apply in specific cases. The American legal system is made up of a number of necessary components. It is basically a two-tiered system consisting of state and federal courts. Each tier includes specific levels of courts. The officers of the court are judges, lawyers, clerks of court, sheriffs, marshals and bailiffs.

Discussion Questions

1. Could a country like the United States function without a federal constitution? Would it be possible for each state to merely abide by its own constitution?

2. Why shouldn't the Constitution include an overall criminal code specifying crimes and punishments that could apply throughout the United States?

3. Why is society considered the victim of a crime rather than the individual victimized?

4. Why must our system provide an appeal procedure?

5. Can you develop an argument against stare decisis?

6. Why shouldn't courts be permitted to argue "what if" questions?

7. Discuss why criminal law is set forth in codified form rather than strictly by common law.

8. If the basic purpose of our legal system is to ensure *fairness* in balancing individual and societal rights and needs, is that end best served by an adversarial system in which the person with the best lawyer often comes out on top? Does our system of justice provide equal access to persons of different socioeconomic classes?

9. Discuss whether you consider our law a "living law."

10. Should people have a right to a defense attorney?

References

Harr, J. Scott and Kären M. Hess. *Criminal Procedure.* St. Paul: West Publishing Company, 1990.

Ross, J. Martin and Jeffrey S. Ross. *Handbook of Everyday Law.* New York: Harper & Row, 1981.

Schulman, William. Review of the manuscript. Middle Tennessee State University, September 1995.

Cases Cited

Moore v. City of Albany, 98 N.Y. 396, 410 (1885).

Roe v. Wade, 410 U.S. 113 (1973).

Chapter 4

The Supreme Court of the United States: The Final Word

The principle is that ours is a government of laws, not of men, and that we submit ourselves to rulers only if under rules.

—JUSTICE ROBERT H. JACKSON, *Youngstown Sheet and Tube Co. v. Sawyer* **(1952)**

The United States Supreme Court.

DO YOU KNOW . . .

What was accomplished by the English Bill of Rights? The United States Bill of Rights?

Under what authority the Supreme Court operates?

What the jurisdiction of the Supreme Court is?

How the Supreme Court has effectively created most of its own power and authority?

Whether the Supreme Court can review acts of Congress? The precedent case?

Whether the Supreme Court can review cases that are pending in state courts or that have been decided in state courts? The precedent case?

What certiorari is?

Why appointments of justices to the Supreme Court are lifetime?

Whether the Supreme Court of the 1990s is liberal or conservative?

CAN YOU DEFINE THESE TERMS?

Certiorari
Judicial review
Opinion
Recesses
Sittings

INTRODUCTION

While the creation of our Supreme Court is uniquely American, like American law itself, it is deeply rooted in the very history of why the framers of the Constitution—representing those who came to America in search of freedom and a better life—created the United States of America. And while already mentioned, visitors to Washington, D.C., cannot help but be drawn to the inscriptions on the two statues outside the National Archives building (in which are displayed, among other things, the Declaration of Independence, the United States Constitution and the Bill of Rights) on which is inscribed: *Study the Past* and *What Is Past Is Prologue.*

This chapter has been included not because many of us will ever find ourselves appearing before the Supreme Court, but because the workings of the Supreme Court are an integral part of our legal system. It is imperative that those studying our law, and particularly our Constitution, have a working knowledge of this aspect of our legal system.

The history and the individuals who make up the Supreme Court combine with its role as defined by the Constitution to create a uniquely effective overseer of our system. To understand this part of the system is to have a better understanding of our system of law.

*National Archives
Building, Washington,
D.C.*

This chapter begins with a review of the Magna Carta and the principles from it that found their way into the United States Constitution. This is followed by a discussion of how the United States Supreme Court gets its authority, its jurisdiction and the powerful influence it has through judicial review and through certiorari. Next the makeup of the Supreme Court is discussed, including the composition of the present-day court and how the jurists' personal philosophies regarding crime and justice affect the entire system. The chapter concludes with a description of some of the Court's traditions, procedures and power.

THE MAGNA CARTA AND THE ENGLISH BILL OF RIGHTS

When the English drafted the Magna Carta in 1215, their intent was to develop a legal system that would no longer be based on an individual ruler's system of laws, but a system of laws that even a ruler would have to abide by. This was the origin of the concept of what was to become the United States Supreme Court.

While the concept of "due process" continued to be a derived ideal in England, the Crown did not accept it. And in 1608 a showdown between what was and what was to be occurred within the British courts that would eventually pave the way to put into practice what the Magna Carta set forth in theory.

In Calvin's case (1608) Lord Chancellor Ellesmere reinforced tradition by stating: "The monarch *is* the law; the king is the law speaking." And as Wiecek (1988, p. 5) contends, King James I did not take kindly to Sir Edward Coke, chief justice of the Court of Common Pleas, asserting that even the king must abide by the law. Wiecek (p. 6) colorfully explains Coke's show of disagreement with the existing system by defiantly standing upright in the presence of the king, rather than falling to the floor and groveling, as was the accepted and expected tradition when judges were before the king. Coke's assertion that even the king was *sub deo et legel* (under God and under the law) proved to be the spark that, in many ways, ignited freedom both in England and, eventually, abroad.

After much bloodshed, in what is referred to as the Glorious Revolution, the Parliamentary Party deposed James II and appointed William and Mary as the new monarchs. Under an imposed condition, the new monarchs were to support the English Bill of Rights (1689), which declared that "pretended power of dispensing laws by regal authority as it hath been assumed and exercised of late is illegal" (Wiecek, p. 6).

The English Bill of Rights was a tremendous step toward the development of a true limited government. And it is through their struggle that one can only imagine the conversations sparking the imaginations of those who were unknowingly laying the groundwork for what was to become not only a new legal system, unlike that existing anywhere in the world, but of an entirely new country.

The English Bill of Rights now had the intended opportunity to develop the ideals of the Magna Carta in creating a much fairer society. Among other things, the English Bill of Rights prohibited the king from forming armies without authorization from Parliament, using "puppet" courts, summarily increasing taxes and using unreasonable fines or cruel and unusual punishment (Wiecek, p. 3).

> The English Bill of Rights provided a mechanism to assure the ideals set forth in the Magna Carta.

Momentum was developing for a new system of law that would influence all the world:

> . . . here is a law which is above the king and which even he must not break. This reaffirmation of a supreme law and its expression in a general charter is the great work of the Magna Carta, and this alone justifies the respect in which men have held it.—Sir Winston Churchill

And while much more time could and arguably should be devoted to delving into the rich history that contributed to what was to become the law of the United States, it is most important at this point to grasp all the importance of what is set forth in the thirty-ninth chapter of the Magna Carta. It is there that we read: ". . . no freeman shall be captured or imprisoned . . . nor will we go against him or send against him, except by the lawful judgment of his peers and by the law of the land." As Wiecek (1988, p. 7) states, it is this portion of the Magna Carta that "embodies the Anglo-American ideal of the rule of law."

Recall that in the United States the Bill of Rights had to be added to the Constitution before most states would ratify it. They considered it important to have a Constitution that would not only establish a workable government, but one that would ensure fairness and freedom by defining what power the federal government would and would not have.

> ⋙ The United States Bill of Rights, guaranteeing citizens freedom from government oppression, assured that the Constitution would be accepted and function as the framework for government.

In the arguments presented to the states in *The Federalist Papers*, Alexander Hamilton stated that the Bill of Rights would also be overseen by the judiciary. This would ensure that neither the executive nor the legislative branches of government would infringe on these important rights.

AUTHORITY FOR THE COURT

The law that emanates from the Supreme Court is the law of the land, and no other judicial or political body can overrule decisions it makes. Because American law is, indeed, a living law capable of change, it is conceivable that the Supreme Court could overrule itself, which it has, in fact, done. But the United States Supreme Court does wield the ultimate power in this country, and some might even argue, beyond.

The constitutional establishment, or authority, is found in Article 3, which provides a framework for the federal judiciary. Goebel (1971) suggests, however, that the framers of the Constitution went a little light on just how it should be organized. Goebel notes that "provision for a national judiciary was a matter of theoretical compulsion rather than of practical necessity . . . more in deference to the maxim of separation of powers than in response to clearly formulated ideas about the role of a national judicial system and its indispensability."

But remembering that the Constitution itself is a rather brief document intended to set forth the framework of the new government, rather than to provide the lengthy specifics that others would find themselves having the responsibility of developing, it should not surprise—nor trouble us—that this article is brief and to the point as well. Article 3 states:

> The judicial power of the United States, shall be vested in one Supreme Court, and in such inferior courts as the Congress may from time to time ordain and establish.

> ⋙ The United States Constitution ordains in Article 3 that there shall be a Supreme Court.

Section 2 of Article 3 of the Constitution defines the jurisdiction (or boundaries) of the Supreme Court.

JURISDICTION OF THE SUPREME COURT

Section 2. The judicial Power shall extend to all Cases, in Law and Equity, arising under this Constitution, the Laws of the United States, and Treaties made, or which shall be made, under their Authority;—to all Cases affecting Ambassadors, other public Ministers and Consuls;—to all Cases of admiralty and maritime Jurisdiction;—to Controversies to which the United States shall be a Party;—to Controversies between two or more States; between a State and Citizens of another State;—between Citizens of the same State claiming Lands under Grants of different States, and between a State, or the Citizens thereof, and foreign States, Citizens or Subjects.

In all Cases affecting Ambassadors, other public Ministers and Consuls, and those in which a State shall be Party, the Supreme Court shall have original Jurisdiction. In all the other Cases before mentioned, the Supreme Court shall have appellate Jurisdiction, both as to Law and Fact, with such Exceptions, and under such Regulations as the Congress shall make.

The Court has jurisdiction over two general types of cases: cases that reach it *on appeal* and cases over which the Court has *original jurisdiction,* meaning the case can actually start at the Supreme Court. Whether a case begins in the state or federal system, the path to appeal a case to the Supreme Court is the same, as shown in Figure 4–1.

Because the framers of the Constitution did not wish for any individual or body to have excessive authority, the Supreme Court has only specific authority itself. It may hear appeals from lower state and federal courts on issues that involve interpretation of either federal law and/or the applicability of the Constitution to the subject at hand. The Supreme Court can also hear appeals on cases dealing with treaties the United States has entered into, admiralty and maritime cases or those involving certain public officials and political entities.

It should not be assumed, however, that the Supreme Court and inferior federal courts have carte blanche to do whatever they want. In the post Civil War case *Ex parte McCardle* (1868), Congress reserved the right to limit the jurisdiction of federal courts, including the Supreme Court. This does not mean that Congress, or any legislature, can override the Constitution by promulgating unconstitutional law. It does mean that Congress retains the authority to determine what types of cases can be heard by these courts, thus affecting their jurisdictional authority.

United States v. Klein (1871) supported the *McCardle* decision in that the Supreme Court held that Congress, indeed, retains the power under Article 3 to determine which federal courts may hear certain types of cases. These two cases dealt with what types of appeals could be presented to federal courts. This is an excellent example of the natural tension that the Constitution creates to prevent any one branch of government from exercising excessive power. These cases show how power with limitations is granted to Congress and the Court to assure the balance sought by a free society through the Constitution—a commendable forethought by those creating it.

The Constitution permits the Court original jurisdiction in cases dealing with foreign dignitaries or cases involving legal disputes between states, with the rationale that a state court could not remain unbiased if its state was a party to the suit. All other cases the Court considers only on appeal.

> The Supreme Court has original jurisdiction in cases dealing with foreign dignitaries and in legal disputes between states. All other cases are only on appeal.

Figure 4-1

The path of a case to the United States Supreme Court.

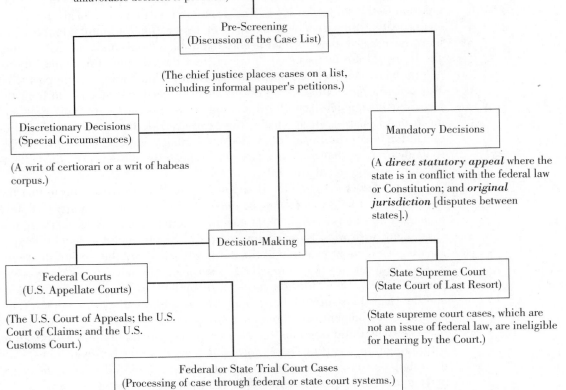

As noted by Goebel (1971, p. 280):

> The brevity of the constitutional description left to Congress and the Court itself the task of filling in much of the substance and all of the details of the new judicial system. One early observer commented, "The convention has only crayoned in the outlines. It is left to Congress to fill up and colour the canvas."

One of the most important ways in which the Court did so was to establish judicial review of laws passed or of cases settled by lower courts.

JUDICIAL REVIEW

The Supreme Court has tremendous power through the process of **judicial review**—the power of the Court to analyze decisions of other government entities and lower courts. The Supreme Court can decide what laws and lower court decisions are constitutional.

> The Supreme Court has effectively created most of its own power and authority through the process of judicial review.

Initially, the Supreme Court did not review state decisions. It is not surprising that lively debate has occurred over just exactly how far the Supreme Court may go in performing its job or what that job actually *is* as well. As in other parts of the Constitution, the brevity leaves room for much interpretation, debate and disagreement.

It was not until 1803 that the Court forcefully asserted its right to judicial review. In 1803 the Supreme Court heard the case of *Marbury v. Madison*, taking advantage of the opportunity to define its own role. William Marbury had been appointed justice of the peace for the District of Columbia in 1801 by President John Adams just before Adams left office. When Thomas Jefferson became president, his new secretary of state, James Madison, would not acknowledge Marbury's position. Marbury took the case to the United States Supreme Court, demanding that the new secretary of state recognize his appointment.

While admittedly a complex case, Chief Justice John Marshall recognized the opportunity to definitively state that, indeed, the United States Supreme Court had the power and prestige to declare an Act of Congress (in this case, the Judiciary Act, passed by Congress in 1789) unconstitutional. Chief Justice Marshall went so far as to say that it was the Supreme Court's *responsibility* to overturn unconstitutional legislation because of the Court's duty to uphold the Constitution. Chief Justice Marshall forcefully established the Supreme Court's authority as the final interpreter of the Constitution:

> If the courts are to regard the Constitution and the Constitution is superior to any ordinary act of the legislature, the Constitution and not such ordinary act must govern the case to which they apply. . . . It is emphatically the province of the judicial department to say what the law is.

In stating that the Constitution is the supreme law of the land and that the justices are required to follow it rather than inconsistent provisions of legislation, the Court denied Marbury his commission.

In short, the legal groundwork (precedent) was established authorizing the Court to maintain a position of the ultimate de facto lawmaker by deciding what legislation is and is not constitutional. Arguably, while Congress could regroup and promulgate additional legislation, the Supreme Court could declare it unconstitutional as well. The Supreme Court does, in fact, have awesome power.

〰️ *Marbury v. Madison* (1803) established that the Supreme Court has the authority to review acts of Congress.

The power of the Supreme Court was further reaffirmed in *Martin v. Hunter's Lessee* (1816). This case established the power Congress had given the Supreme Court to hear cases involving federal law and constitutional issues. The Supreme Court determined that it could reverse state court decisions that involved federal legal issues. This case involved a dispute over land ownership. When the Supreme Court heard the case and made a determination, the Virginia state courts refused to follow the Court's decision, arguing that the Supreme Court had no authority to overrule the state court's decision. Again, while the case is complex, the final determination was that the Supreme Court *did* have the authority to review cases dealing with federal law, even though the case is pending in a state court.

To clarify, Supreme Court Justice Oliver Wendell Holmes asserted that while the *Marbury v. Madison* case gave the Supreme Court the power to declare acts of Congress unconstitutional, it was even more important that, in the case of *Martin v. Hunter's Lessee*, the Supreme Court had the authority and power to review and reverse state court decisions to ensure consistent interpretations of federal law.

〰️ *Martin v. Hunter's Lessee* (1816) held that the Supreme Court can review and reverse state court decisions and can review pending state cases.

Judicial Review over Time

Over time judicial review has been actively pursued and purposefully avoided. Supporters of judicial review see it as the Court's responsibility to monitor any government infringement on civil rights, be it through legislation or the actions of a lower court. Supporters of restraining judicial review, on the other hand, contend that laws should be upheld unless they very obviously violate constitutional rights. Under Chief Justice Earl Warren, the Court clearly supported judicial review and did much to advance individual rights. This trend was reversed under the leadership of Chief Justices Warren Burger and William Rehnquist, with the Court becoming more conservative on criminal justice issues, as will be discussed later in the chapter.

Another source of power of the Supreme Court is its authorization to select which cases it will hear by denying or accepting petitions for certiorari, in essence defining the key justice issues of any given year.

Certiorari

Regardless of what case the Supreme Court *may* hear, what it decides *to* hear is discretionary. A writ of certiorari is issued when at least four of the nine justices of the Supreme Court vote in favor of hearing the case requesting review by the Supreme Court. **Certiorari** is the Latin term meaning "to be informed," which the Supreme Court uses to state which cases it will hear.

> If the Court grants certiorari, it will hear and decide that case.

Because some 7,000 cases are submitted to the Court for review annually, and that number is rapidly increasing, the Court agrees to hear only about 150 cases a year. This agreement is reached behind closed doors.

In determining which cases to hear, and with as many as 75% of the petitions for certiorari denied by the court, the justices are looking for cases that involve matters that directly influence the law and the nation. This is another example of how powerful this institution is. The justices alone determine on which cases a final decision will be made.

WHO SHALL SERVE AND HOW?

The Supreme Court has one chief justice and eight associate justices, appointed by the president of the United States and confirmed by the legislature. It is clear that the framers of the Constitution did not intend for undue influence to be applied to justices serving on the Supreme Court or on any inferior court. Section 1 directs that:

> The Judges, both of the supreme and inferior Courts, shall hold their Offices during good Behavior, and shall, at stated Times, receive for their Services, a Compensation, which shall not be diminished during their Continuance in Office.

So no one trying to influence their decisions can ever hold either their jobs or their paychecks over their heads.

> A Supreme Court appointment is a lifetime appointment so a justice may not be unduly influenced.

Article 2 of the Constitution directs that the president of the United States shall nominate a judge for appointment to the Court, which the Senate must confirm. Article 2 also directs that federal judges, along with all other government officials, could be removed from their offices "on impeachment for and conviction of, treason, bribery, or other high crimes and misdemeanors." And so, even arguably the most secure jobs in the land have their limitations.

Appointing Supreme Court justices is a particularly powerful responsibility. While the president will have no authority over a justice once appointed, considerable research is conducted before the president recommends an individual. By scrutinizing a judicial candidate's past record a president is likely to predict how someone might lean when deciding certain issues of political importance. A conservative president will seek to appoint a conservative judge, and a liberal president will seek a liberal judge. The power of a president to potentially mold the makeup of the Court is a most envied political privilege.

THE JUSTICES

Since the origin of the Supreme Court in 1790, more than 100 justices have served. Appendix C is a list of all past and present members of the Supreme Court, their state, the president who appointed them and their terms.

The 1960s saw a liberal Supreme Court under Chief Justice Earl Warren, with a focus on the rights of the accused. The expansion of criminal procedural rights was slowed in the 1970s and 1980s by President Nixon's appointments of conservatives Warren Burger and William Rehnquist. However, another Nixon appointee, Harry Blackmun, tended to the liberal side. President Ford's single appointee, John Paul Stevens, tended to be moderate to liberal in his views, rather middle of the road, not greatly influencing the direction of the Court.

President Reagan's three appointments continued the trend toward a conservative Court. Sandra Day O'Connor, the first woman to serve on the Court, was seen as moderate to conservative, usually voting to limit prisoner's rights. Antonin Scalia and Anthony Kennedy were both considered very conservative. Also tipping the balance to the conservative side was the appointment of William H. Rehnquist as chief justice.

When conservative David Souter was appointed by President Bush to replace liberal William Brennan in 1990, the trend toward a conservative Court continued, with the Court increasingly favoring the state and law enforcement's position over that of criminal defendants. For example, in *Payne v. Tennessee* (1991), the Court overturned a ban on using evidence about a victim's character and the impact on the victim's family during sentencing.

The trend continued when President Bush appointed another conservative, Clarence Thomas, to replace liberal Thurgood Marshall. President Clinton's appointment of Ruth Bader Ginsburg in 1993 is unlikely to change the "law and order" conservative Court existing in the 1990s. Table 4–1 describes the makeup of the current Supreme Court.

> The Supreme Court of the 1990s is decidedly conservative—a "law and order" court.

The influence of the Supreme Court on the justice system is tremendous, as previously noted. Indeed, most criminal procedure has been established not by legislative acts but by appellate courts, the most important of which is the Supreme Court.

Table 4-1 The Current United States Supreme Court (1996).

Justice	President appointing	Political party	Year nominated	Age at nomination/ current age	Years of previous judicial experience	Views	Home state
Byron R. White	Kennedy	Democrat	1962	44/78	0	Usually conservative	Colorado
John Paul Stevens	Ford	Republican	1976	55/75	5	Moderate to liberal	Illinois
Sandra Day O'Connor	Reagan	Republican	1981	51/66	6.5	Moderate to conservative	Arizona
William H. Rehnquist	Nixon	Republican	1971	47/72	0	Very conservative	Arizona
Appointed chief justice	Reagan		1986				
Antonin Scalia	Reagan	Republican	1986	50/60	4	Very conservative	Illinois
Anthony Kennedy	Reagan	Republican	1988	51/59	12	Very conservative	California
David H. Souter	Bush	Republican	1990	50/56	13	Conservative	New Hampshire
Clarence Thomas	Bush	Republican	1991	43/48	1	Conservative	Georgia
Ruth Bader Ginsburg	Clinton	Democrat	1993	60/63	13	?	New York

The Chief Justice

The current chief justice, William H. Rehnquist, was born October 1, 1924, in Milwaukee, Wisconsin. He served in the United States Army Air Force from 1943 to 1946. Rehnquist earned a BA, MA and LLB from Stanford University and an MA from Harvard University. From 1953 to 1969 he practiced law in Phoenix, Arizona. From 1969 to 1971 he served as assistant attorney general, Office of Legal Counsel. In 1972 President Nixon nominated him to the Supreme Court. He took his seat January 7, 1972, and was nominated chief justice by President Reagan, assuming that office on September 26, 1986.

TRADITIONS AND PROCEDURES

While there is certainly definitive authority as to what the Supreme Court *can* hear, *how* the Court conducts its business is based to a very large degree on tradition, with respect for the process that has endured, along with the Constitution and the findings of the Supreme Court itself. While of little practical importance, except perhaps for the lawyers arguing before the Court, it is interesting and worth a few paragraphs.

By federal statute, a term of the Supreme Court always begins on the first Monday in October, continuing until June or July. Terms are made up of **sittings,** when cases are heard, and **recesses,** during which the Court considers administrative matters at hand and the justices actually write their opinions. Usually each side has 30 minutes to present its arguments, with 22 to 24 cases presented at one sitting. The 10 a.m. entrance of the justices into the courtroom is announced by the marshal and is steeped in history and tradition, as described by the Supreme Court itself (no date, p. 14):

United States Supreme Court chambers. (Photo by Fred Ward. Provided by Black Star.)

Those present, at the sound of the gavel, arise and remain standing until the robed Justices are seated following the traditional chant: "The Honorable, the Chief Justice and the Associate Justices of the Supreme Court of the United States. Oyez! Oyez! Oyez! All persons having business before the Honorable, the Supreme Court of the United States, are admonished to draw near and give their attention, for the Court is now sitting. God save the United States and this Honorable Court!"

The justices all sit at a large conference table and discuss each case. The most junior justice is required to present his or her view of that particular case first. This allows the most senior justices to control the decisions as the votes come in. The decisions reached are then cast into opinions.

Opinions

An **opinion** is a written statement explaining the legal issues involved in a case and the precedents on which the opinion is based. The chief justice assigns the writing of the opinion if he voted with the majority. The justice may assign the case to himself. If the chief justice did not vote with the majority, the most senior justice voting with the majority assigns the writing of the opinion. Any justice is free to write an opinion, even if not assigned to do so. This opinion can be *concurring* (agreeing with the majority) or *dissenting* (disagreeing with the majority and the reasons underlying the disagreement).

Interpretations

The justices not only render decisions, they also interpret the Constitution. The interpretive principles used as the justices deliberate are critical in accomplishing judicial review.

Strict construction means that there is a rigid reading and interpretation of that law. While there is no formal definition of the term, strict construction would not likely expand the specifically set forth law of the particular statute, particularly in expanding the intent of that law. Others may choose to interpret laws more liberally, often referring to the "spirit of the law" rather than the specific wording of the law. As noted by Schulman (1995):

> The recent political history of the Court is the battle for interpretive control between the "strict constructionists" like Robert Bork and the "noninterpretivist" theorists like Michael Perry and Thomas Grey.

The justice's personal views regarding the civil rights of victims and criminals greatly influence the day-to-day operations of the entire justice system as they shape the meaning of the Constitution. In addition, interpretation of the Constitution is inherently subjective, influenced by the long-term political and social pressures of the times.

WHERE SUPREME COURT DECISIONS MAY BE FOUND

Few people read the full text of Supreme Court decisions, relying instead on the news media for such information. These decisions may be found in newspapers and newscasts and in magazines such as *U.S. News & World Report* and *Time*. In addition, the Public Education Division of the American Bar Association, in cooperation with the Association of American Law Schools and the American Newspaper Publishers Association Foundation, publish *The Preview of United States Supreme Court Cases*—an analysis of cases the Court is going to hear. Cases may also be found on the Internet and through Westlaw and Lexis. The next chapter explains how to find and research cases.

THE POWER OF THE SUPREME COURT

The Supreme Court is tremendously powerful. It is so powerful that it has been permitted to actually *create* much of its own immense authority.

As Chief Justice Rehnquist reminds us in *The Supreme Court: How It Was, How It Is*, consider that in No. 78 of *The Federalist Papers*, Alexander Hamilton referred to the Supreme Court as the "least dangerous" division of the federal government. Yet in the cases of *Marbury v. Madison* and *Martin v. Hunter's Lessee*, the Supreme Court was permitted to redefine its powers. Who could stop it? Perhaps diabolical in a sense, perhaps they are merely carrying out the true intentions of the framers of the Constitution. Who else could practically oversee the Bill of Rights? It can be interpreted from *The Federalist Papers* that the Supreme Court was assigned to this awesome task. As Alexander Hamilton so stated, the interpretation of the Constitution was to become the "proper and peculiar province of the United States Supreme Court." For what other reason would the framers of the Constitution have included a supremacy clause declaring that federal law would outweigh state law?

Any system, including ours, must have a final point. Certainly, many argue that "between here and there" are far too many resting points. For example, there is an effort by many to decrease the number of appeals available to condemned prisoners because of the time and expense involved in the system as it currently exists.

Nonetheless, in the end, the Supreme Court has the definitive say. The Supreme Court makes the final determination, even if it is done so by the Court deciding *not* to hear a particular case. The supreme law of the land is created by the United States Supreme Court.

Summary

The English Bill of Rights provided a mechanism to assure the ideals set forth in the Magna Carta. This concept carried over to the United States where citizens refused to accept the Constitution without such a bill. The United States Bill of Rights guaranteeing citizens freedom from government oppression assured that the Constitution would be accepted and function as the framework for government.

The Constitution ordained in Article 3 that there shall be a Supreme Court. The Supreme Court has effectively created most of its own power and authority through the process of judicial review. Two precedent cases confirmed this power. *Marbury v. Madison* (1803) established that the Supreme Court has the authority to review acts of Congress. *Martin v. Hunter's Lessee*

(1816) held that the Supreme Court can review and reverse state court decisions.

Because justices decide matters vital to the national interest, a Supreme Court appointment is a lifetime appointment so a justice may not be unduly influenced. The Supreme Court of the 1990s is decidedly conservative—a "law and order" court.

Discussion Questions

1. Do you think any one court should be given the final say? Why or why not?

2. Is there a negative side to appointment for life on the Court? Does this and the inability to lessen a justice's salary really prevent the influencing of a justice serving on the Supreme Court?

3. Do you think that the Supreme Court is a de facto lawmaker? Why or why not?

4. Is it possible for the justices to provide a fair review of a case when they hear about it so briefly from the lawyers arguing it before them?

5. How do you feel about the Supreme Court deciding to accept so few cases? Does the fact the justices decide this totally in private cause you concern?

6. Do you think the current Supreme Court is carrying out the desires of the founders of our Constitution?

7. Explain where you see the real power of the Supreme Court. In other words, what makes the justices so powerful as individuals and as a group?

8. What does it convey when the Court chooses to not grant certiorari?

9. If you were sitting on the Supreme Court, what sorts of cases would you look for now to review?

10. Do you favor strict construction (rigid reading and interpretation) of the law or a more liberal approach?

References

Goebel, Julius, Jr. "The Oliver Wendell Holmes Devise: History of the Supreme Court of the United States, Volume I." *History of the Supreme Court of the United States. Antecedents and Beginnings to 1801. (Vol. 1).* New York: Macmillan, 1971.

Schulman, William. Review of the manuscript. Middle Tennessee State University, September 1995.

Supreme Court of the United States. *The Supreme Court of the United States.* Published with the cooperation of the Supreme Court Historical Society (no date).

Wiecek, William M. *Liberty under Law: The Supreme Court in American Life.* Baltimore: The Johns Hopkins University Press, 1988.

Cases Cited

Ex parte McCardle, 74 U.S. 506, 19 L.Ed. 264 (1868).
Marbury v. Madison, 5 U.S. (1 Cranch) 137, 2 L.Ed. 60 (1803).
Martin v. Hunter's Lessee, 14 U.S. (1 Wheat.) 304, 4 L.Ed. 97 (1816).
Payne v. Tennessee, 501 U.S. 808, 111 S.Ct. 2597, 115 L.Ed. 2d 720 (1991).
United States v. Klein, 80 U.S. (13 Wall.) 128, 20 L.Ed. 519 (1871).

Chapter 5 Knowing Where to Find the Law

Knowledge is of two kinds. We know a subject ourselves, or we know where we can find information upon it.

—SAMUEL JOHNSON

The Library of Congress main reading room. (Photo provided by the Library of Congress Public Affairs Office.)

DO YOU KNOW . . .

At what levels information about law may be written?

What primary and secondary sources are?

What secondary sources are available?

What a legal citation is and what it includes?

What the *National Reporter System* is?

What the components of a legal opinion are?

What six sections are usually included in a case "brief"?

How to determine if a case has been overturned or expanded upon?

CAN YOU DEFINE THESE TERMS?

Affirm
Brief
Caption
Concur
Dicta
Holding
Legal citation
Legal opinion
Popular literature
Primary information sources
Professional literature
Remand
Reverse
Scholarly literature
Secondary information sources
Shepardizing

INTRODUCTION

The amount of paper dedicated to recording law is simply enormous. With the increasing use of computer data bases, an incredible amount of material is available to research any aspect of the law.

In fact, one might argue that *too much* material is out there. It becomes intimidating, if not overwhelming. While knowing the basics of law is important, it is also important to acquire the skill to identify current law.

Current law may not be the same as the law you are studying! Remember, American law is known as a *living law.* This unique and wonderful attribute of our law permits it to change with our society's needs and expectations. The dilemma this presents is that laws do indeed, change—sometimes before textbooks or other legal sources are updated.

This chapter explains the basic resources you can use to identify the latest law. A word of warning: Legal research has the potential for going on ad infinitum. Like a complex mystery, each lead can produce another avenue to pursue, and on, and on. Our goal is to provide you with the basic skills you may need, as well as an introduction to existing resources. Your knowledge and ability to research the law will expand with experience and practice.

The chapter begins with a discussion of why it is important to have the skills to research the law and the various sources available. This is followed by an explanation of how to read legal citations and how to find and read case law. Next the process of briefing a case and the skills needed are presented. The chapter concludes with some suggested further readings for those wishing to obtain in-depth information on researching the law.

THE IMPORTANCE OF KNOWING HOW TO RESEARCH THE LAW

Researching the law is important for at least two reasons. First, this skill enables you to find answers to legal questions and, perhaps more important at this level, to better understand the judicial system.

When viewed in a basic manner, the law and finding it is not as difficult as it may initially appear. Knowing how and where to find answers for legal questions is a worthwhile skill; and knowing what goes into researching laws, including reading legal opinions and briefs, helps bring the study of law into focus.

You are not expected to be a legal scholar or expert researcher after this short introduction, but it will be a stepping-stone for your efforts to find and understand our laws.

POPULAR, SCHOLARLY AND PROFESSIONAL SOURCES

A wealth of information at a variety of levels is available. It is important to recognize for what audience the information is written.

> Information about law may be written at a popular level for the layperson, at a professional level for the practitioner or at a scholarly level for the researcher.

Popular literature is written for the layperson. It is not necessarily less authoritative; it simply does not go into the depth that professional or scholarly literature does. Examples of popular literature would be articles dealing with constitutional law found in *Time* or in *Newsweek* or even *Reader's Digest*.

While some academicians may not consider magazines and newspapers "legitimate" sources for finding law, they are, in fact, the most popularly used sources. Few people will ever actually conduct formal legal research; however, almost everyone reads about the law in magazines and newspapers.

Always bear in mind, however, the potential for inaccuracy in popular sources. The authors may not be lawyers themselves, or the article may simply not have the time or space to provide the details needed to fully explain the matter.

Anyone using any resource to learn law must understand the limitations of that particular resource. *Reader's Digest* will present material far differently than, for example, *United States Law Week*, one of the best sources for keeping current on law. However, not everyone has the access, nor the desire, to keep current on every case being decided. While there can be no substitute for the carefully detailed research required of lawyers, legislators and academicians, to ignore the popular literature that enables many Americans to learn about the law would be to discount how most Americans do learn about the law.

Many of these sources are sociological and do not, in actuality, report "the law." Such sources are not to be confused with the official reported volumes of cases and statutes. Nonetheless, these popular sources do keep the general population updated on legal changes. If you become interested in a case reported in one of these sources, you can pursue your interest further as discussed next.

Professional literature is written for the practitioner in a given field. In criminal justice this would include articles in such publications as *Police Chief* (published by the International Association of Chiefs of Police), the *FBI Law Enforcement Bulletin, Corrections Today* (published by the American Correctional Association), the *UCLA Law Review,* the *Journal of Municipal Government* and the *NCJA Justice Bulletin.* Professional periodicals are most likely to keep you current on the ever-changing constitutional law. These journals frequently have articles on newly enacted laws and their effect on the criminal justice system. If a criminal justice agency does not subscribe to such magazines, they are affordable enough for individuals to subscribe personally.

However, just as newspapers and magazines are not really "the law," professional sources fall a bit short of what you can learn from going to the next level of authority—scholarly sources.

Scholarly literature, as the term implies, is written for people interested in theory, research, statistical analysis and the like. Examples of scholarly literature would be articles in *Justice Quarterly,* an official publication of the Academy of Criminal Justice.

All the preceding sources of information can be classified as secondary. The most authoritative source of information is primary information—the actual cases and the opinions handed down.

PRIMARY AND SECONDARY SOURCES

Information may be classified according to whether it is primary or secondary.

> **Primary information sources** present the raw data or the original information.

Sources of primary information for legal research include the United States Constitution, the constitutions of the 50 states, the statutes of the United States Congress and of the 50 state legislatures and appellate court decisions of the federal and state courts.

> **Secondary information sources** present data or information based on the original information.

Secondary information involves selecting, evaluating, analyzing and synthesizing data or information. For the nonlawyer, it is usually easier to understand than primary information.

You will rely on both primary and secondary resources if you need to research a specific aspect of the law. Look first at some of the more common secondary sources you might use. These can usually be found in a general library.

> Among the important secondary information sources for legal research are periodicals, treatises/texts, encyclopedias and dictionaries.

Legal Periodicals

Jacobsen and Mersky (1981, p. 268) describe legal periodicals as "recording and critici[zing] of doings of legislators and judges, discussion of current case law, narration of lives of eminent lawyers, and the scientific study of . . . jurisprudedics."

Three groups of legal periodicals can provide important information: law school publications such as the *Harvard Law Review*, bar association publications such as the *American Bar Association Journal* and special subject and interest periodicals such as the *Black Law Journal* and the *Women Lawyers Journal*.

Treatises/Texts

Oran (1985, p. 308) defines a treatise as "a large, comprehensive book on a legal subject." Treatises or textbooks go into a specific subject in great depth. Such works provide the backbone for a great deal of research by legal professionals. Specialized treatises exist in almost every area imaginable.

Although such works are an invaluable resource, they are frequently multivolume and always expensive. They make ideal additions to agency libraries (e.g., law schools, county attorneys' offices, prosecutors' offices) and are readily available at law libraries.

It is worth your time to become acquainted with the treatises/texts available. Stop in and browse. Because many sourcebooks deal with specific areas of the law, the particular source to use can be easily located.

Legal Encyclopedias

According to Jacobsen and Mersky (1981, p. 254):

> Legal encyclopedias are written in narrative form, arranged [alphabetically] by subject and contain supporting footnote references to cases in point. In most instances, they are noncritical and do not attempt to be analytical or evaluative. Instead, they simply state the propositions of law, with introductory explanations of an elementary nature. A legal encyclopedia, because of these features, is a popular and useful research tool.

They go on to identify three types of legal encyclopedias: those dealing with general law, those dealing with local or state law and those dealing with special subjects. Within each, specific articles are arranged alphabetically for easy reference.

Corpus Juris Secundum (C.J.S.) is a general legal encyclopedia that tries to restate the entire body of American law in encyclopedic form. Published by West Publishing Company, it consists of approximately 150 volumes, including supplements and a five-volume index.

American Jurisprudence 2d (AM.Jur.2d) is general legal encyclopedia that contains 400 topics. Published by the Lawyers Co-operative Publishing Company and the Bancroft-Whitney Company, it contains approximately 90 volumes, including an eight-volume index.

Encyclopedia of Crime and Justice contains authoritative articles, often quite lengthy, on all areas of criminal justice. Published by Macmillan, this four-volume set provides a good overview of the major areas of criminal justice.

Guide to American Law is a less voluminous encyclopedia on general topics.

Legal Dictionaries

Legal dictionaries help define words in their legal sense. Among the most popular American law dictionaries are *Ballentine's Law Dictionary* (Lawyers Cooperative Publishing Company, 1969); *Black's Law Dictionary*, 6th ed. (West Publishing Company, 1990); and *Oran's Law Dictionary for Nonlawyers*, 2nd ed. (West Publishing Company, 1985). Whether hardbound or paperback, a legal dictionary makes an excellent addition to anyone's personal library.

READING LEGAL CITATIONS

Although they look as if they were designed to bedevil the unwary, legal citations are actually simple to decipher.

> A **legal citation** is a standardized way of referring to a specific element in the law. It has three basic parts: a volume number, an abbreviation for the title and a page or section number.

Legal citations are usually followed by the date. Following are examples of legal citations.

❖ Supreme Court case: *Horton v. California*, 496 U.S. 128 (1990). This means volume 496 of the *United States Reports* (the official reporter for the United States Supreme Court opinions), page 128, decided in 1990.
❖ Federal law: 42 USC 1983. This means title or chapter 42 of the *United States Code*, section 1983.
❖ Journal: Janice Toran, "Information Disclosure in Civil Actions: The Freedom of Information Act and the Federal Discovery Rules." 49 Geo. Wash. L. Rev. 843, 854-55 (1981). This refers to an article written by Janice Toran that appears in the *George Washington Law Review* #843, pp. 854–855, published in 1981.

The preceding are cites to the official *USSC Reporter*. Sometimes additional cites will be given. These are called *string cites*. The additional cites show where the case could be found in the commercial digests such as West's *Supreme Court Reporter*. For example, the official cite for the Miranda case is *Miranda v. Arizona*, 384 U.S. 436 (1966). This shows where the case is found in the official *Supreme Court Reporter*. A string cite for this case would be *Miranda v. Arizona*, 384 U.S. 436, 86 S.Ct. 1602, 16 L.Ed.2d 694 (1966). This shows that in addition to the official *USSC Reporter*, the case is also in West's *Supreme Court Reporter* (S.Ct.) and the *Lawyers Cooperative Reporter* (L.Ed.2d).

Researching provisions of federal and state constitutions does not present a problem. When it comes to case law, however, the situation is very different. According to Jacobsen and Mersky (1981, p. 13): "There are over three million judicial opinions in the United States, and over 47,000 American cases are published each year." Finding case law can be a real challenge.

CASE LAW

Court decisions are recorded as opinions that describe what the dispute was about and what the court decided and why. The opinion may be written by one member of the court, or there may be many concurring and dissenting opinions. Many landmark cases have as many as eight or nine opinions. As Farnsworth (1983, p. 42) suggests: "The sheer number of decisions is an obvious obstacle to finding case law. Reported decisions of the Supreme Court of the United States and of most of the state appellate courts can be found in the official reports of those courts. Those decided from at least 1887 to date can also be found in a system of unofficial reports, the *National Reporter System*, which contains upwards of 7,000 volumes now running about 1,500 pages per volume."

> ≋ The *National Reporter System* publishes seven regional sets of volumes as well as individual sets for California, Illinois and New York courts.

Figure 5–1 illustrates the eight regions of the National Reporter System.

Another system of unofficial reports, the American Law Reports, publishes only the cases thought to be significant and of special interest and discusses them in depth.

When referring to a case, both official and unofficial reports may be cited. Farnsworth (1983, p. 43) explains:

> Thus, a correct citation would be Wangen v. Ford Motor Co., 97 Wis. 2d 260, 294 N.W. 2d 437, 13 A.L.R. 4th 1 (1980), meaning that the case was decided in 1980, is found at page 260 of volume 97 of the second series of official Wisconsin reports, at page 437 of volume 294 of the second series of the Northwestern set of the National Reporter System, and at page 1 of volume 13 of the fourth series of American Law Reports, where it is followed by an annotation.

Farnsworth (p. 43) goes on to note: "In this manner are collected the more than 40,000 reported decisions that each year add to the existing total of roughly four million." *United States Supreme Court Reports* are published in five current reports (Jacobsen and Mersky, 1981, p. 31):

❖ *United States Reports* (official edition), cited "U.S."
❖ *United States Supreme Court Reports* (Lawyers Cooperative Publishing Company), cited "L.Ed." and "L.Ed. 2d."
❖ *Supreme Court Reporter* (West Publishing Company), cited "Sup.Ct." or "S.Ct."
❖ *United States Law Week* (Bureau of National Affairs), cited "U.S.L.W." or "U.S.L. Week."
❖ *Commerce Clearing House*, United States Supreme Court Bulletin.

Figure 5–1

National Reporter System map.

Source: From *West's Law Finder*. St. Paul: West Publishing Company. Reprinted by permission. All rights reserved.

1   Pacific
2   North Western
3   South Western
4   North Eastern
5   Atlantic
6   South Eastern
7   Southern

READING CASE LAW

You may find yourself challenged with attempting to read actual case law at some time. While this text is not written in traditional casebook style (relying heavily on copying case law, followed by analysis), if you take any other classes on law, you will probably find yourself working your way through cases.

Most legal writing, in whatever format, uses jargon particular to this field. It is foreign to most readers, including students. It is very helpful to become familiar with some of the basic concepts and terminology that you will encounter.

To begin, the **caption** (title of the case) lets you know just who is involved. It may be the government against a criminal defendant (e.g., *The State of Washington v. Smith*), or it may be two individuals disputing an issue (e.g., *Anderson v. Smith*). The parties to the action may be identified by different titles (defendant, plaintiff, petitioner, respondent, etc.), depending on the nature of the case. The particular court and level of legal action (whether it is an appeal, etc.) will determine whose name comes first in the caption. This is usually clarified within the first part of the case.

Most legal disputes, or cases, start out in the trial court. As Dernbach and Singleton (1981, p. 7) explain, the trial court has two basic responsibilities: to find out what happened and to determine what legal rules should be used in deciding the case at hand. The trial court will make its decision based on the facts presented by the lawyers representing both parties (or by the individuals themselves if not represented by legal counsel), using the legal rules the judge determines are appropriate to apply to this case. The party that doesn't emerge victorious may appeal to a higher court on any number of issues. However, only legal issues will be reviewed on appeal, as new evidence is not permitted. In fact, appeals are only considered by the appellate judges reviewing written arguments from the parties, along with transcripts of the case and opinions issued by the previous judge involved. (Not all cases produce opinions, particularly at the trial court level.)

While many issues may be presented in one case, they may not all be addressed by the court deciding the case. Whether to save time or perhaps even to avoid other issues within a case, a court may choose to answer only one issue in its opinion, leaving the others for future cases.

Opinions include more than simply a statement of who won the court case. They tell the story of what occurred, what rules were applied and why the judge(s) decided the case as they did. Dernbach and Singleton (p. 7) explain that opinions contain five important components.

> A **legal opinion** usually contains (1) a description of the facts, (2) a statement of the legal issues presented for decision, (3) the relevant rules of law, (4) the holding and (5) the policies and reasons that support the holding.

A **holding** is the rule of law applied to the particular facts of the case and the actual decision. The court may **affirm, concur, reverse** or **remand.** As noted by Hasse (1982, p. 34):

> The "Holding" of a case is the very narrow statement of a court's final decision about the exact question that the court was asked to answer. When an appeals court reviews a case it passes judgment on the actions of a lower court. The appeals court's holding affirms (okays), concurs (agrees with the lower court's decision, but for different reasons), reverses (decides that the loser should have won) or remands (returns) the case to the lower court for further action.

Three skills are required to read case law. First, you must be able to think in reverse. The opinion provides the end result of the deliberations. The reader must isolate what the dispute involved, what the trial court decided and how it proceeded and what happened when upon appeal.

Second, you must untangle the interplay of the basic components of a judicial opinion. Each affects the others in a process that goes back and forth and around in what may appear to be circles.

Third, not all the elements of the judicial opinion may be included. They must be inferred from the decisions made.

BRIEFING A CASE

Once you locate your case, you will want to make some notes to help you decipher it. Since cases are usually rather long, the best way to do this is to outline, or **brief,** the case. O'Block (1986, pp. 125–26) describes how to brief a case in a nonlawyer way. He suggests that six sections are important: (1) the case name and citation, including the year of the decision; (2) a summary of operable facts, beginning with a one-sentence statement on the type of case or offense involved; (3) legal issues or questions of law involved in the case—the heart of the brief; (4) the court's decision—often phrased as an answer to the questions of law involved; (5) the court's reasoning—why they decided as they did and (6) separate opinions or dissent—the decision need not be unanimous.

> Most case briefs contain the case name and citation, a summary of key facts, the legal issues involved, the court's decision, the reasons for that decision and any separate opinions or dissents.

Traditionally law is taught through case law. This is an arduous process by which issues and rules are dissected from court opinions. This discipline is necessary for those intending to become lawyers because case analysis is the cornerstone of understanding *how* and *why* cases are decided the way they are, and why the law in any particular area developed as it did.

Common law itself depends on comparing one case with others. As difficult as the case analysis approach to learning law is, it definitely has its place. However, this complex approach can hinder your understanding of the basics of constitutional law as they apply to criminal justice—the focus of this text.

You should, however, know what a case opinion looks like as well as how a brief of that case might be used to analyze the issues and rules drawn from it. Opinions also provide judges with an opportunity to express thoughts that may not be rules of law, but indicate the thoughts of the majority, which could be relevant to how future cases might be determined. This is called **dicta.** The dissenting judges may also state their thoughts at the end of the opinion. Consequently, an opinion holds a great deal of information to be scrutinized.

Two relevant and famous cases have been selected to illustrate opinions and the briefs that might be written from them. *Marbury v. Madison* (1803) was selected because it is the pivotal case of constitutional law granting the Supreme Court authority to review legislation to determine if it is constitutional—and thus legal. *Miranda v. Arizona* (1964) was selected because it is perhaps the most famous of constitutional law cases. The opinions for these two cases are contained in Appendix C. You may wish to read them before reading the briefs that follow.

Brief of **Marbury v. Madison**

TYPE OF CASE   This case deals with a petition to the United States Supreme Court for a writ of mandamus to compel a government official to deliver a commission, subsequently requiring a determination of whether the United States Supreme Court may review an act of Congress to determine its constitutionality.

FACTS OF THE CASE   Just before President John Adams left office after his defeat by Thomas Jefferson in 1800, Adams made several judicial appointments. While Adams signed these appointments under the authority granted left office, for no other reason than time pressures. President Jefferson ordered his new secretary of state, James Madison, to withhold delivery of several commissions made by the previous president, including that of justice of the peace to William Marbury. Marbury, along with several others, petitioned the United States Supreme Court to require Secretary of State Madison to deliver their commissions.

LEGAL ISSUE Does the United States Supreme Court have the authority to declare congressional acts unconstitutional?

HOLDING AND DECISION Yes. Because the government of the United States is one of laws, not men, the law needs to be able to remedy wrongs that result in taking away a legally bestowed right. In this case, Marbury had a right to have his commission delivered, and the use of the Judiciary Act as passed by Congress to withhold the commission is unconstitutional.

Because the Constitution limits the Supreme Court's original jurisdiction to only certain areas, giving the Court only appellate jurisdiction in all other areas, the Judiciary Act may not grant the Supreme Court original jurisdiction to issue writs of mandamus. It is the Constitution that limits the rights and powers of the legislature, and the legislature cannot change the Constitution, which itself provides that it is the "supreme law of the land."

If an act of the legislature is repugnant to the Constitution, are courts bound by that law? No. If a law is not in accordance with the United States Constitution, the Supreme Court may determine which of the conflicting rules will govern the particular case. If the Constitution is to have the power it was meant to have, it must prevail pursuant to Article 3, Section 2.

The framers of the Constitution meant for it to govern courts as well as Congress. Why else are judges required to take an oath to uphold the United States Constitution? The Supreme Court has the authority to review acts of Congress, and in this case, Section 13 of the Judiciary Act of 1789 is unconstitutional.

RULE Under the supremacy clause and Article 3, Section 2 of the United States Constitution, the Supreme Court has the authority to review acts of Congress to determine whether they are unconstitutional.

Brief of Miranda v. Arizona

TYPE OF CASE This case deals with the issue of whether the police must advise certain criminal suspects who are being questioned of their constitutional rights to not speak.

FACTS OF THE CASE After being arrested, the defendant was taken to an interrogation room where he gave a confession to the police. He had not been told of his constitutional right to remain silent or to have a lawyer present because the police assumed he knew about these rights since he had been arrested before.

LEGAL ISSUE Must government agents advise certain suspects of their constitutional Fifth Amendment rights?

HOLDING AND DECISION   Yes. Suspects held for interrogation must be clearly informed that they have the right to consult with a lawyer and to have the lawyer with them during interrogation. They must also be advised of their right to remain silent and that anything stated can be used in evidence against them.

If individuals indicate that they wish the assistance of counsel before any interrogation occurs, the authorities cannot deny this request. If a person cannot afford legal counsel, it must be provided without cost. Suspects must be advised that they have a right to have legal counsel present during any questioning.

Once the warnings have been given, interrogation must cease at any time before or during questioning if suspects indicate in any manner that they wish to remain silent. If the questioning continues, the burden is on the government to demonstrate that the suspect knowingly and intelligently waived the privilege against self-incrimination and the right to retained or appointed counsel.

RULE   When government agents question people in custody, they must be advised of their specific Fifth Amendment rights dealing with self-incrimination and must knowingly and intelligently waive such privileges.

A great deal more could be addressed regarding the legal process and how to decipher legal cases and their resulting opinions. However, this text was not intended to address these specific issues. The goal in this chapter is to provide you with the basic information to seek out the law as needed. One last skill is needed: going beyond the case itself to determine if it is still a precedent or if it has been overturned or expanded—a process known as **shepardizing.**

SHEPARDIZING

Once a case has been researched, the current status of the case should be determined. As noted by Hasse (1982, p. 49):

> Shepardizing is a process with one goal and two uses. The goal is to make sure that the case or statutory law that you are reading has not been overturned or modified by later case decisions. The two uses are to update the law (to see how it has developed through later cases) and to find cites to other sources which analyze or explain the same points of view.
>
> Many researchers save time in reading case decisions by turning to Shepard's before they follow a case citation to a reporter. If the case cited has been overturned by a later case, they go directly to the later case. This saves them from reading and taking notes on a case that is no longer legally significant.

Shepardizing a case involves using *Shepard's,* the set of bound volumes and pocket parts published for each set of official volumes of cases, indicating if a case's status has changed.

FURTHER READING

Two texts written for general public legal research might be of interest to you:

❖ Alfred J. Lewis, *Using Law Books* (Dubuque, IA: Kendall/Hunt, 1976).
❖ Stephen Elias, *Legal Research: How to Find and Understand the Law* (Berkeley, CA: Nolo Press, 1982).

Another source of information that might be of value to you is Robert L. O'Block's *Criminal Justice Research Sources* (Anderson Publishing Company, 1986). This is a comprehensive listing of various sources, including books, indexing services, journals, bibliographies, computerized literature searches, general reference sources (including reference books, career information guides, encyclopedias, dictionaries, newspapers, annuals and yearbooks), directories, government documents (including national commission reports), federal agencies, statistical data (including the FBI's Uniform Crime Reports) and the National Criminal Justice Reference Service (NCJRS).

COMPUTERS AS AN INVALUABLE AID TO FINDING THE LAW

The computer is redefining the research practices of the legal profession and of the layperson seeking to understand the law. In just the time during which this text has been written, the Internet has become a legitimate source of legal information for everyone. While computerized legal research through such sources as Westlaw has been standard practice for law offices, expense and complexity prevented the general public from using them for their legal questions. The Internet has changed all that.

Now anyone with Internet access can acquire astounding amounts of material and conduct quality research without great difficulty. With all levels of jurisdictions striving to present their material on the World Wide Web in user-friendly ways, the Internet has the potential to bring the law "home" to everyone in ways never before considered.

Following are some examples of the Uniform Resource Locators (URL), or "addresses" that can be used to access sources on the World Wide Web:

Internet Law Library	http://www.pls.com:8001/
Supreme Court	http://www.law.cornel
National Criminal Justice Reference Service	askncjrs@ncjrs.aspensys.com

Summary

Information may be written at a popular level for the layperson, at a professional level for the practitioner or at a scholarly level for the researcher. Information may be classified as primary or secondary. Primary information is raw data or the original information. Secondary information is based on the raw data or original information.

Among the important secondary information sources for legal research are periodicals, treatises/texts, encyclopedias and dictionaries. Within these information sources you will find many legal citations. A legal citation is a standardized way of referring to a specific element in the law. It has three basic parts: a volume number, an abbreviation for the title and a page or section number. The *National Reporter System* publishes seven regional sets of volumes as well as individual sets for California, Illinois and New York courts.

As you research the law, you may find yourself reading legal opinions. An opinion usually contains (1) a description of the facts, (2) a statement of the legal issues presented for decision, (3) the relevant rules of law, (4) the holding and (5) the policies and reasons that support the holding.

You may also find it helpful to be able to brief, or outline, a case. Most case briefs contain the case name and citation, a summary of key facts, the legal issues involved, the court's decision, the reasons for that decision and any separate opinions or dissents.

Shepardizing a case involves using *Shepard's,* the set of bound volumes and pocket parts published for each set of official volumes of cases, indicating if a case's status has changed.

Discussion Questions

1. Why is it necessary to know how to research the law?
2. What is the danger of relying on only textbooks to learn the law?
3. Discuss what information can be obtained from reading a legal opinion.
4. Why can legal research become frustrating?
5. What are the benefits to actually reading and briefing a case that is relevant to your specific legal question?
6. Why is the newspaper a legitimate source of legal information?
7. What shortcoming do you think the newspaper might have in providing legal information?
8. What problems could arise for any professional not keeping up with the law?
9. What legal sources are available in your profession or area of interest?
10. What reasons are there for the general public to maintain a current awareness of the law?

References

Dernbach, John C. and Richard V. Singleton II. *A Practical Guide to Legal Writing and Legal Method.* Littleton, CO: Fred B. Rothman & Company, 1981.

Farnsworth, E. Allen. *An Introduction to the Legal System of the United States.* New York: Oceania Publications, Inc., 1983.

Hasse, Paul. *Citizens Legal Manual: Using a Law Library.* Washington: HALT, Inc., 1982.

Jacobsen, J. Myron and Roy M. Mersky. *Legal Research Illustrated.* 2nd ed. New York: The Foundation Press, Inc., 1981.

O'Block, Robert. *Criminal Justice Research Sources.* Cincinnati: Anderson Publishing Company, 1986.

Oran, Daniel. *Law Dictionary for Nonlawyers.* 2nd ed. St. Paul: West Publishing Company, 1985.

Cases Cited

Horton v. California, 496 U.S. 128 (1990).
Marbury v. Madison, 5 U.S. 137 (1803).
Miranda v. Arizona, 384 U.S. 436 (1966).

The Guarantees of the Constitution to Citizens: Civil Rights and Civil Liberties

*The Thirteenth
Amendment:
Proclamation of
Emancipation.*

THE ESSENCE OF the United States Constitution is "liberty and justice for all." The significance of these words, generally learned in the Pledge of Allegiance, is what the legal system in the United States strives to achieve, and what our system of laws, beginning with the framework provided by the Constitution, is all about: guaranteeing the rights and liberties of the *individual*.

Sections One and Two helped build the framework of understanding how the constitutional machine was conceived and built. Understanding *why* the constitution was considered necessary when this country was begun and *how* the Constitution was worded to address specific idealistic goals, enables those studying it to understand what it seeks to achieve: individual rights and liberties.

As you begin your in-depth look at the Constitution and its amendments, remember that the Constitution simply provides a basic framework within which all other laws, whether federal, state or local, must remain. While this basic framework necessarily provides for how the legal system should be constructed, i.e., establishing Congress, the presidency, the Supreme Court, etc., the guarantees of the Constitution for individual rights and liberties are why those who established the document met in the first place: to protect the individual from the government.

This section begins with a look at two amendments that delineate civil rights and civil liberties, the Thirteenth and Fourteenth Amendments (Chapter 6). This is followed by an up-close look at the First Amendment and the basic freedoms it guarantees (Chapter 7). The section concludes with a discussion of the Second Amendment and the controversial issue of gun control (Chapter 8).

Throughout the section, keep in mind that although the Constitution and its amendments are relatively simple, interpretation of them can become complex. Do not let the complexities obscure the basic purpose of these documents: to prevent government from unnecessarily infringing on the citizens' basic rights to liberty and justice.

Chapter 6

Equal Protection under the Law: Balancing Individual, State and Federal Rights

All Persons Born or Naturalized *in the United States and subject to the jurisdiction thereof, are* citizens *of the United States and of the state wherein they reside.* No state *shall make or enforce any law which shall* abridge the Privileges or Immunities *of citizens of the United States; nor shall any state deprive any person of life, liberty, or property, without* Due Process of Law; *nor deny to any person within its jurisdiction the* Equal Protection of the Laws.

—FOURTEENTH AMENDMENT OF THE UNITED STATES CONSTITUTION

Segregated sleeping cars.

DO YOU KNOW . . .

What the Thirteenth Amendment did?

What the Fourteenth Amendment did?

How discrimination differs from prejudice?

What significance the *Dred Scott* decision had?

What the Court held in *Plessy v. Ferguson?*

What Jim Crow laws are?

What is significant about *Brown v. Board of Education?*

What was accomplished by the 1964 Omnibus Civil Rights Law? The Equal Employment Opportunity Act?

What the intent of affirmative action programs was?

What reverse discrimination is?

What the American Dream refers to?

What the greatest barrier to equality is?

CAN YOU DEFINE THESE TERMS?

Affirmative action
American Dream
Discrimination
Jim Crow laws
Prejudice
Reverse discrimination
Selective incorporation

INTRODUCTION

A shortcoming of the Constitution and the Bill of Rights was their failure to address the issue of slavery. In addition, although the Bill of Rights guaranteed American citizens basic freedoms that the federal government could not infringe upon, it did not apply to the states, each of which had its own constitution and statutes. To assure that the states did not deny the basic rights set forth in the Constitution and the Bill of Rights, Congress passed the Fourteenth Amendment.

This chapter begins with a brief look at the abolition of slavery through the Thirteenth Amendment and a discussion of the Fourteenth Amendment, which granted slaves citizenship and required that states abide by the federal Constitution and specific provisions in the Bill of Rights. This is followed by an examination of discrimination and prejudice, the roots of racial discrimination, the issue of "separate but equal" and the struggle for equality. Next the rise of affirmative action programs is discussed, including the claims of reverse discrimination and the challenges to affirmative action programs mounted in the 1990s. The chapter concludes with a discussion of the balancing of state and federal powers.

THE THIRTEENTH AMENDMENT

The Civil War resulted from several issues, most involving interpretation of the Constitution. Among the issues were state banks and money versus national banks and currency, federal aid versus state aid for improvements on highways and railways and freedom versus slavery in the territories. During the course of debates involving these issues, two theories as to the nature of the Constitution emerged, articulated in the Great Debate in the Senate in 1830 between Robert Hayne of South Carolina and Daniel Webster of Massachusetts.

Hayne asserted that the Union created by the Constitution was merely a compact between sovereign states, a league of independent states and, as such, states may lawfully withdraw from the Union if they so wish. Webster, on the other hand, asserted that the Constitution established a perpetual, indivisible Union, that its laws were binding on the states and that states could not lawfully leave the Union.

These issues came to a head when Abraham Lincoln was elected president in 1860. That December South Carolina passed a resolution to withdraw from the Union. Early in 1861 Florida, Georgia, Alabama, Mississippi, Louisiana and Texas followed suit.

President Lincoln was faced with the task of trying to hold the Union together. He had been elected on a promise to abolish slavery in the territories, but he conceded that under the Constitution slavery was legal in the states where it had been established. Lincoln tried to assure the southern states that he had neither the right nor the intent to disturb slavery there. The Supreme Court had ruled in *Dred Scott v. Sandford* (1856) that even free blacks could not be citizens of the United States and that they "had no rights which a white man was bound to respect." The southern states were not convinced, however, and the Civil War ensued.

While debating and passing bills regarding conducting the war, taxes, tariffs, banking and the like, Congress also dealt with the slavery issue. In April 1862 it abolished slavery in the District of Columbia and two months later in all the existing territories. In the summer of 1862 Lincoln boldly announced that unless they returned to the Union he would call for an end to slavery in all rebelling states. In the Emancipation Proclamation, issued January 1, 1863, under his war powers, Lincoln declared forever free all the slaves in all the districts of the United States in rebellion against the Union. In effect, this proclamation did little. Those in the South retained their slaves as did those slave states that remained loyal to the Union. It did, however, provide a strong push toward abolishing slavery.

In January 1864 a resolution to amend the Constitution to abolish slavery throughout the United States was introduced into Congress and after a year of prolonged discussion was ratified by the required two-thirds vote in both houses. It was then sent to the states for consideration and ratification and went into effect in December 1865.

🌊 The Thirteenth Amendment, ratified in 1865, abolished slavery.

Neither slavery nor involuntary servitude . . . shall exist within the United States or any place subject to their jurisdiction—Thirteenth Amendment

Although the Thirteenth Amendment abolished slavery in 1865, after the Civil War many southern states continued discrimination by passing "Black Codes," which forbid blacks to vote, serve on juries, hold certain jobs, move freely, own firearms or gather in groups. As noted by Klotter and Kanovitz (1985, pp. 493–494):

> Hostile Southern legislatures responded to the Thirteenth Amendment with the enactment of Black Codes which were designed to compel the newly freed slaves to return to the service of their former masters. . . . A period of racial turbulence and violent unrest followed as terrorist organizations like the Ku Klux Klan and the Knights of the White Camelia sprang up in numerous local communities.

To remedy this situation, Congress passed the Fourteenth Amendment, which gave blacks citizenship, a status previously defined only by the states.

THE FOURTEENTH AMENDMENT

The Fourteenth Amendment, in addition to giving blacks citizenship, also promised due process and equal protection of the laws at the state level. Southern states were required to ratify the Fourteenth Amendment before reentering the Union.

John Bingham, representative of Ohio and author of the Fourteenth Amendment, argued during congressional debates that the amendment, through its privileges or immunities clause, extended the protection of the Bill of Rights to the states. The Supreme Court refused to go along with this interpretation. In the *Slaughterhouse* case (1873), the Court held that the privileges or immunities clause of the Fourteenth Amendment did *not* apply the Bill of Rights to the states. Doing so would "change the whole theory of the state and federal governments" and "would [make] this court a perpetual censor upon all legislation of the states."

Twenty-four years later, however, the Supreme Court did begin to apply the Bill of Rights to the states, using the due process clause of the Fourteenth Amendment. As Justice William Brennan viewed it, the Fourteenth Amendment extended to Americans "a brand new Constitution after the Civil War." It extended citizenship to former slaves and promised them equal treatment under the law. The Fourteenth Amendment also specifically restricted the states by requiring them to apply fundamental provisions of the Bill of Rights to their citizens. This greatly expanded the scope of citizens' constitutional rights as well as the resultant case load of the Supreme Court.

➣ **The Fourteenth Amendment, in addition to granting citizenship to all persons born or naturalized in the United States, forbid the states to deny their citizens due process of law or equal protection of the law, that is, it made certain provisions of the Bill of Rights applicable to the states.**

According to Currie (1988, p. 12):

The Fourteenth Amendment, which has proved one of the most significant parts of the Constitution, contains several important provisions:

In order to overrule the infamous *Dred Scott* decision . . . Section 1 declares virtually all persons born or naturalized in the United States "citizens of the United States and of the State wherein they reside."

Most important, it also forbids the states to abridge the "privileges or immunities" of United States citizens, to deny anyone within its jurisdiction "equal protection of the laws" or . . . to deprive any person of life, liberty, or property "without due process of law."

The Fourteenth Amendment has five sections dealing with many issues that arose after the Civil War, such as paying war debts and barring Confederates from holding public office. Section 1 has had the most lasting significance. This section provides that no person shall be denied "due process of law" (fairness in government actions) or "equal protection of the laws" (protection from unreasonable discrimination). These two rights have been the basis of most twentieth century cases in constitutional law.

Despite the ratification of the Fourteenth Amendment by all states, and despite the Supreme Court's ruling that this amendment made specific provisions of the Bill of Rights applicable to the states, prejudice and discrimination were not automatically eliminated, as evidenced by the following "Great Moments in History" reported by the Associated Press:

Rosa's Refusal. Montgomery, Alabama, December 5, 1955. Rosa Parks refuses to give up her bus seat to a white man and is fined ten dollars. One year later, a federal court banned bus segregation. "Congress" 1600

Martin Luther King, Jr. delivers his "I Have a Dream" speech. (Provided by UPI/Corbis-Bettmann.)

Rocking the Boat. Little Rock, Arkansas, September 1957. President Eisenhower orders troops to admit nine black students into a previously all-white, southern school. "Congress" 1600

King's Crusade. Birmingham, Alabama, April 3, 1963. In a quest for equality and civil rights, Dr. Martin Luther King, Jr. led mass demonstrations down the streets and in the parks of Birmingham. "Congress" 1600

A few years later, King would be shot to death as he stood on the balcony of his hotel suite.

"Liberty and justice for all," while an intellectual ideal, has been more than difficult to achieve. Laws, programs and great leaders have tried to achieve equality, but laws cannot change attitudes or long-held beliefs. This chapter addresses the issue of whether our nation of laws is also a nation of equal treatment and opportunity.

DISCRIMINATION VERSUS PREJUDICE

In addition to the guarantees contained in the Constitution and the Bill of Rights, laws have been passed forbidding discrimination, but they do *not* address individual prejudices. Ironically, America began mainly because people despised being ruled by others, yet those people fostered slavery and racism. And as the Civil War was to prove, some would go to their graves for the belief they were so superior to others that they could dictate over or even own other humans. The tendency to form prejudices is explained by Hageman (1985, p. 51):

> We as human beings, as part of processing information, have a tendency to prejudge—to classify information into meaningful categories. Prejudgments are natural for human beings, whose eyes are able to receive more bits of stimuli than their brains are able to process. Thus, each one of us is carrying around "preconceived notions" of specific persons or groups of persons. . . .
>
> These prejudgments do not always involve minority groups, such as blacks and American Indians. Prejudgments can also center on the categories developed and labeled as "old people," "teenagers," "the handicapped," "gay people," and "women."

In a democratic society, individuals are free to think what they want. If these thoughts translate into behavior, problems may arise.

> **Prejudice** is an attitude; **discrimination** is a behavior.

Hageman (1985, p. 55) illustrates this distinction:

> The difference between the *attitude* reflected in the word "prejudice" and the *overt behavior* of prejudice, as in the word "discrimination," was summed up by an English judge in his comments to nine youths convicted of race rioting in the Notting Hill section of London:
>
> Think what you like. . . . But once you translate your dark thoughts into savage acts, the law will punish you, and protect your victim.

SCENE ON A COTTON PLANTATION.   GATHERING COTTON.

A southern cotton plantation. (Provided by Corbis-Bettmann.)

THE ROOTS OF RACIAL DISCRIMINATION

Racial discrimination existed before the time of colonial America and the framing of the Constitution. To people such as Washington, Hamilton and Jefferson, slavery was an accepted part of life.

> The *Dred Scott* decision ruled that a freed slave did not have the right to remain free in territory where slavery was still legal.

The Thirteenth Amendment to the Constitution later declared slavery illegal, but it could not outlaw unequal treatment or change racial attitudes so prominent in southern states.

In 1896 the case of *Plessy v. Ferguson* was brought before the Supreme Court. Plessy had refused to abide by a law that required black people to give up their train seats to white passengers. Plessy brought suit, arguing a violation of his Thirteenth and Fourteenth Amendment rights.

It is of interest that *Plessy* was a test case engineered by the Union League and the railroad companies, who saw the economic costs of segregation. The Court ruled against Plessy, stating:

> If the two races are to meet upon terms of social equality, it must be the result of . . . a voluntary consent of individuals. . . . Legislation is powerless to eradicate racial instincts. . . . and the attempts to do so can only result in accentuating the difficulties of the present situation.

Only Justice Harlan dissented, saying: "[O]ur constitution is color-blind" . . . and that "[i]n respect of civil rights, all citizens are equal before the law."

Thus was set forth one of the Court's most famous decisions. Interestingly enough, the Court hardly considered whether the law was a violation of his

Segregated lunch counter where a well-known sit-in occurred.

civil rights, and if it was, the Court did not get involved because in its view, discrimination was a problem to be dealt with by society, not the court.

≋ *Plessy v. Ferguson* (1896) showed the Court's desire to avoid civil rights issues, declaring discrimination to be outside the realm of the Court.

Racial tension mounted as states passed laws to assure that whites could maintain their privileged status.

≋ **Jim Crow laws** strictly segregated blacks from whites in schools, restaurants, street cars, hospitals and cemeteries.

These Jim Crow laws supposedly kept blacks "separate but equal." The compelling question became: Is "separate but equal" really equal?

THE ISSUE OF "SEPARATE BUT EQUAL"

The issue of "separate but equal" was decided in *Brown v. Board of Education of Topeka I* (1954) when a group of black children sought admission to an all-white public school. The plaintiffs claimed they were being denied their constitutional right to equal protection and that the laws of "separate but equal" were not equal. When comparing the quality of black and white facilities, black facilities were definitely of lesser quality.

The Court ruled unanimously that "[s]eparate educational facilities are inherently unequal" and legally ended the years of Jim Crow that segregated facilities in the South.

The beginning of integregation. (Provided by UPI/Corbis-Bettmann.)

〜 *Brown v. Board of Education of Topeka I* (1954) established that "separate but equal" schools were illegal.

The Court's reasoning was that barring children from an educational facility based solely on race was a blow to the "hearts and minds" of those being discriminated against. Separation may create "a feeling of inferiority" that may affect children's ability to cope, to learn and to dream of one day being successful.

A powerful advocate for equality and for the dream of a future was Dr. Martin Luther King Jr., who on a summer afternoon in 1963 stood at the foot of the Washington Monument and delivered his renowned "I have a dream" address.

THE STRUGGLE FOR EQUALITY

Through the difficulties with communism, racism and segregationism of the fifties and sixties, this nation of races tugged and pulled at the issue of equality. Some chose to accept it while others chose to don a white sheet as the Klan had before and burn crosses, believing that this country was created by and for whites. Now the courts were saying that the color of one's skin didn't matter, everyone was equal.

The *Brown* decision led to one of the greatest civil-rights advances in our history, the 1964 Civil Rights Act. The passing of this act "put statutory 'teeth' into the 'color blind' language . . . in *Plessy's* dissent and *Brown's* majority" (Magill, 1992, p. 1254).

~~~ The 1964 Omnibus Civil Rights Law prohibited discrimination in employment opportunities in private business. The 1972 Equal Employment Opportunity Act prohibited discrimination based on race, color, religion, sex or national origin in employment of any kind, public or private, local, state or federal.

The Civil Rights Act put teeth into the lengthy section of Title VII, which sets out the provisions for equal employment opportunities for the minority classes. And the teeth it provided stated that it will be unlawful for employers to hire or fire on the basis of "race, color, religion, sex or national origin." It also made it unlawful to place job advertisements stating preference to race, although employers could indicate desired qualifications with regard to ability.

THE RISE OF AFFIRMATIVE ACTION PROGRAMS

Many argued that the provisions of the Civil Rights Act of 1964 were nothing but a "hollow promise" that did little to rid society of discrimination in employment and education opportunities (Magill, p. 1254). That argument prompted the Nixon administration to form a coalition to work toward equalizing the years of unequal treatment experienced by the minority populations and women. The result was affirmative action programs. **Affirmative action** programs, sometimes referred to as ethnic- and gender-preference programs, were designed to cure discrimination in hiring, and eliminate past, present and future discrimination using race, color, sex and age as deciding criteria ("Affirmative Action Programs," 1991, p. 59). That was the Act's intention when it began, "[B]ut with the passing of time its meaning changed" (Graglia, 1993, p. 26).

~~~ Affirmative action was created to spread equal opportunity throughout the diverse American population.

The idea was that minorities and women would no longer be discriminated against in employment and educational opportunities. Through the decades, this subject has led to intense controversy over "whether governmental intervention . . . should be aimed at *equalizing* the *opportunities* for achievement. . . . [or] ensure instead the *equality of achievement itself* for that group . . ." (Trow, 1992, p. 597). Affirmative action can be seen as a line that separates those with different views (Taylor and Liss, 1992, p. 31). And those different views sharply split scholars and laypersons alike over the meaning of equal opportunity.

Those against affirmative action say that it is only a vehicle that heightens racial awareness. And if affirmative action groups are constantly working to make the public racially aware, the public will never forget the conflict over race. It impedes America's ability to achieve equality without being constantly reminded of racial differences. But, opponents say, as Justice Blackmun wrote in *Bakke* (1978): "[I]n order to get beyond racism, we must first take race into account. There is no other way."

Opponents of affirmative action also argue forcibly that such programs are, themselves, discriminatory.

REVERSE DISCRIMINATION

Opponents of affirmative action programs contend that civil rights laws cannot remedy the effects of past discrimination. For example, a black person may be severely disadvantaged in the job market because of unequal education even though formal discrimination has been outlawed. Therefore, the federal government through its affirmative action policy requires those who receive federal funding to provide training and job opportunities for those who have traditionally been discriminated against in the past.

Some people would charge that this policy leads to reverse discrimination because women or racial minorities are hired over white males who may be better qualified.

> **Reverse discrimination** consists of giving preferential treatment in hiring and promoting to women and minorities to the detriment of white males.

Critics of affirmative action programs argue that discrimination cannot be cured by counterdiscrimination. This is divisive and fundamentally unfair. Further, it usurps the fundamental American concept of individual rights in favor of group entitlement.

The issue of reverse discrimination was raised in *Regents of the University of California v. Bakke* (1978). The University's medical school at Davis each year reserved a fixed number of slots for nonwhite students. Alan Bakke, a white male, had twice been denied admission to medical school, even though less qualified minorities had been admitted. Bakke charged that the University's quota system violated the equal protection clause. And as the Court said in *Regents v. Bakke:*

> Preferring members of any one group for no reason other than race or ethnic origin is discrimination for its own sake. This the Constitution forbids.

But the Court also said that a "black applicant may be examined for his potential contribution to diversity without the factor of race being decisive."

The question then becomes whether admission to a college based on diversity is simply a nice way of saying we are going to take race into account. Something must guide the decisions of those who determine who will be hired, fired or admitted to the college of their choice.

The Supreme Court ruled that a strict quota system in which race was the sole factor for admission *did* violate the Fourteenth Amendment. But the Court also held that the University could consider race as one of many factors in an admission decision. Generally, the Court has held in subsequent decisions that affirmative action in employment must result from specific acts of discrimination against specific individuals, rather than a general claim that blacks and women have been discriminated against in the past.

The nine justices could not come to total agreement on this controversial issue. Wrobleski and Hess (1997, pp. 574–575) note:

> This issue [reverse discrimination] has separated whites from minorities, men from women, and the advocates of affirmative action from those who believe in a strict "merit" principle for employment and advancement. A growing number of majority member workers are complaining bitterly about their own civil rights being abridged, and some are filing reverse discrimination suits in court.
>
> The majority position has been summarized as a concern that for every deserving minority group member who is provided a job or promotion through preferential quotas, there is also a deserving, and often more qualified nonminority person who is thereby deprived of a job or promotion. The courts themselves have been deeply divided over the constitutionality of the reverse discrimination that some believe is implicit in minority quotas and double standards.

Through time, according to Kuran (1993, p. 56), the idea of affirmative action and opportunity have been lost in a system of "racial quotas, time-tables, and standards." The action plan is no longer concerned so much with equal opportunity, but with meeting the racial quota required in education and employment. Graglia (p. 28) argues that affirmative action has become obsessed with numbers: "[T]he underrepresentation of any racial group . . . can be taken as evidence of discrimination." Reynolds (1992, p. 44) suggests that group equality has become the focus of affirmative action policies, and the opportunity of the individual has been left behind for the sake of meeting a desired numerical result.

In this sea of numbers, the true intention of affirmative action has been lost, and the public's view of minorities has become distorted. As noted by Trow (1992, p. 596): "A culture is defined, in part, by what it feels guilty about." According to many people, that guilt has virtually *given* blacks the opportunity that their white counterparts have had to work for. The result is that minority students are admitted to colleges without the proper qualifications, and that "preferential programs may only reinforce common stereotypes . . . that certain groups are unable to achieve success without special protection" *(Bakke)*.

Those in favor of affirmative action say that this is a much needed policy to remedy the "decades of second class citizenship . . . legalized discrimination . . . [and] educational deprivation" experienced by minorities and women. According to Trow (p. 586), opportunity in education "celebrates the American Dream," and all people need the chance to raise their aspiration in hope of accomplishing what every person, of any color, hopes for.

> ≋ The **American Dream** refers to the belief that through hard work anyone can have success and ample material possessions.

The Civil Rights Act, the Fair Housing Act, the Voting Rights Act and numerous court decisions have, on paper, outlawed racial discrimination in this nation. But discrimination still exists, as noted by Kuran (p. 59):

> Controlled studies reveal that when a black and a white apply for a job, stating identical credentials, the black is more likely to hear the job has been filled.

The interment of Japanese-Americans during World War II, Smithsonian Institute, Washington, D.C.

Why does this happen? Employers say that by hiring a white person over a black, they run less risk of being sued for discrimination if that person ends up being fired. Affirmative action programs have put fear into many employers who hesitate to hire a minority member even though they have a quota to meet. So the question that must be asked is whether affirmative action programs are truly effective.

EQUALITY IN THE 1990S AND BEYOND

A look at this nation's history helps explain why affirmative action programs developed. In the 1990s, however, such programs are being increasingly challenged as unconstitutional. For example, the California Civil Rights Initiative (CCRI) passed unanimously. This initiative forbids the government to use ethnicity or gender as a criterion for either discriminating against or giving preferential treatment to any individual or group. It is now tied up in the courts however, its constitutionality in question. As noted by *Law Enforcement News* ("Affirmative-Action . . . ," 1995, p. 1):

> The continued need for affirmative-action programs is under renewed challenge from critics who contend that they have achieved their original goals of ending discrimination against minorities and providing parity with white males.
>
> Congress is currently scrutinizing the issue, and several Republican presidential candidates say they oppose the programs, thus ensuring that affirmative action will be an issue in the 1996 campaign . . . [Likewise,] the Clinton administration is reviewing more than 100 federal programs that seek to give special help to minorities and women.
>
> This month [April] , the U.S. Supreme Court refused to review a lower-court decision which found that race-based promotions were unfair to whites in Birmingham, Alabama.

A leading case in applying strict scrutiny to government affirmative action programs is *Adarand v. Pena* (1995), in which the United States Supreme Court considered the case of a Colorado business operated by a white man that low-bid a highway contract, but lost to a Latino-owned company that took advantage of an affirmative-action bonus to the contractor.

The greatest barrier to equality is public attitude.

Many Americans have closed their minds to the intent of affirmative action, contending that programs that help minorities are unfair. They question why minorities and women are given programs that help them achieve success while the white male has to make it on his own.

Whether affirmative action is fair is controversial, but fairness does not always mean going by the letter of the law. Law making involves a give and take. Some laws are not fair to everyone, and exceptions have to be made. Such exceptions are known as compromise, and affirmative action is a creature of compromise.

This country was built on freedom, with liberty and justice for *all*—concepts written into the Constitution that make no mention of race, color, creed, religion, sex or sexual orientation. People flock to this country for that very reason with the hope of attaining the American Dream. Everyone has the right to dream and to have access to the vehicles that can take them there.

Unfortunately, as noted by Eitzen (1992, p. 584): "Some young people act in antisocial ways because they have lost their dreams." He describes the economic inequality using the analogy of a boat and the traditional argument that "a rising tide lifts all boats." This may have been true during the fifties and sixties as the average standard of living increased steadily. This has *not* been the case during the last 20 years, as noted by Eitzen: "But since 1973 the water level was not the same for all boats, some boats leaked severely, and some people had no boat at all."

As Justice Holmes stated: "While justice may wear a blindfold, it should not be blind to inequality."

BALANCING STATE AND FEDERAL POWER AND INDIVIDUAL RIGHTS

Although this text specifically addresses the overall importance of the United States Constitution and its amendments, state constitutions also play a role in the formation of laws that people are protected by and expected to abide by. It is sometimes confusing that two constitutions can be in effect at the same time. In fact, some people are surprised that state constitutions even exist. They do, but they play a role different from the United States Constitution.

Like the bylaws of a company, the constitution of a state sets forth some general guidelines that the particular state has chosen to operate under. But because the United States Constitution is overriding, state constitutions are used more to set forth some specific ideals that the particular state asserts. They do have the more practical use of establishing the organization of a state's governing bodies.

As noted by Marks and Cooper (1988), state constitutions serve several purposes:

❖ The first and paramount purpose of a state constitution is to impose limitations and restrictions on the exercise of state government's inherent power.

❖ The second purpose of a state constitution is to prescribe the manner in which the state is required to exercise its inherent power.

❖ The third purpose of a state constitution is to affirm the continuing existence in state government of certain powers, e.g., to appropriate state funds to school districts.

❖ One of the primary functions of a state constitution is to establish the structure of state and local government.

As noted, the Fourteenth Amendment established that neither the federal nor state governments could infringe upon our constitutionally guaranteed rights. Reflecting that the Constitution itself was drafted as a tool with which to limit federal government, it made no sense to then permit states to tread on these very rights.

The Fourteenth Amendment is important because it serves to limit both national (federal) power and state power, either of which abused could assault the same liberties the Constitution sought to guarantee.

In the 1833 case of *Barron v. Mayor and City Council of Baltimore*, the Supreme Court held that the first ten amendments to the Constitution, that is, the Bill of Rights, were not applicable to state governments. As noted by Nowak and Rotunda (1991, p. 332):

> This holding was correct historically because the drafters of the Bill of Rights designed the amendments as a check on the new national government. This judicially perceived intent of the drafters, however, limited the ability of the courts to control the substance of state law under the federal constitution.

The passage of the Fourteenth Amendment provided through its privileges and immunity and due process clauses that the *fundamental* provisions of the Bill of Rights would apply to all levels of governmental powers (national, state and local).

Some confusion arises here because, for reasons that have confounded many who have argued over the course of history that the entire Bill of Rights should be directly applied to the states, the doctrine of selective incorporation as upheld by the Supreme Court has prevented this from occurring.

Selective Incorporation

The doctrine of **selective incorporation** holds that only the provisions of the Bill of Rights that are *fundamental to the American legal system* are applied to the states through the due process clause. For example, if a state law were to abridge freedom of religion, it would be violating the First Amendment as applied to it through the Fourteenth Amendment.

According to Nowak and Rotunda (pp. 332–334), the Ninth and Tenth Amendments appear to be inapplicable to the states. Of the first eight amendments, they suggest that only three individual guarantees have been made inapplicable to the states by the Supreme Court:

❖ The Second Amendment guarantee of the right to bear arms.
❖ The Fifth Amendment clause guaranteeing criminal prosecution only on a grand jury indictment.
❖ The Seventh Amendment guarantee of a jury trial in a civil case.

They note that the Third Amendment prohibiting the quartering of soldiers in private houses and the Eighth Amendment prohibiting excessive fines have not been addressed as yet by the Court.

A Check on Federal Power

Just as states may exceed their power, so too, can the federal government. A prime example of this is *United States v. Lopez* (1995) in which the United States Supreme Court struck down a 1990 federal law aimed at banning firearms in schools, ruling five to four that Congress had exceeded its power under the commerce clause of the United States Constitution when it enacted the law.

The *NCJA Justice Bulletin* ("Supreme Court . . .", 1995, p. 1) describes the case that involves Alfonso Lopez, a 12th-grade student, arrested for carrying an unloaded .38-caliber handgun and five bullets on high school grounds in San Antonio, Texas, on March 10, 1992. Federal officials charged him with violating the federal gun-free schools statute. The United States Court of Appeals for the Fifth Circuit ruled that Congress had exceeded its power in enacting the law, and the Supreme Court agreed.

According to Professor Charles Whitebread of the USC Law School, this was the "blockbuster case of the term" because it shows that the "conservative majority" is now firmly in control and that future limitations on congress' attempts to regulate will follow. Whitebread believes that the power of Congress in the next few years will be severely restricted in favor of individual state regulation in many fields. He has stated that from now on the "United States is a plural noun."

Summary

To assure "liberty and justice for all," two additional amendments were passed. The Thirteenth Amendment abolished slavery. The Fourteenth Amendment granted citizenship to all persons born or naturalized in the United States, and forbid states to deny their citizens due process of law or equal protection of the law, that is, it made certain provisions of the Bill of Rights applicable to the states.

These amendments, however, did not eliminate prejudice and discrimination. *Prejudice* is an attitude; *discrimination* is a behavior. Racial discrimination has its roots in our nation's history of slavery. The *Dred Scott* (1856) decision ruled that a freed slave still did not enjoy the right to remain free in those parts of the United States where slavery was legal. *Plessy v. Ferguson* (1896) showed the Court's desire to avoid civil rights issues, declaring discrimination to be outside the realm of the Court. Jim Crow laws strictly segregated blacks from whites in schools, restaurants, street cars, hospitals and even cemeteries by permitting "separate but equal" accommodations.

It was not until the fifties and sixties that the Court directly confronted civil rights. *Brown v. Board of Education of Topeka I* (1954) established that "separate but equal" schools were illegal. The 1964 Omnibus Civil Rights Law prohibited discrimination in employment opportunities in private business. The 1972 Equal Employment Opportunity Act prohibited discrimination based on race, color, religion, sex or national origin in employment of any kind, public or private, local, state or federal.

Affirmative action was created to spread equal opportunity throughout the diverse American population. Reverse discrimination consists of giving preferential treatment in hiring and promoting to women and minorities to the detriment of white males. And yet, affirmative action may be needed to assure belief in the American Dream, which suggests that through hard work anyone can have success and ample material possessions. The greatest barrier to true equality is public attitude.

Discussion Questions

1. Why was the Fourteenth Amendment necessary?

2. Why has the entire Bill of Rights not been embraced by the Fourteenth Amendment?

3. Were the framers of the Constitution racist?

4. Why are people prejudiced? Do you recognize your own prejudices?

5. Do you think quota laws improve things or worsen them? For whom?

6. Is "separate but equal" possible?

7. Can it be argued that government has "gone too far" by requiring that all people be treated equally? Can you think of instances in which different people might not be equally able to do a job?

8. What is your definition of the American Dream? Do you feel it is within your reach? Why or why not?

9. Can all people's dreams be possible?

10. Can law shape attitude?

References

"Affirmative Action Programs." *Black's Law Dictionary.* 6th ed. 1991.

"Affirmative-Action Programs Looking a Little Black and Blue." *Law Enforcement News.* April 30, 1995, pp. 1, 7.

Currie, David P. *The Constitution of the United States: A Primer for the People.* Chicago: The University of Chicago Press, 1988.

Eitzen, Stanley. "Problem Students: The Sociocultural Roots." *Phi Delta Kappan.* April 1992, pp. 584–590.

Graglia, Lino A. "Affirmative Discrimination." *National Review.* July 5, 1993, pp. 26–31.

Hageman, Mary Jeanette. *Police-Community Relations.* Beverly Hills: Sage Publishing, 1985.

Klotter, J. C. and J. R. Kanovitz. *Constitutional Law.* 5th ed. Cincinnati: Anderson Publishing, 1985.

Kuran, Timur. "Seeds of Racial Explosion." *Social Science and Modern Society.* September-October 1993, pp. 55–67.

Magill, Frank M., ed. *Great Events from History.* Human Rights Series 1960–1971. California: Salem, 1992.

Marks, Thomas C., Jr. and John F. Cooper. *State Constitutional Law.* St. Paul: West Publishing Company, 1988.

Nowak, John E. and Ronald D. Rotunda. *Constitutional Law.* 4th ed. St. Paul: West Publishing Company, 1991.

Reynolds, Wm. Bradford. "Affirmative Action and Its Negative Repercussions." *The Annals of the American Academy of Political and Social Science.* September 1992, pp. 38–49.

"Supreme Court Strikes Down Gun-Free School Zones Act." *NCJA Justice Bulletin.* April 1995, vol. 15, no. 4, pp. 1–2.

Taylor, William M. and Susan M. Liss. "Affirmative Action in the 1990s: Staying on Course." *The Annals of the American Academy of Political and Social Science.* September 1992, pp. 30–37.

Trow, Martin. "Social Class and Higher Education." *American Behavioral Scientist.* March-June 1992, pp. 585–605.

Wrobleski, Henry M. and Kären M. Hess. *Introduction to Law Enforcement and Criminal Justice.* 5th ed. St. Paul: West Publishing Company, 1997.

Cases Cited

Adarand v. Pena, ___ U.S. ___, 115 S.Ct. 2097, 132 L.Ed. 2d 158 (1995).

Barron v. Mayor and City Council of Baltimore, 32 U.S. (7 Pet.) 243, 8 L.Ed. 672 (1833).

Brown v. Board of Education of Topeka I, 347 U.S. 483, 74 S.Ct. 686, 98 L.Ed. 873 (1954).

Dred Scott v. Sandford, 60 U.S. 393, 19 How. 393, 15 L.Ed. 691 (1856).

Plessy v. Ferguson, 16 S.Ct. 1138, 41 L.Ed. 256 (1896).

Regents of the University of California v. Bakke, 438 U.S. 265, 98 S.Ct. 2733, 57 L.Ed. 2d 750 (1978).

Slaughterhouse (1873).

United States v. Lopez, ___ U.S. ___, 115 S.Ct. 1624, 131 L.Ed. 2d 626 (1995).

Chapter 7

The First Amendment: Basic Freedoms

Congress shall make no law respecting an establishment of religion, or prohibiting the free exercise thereof; or abridging the freedom of speech, or of the press, or the right of the people peaceably to assemble, and to petition the Government for a redress of grievances.

—FIRST AMENDMENT OF THE UNITED STATES CONSTITUTION

An antiwar demonstrator burns an American flag on the steps of the Capitol. (Photo by Matt Mendelsohn. Provided by UPI/Corbis-Bettmann.)

What basic freedoms are guaranteed in the First Amendment?

What freedoms are included in religious freedom?

What the establishment clause guarantees? The free exercise clause?

What freedom of speech guarantees American citizens?

How the Smith Act relates to the First Amendment?

What the "imminent lawless action" test involves and when it is likely to be used?

Whether symbolic acts are protected under the First Amendment?

What is included in freedom of the press?

CAN YOU DEFINE THESE TERMS?

Balancing test
"Clear and present danger" test
Establishment clause
Free exercise clause
Judicial activism
Preferred freedoms approach
Prior restraint
Resolution

INTRODUCTION

Perhaps the best known provision of the Bill of Rights as far as the public is concerned is the First Amendment. Being able to speak out, particularly against the government, has remained a cornerstone of American freedom and one that continues to be examined and argued—for and against.

> The First Amendment prohibits Congress from making any laws that restrict freedom of religion, freedom of speech, freedom of the press or the right to gather or assemble peaceably and to request the government to respond to complaints from its citizens.

In *Gitlow v. New York* (1925) and in other important cases (*Near v. Minnesota*, 1931; *DeJonge v. Oregon*, 1937; *Cantwell v. Connecticut*, 1940), the Supreme Court held that protecting these fundamental liberties applied also to the states under the due process clause of the Fourteenth Amendment. Remember, the Constitution as originally drafted served to restrict only the federal government. The Fourteenth Amendment applied the majority of the Bill of Rights to state governments as well.

Differences and difficulties in interpretation have characterized much of the later history of the First Amendment. For example, despite the apparent absolute prohibition in the phrase "Congress shall make no law . . .," Congress has, in fact, many times passed laws "in the public interest" that restrict

Figure 7–1
Balancing individual and societal rights.

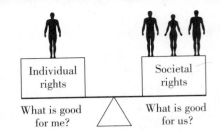

freedom of religion, speech and press. Keep in mind that the framers of our Constitution intended to construct only the basic framework of American law. Those very general terms like "religion," "speech" and "press" have proven worthy of great debate as our law continues to grow and change.

In addition, federal agencies and prosecutors have initiated actions that have resulted in certain limitations on freedom of speech and press. In ruling on the constitutionality of various restrictions on these civil rights, the Supreme Court has at various times tended to support either the individual's rights or society's interests. Consider that for a moment: either the interests of the individual or of society. It sounds simple, but it is not. Private versus public interests continue to be at odds while giving courts continual opportunities to provide solutions that will best serve all involved, including those who will rely on past law to determine future decisions.

Since the early 1950s, the Court has sought a balanced approach whereby both private and public interests are weighed in each case, as illustrated in Figure 7–1. It is worth mentioning again that the framers of our Constitution looked forward to our interpreting all provisions. Surely, if they had intended for the document to be an absolute, it would not be as brief as it is. By providing future lawmakers with the cornerstones of what America was to become, law has been able to be the living law that was desired—able to grow and develop to continue to serve the perceived needs of present society. Interpretation plays an important role in constitutional law, and must have been why those who drafted the document kept it so fundamental. The basic nature of the Constitution permits courts to continue to interpret law to let it grow along with our society.

This chapter provides an in-depth look at how the First Amendment has been interpreted over the years, beginning with freedom of religion followed by freedom of speech. Next freedom of the press is examined. The chapter concludes with a discussion of the right to peaceful assembly.

FREEDOM OF RELIGION

Freedom of religion is at the "top of the list" of rights set forth in our Bill of Rights. Many of the colonists fled religious persecution and cherished their right to worship as they believed in their new country. And because the religions differed from colony to colony, our founding fathers wanted to guarantee every individual religious freedom. As noted by Killian (1987, p. 964):

In some of the states, Episcopalians constituted the predominant sect; in others Presbyterians; in others, Congregationalists; and in others, Quakers; and in others again, there was a close numerical rivalry among contending sects. It was impossible that there should not arise perpetual strife and perpetual jealousy on the subject of ecclesiastical ascendancy, if the national government were left free to create a religious establishment.

Freedom of religion is a political principle that strives to forbid government constraint on people's choices of beliefs. It requires also that people be free to act upon their beliefs.

> Religious freedom includes the freedom to worship, to print instructional material, to train teachers and to organize groups for their employment and schools in which to teach, including religion.

Thus, freedom of religion is closely linked with other freedoms such as freedom of speech, freedom of the press and freedom of assembly. This area reflects the importance that religious freedom played in the formation of the United States.

The concept of separation of church and state is an important legal issue related to freedom of religion in the United States. Such a separation is not widespread in other parts of the world, nor does it necessarily indicate the presence or absence of religious freedom. Because religion tends to be so important to many people, many governments attempt to control their society by controlling religion. Some dictatorships have banned certain religions altogether. Governments still provide some restrictions on practicing religions, such as controlling the use of certain drugs or use of animals in ceremonies. England, Scotland and Sweden, for example, have officially established churches, but also permit religious freedom.

It has been difficult to separate church and state in the United States. Churches are required to conform to building codes, fire regulations and sanitation laws. The government is expected to decide whether a group claiming to be religious should be exempt from property taxes. The First Amendment pledges the federal government to neither favor nor be hostile, but to be *neutral*.

The Establishment Clause

Currie (1988, p. 81) notes: "The most obvious effect of the Establishment Clause was to preclude the creation of a national church."

> The **establishment clause** of the First Amendment states clearly that "Congress shall make no law respecting an establishment of religion."

The "establishment clause" has been interpreted at various times to mean either the government cannot show preference to any particular religion or that there must be complete separation of church and state.

Large areas of dispute exist resulting in constant litigation over such issues as government assistance to religiously sponsored schools, devotional practices in public schools and the treatment of sectarians, whose religious convictions are not easily accommodated by local law.

Nowak and Rotunda (1991, p. 1160) suggest: "The religion clauses were among the first portions of the Bill of Rights incorporated into the Fourteenth Amendment and made applicable to the states by the Supreme Court." The establishment clause was made applicable to the states in *Everson v. Board of Education* (1947). In this case, the Supreme Court held that state reimbursement to parents for money spent to transport their children to parochial schools on the public bus system does *not* constitute an establishment of religion. Further, in public schools a period of silence may be observed in which children may pray if they wish, but the schools may not conduct devotional exercises, compose prayers, read the Bible or otherwise enter the field of religious instruction (*Engle v. Vitale,* 1962).

However, the Court, in *Wallace v. Jeffries* (1985), ruled that even permitting a "moment of silence" for "meditation or voluntary prayer" in public schools was unconstitutional. The Court held that authorizing such a silence period had as a purpose to promote religious values and, therefore, violated the establishment clause of the First Amendment.

In 1980 the Courts struck down a Kentucky law requiring the posting of the Ten Commandments in all classrooms (*Stone v. Graham,* 1980). The "Equal Access" law of 1984, however, gave students the right to hold religious meetings in public high schools outside class hours.

In some instances, the government can assist religion, for example, providing police and fire protection to churches. This certainly aids the practice of religion, but to withhold such services would not be in the interest of the public good.

If a law is challenged under the establishment clause, a three-part test is usually applied. Nowak and Rotunda (p. 1159) explain the standards applied in this test that have been applied by the Supreme Court "in virtually all of its establishment clause cases since 1971":

> Those establishment clause standards require that any statute that has the incidental effect of aiding religion must (1) have a secular purpose, (2) have a principle or primary effect that does not advance or inhibit religion, and (3) not give rise to an excessive entanglement between government and religion.

They note that this three-part test—purpose, primary effect and excessive entanglement—is often referred to as the "*Lemon* test" because it resulted from the landmark decision in *Lemon v. Kurtzman* (1971). In this case Rhode Island was providing a 15% salary supplement to teachers of secular subjects in private schools. The Court invalidated the state's attempt to subsidize costs of parochial school education by ruling that the statutes fostered an excessive entanglement between church and state. Nowak and Rotunda (p. 1171) explain:

> Chief Justice Burger, writing for the majority, held that, in assessing the degree of entanglement, three factors were to be considered:

1. The character and purpose of the institution benefited.
2. The nature of the aid.
3. The resulting relationship between government and religious authorities. . . .

This three part analysis showed that the program would result in an excessive entanglement violative of the establishment clause.

The Chief Justice also stressed the fact that these types of programs were politically divisive. The provision of significant ongoing aid to parochial elementary and secondary schools injected an explosive political issue which caused division along religious lines. These programs virtually guarantee that there will be yearly public debate and political conflict between religious factions.

Killian (1987, p. 975) explains that the Court found the program uncon- stitutional because "the state supervision necessary to ensure a secular pur- pose and a secular effect inevitably involved the state authorities too deeply in the religious affairs of the institutions aided."

Currie (p. 84) explains further that in *Lemon v. Kurtzman* the Court found:

[S]ecular and religious education were so tightly interwoven that it would be practically impossible to support one without supporting the other. Any effort to separate the two, the Court continued, would so entangle the state in the administration of the religious body as to impair its independence, and such an "entanglement" would offend a central purpose of the Establishment Clause.

The Free Exercise Clause

〰️ The **free exercise clause** of the First Amendment declares that "Congress shall make no law . . . prohibiting the free exercise [of religion]."

In *Davis v. Beason* (1890) the Court described the First Amendment free exercise clause:

The First Amendment was intended to allow everyone under the jurisdiction of the United States to entertain such notions respecting his relations to his Maker and the duties they impose as may be approved by his judgment and conscience, and to exhibit his sentiments in such form of worship, as he may think proper, not injurious to the rights of others.

In other words, the freedom to believe is an absolute established by the First Amendment. However, the freedom to act is not so protected. According to Killian (1987, p. 992):

The Court's first encounter with free exercise claims occurred in a series of cases in which the Federal government and the territories moved against the Mormons because of their practice of polygamy. Actual prosecutions and convictions for bigamy presented little problem for the Court, inasmuch as it could distinguish between beliefs and acts (*Reynolds v. United States*, 1879).

The free exercise clause was first applicable to the states in *Cantwell v. Connecticut* (1940). This case established that although freedom to believe is an absolute, freedom to act is not absolutely protected by the First Amendment:

> Freedom of conscience and freedom to adhere to such religious organization or form of worship as the individual may choose, cannot be restricted by law. On the other hand, it safeguards the free exercise of the chosen form of religion. Thus, the Amendment embraces two concepts—freedom to believe and freedom to act. The first is an absolute, but, in the nature of things, the second cannot be. Conduct remains subject to regulation for the protection of society. The freedom to act must have appropriate definition to preserve the enforcement of that protection.

In *Cantwell v. Connecticut* (1940) three Jehovah's Witnesses were convicted under a statute that forbade the unlicensed soliciting of funds on the representation that they were for religious or charitable purposes, as well as a charge of breach of the peace when an altercation occurred in a strongly Catholic neighborhood after the Jehovah's Witnesses played a phonograph recording that insulted the Christian religion, and the Catholic Church in particular. Both counts were voided by the court.

Another example of weighing the individual's right to freedom of religion versus the good of society was an incident in St. Paul, Minnesota, where officers ticketed a Muslim woman for wearing a veil as part of her religious practice. St. Paul had a city ordinance prohibiting people from hiding their identity "by means of a robe, mask or other disguise." As noted by Shafer (1995, p. 329): "[D]ue to bank robberies, thefts and crimes at the mall, officers were utilizing the ordinance as a prevention tactic. The somewhat predictable result is concern and anger among the Muslim community in the Minneapolis-St. Paul area." The court ruled the ordinance unconstitutional.

Courts have had to weigh the requirements of the free exercise clause of the First Amendment against certain legal, social and religious needs of society. For example, the Court has never held that the free exercise clause required the government to exempt from military service those who object to such service on religious grounds.

In *Employment Division v. Smith* (1990) the Court stated: "We have never held that an individual's religious beliefs excuse him from compliance with an otherwise valid law prohibiting conduct that the State is free to regulate." In this case, two American Indian drug counselors in Oregon lost their jobs because they used peyote, a hallucinogenic drug, as part of a religious ritual in the Native American church. Some states allowed such a practice, but Oregon did not. The court decreed: "Because respondents' ingestion of peyote was prohibited under Oregon law, and because that prohibition is constitutional, Oregon may, consistent with the Free Exercise Clause, deny respondents unemployment compensation when their dismissal results from use of the drug." Under this 1990 ruling, restrictions on religion were acceptable as long as they were not aimed specifically at religious groups. The state had only to show a "compelling state interest" in enacting the law.

Some examples of how this ruling affected other religious groups were the performance of autopsies despite families' religious beliefs and members of the Amish community being compelled to put orange reflectors on the backs of their buggies.

When Congress passed and President Clinton signed the Religious Freedom Restoration Act, however, interference with religious practices by the government was made more difficult. This act, in effect, overturned *Employment Division v. Smith* and held the government to a very high level of proof before interfering with free exercise of religion. As Clinton stated: "Congress should rarely reverse the Supreme Court, but this is an issue in which extraordinary measure was clearly called for."

The free exercise clause has taken some interesting paths as various issues have been presented to the Court. While *Cruz v. Beto* (1972) protected inmates' freedom to worship, in *West Virginia State Board of Education v. Barnette* (1943) the Supreme Court held that states could not require children to pledge allegiance to the United States each school day. In his opinion, Justice Jackson said that everyone has a First Amendment right to not pledge allegiance because of the "freedom of thought and belief that is central to all First Amendment freedoms."

In *Lynch v. Donnelly* (1984), a government subsidized Christmas display of a creche was found not an advancement or endorsement of religion, and, therefore, permitted. In *Wooley v. Maynard* (1977), the Supreme Court stated that a state could not punish someone for blacking out the part of his car's license plate that set forth the state's motto, "Live Free or Die." The government is not permitted to force citizens to advertise government or religious beliefs, or to comply with the advertisement or assertion of them.

However, in balancing this, the Court held in *Wooley v. Maynard* that printing "In God We Trust" on money did not violate the Constitution because money is passed among people, and, therefore, does not indicate that a particular individual agrees with a religious or governmental belief, like a motto on a license plate might. Also, money is transported in such a manner as to not be a public display.

In effect, the free exercise clause establishes that the government may not require people to assert certain religious or political beliefs, nor may the government subsidize activities that would support beliefs favorable to the government but in violation of anyone's First Amendment rights.

In June 1993 the Supreme Court ruled unanimously that a Miami suburb, Hialeah, could not suppress an African religion by banning ritualistic sacrifice of animals (*Church of Lukumi Babalu Aye v. Hialeah*, 1993). In the past few years an estimated 50,000 Santerians have settled in southern Florida. Their worship services routinely include sacrificing chickens, goats, ducks and other small animals. Angry residents of Hialeah urged their city council to pass an ordinance forbidding such sacrifices, which it did. The case eventually found its way to the Supreme Court, which ruled: "The record in this case compels the conclusion that suppression of the central element of the Santeria worship was the object of the ordinances" ("High Court Protects . . .," 1993, p. A12).

In December 1993 the Supreme Court ruled that the Boy Scouts could require applicants to promise to "love God" and to "do my duty to God and my country." The suit was brought by Mark Welsh and his father, Elliott, in 1990 when Mark was denied membership in the Tiger Cub Group because he refused to sign the required pledge. The Court ruled this was not a violation of the First Amendment or of Title III of the Civil Rights Act of 1964, which applied to public accommodations ("Scouts Allowed to Require Vow on God," 1993, p. A2).

Table 7–1 summarizes conduct not protected by the freedom of religion clause.

Table 7–1   **Conduct not protected by the freedom of religion clause.**

We have never held that an individual's religious beliefs excuse him from compliance with an otherwise valid law prohibiting conduct that the State is free to regulate.

UNITED STATES SUPREME COURT,
Employment Division v. Smith, 108 L.Ed.2d 876 (1990).

Conduct not protected	Case
Multiple marriages in violation of state polygamy laws (obsoleted crime of bigamy)	*Reynolds v. United States*, 98 U.S. 145, 25 L.Ed. 244 (1879)
Handling poisonous snakes in a public place in violation of state law as part of a religious ceremony	*State v. Massey*, 229 N.C. 734, 51 S.E.2d 179 (1949)
Requirements at airports, state fairs, etc. that religious, political and other groups distribute or sell literature from booths provided for that purpose	*Heffron v. International Society for Krishna Consciousness*, 452 U.S. 640, 101 S.Ct. 2559 (1981)
Using a mailbox to put religious, political or other literature can be in violation of the federal postal statute 18 U.S.C. 1725. The Supreme Court held that a letter box is not a "soap box" and upheld the statute.	*Council of Greenburgh Civic Assn. v. U.S. Postal Service*, 453 U.S. 917, 101 S.Ct. 3150 (1981)
Violation of Sunday retail store closing law is not protected by First Amendment	*Braunfeld v. Brown*, 366 U.S. 599, 81 S.Ct. 1144 (1961)
Violation of child labor laws	*Prince v. Massachusetts*, 321 U.S. 158, 64 S.Ct. 438 (1944)
Failure to comply with compulsory military service by defendants who conscientiously objected only to the Vietnam War	*Gillette v. United States*, 401 U.S. 437, 91 S.Ct. 828 (1971)
Air Force officer continued to wear his yarmulke (Jewish skullcap) after repeated orders to remove it. He was dropped from service. Affirmed for Air Force.	*Goldman v. Weinberger*, 475 U.S. 503, 106 S.Ct. 1310 (1986)
Illegal importation of aliens in violation of Immigration and Nationality Act 8 U.S.C.A. Sec. 1324	*United States v. Merkt*, review denied, 794 F.2d 950, 41 CrL 4001 (5th Cir. 1987)
Members of the Old Order Amish who do not use motor vehicles and travel in horse-drawn buggies would not obey a state law requiring reflecting triangles on the rear of all slow-moving vehicles. Held not exempted from complying with this highway safety law.	*Minnesota v. Hershberger*, ____ U.S. ____, 110 S.Ct. 1918, vacating 444 N.W.2d 282 (1990)
There was also no exemption on religious grounds from complying with required vehicle liability insurance. South Dakota law makes it a crime not to carry the insurance.	*South Dakota v. Cosgrove*, 439 N.W.2d 119, review denied, ____ U.S.____ , 110 S.Ct. 140, 46 CrL 3008 (1989)

The freedom of religion clause could not be used as a defense for:

Destroying government property (760 F.2d 447); extortion and blackmail (515 F.2d 112); racketeering (695 F.2d 765, rev. den., 460 U.S. 1092); refusal to testify before a grand jury (465 F.2d 802, see 409 U.S. 944); photographing of arrested person (848 F.2d 113); putting logging road through area sacred to Indian tribes (108 S.Ct. 1319); vaccination of children (25 S.Ct. 358); participating in social security system (102 S.Ct. 1051).

Source: Thomas J. Gardner and Terry M. Anderson. *Criminal Law: Principles and Cases.* 6th ed. St. Paul: West Publishing Company, 1994, p. 277. Reprinted by permission. All rights reserved.

Interpretations

What exactly did the framers and ratifiers of the First Amendment freedom of religion clause intend? Did they mean, as Justice Black argued, that the statement "Congress shall make no law" means just that, Congress (and through the Fourteenth Amendment, the states) could not in any way, shape or form do anything that might breech the "wall of separation"? Or did they mean that while government could not prefer one sect over another, it might provide aid to all religions equally?

Some scholars believe the historic record is confused and contradictory. At the core of the problem is one's view of the Constitution and its role in American government. Advocates of the original intent believe that the vision of the framers is as good today as it was 200 years ago. Any deviation from that view abandons the ideals that have made this country free and great. Judges should go strictly by what the framers intended. Any revisions must be made through the amendment process.

On the other side, defenders of **judicial activism** say that amendments are not necessary. Judges should be allowed to interpret the Constitution and its amendments. Such defenders believe that for the document to remain true to the framers' intent, the framers' spirit must reach a balance with the realities of modern society. They suggest that the framers set out a series of ideals expressed through powers and limitations and deliberately left details vague so that those who came after could apply those ideals to the world in which they live.

FREEDOM OF SPEECH

Freedom of speech is the liberty to speak openly without fear of government restraint. It is closely linked to freedom of the press because this freedom includes both the right to speak and the right to be heard. In the United States, both freedoms, commonly called *freedom of expression,* are protected by the First Amendment.

> Freedom of speech/expression includes the right to speak and the right to be heard.

Freedom of speech and the constitutional limits to it have been defined in practice by Supreme Court rulings.

Originally the free speech guarantee of the First Amendment applied only to acts of Congress, that is, the federal government could not pass a law "abridging the freedom of speech." In the twentieth century, however, the Supreme Court began to interpret the due process clause of the Fourteenth Amendment to mean that states, as well as the federal government, are bound by the provisions of the First Amendment (*Gitlow v. New York,* 1925).

Restrictions on Freedom of Speech

As noted by Currie (1988, p. 71): "Freedom to speak was certainly not absolute at the time the Constitution was adopted. Defamation, among other things, was traditionally prohibited." He notes that surely the founding fathers did not intend to protect speech that incited to murder or false advertising.

Restrictions on freedom of speech have occurred most often in time of war and national emergency. The Alien and Sedition Acts of 1798 were the first incursions by Congress on this freedom. These acts were passed when war with France threatened. They empowered the president to expel "dangerous" aliens and provided for indicting those who should "unlawfully combine or conspire" against the administration or write or speak "with intent to defame" the government, the Congress or the president. These laws were never tested in the courts and were allowed to expire after several years.

The first clear-cut test came over the Espionage Act (1917) passed by Congress during World War I. This act made it illegal to interfere with recruiting or drafting soldiers or to do anything adversely affecting military morale.

In *Schenck v. United States* (1919), the Court upheld the conviction of a socialist indicted under the Espionage Act on the grounds that freedom of speech is not absolute. In this case the defendant was convicted of conspiracy to obstruct troop recruiting by issuing a circular urging draftees to assert their right to oppose the draft. As noted by Currie (1988, p. 73):

> The government was protecting itself against the possible commission of a crime—the illegal refusal of draftees to serve. That crime, moreover, was one that in some circumstances could seriously threaten the national security.
>
> In order to reconcile these competing interests to the extent possible, Holmes enunciated the familiar "clear and present danger" test.

Delivering the Court's unanimous opinion, Justice Holmes argued: "[T]he most stringent protection of free speech would not protect a man in falsely shouting fire in a theater and causing a panic. . . . The question in every case is whether the words used are used in such circumstances and are of such a nature as to create a clear and present danger that they will bring about the substantive evils that Congress has a right to prevent."

The Court began to apply the **"clear and present danger" test** to subsequent cases involving freedom of speech. Another test restricting freedom of speech was whether an expression tended to lead to bad results for the public. In *Gitlow v. New York* (1925) the Court held that "a state in the exercise of its police power may punish those who abuse this freedom by utterances inimical to the public welfare, tending to corrupt public morals, and incite to crime, or disturbing the public peace. . . ." Gitlow had been indicted under a New York state law prohibiting the advocacy of the overthrow of the government by force or violence.

≫ In 1940 Congress enacted the Smith Act, which declared it unlawful to advocate overthrowing the government by force or violence.

Eleven leaders of the Communist Party were convicted under the Smith Act and appealed on the ground that it was unconstitutional. The Court upheld the act's constitutionality in *Dennis v. United States* (1951), but not on the grounds of the "clear and present danger" doctrine. Instead, the majority adopted a standard put forward by Judge Learned Hand: "Whether the gravity of the evil discounted by its improbability, justifies such invasion of free speech as is necessary to avoid the danger." This standard has sometimes been called the "clear and probable danger" test.

In *Brandenburg v. Ohio* (1969), the Court replaced the "clear and present danger" test with the "imminent lawless action" test. While government has a justifiable interest in preventing lawless conduct, the mere discussion of such conduct would not necessarily cause imminent lawless action.

The Court in *Brandenburg* set a three-part test that the government must meet if certain communication is not to be protected by the First Amendment:

1. The speaker subjectively intended incitement.
2. In context, the words used were likely to produce imminent, lawless action.
3. The words used by the speaker objectively encouraged and urged incitement.

> 〰 The "clear and present danger" test was replaced by the "imminent lawless action" test in determining when speech should not be protected by the First Amendment.

This approach, modified by other cases, has been termed the **balancing test.** When applying the balancing approach, the Supreme Court strives to strike a balance between the value of liberty of expression and the demands of ordering a free society. Many critics of the balancing approach contend that a balance is rarely struck, and in most cases in which it is involved, society prevails over the individual.

The **preferred freedoms approach,** a position originally set forth by Justice Harlan F. Stone, has been important in constitutional law since World War II. This approach stresses that civil liberties have a preferred position among other constitutional values since they are requisite to a democracy. Under this concept, the burden lies largely with the government to prove clear and present danger exists when a freedom is exercised. This concept tends to change the balance sought in judicial decisions, as shown in Figure 7–2.

Some Supreme Court justices have argued that free speech is an absolute right, by definition, and not subject to balancing. Justice Black, in *Konigsberg v. State Bar of California* (1961), stated:

> I do not subscribe to that doctrine [the balancing approach] for I believe that the First Amendment's unequivocal command that there shall be no abridgement of the rights of free speech and assembly shows that the men who drafted our Bill of Rights did all the "balancing" that was to be done in the field.

Figure 7–2
The preferred freedoms approach.

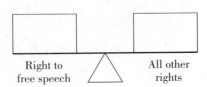

Right to free speech

All other rights

In opposition to this view and in support of the balancing approach, Justice Harlan, in the same case, wrote:

> [W]e reject the view that freedom of speech and association . . . as protected by the First and Fourteenth Amendments, are "absolutes," not only in the undoubted sense that where the constitutional protection exists it must prevail, but also in the sense that the scope of that protection must be gathered solely from a literal reading of the First Amendment (Nowak and Rotunda, 1991, p. 943).

The importance of freedom of speech was highlighted in the Free Speech Movement of student protestors in the 1960s and 1970s. Thirty years ago the University of California, Berkeley, banned political activity on campus. Students wanted to raise money and recruit students to civil rights work, but Berkeley officials said they could not. The students rebelled, claiming that their First Amendment rights were being denied. The riot at Berkeley became a catalyst for years of political unrest on the country's college campuses ("30 Years Ago . . .," 1994, p. A2). Ultimately freedom of speech was established in most colleges and universities.

As noted, some justices, notably Hugo Black and William Douglas, tend to see freedom of speech as nearly an absolute right. The difficulty of the absolute approach to free speech was shown in 1978 when a group of American Nazis sought to hold a rally in Skokie, Illinois. The municipality denied them a permit on the grounds that the Nazi rally would incite hostility in the largely Jewish population, which included many survivors of Nazi concentration camps. Lawyers for the American Civil Liberties Union (ACLU) repre-

The "American Nazi" party. (Provided by UPI/Corbis-Bettmann.)

sented the Nazis, arguing that Skokie laws limiting public demonstrations were unconstitutional. A United States Court of Appeals agreed with the ACLU, but many Americans were outraged at the defense of those they considered the enemies of free speech.

To this day, while many Americans may disagree with the work of the ACLU, it is such input and additional perspective that ensure that all ideas are considered when maintaining the balance of our Constitution as it continues to grow and develop.

In some instances, however, the Supreme Court has ruled that groups can be excluded ("Supreme Court Limits Groups . . .," 1994, p. A7):

> The Supreme Court on Tuesday allowed government-sponsored events such as fairs, festivals and parades to bar "inappropriate" groups from participating.
>
> The Court turned down the appeal of a group opposed to abortion that said its free-speech rights were violated when it was excluded from the 1990 "Great Pumpkin Festival" in Frankfort, Kentucky, aimed at promoting the capital city's downtown revitalization.

Exclusion of groups with political agendas from shopping malls is another controversial area. According to Kaszuba (1995, p. B1):

> In courtrooms around the country, enclosed shopping malls long have been a legal enigma—private property that is essentially a public place. . . .
>
> Since 1968, when the U.S. Supreme Court first said the public had some speech rights in malls, the issue has seesawed between civil libertarians and mall owners.

Kaszuba (p. B5) notes that in the past decade most state courts that have ruled on this issue have ruled in favor of the malls, with only a few states, including California, Oregon, Massachusetts, Washington, Colorado and New Jersey, recognizing free speech rights in malls. He also notes:

> Only last year, the Ohio Supreme Court overwhelmingly rejected arguments that malls have become public squares, saying they remained essentially private property. The case involved a man who distributed leaflets and wore a sandwich board at a mall that read "Eating at McDonald's is hazardous to your health." The court's majority opinion stated "the privilege of free speech cannot be used to the exclusion of other constitutional rights nor as an excuse for unlawful activities with another's business."

The judicial interpretation of the right to free speech has yet to produce a clear definition of what is permissible. In so far as cetaceous, or bristlelike, speech is concerned, the courts have held language permissible if it does not tend to incite the violent overthrow of government. In other free speech areas such as obscenity and pornography, "fighting words," picketing or demonstrating, symbolic speech and loyalty oaths, the courts have also had to consider the various interests of society in their requirements of the Constitution. Table 7–2 summarizes some typical "fighting words" and obscenity violations. Table 7–3 summarizes several types of verbal offenses and what they consist of.

More recently the Court has been involved in interpreting free speech concerns related to symbolic expression.

Table 7–2 "Fighting word" violations.

Words (or other communication) may be offensive, profane and vulgar . . .	but not be "fighting words" (see *Cohen v. California*, in which the words "Fuck the draft" were offensive but not "fighting words").
Words may be insulting and even outrageous . . .	but not be "fighting words" because there was no face-to-face confrontation, as in *Falwell v. Hustler Magazine*.
Words may make a person or an audience angry . . .	and may be protected by the First Amendment and thus not be forbidden by government.
Words may be rude, impolite and insulting . . .	but may fall short of the "fighting word" violation.
If the person to whom the words are addressed is not angered by the words, . . .	there is no "fighting word" violation.
If the person to whom the words are addressed is not likely to make an immediate violent response, . . .	there is no "fighting word" violation.
Obscenity is a different concept than "fighting words." . . .	To be obscene, the state must show as a matter of law that (a) the work taken as a whole appeals to the prurient (lustful) interest in sex; (b) "portrays sexual conduct in a patently offensive way"; (c) the work "taken as a whole does not have a serious literary, artistic, political or scientific value." *Miller v. California*, 413 U.S. 15, 93 S.Ct. 2607 (1973).
"Fighting words" and obscenity cause different reactions in persons. . . .	"Fighting words" cause persons to become very angry while obscenity appeals to the prurient interest (erotic interest), causing persons to become sexually aroused.
Graphic sex scenes on television or scenes that are sexually explicit . . .	are not necessarily obscene.
Because it is absolutely disgusting . . .	it is not necessarily obscene.
Nudity in itself is not obscene or lewd, . . .	but a state or community may regulate (a) when nudity is in a place where liquor is sold (see *California v. LaRue*, 409 U.S. 109, 93 S.Ct. 390 [1972]) and (b) when public nudity is forbidden by a specific ordinance or law.

Source: Thomas J. Gardner and Terry M. Anderson. *Criminal Law: Principles and Cases.* 6th ed. St. Paul: West Publishing Company, 1996, p. 229. Reprinted with permission. All rights reserved.

➤ Symbolic acts are included within the protection of the First Amendment.

Speech That Is Somewhat Protected

Many symbolic acts fall under the protection of the First Amendment. Such acts range from flag desecration and burning to burning of crosses and controversial ideological art, from entering forbidden property to nude dancing and from proscribing hair and dress styles to sanctioning statements coming from counter cultures. More recently it has involved the issue of yard signs.

Table 7–3 Verbal offenses.

Type of verbal offense	To constitute the verbal offense, there must be:
"Fighting words"	1. Insulting or abusive language 2. Addressed to a person on a face-to-face basis 3. Causing a likelihood that "the person addressed will make an immediate violent response"
Obscenity	1. A communication that, taken as a whole, appeals to the prurient (lustful) interest in sex 2. And portrays sexual conduct in a patently offensive way 3. And the communication, taken as a whole, does not have serious literary, artistic, political or scientific value
Urging unlawful conduct (inciting)	1. Language or communication directed to inciting, producing or urging 2. ***Imminent*** lawless action or conduct, or 3. Language or communication likely to incite or produce such unlawful conduct
Obstruction of a law enforcement officer (or of justice)	1. Deliberate and intentional language (or communication) that hinders, obstructs, delays or makes more difficult 2. A law enforcement officer's effort to perform his official duties (the scienter element of knowledge by the defendant that he or she knew the person obstructed was a law enforcement officer is required) 3. Some states require that the "interference would have to be, in part at least, physical in nature" (see the New York case of *People v. Case*)
Defamation (libel and slander)	1. Words or communication that are false and untrue 2. And injure the character and reputation of another person 3. Defamation must be communicated to a third person ***When a public official is the victim, it must also be shown*** that the words or communications were uttered or published with a reckless disregard as to the truth or falsity of the statement. (See also the case of *Falwell v. Hustler Magazine* as Rev. Falwell is a public figure.)
Abusive, obscene or harassing telephone calls	1. Evidence showing that the telephone call was deliberate 2. And made with intent to harass, frighten or abuse another person 3. And any other requirement of the particular statute or ordinance

	Cities and states may:
Loud speech and loud noise	1. Forbid speech and noises meant by the volume to disturb others 2. And forbid noise and loud speech that create a clear and present danger of violence

FLAG BURNING   One case involving symbolic expression decided by the Supreme Court demonstrates the centrality of such issues and the danger of assuming easy answers to First Amendment dilemmas. This case began during the Republican National Convention. In 1984, Gregory Johnson participated in a demonstration dubbed "The Republic War Chest Tour" to protest the policies of the Reagan administration in certain Dallas-based corporations. The demonstrators marched through the streets chanting slogans and staging die-ins outside various corporate locations to dramatize the consequences of nuclear war. The demonstration ended in front of the Dallas City Hall, where Johnson unfurled an American flag, doused it with kerosene and set it on fire. While the flag burned, the protestors chanted: "America, the Red, White and Blue, we spit on you."

Johnson was subsequently convicted for violating a Texas law prohibiting "the desecration of venerated objects," including the national flag. The law defines *desecrate* as "an act which defaces, damages or otherwise physically mistreats in a way that the actor knows will seriously offend one or more persons likely to observe or discover his actions." The opinion was delivered by

Justice Brennan, with the State of Texas conceding for purposes of its oral argument that Johnson's conduct was expressive conduct. Under these circumstances, Johnson's burning of the flag was conduct "sufficiently imbued with elements of communication" to implicate the First Amendment.

"If there is a bedrock principle underlying the First Amendment," Brennan wrote, "it is that the government may not prohibit the expression of an idea simply because society finds the idea itself offensive or disagreeable." Brennan contended that nothing in the courts' precedents suggests that the state may foster its own view of the flag by prohibiting expressive conduct relative to it.

Justice Anthony Kennedy concurred. "The ruling," Kennedy stated, was simply "a pure command of the Constitution. It is poignant and fundamental that the flag perplexes those who hold it in contempt."

Four justices, speaking through Chief Justice William Rehnquist, dissented. Rehnquist wrote a highly emotional opinion stressing that millions of Americans have "a mystical reverence" for the flag and deriding the majority for "bundling off" under the rubric of "designated symbols that uniquely deep awe and respect for our flag felt by virtually all of us." Reaction to the ruling was strong and highly negative. Then-President George Bush cited as supporting documentation a *Newsweek* poll that found that 65% of American's disagreed with it and by a vote of 97 to 3 the United States Senate passed a **resolution**—a formal statement—expressing profound disappointment with the ruling.

Members of Congress called for constitutional action to overrule the Court, proposing an amendment to the First Amendment to exclude flag burning from this protection and to deny flag burning as free speech. In 1989, federal legislation passed a flag protection act. The House voted 317 to 43 to complete congressional action on the bill. President Bush allowed the measure to become law without his signature. But the law did not survive long. On June 11, 1990, the Supreme Court declared the statute unconstitutional as an unwarranted restriction on symbolic expression and, so, on the First Amend-

Pro-flag demonstrators outside the United States Supreme Court. (Provided by UPI/Corbis-Bettmann.)

ment, thus ruling this federal statute unconstitutional. This issue has been hotly debated for decades and may be an issue in future elections.

CROSS BURNING AND BIAS/HATE CRIMES   In 1989 St. Paul, Minnesota, like a number of other cities, passed an ordinance against various forms of expression based on bias or hatred. "We are seeing more racially motivated and religion oriented crimes," explained the city council president. The city wanted to send a message that crimes against people because of their race or religion would not be tolerated.

Several months later in June 1990, a teenager was arrested under the ordinance and charged with burning a cross at the home of the only black family in a St. Paul neighborhood. A county district judge initially held the ordinance unconstitutional as a violation of the First Amendment. The Minnesota Supreme Court, however, overturned this decision and upheld the ordinance maintaining that it could be narrowly interpreted to ban acts of bigotry that arouse anger in others and still protect free speech. The state court said: "Burning a cross in the yard of an African American family's home is deplorable conduct that the City of St. Paul may without question prohibit. The burning of a cross is itself an unmistakable symbol of violence and hatred based on virulent notions of racial supremacy."

The case was subsequently appealed to the United States Supreme Court, which held that the ordinance was unconstitutional (*R.A.V. v. City of St. Paul*, 1992). Justice Scalia delivered the opinion of the Court. He accepted the Minnesota court's narrowing of the ordinance to apply only to so-called fighting

The Ku Klux Klan.
(Provided by
UPI/Corbis-Bettmann.)

words, which Scalia termed constitutionally prescribable, but even so he found the ordinance to be unconstitutional on its face because "it prohibits otherwise permitted speech solely on the basis of the subjects the speech addresses." Cross burning and other reprehensible acts, Scalia argued, could be prosecuted under a variety of existing statutes. These means were sufficient for St. Paul to prevent such behavior "without adding the First Amendment to the fire."

Balancing what the Constitution means and what the public wants it to mean at the time is often difficult to effectively accomplish.

NUDE DANCING   In 1991 the Supreme Court took up the question of nude dancing as a form of symbolic speech. The case involved nude dancers in the Kity Cat Lounge in South Bend, Indiana, arrested for violating the state's public indecency law. A federal appeals court in Chicago had ruled the dancing was inherently expressive, communicating an emotional message of eroticism and sensuality and that the ban, therefore, violated the First Amendment. Five Supreme Court justices voted to reverse, but were unable to isolate a single reason for the reversal. The essence of the 1991 ruling in *Barnes v. Glen Theatre* (1991) was that requiring dancers to wear at least pasties and a g-string did not violate their freedom of speech. It thus gave local prosecutors a new option to restrict totally nude entertainment in their communities.

Civil liberty lawyers who had feared that the Court might apply a sweeping analysis that could call into question constitutional protection for many forms of artistic expression were relieved by the Court's relatively narrow approach. Chief Justice Rehnquist for the majority made clear that nude dancing enjoyed some marginal First Amendment protection. But, due to the state's interest in promoting order and morality, nude dancing *could* be pro-

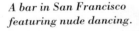

A bar in San Francisco featuring nude dancing.

hibited just as can other forms of public nudity. He observed that the pasties and g-string requirement of the statute was a modest imposition and the bare minimum necessary to achieve the state's purpose.

YARD SIGNS   Another area of expression that some city ordinances seek to limit is use of yard signs. Many cities prohibit such signs altogether. Other cities have restrictions on the size or number of signs that can be placed in a person's yard or window of the home.

Such restrictions were tested in a case involving Margaret Gilleo, a resident of Ladue, an exclusive suburb of St. Louis, Missouri. In late 1990 Gilleo put up an antiwar sign in the second-floor window of her home reading: "Peace in the Gulf." Ladue's city ordinance prohibits all signs within its boundaries except for real estate signs, road and safety hazards, inspection signs, public transportation markers and commercial signs in commercially zones areas. According to officials, the ordinance is intended to protect the aesthetics of their community. Lower courts ruled for Gilleo, saying Ladue was wrong in favoring some signs over others, for example, real estate signs over political protest signs ("High Court Backs Yard Signs . . .," 1994, p. A7).

The Supreme Court to which it was appealed agreed. In June of 1994 the Supreme Court ruled 9 to 0 that cities may not prohibit residents from putting political or personal signs in their yards (*City of Ladue v. Gilleo*, 1994). Justice John Paul Stevens, writing for the court, declared:

> A special respect for individual liberty in the home has long been part of our culture and our law. That principle has special resonance when the government seeks to constrain a person's ability to speak there.

FREEDOM OF SPEECH AND CYBERSPACE   Of recent concern is the issue of free speech and the various computer networks. For example, in December 1995, CompuServe, the world's largest Internet access provider, under pressure from a German prosecutor, blocked access to over 200 computer discussion groups that the German authorities considered pornographic. While some groups applauded the decision, others, such as Lori Fena, executive director of the Electronic Freedom Foundation, warned, "This is really the wake-up call for civil rights and individual freedom in the electronic world" ("Limited Access . . .," 1995, p. A10).

WHAT'S AHEAD?   Lehigh (1995, p. A25) suggests: "Free-speech issues are political hot buttons these days, from the Internet to militia movements to a resurgence of the flag-burning debate. The political response to these real or imagined threats will determine which issue is paramount—the urge to ban that which offends, or the insistence on honoring fundamental principles" contained in our Constitution.

FREEDOM OF THE PRESS

Freedom of the press protects the right to obtain and publish information or opinions without governmental control or fear of punishment.

⁓ Freedom of the press applies to all types of printed and broadcast material, including books, newspapers, magazines, pamphlets, films and radio and television programs.

Historically, freedom of the press has been bound up with the general question of censorship. In countries with extensive censorship, the right to publish news, information and opinions is usually tightly restricted. By comparison, the British government was able to restrict almost anything that arguably related to the government through use of the Official Secret Act. Simply, anything the government wished to remain secret, would. Period. Under such a law, for example, news of the Three Mile Island nuclear accident in the United States would not have been released if it had happened in the United Kingdom.

But even in the United States where censorship is light, the right to publish is not absolute. The constraints on freedom of the press in a free society are controversial and are constantly being redefined by the judiciary.

Governments have restricted the right to publish in two ways. One, by restraining the press from publishing certain materials, and two, by punishing those who publish matter considered seditious, libelous or obscene. The first kind of restriction, often called **prior restraint,** is rare in the United States and most other democratic countries. One of the first attacks on prior restraint can be found in John Milton's essay *Areopagitica* (1644), which was directed against the English licensing and censorship laws enacted in 1534 under Henry VIII. These laws were abolished in England in 1695, but the government was still able to take action on grounds of seditious libel against those who published material, whether true or false, and criticized government policies.

Freedom of the press— many words by many people. Newspaper boxes in Washington, D.C.

In the American colonies, prosecutions of this kind were made more difficult by a jury's decision in the *Zenger* case of 1735. John Peter Zenger, a New York newspaper publisher, was charged with libel because he had published articles criticizing policies of the colonial governor. The jury acquitted Zenger on the grounds that his charges were true and, therefore, could not be considered libelous. Not until 1868 did the truth of the published material become an accepted defense in England.

Freedom of the press was protected in the Constitution by including the First Amendment, which states: "Congress shall make no law . . . abridging freedom of speech or the press." This restraint on the federal government was later made binding on state governments via the Fourteenth Amendment in *Near v. Minnesota* (1931). In that case, the Court ruled that no newspaper could be banned because of its contents regardless of how scandalous they might be. Still, freedom of the press has frequently been denied in the areas of obscenity and pornography. The courts have, however, had some difficulty delineating appropriate standards of censorship.

For example, in *Roth v. United States* (1957) the Court ruled that obscenity is not a constitutionally protected freedom of speech. The standard to be used is "whether to the average person, applying contemporary community standards, the dominant theme of the material, taken as a whole, appeals to prurient interest, that is, having a tendency to excite lustful thoughts."

In 1966, in *Memoirs v. Attorney General of Massachusetts,* the Court set forth more specific criteria for what constitutes obscenity:

❖ The dominant theme of the material taken as a whole appeals to a prurient interest in sex.
❖ The material is patently offensive because it affronts contemporary standards for the description or representation of sexual matters.
❖ The material is utterly without redeeming social value.

Also, in *Miller v. California* (1973) the Court established the following tests and standards to define obscenity (Gardner and Anderson, 1992, p. 277):

❖ Whether "the average person applying contemporary community standards" would find that the work, taken as a whole, appeals to the prurient interest (prurient interest would be appealing to the sexual interests, causing a person to become sexually aroused).
❖ Whether the work or communication depicts or describes, in a patently offensive way, sexual conduct specifically defined by the applicable state law.
❖ Whether the work or communication, taken as a whole, lacks serious literary, artistic, political, or scientific value.

Restrictions on the press have often occurred during national emergencies. Censorship during World War I led to the first clear articulation of the limits to freedom of speech with which free press issues are closely tied. Justice Oliver Wendell Holmes Jr. stated in *Schenck v. United States* (1919) that abridgement of free speech was justified only if the words used constituted a "clear and present danger" to the American public's best interests. This test was used to strike down contempt citations levied on members of the press for being critical of certain judges (*Bridges v. California*, 1941).

During World War II, freedom of the press was greatly curtailed for security reasons, but the press willingly complied with censorship restrictions. Other than in war time, censorship for national security reasons has been carefully limited.

In 1971 the United States government attempted to halt publication of *The Pentagon Papers* on the grounds that it could endanger national security. The Supreme Court ruled (*New York Times v. Sullivan*, 1964) that this case of prior restraint was unconstitutional. Other cases involving national security have concerned attempts to censor or halt publication of books about the Central Intelligence Agency. In 1983, when U.S. troops invaded the Caribbean island of Grenada, the press was initially barred from the island. The restrictions later imposed were thought to be unprecedented in United States practice and generated much controversy.

Control of the press during the Persian Gulf War (1991) was close to 100%. Many criticized the press for accepting conditions that made complete reporting impossible. After the war ended, the accuracy of some press reports disseminated was questioned. Constraints upon the press are always controversial.

In Minnesota, reporters promised anonymity to a political campaign worker who gave them information. Later the editors of the papers revealed his name, and he sued them. The Supreme Court ruled (*Cohen v. Cowles Media Company*, 1991) that the First Amendment does not give the press a constitutional right to disregard promises that otherwise would be enforced under state law. It returned the case to the Minnesota Supreme Court to reconsider. Further complicating the issue, several previous decisions appeared to narrow the newspaper reporters' right to withhold information given to them in confidence. In April 1991 a *Washington Post* reporter was held in contempt in court and jailed for refusing to identify a source.

The Zenger case had established the precedent that truthful statements were not to be considered libelous. The obvious corollary was that damages could be collected for false statements. In *New York Times v. Sullivan* (1964), however, the Supreme Court held that public officials can win damages only if they can show that a statement defaming them was made with actual malice, that is, knowing it was false or recklessly disregarding whether it was false.

Other court rulings have extended the principle to include public figures not in government office but involved in public controversy. In 1979 the Supreme Court held *(Hutchinson v. Proxmire)* that a person who involuntarily receives publicity is not necessarily a public figure and, therefore, need not prove that the statements by the press were made with "actual malice" to obtain liable damages.

The privileges of the press have had to be constantly weighed against other considerations. In 1976, for example, the Supreme Court ruled as unconstitutional so-called gag orders by trial courts forbidding publication of certain information about a defendant.

The Supreme Court has also held (*Zurcher v. Stanford Daily,* 1978) that newspapers enjoy no special immunity from searches of their premises by police with warrants. In 1980, however, Congress passed a privacy protection act that required the police in most cases to obtain subpoenas for such searches. In 1979, in a controversial effort to curb prejudicial pretrial publicity, the court ruled *(Gannett v. DePasquale)* that judges can bar the press and the public from criminal proceedings. In other cases, however, the courts have allowed televised proceedings.

Recently, the Supreme Court held that Americans have a free-speech right to pass out anonymous political pamphlets (*McIntyre v. Ohio Elections Commission,* 1995). In a 7 to 2 decision, the Court said: "'[A]nonymous pamphleteering' has a long and honorable history in this country that extends back to the authors of Federalists Papers and is deeply ingrained as the secret ballot. 'Anonymity is a shield from the tyranny of the majority'" ("Court Allows Anonymous Leaflets," 1995, p. A2).

Balancing Freedom of the Press with the Right to a Fair Trial

A delicate balance exists between the people's right to know, the press' right to publish and the due process rights of those accused of crimes as well as the needs of the agencies charged with investigating such crimes. As noted by Gardner and Anderson (1992, p. 294):

> A free and unfettered press that seeks out and publishes the news is necessary to the functioning of a democracy. The people must be fully and adequately informed in order that they may intelligently discharge their responsibilities as citizens. On the other hand, we as a nation have long cherished the fundamental principles that a defendant in a criminal case shall be afforded all the safeguards of due process of law and shall be given a fair and impartial trial. These two principles come into conflict when newspapers and other communication media publish detailed information before a defendant has been tried.

The question is whether events reported in the press prior to the trial may unduly influence jurors. In *Sheppard v. Maxwell* (1966) the defendant, Dr. Samuel Sheppard, was accused of brutally murdering his pregnant wife in their home. The pretrial publicity was intensely prejudicial and Sheppard was convicted of the crime. On appeal, the conviction was overturned, with the Court quoting the Ohio Supreme Court:

> Murder and mystery, society, sex and suspense were combined in this case to such a manner as to intrigue and captivate the public fancy to a degree perhaps unparalleled in recent annals. Throughout the preindictment investigation, the subsequent legal skirmishes and the nine-week trial, circulation-conscious editors catered to the insatiable interest of the American public in the bizarre. . . . In this atmosphere of a "Roman holiday" for the news media, Sam Sheppard stood trial for his life.

Other high-profile cases include the very political, highly publicized trial of Oliver North, the highly publicized ten-day rape trial of William Kennedy

Table 7–4   Types of public and "quasi-public" property.

Property	Extent of use by the public and social protesters	Restrictions that may be placed on use
Publicly owned streets, sidewalks and parks	Are used extensively by the public and ordinarily will accommodate the exercise of most First Amendment rights.	Reasonable regulations may be imposed to assure public safety and order (for example, traffic regulations).
Government buildings, such as courthouses and city halls	Are used for the business of government during business hours. Open to the public at these times so that the public may ordinarily come and go as they wish.	Greater restrictions may be imposed to assure the functioning of government or the regular use of the facilities by the public. Can accommodate only limited expressions of social protest.
Public hospitals, schools, libraries, etc.	Use of these public facilities is ordinarily limited to the specific function for which they are designed.	As these facilities need more order and tranquility than do other public buildings, there are generally more restrictions concerning use by the public.
Quasi-public facilities, such as shopping centers, stores and other privately owned buildings or property to which the public has access	Many quasi-public facilities are as extensively used by the public as are public streets, sidewalks and parks.	Private owners of quasi-public facilities have greater authority to regulate their property than does the government of public streets and parks.
Public property whose access by the public is limited and restricted	Government may limit and restrict in a reasonable manner the access by the public to jails, executive offices (mayor, police chief, etc.) and other facilities that must be restricted to permit government to function effectively.	Such restrictions must be made in a reasonable and nondiscriminating manner.

Source: Thomas J. Gardner and Terry M. Anderson. *Criminal Law: Principles and Cases.* 6th ed. St. Paul: West Publishing Company, 1996, p. 242. Reprinted with permission. All rights reserved.

Smith, the trial of Mike Tyson for raping a Miss Black America contestant and, of course, the trial of O. J. Simpson.

It is the duty of the court to protect those who come before it from undue adverse publicity. To fail to do so may result in a higher court declaring that the trial was unfair and overturning the conviction.

THE RIGHT TO PEACEFUL ASSEMBLY

The right to peaceful assembly often involves the right to assemble in public places. This is a long-cherished right of Americans and one frequently exercised. Demonstrators and protestors are entitled to assemble and to speak and be heard—as long as they remain nonviolent. It is not what they say so much as what they do that will determine if they are protected under the First Amendment. Table 7–4 summarizes several types of property and the types of restrictions that lawfully may be placed on their use.

Summary

The First Amendment prohibits Congress from making any laws that abridge or restrict freedom of religion, freedom of speech, freedom of the press or the right to assemble peaceably and to petition the government for redress of grievances.

Religious freedom includes the freedom to worship, to print instructional material, to train teachers and to organize societies for their employment. The establishment clause of the First Amendment states clearly that "Congress shall make no law respecting an establishment of religion." The free exercise clause of the First Amendment declares that "Congress shall make no law . . . prohibiting the free exercise [of religion]."

Freedom of speech/expression includes the right to speak and the right to be heard. The "clear and present danger" test was replaced by the "imminent lawless action" test in determining when speech should not be protected by the First Amendment. In 1940 Congress enacted the *Smith Act,* which declared it unlawful to advocate overthrowing the government by force or violence. Symbolic acts are included within the protection of the First Amendment.

Freedom of the press applies to all types of printed and broadcast material, including books, newspapers, magazines, pamphlets, films and radio and television programs.

Discussion Questions

1. Discuss whether you personally believe that the First Amendment is the most important amendment.

2. On a scale of one to ten, with one being "not important" and ten being "very important," how important do you think free speech is? Why?

3. Speaking from a historical perspective, why do you think the framers of the Constitution placed so much importance on the First Amendment?

4. Why should the government tolerate people speaking against or criticizing it?

5. Do you believe an amendment banning burning of the American flag should be passed? Why or why not?

6. Imagine that you are an attorney who has been asked to defend nude dancing as an act of expression that should be allowed in a small town bar. What would you say to represent your client's interests? Include an explanation of how nude dancing could ever be considered "speech."

7. Discuss whether you think Nazi Germany could have gone as far as it did if there was a similar First Amendment present in Germany.

8. Should all schools, public and parochial, receive equal support from the government?

9. Has government gone too far in prohibiting school prayer, prohibiting nativity scenes at public schools and the like? How do you feel about not permitting Christmas trees in public schools or prohibiting Christmas displays in government buildings or parks? If you were the principal of a public elementary school, on what basis would you decide whether to allow Christmas terminologies, displays and programs?

10. Discuss whether you think the United States government is hypocritical when, on the one hand, freedom of religion is guaranteed, but, on the other hand, Christianity is so obviously stated in the words of the Pledge of Allegiance, the fact that there is a clergyman assigned to the Congress and the like.

References

"Court Allows Anonymous Leaflets." (Minneapolis/St. Paul) *Star Tribune*. April 20, 1995, p. A2.

Currie, David P. *The Constitution of the United States: A Primer for the People.* Chicago: University of Chicago Press, 1988.

Gardner, Thomas J. and Terry M. Anderson. *Criminal Law: Principles and Cases.* 5th ed. St. Paul: West Publishing Company, 1992.

"High Court Backs Yard Signs in Free Speech Case." (Minneapolis/St. Paul) *Star Tribune*. June 14, 1994, p. A7.

"High Court Protects Florida Sect's Use of Animal Sacrifice." (Minneapolis/St. Paul) *Star Tribune*. June 12, 1993, p. A12.

Kaszuba, Mike. "Can Malls Tell Protesters to Bag it? Courts Reconsider Speech Rights in those Public-but-Private Places." (Minneapolis/St. Paul) *Star Tribune*. January 29, 1995, pp. B1, B5.

Killian, Johnny H., ed. *The Constitution of the United States of America: Analysis and Interpretation.* Washington: U.S. Government Printing Office, 1987.

Lehigh, Scot. "Speaking Terms: Censorious Zeal Sweeps Old and New Political Fronts." (Minneapolis/St. Paul) *Star Tribune*. June 30, 1995, p. A25.

"Limited Access Sparks Free-Speech Row." (Minneapolis/St. Paul) *Star Tribune*. December 30, 1995, p. A10.

Nowak, John E. and Ronald D. Rotunda. *Constitutional Law.* 4th ed. St. Paul: West Publishing Company, 1991.

"Scouts Allowed to Require Vow on God." (Minneapolis/St. Paul) *Star Tribune*. December 7, 1993, p. A2.

Shafer, Kent H. "A Large Dose of Common Sense." *Law and Order*. January 1995, p. 329.

"Supreme Court Limits Groups at Public Events: 'Inappropriate' Organizations Can Be Barred." (Minneapolis/St. Paul) *Star Tribune*. June 1, 1994, p. A7.

"30 Years Ago, They Sat Down to Speak Up." (Minneapolis/St. Paul) *Star Tribune*. November 26, 1994, pp. A2, A10.

Cases Cited

Barnes v. Glen Theatre, 501 U.S. 560, 111 S.Ct. 2456, 115 L.Ed.2d 504 (1991).

Brandenburg v. Ohio, 395 U.S. 444 (1969).

Braunfeld v. Brown, 366 U.S. 599, 81 S.Ct. 1144 (1961).

Bridges v. California, 314 U.S. 252, 62 S.Ct. 190, 86 L.Ed. 192 (1941).

California v. LaRue, 409 U.S. 109, 93 S.Ct. 390 (1972).

Cantwell v. Connecticut, 310 U.S. 296, 60 S.Ct. 900, 84 L.Ed. 1213 (1940).

Church of Lukumi Babalu Aye v. Hialeah (1993).

City of Ladue v. Gilleo, 512 U.S. 43, 114 S.Ct. 2038, 129 L.Ed.2d 36 (1994).

Cohen v. California.

Cohen v. Cowles Media, 111 S.Ct. 2513, 115 L.Ed.2d 586 (1991).

Council of Greenburgh Civic Assn. v. United States Postal Service, 453 U.S. 917, 101 S.Ct. 3150 (1981).

Cruz v. Beto, 405 U.S. 319, 92 S.Ct. 1079, 31 L.Ed.2d 263 (1972).

Davis v. Beason, 133 U.S. 333, 10 S.Ct. 299, 33 L.Ed. 637 (1890).

DeJonge v. Oregon, 299 U.S. 353, 57 S.Ct. 255, 81 L.Ed. 278 (1937).

Dennis v. United States, 341 U.S. 494, 71 S.Ct. 857, 95 L.Ed. 1137 (1951).

Employment Division v. Smith, 494 U.S. 872, 110 S.Ct. 1595, 108 L.Ed.2d 876 (1990).

Engle v. Vitale, 370 U.S. 421, 82 S.Ct. 1261, 8 L.Ed. 2d 601 (1962).

Everson v. Board of Education, 330 U.S. 15, 67 S.Ct. 504, 91 L.Ed. 711 (1947).

Falwell v. Hustler Magazine.

Gannett v. DePasquale, 443 U.S. 368, 99 S.Ct. 2898, 61 L.Ed.2d 608 (1979).

Gillette v. United States, 401 U.S. 437, 91 S.Ct. 828 (1971).

Gitlow v. New York, 268 U.S. 652, 45 S.Ct. 625, 69 L.Ed. 1138 (1925).

Goldman v. Weinberger, 475 U.S. 503, 106 S.Ct. 1310 (1986).

Heffron v. International Society for Krishna Consciousness, 452 U.S. 640, 101 S.Ct. 2559 (1981).

Hutchinson v. Proxmire, 443 U.S. 111, 99 S.Ct. 2675, 61 L.Ed.2d 411 (1979).

In the Matter of the Welfare of R.A.V., 464 N.W.2d 507 (Minn.1991).

Konigsberg v. State Bar of California (1961).

Lemon v. Kurtzman, 403 U.S. 602, 91 S.Ct. 2105, 29 L.Ed.2d 745 (1971).

Lynch v. Donnelly, 465 U.S. 668, 104 S.Ct. 1355, 79 L.Ed.2d 604 (1984).

McIntyre v. Ohio Elections Commission, ___ U.S. ___, 115 S.Ct. 1511, 131 L.Ed.2d 426 (1995).

Memoirs v. Attorney General of Massachusetts, 383 U.S. 413, 86 S.Ct. 975, 16 L.Ed.2d 1 (1966).

Miller v. California, 413 U.S. 15, 93 S.Ct. 2607, 37 L.Ed.2d 419 (1973).

Minnesota v. Hershberger, ___ U.S. ___, 110 S. Ct. 1918, vacating 444 N.W.2d 282 (1990).

Near v. Minnesota, 283 U.S. 697, 51 S.Ct. 625, 75 L.Ed. 1357 (1931).

New York Times v. Sullivan, 376 U.S. 254, 84 S.Ct. 710, 11 L.Ed.2d 686 (1964).

People v. Case.

Prince v. Massachusetts, 321 U.S. 158, 64 S.Ct. 1144 (1994).

R.A.V. v. City of St. Paul, 505 U.S. 377, 112 S.Ct. 2538, 120 L.Ed.2d 305 (1992).

Reynolds v. United States, 98 U.S. 8 Otto 145, 25 L.Ed. 244 (1879).

Roth v. United States, 354 U.S. 476, 77 S.Ct. 1304, 1 L.Ed.2d 1498 (1957).

Schenck v. United States, 249 U.S. 47, 39 S.Ct. 247, 63 L.Ed. 470 (1919).

Sheppard v. Maxwell, 384 U.S. 333, 86 S.Ct. 1507, 16 L.Ed.2d 600 (1966).

South Dakota v. Cosgrove, 439 N.W.2d 119, review denied, ___ U.S. ___, 110 S.Ct. 140, 46 CrL 3008 (1989).

State v. Massey, 229 N.C. 734, 51 S.E.2d 179 (1949).

Stone v. Graham, 449 U.S. 39, 101 S.Ct. 192, 66 L.Ed.2d 199 (1980).

United States v. Merkt, review denied, 794 F.2d 950, 41 CrL 4001 (5th Cir. 1987).

Wallace v. Jeffries, 472 U.S. 38, 105 S.Ct. 2479, 86 L.Ed.2d 29 (1985).

West Virginia State Board of Education v. Barnette, 319 U.S. 624, 63 S.Ct. 1178, 87 L.Ed. 1628 (1943).

Wooley v. Maynard, 430 U.S. 705, 97 S.Ct. 1428, 51 L.Ed.2d 752 (1977).

Zenger (1735).

Zurcher v. Stanford Daily, 436 U.S. 547, 98 S.Ct. 1970, 56 L.Ed.2d 525 (1978).

Chapter 8 — The Second Amendment: The Gun Control Controversy

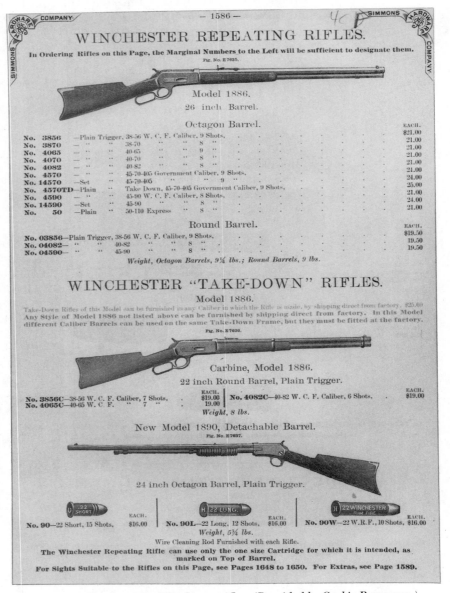

A well-regulated militia, being necessary to the security of a free state, the right of the people to keep and bear arms shall not be infringed.

—SECOND AMENDMENT OF THE UNITED STATES CONSTITUTION

Mail-order catalog featuring Winchester rifles. (Provided by Corbis-Bettmann.)

DO YOU KNOW . . .

Historically, who was included in the militia and what was required of them?

What the central controversy over the Second Amendment involves?

Whether the federal courts uphold the view that the Constitution guarantees the right of the individual to keep and bear arms?

What two opposing interpretations of the Second Amendment have clashed over the years?

What the primary claim of individuals' rights proponents is? That of states' rights proponents?

Why *United States v. Miller* is important in the gun control controversy? *Stevens v. United States?*

How Congress can constitutionally enact federal gun control legislation?

What was accomplished by the Brady Bill?

Who has near absolute authority to regulate firearms?

CAN YOU DEFINE THESE TERMS?

Demurrer
In dictum
Militia
Prohibited persons

INTRODUCTION

The Second Amendment protects the "right of the people to keep and bear arms." But the amendment also begins with a phrase explaining its purpose. This phrase states that a "well-regulated militia" is "necessary to the security of a free state."

At a time when personal freedoms and concerns for self-protection are on the minds of Americans, the Second Amendment is being subjected to careful scrutiny. What exactly does this brief but important amendment mean? Does this phrase mean that the people are allowed to bear arms only if they are part of a militia or defending this country? Can guns be used for national defense but not for self-defense?

These questions are part of the ongoing debate over gun control and the Second Amendment. One critical question is the definition of a **militia,** a group of citizens who defend their community as emergencies arise.

In many ways, this chapter, although brief, is extremely challenging. First, relatively few cases have been litigated at the Supreme Court level. And when you consider that the Second Amendment is one of the hottest current topics of legal discussion, it becomes difficult to address it without emotion and without taking a side.

When passionate convictions are combined with reading any material that addresses that conviction, some won't agree with how it was presented. This is a challenge for those responsible for presenting it objectively. The option of not addressing the Second Amendment, excluding it for fear of not presenting it in a way that makes everyone comfortable, would be the easy way out.

This text addresses the Second Amendment because the text is intended as a tool to help you consider the Constitution, including the questions it raises. Controversy is what ignited the movement that resulted in the formation of the Constitution, and controversy is what will continue to fuel the presumably continuing demand by the American people for legal interpretations of the document.

This text seeks more to help you learn to ask questions than to have answers presupposed. If there were absolutes, there would be no need for anything but an introductory course on the topic. But the beauty of the American law is that it is open to interpretation and question by those it was drafted to serve—the people of this country.

This chapter begins with a brief historical background on the Second Amendment and then a discussion of the current controversy regarding gun control and individual versus state rights. This is followed by an examination of case law and of federal regulations as they relate to the Second Amendment. The chapter concludes with an explanation of gun control as a political rather than a legal issue.

HISTORICAL BACKGROUND

A brief history will help put the current gun control controversy into perspective. The Second Amendment, like the rest of the Constitution, was drafted in a time when fear of tyranny from a strong central government was very strong. During the colonial period and the earliest years of the country, a permanent army was not possible. At that time it would have been nearly impossible to fund such an army and the necessary personnel. Therefore, the concept of the militia was conceived. The militia consisted mainly of civilians and professional soldiers when necessary.

> The militia was considered to be the entire male populace. They were not simply allowed to keep arms, but were generally required to do so by law.

If members of the militia were called to service, they were to bring their own arms and ammunition. The arms of the private populace made up the arms of the militia. Most states mandated that all persons between certain ages be members of the militia. States directed that these persons were to be armed and taught the knowledge of military duty.

According to Black (1995, p. 4): "The generation that wrote and ratified the Constitution and the Bill of Rights lived in a world in which armed citizen militias were the norm, while standing armies or even an armed, full-time police force were the exception." In addition, notes Black (p. 6): "In Federalist Paper Number 46, Madison reminded his readers that they had 'the advantage of being armed, which the Americans possess over the people of almost every other nation.'"

Indeed the United States "gun culture" arose out of the *practical* need for the pioneers to protect themselves against thieves, bandits and Native Americans whose land they were crossing, as well as the *philosophical* belief that they needed to protect themselves from political tyranny.

THE CURRENT CONTROVERSY

In 1794 the militia was composed of all free male citizens, armed with muskets, bayonets and rifles. Now the militia is generally considered to consist of National Guard units in every state armed with sophisticated modern weaponry. Is a militia in 1997 the same as in 1794? How does that affect the meaning of the Second Amendment?

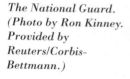 The central controversy over the Second Amendment is whether people have a right to bear arms as individuals rather than only as part of a militia.

"There can be no question that an organized society which fails to regulate the importation, manufacture and transfer of the highly sophisticated

The National Guard. (Photo by Ron Kinney. Provided by Reuters/Corbis-Bettmann.)

lethal weapons in existence today does so at its peril" (*United States v. Warin,* 1976).

As this text goes to press, significant activity is occurring regarding organized groups that some refer to as militias. For example, the standoff between the FBI and the Freemen in Montana involved such a group. This situation was finally peacefully resolved. However, the subject will no doubt continue to address the tension between the Constitution and the individual. Some people feel very much like those more than 200 years ago—that the government has become too powerful and that individuals need to reclaim that power.

The number of gun-related deaths is rising at a rate that causes concern in our society. Table 8–1 summarizes the incidence of crimes involving handguns from 1987 to 1992. According to Brady (1995, p. 54):

> Just to give you one idea of how severe the problem is with guns, the Centers for Disease Control have now begun to treat it as an epidemic in this nation. Violence and homicide rates actually have gone down in the nation in recent years. But homicides with guns have skyrocketed. The difference is it's not hard-core criminals. It's our kids. It's young people. Today, according to the Centers for Disease Control, there are now six states in which more people are injured and die because of guns than because of automobiles. . . .

According to Zawitz (1995, p. 1), in 1993 about 582,000 reported murders, robberies and aggravated assaults were committed with firearms. In addition, 70% of the 24,526 murders in 1993 were committed with firearms. Says Zawitz: "Although most crime is not committed with guns, most gun crime is committed with handguns."

Zawitz (1996, p. 1) reports on the findings of the 1994 BJS National Crime Victimization Survey, which found that 29% of victims of nonfatal violent crime, excluding simple assault, faced an offender armed with a gun.

Vassar and Kizer (1996, p. 1734) put the figure even higher: "Firearm-related violence has become epidemic in the United States, with 39,720 firearm-related fatalities in 1994 alone." Interestingly, these figures were not from a criminal justice publication, but from the *Journal of the American Medical Association (JAMA).*

Table 8–1   Handguns and crime, 1987–1992.

	1992	Annual average, 1987–91
Handgun crimes	930,700	667,000
Homicide	13,200	10,600
Rape	11,800	14,000
Robbery	339,000	225,100
Assault	566,800	417,300

Note: Detail may not add to total because of rounding. Data for homicide come from the FBI's Uniform Crime Reports.
Source: Michael R. Rand. "Guns and Crimes." *Security Concepts.* July 1994, p. 9. Reprinted by permission.

This illustrates the broadening of the gun control debate, which is also described by Blendon, et al. (1996, p. 22):

> Traditionally, gun control debates have involved professionals from the field of law, the police, and others concerned with the criminal justice system. However, in the past decade a number of physicians and public health professionals have entered the debate over gun control. For example, in a 1994 *JAMA* commentary, firearm violence was called "a public health emergency" and recommendations were made for stiffer gun control measures.

Gun control opponents claim that gun control will only put guns where they don't belong—in the hands of criminals. Advocates of gun control claim something must be done and that every gun not sold is one that won't take a life.

Current Legal Status

Despite all the controversy over gun control, there is no question where the courts stand. Gun control by the states is not constitutionally prohibited. Nor under most circumstances is legislation by the federal government.

> ≋ Federal courts to date have held that the Constitution does *not* guarantee the absolute right of the individual to keep and bear arms.

The Supreme Court has ruled on the amendment relatively few times when compared to contests over other amendments. *United States v. Miller* (1939) is the only Supreme Court case that specifically addresses that amendment's scope, as will be discussed shortly. Most of the adjudication has been done at the federal district level and has seldom gone beyond the court of appeals. The Supreme Court has repeatedly denied certiorari (refused to review) in cases in which the individual right to bear arms is at issue.

According to Nowak and Rotunda (1991, p. 333): "The Court in *Presser v. Illinois* [1886] refused to incorporate the Second Amendment into the Fourteenth Amendment; the result of this case is that the Second Amendment at this time does not apply to state governments."

The history of the courts suggests that they will defer to the discretion of Congress on almost all matters concerning gun control. Thus far it appears the only action that the courts may find constitutionally offensive is a complete nationwide ban on firearms.

INDIVIDUAL RIGHTS VERSUS STATES' RIGHTS

Two opposing interpretations of the Second Amendment have clashed over past decades.

> ≋ The two opposing interpretations of the Second Amendment involve whether the amendment guarantees the

right of *individuals* to keep and bear arms or whether it
guarantees the *states* freedom from federal government
infringement on this right.

Individual Rights

Proponents of "the right to bear arms," including the National Rifle Association (NRA), endorse an individual rights interpretation that would guarantee that right to all citizens.

Individual rights proponents see the amendment as primarily guaranteeing the right of the people, not the states. While they concede that a state right is embodied within the amendment, that right is a product of the more central individual right. By guaranteeing the arms of the individuals who make up the militia, the Constitution guaranteed the arms of the militia. The collective right that preserves the states' militia is guaranteed only if the individual right is first maintained.

> Individual rights proponents claim that the framers intended to preserve the individual right, above the right of the state.

The amendment is placed in close proximity to other individual rights while the states are not expressly mentioned until the Tenth Amendment. Madison's notes state the amendments were to relate first to private rights. Further, arms were such a pervasive part of colonial life that five state conventions recommended an amendment guaranteeing the right to bear arms.

Leroy Pyle (1991, p. 19), former police officer, member of the board of directors of the NRA and executive director of Law Enforcement Alliance of

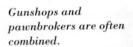

Gunshops and pawnbrokers are often combined.

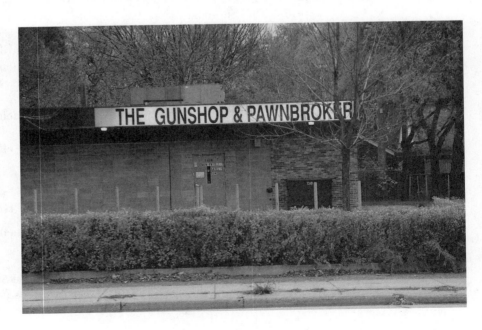

America contends: "All this recent legislation that is being rammed down our throats is completely wrong for two major reasons: One, they are confiscation laws and prohibition laws, and they have nothing to do with crime; and two, they are being promoted by the political police, not by the working police." He further claims: "In the current situation, these gun control laws are like locks, they keep honest people honest."

Another advocate of individual rights is Chief Kevin D. Cavanaugh, Pratt, Kansas (1991, p. 18), who suggests that gun control will not affect crime:

> I am a firm supporter of the Second Amendment, that the citizenry of a free country has the right to bear arms to combat oppressive government. Additional restrictions on law-abiding people purchasing firearms is nowhere near crime control.
>
> The first line of defense to crime is not the police department, it's ordinary people, the potential victims of violent crime. It is in law enforcement's best interests to teach and encourage the citizens to determine their own fate.

Support for this view may be found in the Los Angeles riots that followed the not-guilty jury verdict in the Rodney King case. Citizens cheered the shopkeepers in Koreatown as they defended their property with weapons. As noted by Farah (1992, p. A15):

> Suddenly, restrictive gun-control laws, 15-day waiting periods and even bans on those nasty "assault rifles" didn't seem like such a great idea anymore. Could it be that the Founding Fathers knew what they were doing, after all, when they drafted the Second Amendment: . . .
>
> The single most sobering lesson of the Los Angeles uprising for most people was that the police cannot be counted on for protection in citywide emergencies.
>
> Would the kind of widespread looting and violence Los Angeles witnessed in the aftermath of the verdict have been likely, or even possible, if more law-abiding citizens were armed? . . . That's called deterrence. . . .
>
> A well-armed population might be just what is needed to take back the streets from the hoodlums who plague cities like Los Angeles 365 days a year.

Likewise, militant groups argue that an armed citizenry is the best defense against tyranny and that their thinking is in line with those who wrote the Second Amendment.

This view has not been supported by the courts. The courts throughout history have consistently rejected the individual rights view in favor of the states' rights interpretation.

States' Rights

Those favoring a states' right interpretation see the Second Amendment as protecting and modifying Article 1, Section 8 of the Constitution, which grants Congress the power "to provide for the calling forth of the Militia to execute the laws of the Union. . . ." The purpose of the amendment is obviously to "assure the continuation and render possible the effectiveness of such forces" (*United States v. Miller*, 1939). Further, as Tribe and Dorf (1991, p. 11) suggest:

Unique among the provisions of the Constitution, the Second Amendment comes with its own mini-preamble, setting forth its purpose: to foster a "well regulated Militia." This purpose has little to do with individuals possessing weapons to be used against their neighbors; as a result, the Second Amendment has not been interpreted by the courts to prohibit regulation of private gun ownership.

> ≈ States' rights proponents claim that the Second Amendment was adopted with the primary purpose of preserving the state militia.

This interpretation is linked to the traditional Whig fear of standing armies. Not only does the amendment preserve the states' power to defend against foreign and domestic enemies, it also reduces the need for a large standing army. A large standing federal army was seen as inherently contrary to the preservation of a free, democratic people.

One advocate of gun control is Dewey Stokes (1991, p. 20), national president of the Fraternal Order of Police, who states: "We prefer to refer to the issue as 'crime control' and not just 'gun control.'" Stokes also states of their 220,000 members, the majority being rank and file police officers, that they have "expressed overwhelming support for a seven-day waiting period and a ban on 'specifically named' assault weapons." Stokes' concluding statement is that: "Last year we lost 46 officers to gun fire, and we have to stand up as an organization and say something."

Another advocate of gun control is Chief Charles Gruber (1991, p. 20), past president of the International Association of Chiefs of Police: "We need to figure out a way to allow law abiding citizens to purchase and own guns, and a way to keep non-law abiding citizens from owning guns."

Public Attitudes toward Gun Control

The controversy is likely to continue, but support seems to be shifting toward more control of handguns and assault weapons. A Harris Survey released in June of 1993 reported that more than half of all Americans favor gun control of some form, with 90% supporting a waiting period for purchasing handguns ("Polls Find Broad Public Support . . .," 1993, p. 1).

CASE LAW AND THE SECOND AMENDMENT

Before 1934 the federal government made little effort to regulate the possession of firearms, giving the court little reason to interpret the amendment. The National Firearms Act of 1934 was the first such effort at federal regulation. Section 11 of the act made it illegal for a person "who has not in his possession a stamp-affixed order (from the person requesting the firearm) to ship, carry, or deliver any firearm in interstate commerce."

One of the first important rulings on the Second Amendment involved this act. Jack Miller was convicted of violating the National Firearms Act of 1934. Miller was convicted of feloniously transporting a double-barreled 12-gauge shotgun (having a barrel less than 18 inches) from Oklahoma to Arkansas (*United States v. Miller*, 1939). The district court granted the defense a **demurrer,** a request that a suit be dismissed because while the facts are true, they do not sustain the claim against the defendant. The United States appealed the demurrer and certiorari was granted. The Supreme Court interpreted the Second Amendment as providing for maintaining a militia:

> With the obvious purpose to assure the continuation and render possible the effectiveness of such forces[as outlined in Article 1, Section 8 of the Constitution] the declaration and guarantee of the Second Amendment were made. It must be interpreted and applied with that view in mind.

This case indicates that only arms that bear some relation to the preservation of the militia would be protected under the amendment. The Court held that: "[I]n the absence of any evidence tending to show that possession or use of a 'shotgun having a barrel of less than 18 inches in length, at this time has some reasonable relationship to the preservation or efficiency of a well-regulated militia, we cannot say that the Second Amendment guarantees the right to keep and bear such an instrument" (Killian, 1987, p. 1148). Therefore, a law prohibiting transportation of unregistered shotguns in interstate commerce is not unconstitutional.

> *Miller* is important in that the court recognized a state right rather than an individual one.

It was not intended to be a broadly sweeping decision that designated which arms are protected and which are not. The courts clarified the decision in *Miller* three years later.

In 1942 a circuit court of appeals ruled: "The rule which it [*Miller*] laid down was adequate to dispose of the case before it and that we think was as far as the Supreme Court intended to go" *(Cases v. United States)*. The court also clearly stated its position on individual rights and the Second Amendment:

> The right to keep and bear arms is not a right conferred upon the people by the federal constitution. Whatever rights in this respect the people may have depend upon local legislation; the only function of the Second Amendment being to prevent the federal government and the federal government only from infringing on that right.

> In 1971 the courts ruled that there was no express right of an individual to keep and bear arms *(Stevens v. United States).*

A federal circuit court ruled that the Second Amendment applies "only to the right of the state to maintain a militia and not to the individual's right to bear arms, there can be no serious claim to any express constitutional right of an individual to possess a firearm" (*Stevens v. United States,* 1971).

FEDERAL REGULATION AND THE SECOND AMENDMENT

Although the Second Amendment has repeatedly been interpreted to protect the states' rights from federal intervention, the federal government has managed to pass several gun control laws.

    〜 Congress, using its broad authority to regulate interstate commerce, has enacted federal gun control legislation.

In 1967 Congress passed the Omnibus Crime Control and Safe Streets Act. A portion of that act made it unlawful for convicted felons to possess a firearm. The constitutionality of this act was called into question in the case just described. Stevens, a felon, was convicted under the act and appealed on the grounds that his right to bear arms had been infringed and that Congress did not have the constitutional authority to regulate possession of firearms.

The Court again ruled that the Second Amendment guaranteed no individual right. On the question of constitutional authority, the Sixth Circuit Court of Appeals held that the power to regulate interstate commerce gave Congress the power to regulate firearms (*Stevens v. United States*, 1971): "There can be no serious doubt that the possession of firearms by convicted felons is a threat to interstate commerce." It was also ruled that Congress need not wait for "the total dislocation of commerce before it may provide reasonable preventative measures." The Supreme Court denied certiorari on this case.

In 1968 the Gun Control Act was passed, prohibiting federal licensees from selling firearms to anyone they knew or had reasonable cause to believe was or had been:

❖ Under indictment for—or convicted of—a felony.
❖ A fugitive.
❖ A drug user.
❖ Adjudicated a mental defective or committed to a mental institution.
❖ Or who fit into other limited categories.

Such individuals are referred to as **prohibited persons.**

In *United States v. Warin* (1976) the Sixth Circuit Court of Appeals further defined the relationship between militia and the right to keep and bear arms. The court heard claims of unconstitutionality of federal taxation on guns and a Ninth Amendment violation. Both claims were rejected.

In this case, Warin was convicted of possessing an unregistered submachinegun. He appealed on several counts. First, he argued since he was subject to enrollment in (although not actually a member of) the state militia, the amendment granted him the right to bear arms. Second, he argued that the National Firearms Act taxed the right to keep and bear arms. Finally, he argued as a member of the sedentary militia the right to bear and keep arms was a fundamental right under the Ninth Amendment.

The court held that being subject to enrollment in the state militia does not grant a special right to keep and bear arms. On the matter of taxation it held: "Even where the Second Amendment is applicable it does not constitute an absolute barrier to congressional regulation of firearms." It also held that the Ninth Amendment confers no additional fundamental right to an "unregistered submachine gun."

In 1986 Congress banned the purchase and sale of all fully automatic weapons. All privately owned automatic weapons bought before 1986 were to be registered, but would remain in the hands of their owners. The NRA criticized the law as "the first ban on firearms possession by law abiding citizens in American history" (*Washington Post*, January 15, 1991).

This ban was tested by a gun collector, Farmer, who applied for a permit to legally make and register a machine gun for his private collection. The Bureau of Alcohol, Tobacco and Firearms (ATF) denied his application. When the district court ruled in favor of Farmer, the court of appeals stayed the order.

The court of appeals ruled that the ATF was not abusing its discretion by denying the permit. In its decision the court did not consider the constitutional issue of the right to keep and bear arms but dealt with the case only on its statutory merits.

The Brady Bill

Congress passed and on November 30, 1993, President Clinton signed the Brady Handgun Violence Prevention Act. The Brady Bill is named in honor of Jim Brady, press secretary to Ronald Reagan, who was shot during

Assassination attempt on President Reagan in which Press Secretary James Brady was wounded. (Photo by Don Rypka. Provided by UPI/Corbis-Bettmann.)

an attempt on the president's life. According to John Magaw (1994, p. 14), director of the Bureau of Alcohol, Tobacco and Firearms: "This is the most important piece of firearms legislation since 1978."

> The Brady Bill requires a waiting period of five business days or a background check in order to buy or obtain a license to carry a handgun.

More specifically, the bill requires that dealers can sell a handgun only under the following conditions (Magaw, 1994, p. 14):

❖ The dealer complies with the new five-day waiting period requirements, or
❖ The buyer presents a state permit issued after a background check, or
❖ State law already requires that every sale is subject to a background check, or
❖ The transaction fits within one of the other very limited circumstances relating to threats to individuals, or specific approvals by the Treasury secretary.

The purpose of the bill is to stop prohibited persons from obtaining handguns. According to Kime (1994, p. 10):

> While the law initially requires a five-day waiting period, this waiting period is eventually to be replaced by a nationwide "instant check" system for criminal records. In those states that already require a background check in order to purchase a handgun or obtain a permit to carry a handgun, purchasers will be unaffected by this provision of the law.

The Brady Bill does not prohibit states from enacting their own, longer waiting periods. The constitutionality of this bill is being challenged in several states. In other jurisdictions, officials have taken steps to circumvent the law. For example, according to *Law Enforcement News* ("Coast-to-Coast Activity on Gun Laws," 1994, p. 7):

> The Brady Law has spawned an unlikely response from officials of Santa Rosa County [Florida] who resent the Federal Government's intrusion on the rights of citizens to bear arms. The County Commission has established a militia and made every able-bodied man, woman and child a member. . . .
> County Commissioner H. Byrd Mapoles, who sponsored the resolution, . . . [said] "Most folks in this part of the country are not willing to give up their guns."

In general, however, the public appears to becoming more supportive of gun control laws ("Taking Better Aim at Gun Crime, 1994, p. 13):

> Public awareness about the proliferation of fire-arms, the increasing willingness of youths to use guns to settle disputes, and the incalculable toll gun violence has wreaked on all sectors of American society all appear to have grown by quantum leaps—as witness the success of the innumerable gun-buyback programs that sprang up nationwide early this year.

Playing "cops and robbers."

This article concludes with the observation: "1994 may also go down as the year that the children's games such as 'Cops and Robbers,' 'War' and 'Cowboys and Indians' became relics of a more innocent time."

The Violent Crime Control and Law Enforcement Act of 1994

In September 1994, Congress passed and President Clinton signed into law the Violent Crime Control and Law Enforcement Act of 1994, which went into effect in October. This act places a ban on the manufacturing of 19 different semiautomatic guns with multiple assault-weapon features as well as copies or duplicates of such guns. The act also:

❖ Prohibits transferring to or possession of handguns and ammunition by juveniles.
❖ Prohibits possessing firearms by persons who have committed domestic abuse.
❖ Provides for stiffer penalties for criminals who use firearms in committing federal crimes.

STATES AND THE SECOND AMENDMENT

Providing that a statute does not violate a state's constitution, the federal courts have ruled that a complete ban on certain types of guns is acceptable.

🍃 **The states' power to regulate firearms appears to be nearly absolute.**

In dictum (the court's side opinion) on a case involving illegal search and seizure, Douglas summed up the federal position on gun control (*Adams v. Williams*, 1972):

> A powerful lobby dins into the ears of our citizenry that these gun purchases are constitutional rights protected by the Second Amendment. . . . There is under our decisions no reason why stiff state laws governing the purchase and possession of pistols may not be enacted.

In 1982 the village of Morton Grove, Illinois, banned from the town all handguns, shotguns with barrels less than 18 inches and guns firing more than eight shots in repetition. Exceptions were made for law enforcement officials and for armed services personnel performing official duties. (Several other exceptions were also made, e.g., licensed gun collectors and gun clubs, providing the guns were kept securely on the premises.)

The village ban on guns was contested by Quilici who brought suit, claiming the ordinance went too far in restricting the right to bear arms according to both the Illinois and United States Constitution. He also claimed that the ban violated the Ninth Amendment. The district court upheld the ordinance which was taken to the United States Court of Appeals for the Seventh District.

The Court of Appeals considered the scope of the ban irrelevant and dismissed the issue *(Quilici v. Village of Morton Grove*, 1982): "Since we hold that the Second Amendment does not apply to the states, we need not consider the scope of its guarantee of the right to bear arms." The court went on to conclude that according to the plain language of the amendment: "[I]t seems clear that the right to bear arms is inextricably connected to the preservation of a militia."

Before leaving the issue of the Second Amendment and the states, recall the case of *United States v. Lopez* (1995) discussed in Chapter 6. This case found the federal law banning guns near schools to be unconstitutional. This Supreme Court five-to-four decision struck down the Gun-Free School Zones Act. Although Justice Department lawyers argued that the law was a legitimate extension of Congress' power to regulate interstate commerce, Chief Justice Rehnquist found that the law "has nothing to do with commerce or any sort of enterprise."

This overturning of the Gun-Free School Zones Act may not have much practical effect, however, as more than 40 states have banned possession of handguns near schools, exercising their right to pass laws controlling guns.

GUN CONTROL AS A POLITICAL ISSUE

In *Quilici v. Village of Morton Grove* the court began its opinion: "While we recognize that this case raises controversial issues which engender strong emotions, our task is to apply the law as it has been interpreted by the Supreme Court, regardless of whether that Court's interpretation comports with various personal views of what the law should be." The trend for the judiciary is to leave gun control laws to the states to be determined through the political process.

Courts have tended to rule in support of states' interpretations of the Constitution. While significant political pressure has been exerted on both sides, the arguments for and against have only become stronger and more emotional. The gun control issue is sure to remain in the forefront of debate as society examines its needs, rights and desires in the 1990s.

Summary

Historically, the militia was considered to be the entire male populace. They were not simply allowed to keep arms, but were generally required to do so by law. The central controversy over the Second Amendment is whether people have a right to bear arms as individuals rather than only as part of a militia. Federal courts have held that the Constitution does *not* guarantee the right of the individual to keep and bear arms.

The two opposing interpretations of the Second Amendment involve whether the amendment guarantees the right of *individuals* to keep and bear arms or whether it guarantees the *states* freedom from federal government infringement on this right. Individual rights proponents claim that the framers intended to preserve the individual right, above the right of the state. States' rights proponents claim that the Second Amendment was adopted with the primary purpose of preserving the state militia.

In 1967 the courts ruled that there was no express right of an individual to keep and bear arms. Despite the federal interpretation of the Second Amendment, giving authority over gun control to the states, Congress has been able to enact federal gun control legislation by using its broad authority to regulate interstate commerce. The federal government has passed legislation regulating the sale of handguns, including the Brady Bill, which requires a waiting period of five business days or a background check in order to buy or obtain a license to carry a handgun. In general, however, the states' power to regulate firearms appears to be nearly absolute.

Discussion Questions

1. Why do you think gun control is such a volatile issue?
2. Do you think the government should control the possession of guns? Why or why not?
3. Should the government restrict certain types of firearms? Why or why not?
4. Does the Brady Bill serve a legitimate function? Why or why not?
5. Considering the history behind the drafting of the Second Amendment, can any original interpretations reasonably be used today? If so, how?

6. In Great Britain police officers do not carry firearms because, among other reasons, firearms are generally not a threat from the public. Discuss whether you think this could ever occur in the United States.

7. Discuss whether you think gun control is crime control.

8. Do you think the so-called "cooling off" period for gun permits is reasonable?

9. Does it make sense to regulate handguns and not rifles and shotguns in a similar manner?

10. Rewrite the Second Amendment as though you were asked to in order to address today's concerns.

References

Black, Eric. "The Second Amendment: Necessary Safeguard or Constitutional Fossil?" (Minneapolis/St. Paul, *Star Tribune*) *World & Nation.* June 26, 1995, pp. 4–7.

Blendon, Robert J., John T. Young and David Hemenway. "The American Public and the Gun Control Debate." *JAMA.* June 12, 1996, vol. 275, no. 22, pp. 1719–1722.

Brady, Sarah. "Registration, Regulation and Education Will Help Stop the Nation's Gun Violence." *Corrections Today.* April 1995, pp. 52–56.

Cavanaugh, Kevin D. "The Fiery Issue of Gun Control: Voices for and Against." *Law Enforcement Technology.* October 1991, p. 18.

"Coast-to-Coast Activity on Gun Laws." *Law Enforcement News.* June 30, 1994, p. 7.

Farah, Joseph. "L.A. Riots Prove That We Need More Guns for Our Protection." (Minneapolis/St. Paul) *Star Tribune.* May 13, 1992, p. A15.

Gruber, Charles. "The Fiery Issue of Gun Control: Voices for and Against." *Law Enforcement Technology.* October 1991, p. 20.

Killian, Johnny H. *The Constitution of the United States of America: Analysis and Interpretation.* Washington: U.S. Government Printing Office, 1987.

Kime, Roy Caldwell. "Congress Passes Brady Bill, Addresses Other Gun Control Measures." *The Police Chief.* January 1994, p. 10.

Magaw, John W. "The Brady Law: An Implementation Summary." *The Police Chief.* March 1994, pp. 14, 18.

Nowak, John E. and Ronald D. Rotunda. *Constitutional Law.* 4th ed. St. Paul: West Publishing Company, 1991.

"Polls Find Broad Public Support for Tougher Controls on Handguns, Assault Weapons." *Law Enforcement News.* June 15, 1993, pp. 1, 9.

Pyle, Leroy. "The Fiery Issue of Gun Control: Voices for and Against." *Law Enforcement Technology.* October 1991, p. 19.

Stokes, Dewey. "The Fiery Issue of Gun Control: Voices for and Against." *Law Enforcement Technology.* October 1991, p. 20.

Tribe, Laurence H. and Michael C. Dorf. *On Reading the Constitution.* The President and Fellows of Harvard College, 1991.

Vassar, Mary J. and Kenneth W. Kizer. "Hospitalizations for Firearm-Related Injuries." *JAMA.* June 12, 1996, vol. 275, no. 22, pp. 1734–1743.

Zawitz, Marianne W. *Firearm Injury from Crime.* Washington: Bureau of Justice Statistics Selected Findings, April 1996.

Zawitz, Marianne W. *Guns Used in Crime.* Washington: Bureau of Justice Statistics Selected Findings, July 1995.

Cases Cited

Adams v. Williams, 407 U.S. 143, 92 S.Ct. 1921, 32 L.Ed.2d 612 (1972).

Cases v. United States, 131 F.2d 916 (1942).

Presser v. Illinois, 116 U.S. 252, 6 S.Ct. 580, 29 L.Ed. 615 (1886).

Quilici v. Village of Morton Grove, 695 F.2d 261 (1982).

Stevens v. United States, 440 F.2d 144 (1971).

United States v. Lopez, ___ U.S. ___, 115 S.Ct. 1624, 131 L.Ed.2d 626 (1995).

United States v. Miller, 307 U.S. 174, 59 S.Ct. 816, 83 L.Ed. 1206 (1939).

United States v. Warin, 530 F.2d 103 (1976).

Section Four

Constitutional Amendments Influencing the Criminal Justice System

Whether a person is in custody determines what measures the Constitution will permit.

THE PRECEDING SECTION examined amendments to the Constitution that guaranteed citizens' civil rights and civil liberties—basic freedoms promised to everyone. To ensure such freedoms our country is based on laws that all are expected to obey and has a criminal justice system in place to deal with those who break the law. It also has a Bill of Rights to ensure that the government does not carry its policing powers too far.

This section examines the amendments affecting the criminal justice system, those who are employed in it, those who are protected by it as well as those who become involved with it. At the very core of restrictions on government infringing on citizens' freedom is the Fourth Amendment, which forbids unreasonable search and seizure. Chapter 9 provides an overview of this amendment as well as a discussion of how it and other amendments are enforced—through the exclusionary rule. Chapter 10 provides an in-depth discussion of the restrictions placed on searches, Chapter 11 an in-depth discussion of the law of arrest. Next, Chapter 12 explains the Fifth Amendment, including its protection for citizens against self-incrimination and their guarantee of due process of law. Chapter 13 discusses the Sixth Amendment and the guarantees of right to counsel and to a fair trial. The section concludes with Chapter 14 and a discussion of the Eighth Amendment and how it restricts bail, fines and punishment.

Chapter 9

The right of the people to be secure in their persons, houses, papers, and effects, against unreasonable searches and seizures, shall not be violated, and no warrants shall issue but upon probable cause, supported by oath or affirmation, and particularly describing the place to be searched, and the persons or things to be seized.

—FOURTH AMENDMENT OF THE UNITED STATES CONSTITUTION

The Fourth Amendment: Constitutional Searches and Seizures and the Exclusionary Rule

Facts will determine if a stop or frisk has occurred, and the Fourth Amendment will then determine what the police are permitted to do.

INTRODUCTION*

The essence of being an American to many means the right to be left alone by the government. While most of us take it for granted, one of the greatest advantages of living in the United States is to be able to live unimpeded by government. A continuing argument in our country, and one our First Amendment permits to be pursued, is whether we, indeed, have "too much" government. Two hundred years after the drafting of the Constitution, it is clear that governmental controls remain important to Americans.

---

*Much of this chapter's material is adapted from *Criminal Procedure*, Harr and Hess, West Publishing Company, 1990.

155

Governmental controls assure that you can drive to and from your destinations without the fear of being pulled over by an overly zealous police officer who simply doesn't like the color of your car—or skin. It means that you can enjoy the security of your home without fearing an intrusion by the government seizing assets, property or records just because you are engaged in an unpopular line of work.

Of course, this security does not mean that the government is barred from carrying out its responsibility. Limited governmental power is necessary for the laws of our country to be enforced and for the business of government to be carried out. But a balance is required for a democracy such as ours to exist—a balance between the power of the government and the freedom of its people; and that is what the law of search and seizure is all about. Because Americans take this freedom very seriously, American law has developed to firmly regulate just what government agents can—and cannot —take from you.

> The Fourth Amendment forbids unreasonable searches and seizures and requires that any search or arrest warrant be based on probable cause.

This chapter will explain what power the government has when it comes to searching and seizing property or people. As the chapter develops, it is important to think about not only how important these freedoms are, but also how important it is that government be able to take action to enforce our laws. This balance is vital to our democracy.

The chapter begins with an examination of the two main clauses of the amendment, the reasonable clause and the warrant clause. This is followed by an explanation of other requirements of warrants and a discussion of how the Fourth Amendment clauses have been interpreted. Next an examination is made of who is governed by this amendment. After this discussion, the continuum of contacts citizens may have with the criminal justice system and the law of stop and frisk is described as one of the most basic situations in which the Fourth Amendment applies. The chapter concludes with an explanation of the exclusionary rule as a means to enforce the provisions of the Fourth Amendment as well as other amendments related to the criminal justice system.

THE CLAUSES OF THE FOURTH AMENDMENT

The Fourth Amendment contains two clauses of importance to the issue of search and seizure:

The reasonableness clause: "The right of the people to be secure in their persons, houses, papers, and effects, against unreasonable searches and seizures shall not be violated."

The warrant clause: ". . . and no warrants shall issue but upon probable cause, supported by oath or affirmation, and particularly describing the place to be searched, and the persons or things to be seized."

Two Interpretations

These two clauses have been viewed differently by the Supreme Court. Until the 1960s the Court used the **conventional Fourth Amendment approach,** viewing the two clauses as intertwined and firmly connected. This interpretation holds that all searches not conducted with *both* a warrant and probable cause are unreasonable.

Since the 1960s, however, the Court has broadened government's power by adopting what has been called the **reasonableness Fourth Amendment approach.** This interpretation sees the two clauses as separate, distinct and addressing two separate situations. In some instances, searches can be reasonable without either warrants or probable cause.

Two key terms in understanding the Fourth Amendment are *reasonable* and *probable cause.*

Reasonable

How would you define *reasonable?* Most people have a general idea of what would be reasonable—in their opinion. Reasonable means sensible, logical, fair, showing good judgment.

> **Reasonable** means sensible, rational, justifiable.

Oran (1985, p. 254) defines reasonable:

A broad, flexible word used to make sure that a decision is based on the facts of a particular situation rather than on abstract legal principles. It has no exact definition, but can mean fair, appropriate, moderate, rational, etc. Its definition tends to be circular. For example, reasonable care has been defined as "that degree of care a person of ordinary prudence would exercise in similar circumstances."

Samaha (1996, p. 106) describes two approaches that have been used to determine reasonableness:

Bright line approach—The determination of reasonableness according to a specific rule that applies to all cases.
Case-by-case method—The determination of reasonableness by considering the totality of circumstances in each individual case.

He notes that usually the case-by-case method is used by our courts. A key consideration in determining whether a search or seizure is reasonable is the balancing of individual rights and the needs of society, as stressed earlier. Samaha (p. 107) describes this **reasonableness test:** "The reasonableness of searches and seizures depends on balancing government and individual interests and the objective basis of the searches and seizures." This is also referred to as a **balancing approach** to the Fourth Amendment (Samaha, p. 106): "The element of reasonableness that balances government interest in law enforcement against individual interests in privacy and liberty." He suggests (p. 112):

The reasonableness of searches and seizures generally . . . depends on two elements:

1. The application of a balancing approach to the Fourth Amendment.
2. The existence of an adequate objective basis for the search and seizure.

The balancing approach element requires weighing:

1. the *government interest* furthered by conducting the search or seizure, and
2. the *invasions against citizens* caused by the searches and seizures.

According to the reasonableness test, a search or seizure is reasonable if it meets three conditions:

1. The search or seizure furthers a government interest.
2. The government interest outweighs the invasions of the privacy, liberty, and property of individuals.
3. The invasions of individual privacy, liberty, and property are supported by a sufficient objective basis.

Expectation of Privacy

An important consideration in determining the reasonableness of a search or seizure is the expectation of privacy involved, that is, whether the search or seizure violates a person's Fourth Amendment right to a "reasonable expectation of privacy." The precedent landmark case, *Katz v. United States* (1967), involved an appeal by Charles Katz, convicted in California of violating gambling laws. Investigators had Katz under surveillance for several days as he made calls from the same phone booth at the same time each day. The investigators suspected that he was placing horse racing bets, so they attached an electronic listening/recording device to the phone booth and recorded Katz's conversations. The recordings were used in obtaining his conviction. The Supreme Court reversed the California decision saying: ". . . the Fourth Amendment protects people not places. . . . Wherever a man may be, he is entitled to know that he will remain free from unreasonable searches and seizures."

The issue of electronic surveillance as a form of search and seizure is discussed in depth in Chapter 10. The Katz case shows that the investigators had facts on which to support their suspicions that a crime was being committed—that is, they had probable cause, another critical concept contained in the Fourth Amendment and the heart of the warrant clause.

Probable Cause

Probable cause is stronger than **reasonable suspicion**. The question is: "Would a reasonable person believe that either the individual committed the offense, or that the contraband or evidence would be where it is said to be?" Oran (1985, pp. 239–240) says:

〰️ "Probable cause to search means it is more likely than not that the items sought are where the officers believe them to be. Probable cause to arrest means that it is more likely than not that a crime has been committed by the person whom a law enforcement officer seeks to arrest."

Smith v. United States (1949) defined probable cause as: "The sum total of layers of information and the synthesis of what the police have heard, what they know, and what they observe as trained officers. We[the Court] weigh not individual layers but the laminated total." According to Creamer (1980, p. 9):

> Probable cause for the issuance of a search warrant is defined as facts or apparent facts, viewed through the eyes of an experienced police officer, which would lead a man of reasonable caution to believe that there is something connected with a violation of law on the premises to be searched.

Creamer notes that probable cause is one of the oldest and most important concepts in criminal law, having existed for more than 2,000 years. He suggests (p. 8): "This concept of probable cause has acquired its legal potency in the United States because it has constitutional dimensions and because it is interpreted in the final analysis by impartial judges rather than by the police."

The Supreme Court has defined probable cause this way: "Probable cause exists where the facts and circumstances within their [the arresting police officers'] knowledge and of which they had reasonably trustworthy information [are] sufficient in themselves to warrant a man of reasonable caution in the belief that more likely than not an offense has been or is being committed [by the one about to be arrested]" (*Brinegar v. United States*, 1948).

This concept exemplifies how law becomes confusing. With all the resources, intellect and precedent involved, shouldn't there be a precise definition of such a term rather than "more likely than not"? Such a definition demands that those dealing with the tool of probable cause stretch their understanding of the concept to effectively and lawfully deal with it. This is what the Constitution wants us to do, to have the freedom to make the document work for us, without unnecessarily restricting government or the people it serves.

Probable cause must be established *before* a lawful arrest can be made. Facts and evidence obtained *after* an arrest cannot be used to establish probable cause. They *can* be used, however, to strengthen the case *if* probable cause was established before the arrest, making the arrest legal.

SOURCES OF PROBABLE CAUSE   Probable cause is based on a "totality of circumstances." It may come from what government agents see, hear and smell and from information given to them by other agencies, victims or informants.

OBSERVATIONAL PROBABLE CAUSE   Observational probable cause includes anything government agents become aware of through their senses, interpreted by their past experiences, training and knowledge of criminal behavior. It includes suspicious conduct, being under the influence of drugs, associating with known criminals, having a criminal record, running away from officials, being present in an unusual place or at an unusual time, being present in a high crime area or being present at a crime scene. It also includes failing to answer questions, failing to provide identification or providing false information to authorities.

INFORMATIONAL PROBABLE CAUSE   Most crimes are not committed in the presence of the authorities. They must rely on information provided by others. These sources of information include official sources such as roll call, dispatch, police bulletins and wanted notices; or unofficial sources such as witnesses, victims and informants.

Two Supreme Court decisions set forth the legal requirements for establishing probable cause when working with informants. *Aguilar v. Texas* (1964) and *Spinelli v. United States* (1969) established a two-pronged test, with each prong considered independent of the other. The first prong tested the informant's basis of knowledge. Was the information accurate? Did the informant personally witness the information given? If not, did the information come from another source? Is there still reason to believe it?

The second prong tested the informant's credibility. Was the person reliable? Was the informant's identity known? Is the informant a common citizen or a criminal?

In other words, the historical two-pronged test for using an informant to establish probable cause looked at (1) the basis of knowledge and (2) the informant's credibility.

This two-pronged approach was abandoned in 1983 in *Illinois v. Gates*. This case involved executing a search warrant for drugs on the basis of an anonymous informant tip. Judge Rehnquist held that because "the most basic function of any government is to provide for the security of the individual and of his property," it better served the spirit of the law to determine the exis-

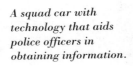

A squad car with technology that aids police officers in obtaining information.

tence of probable cause by considering the totality of the circumstances in deciding whether a "reasonable and prudent person" would believe that, in this case, contraband was located in a particular location, thus indicating criminal activity. Justice Rehnquist noted that "probable cause is a fluid concept—turning on the assessment of probabilities in a particular factual context—not readily, or even usefully reduced to a neat set of legal rules." This "totality of circumstances" test made it easier for police to establish probable cause using informants.

No matter what the source, if an officer can establish probable cause, the next step is to obtain a search warrant or an arrest warrant—or both.

SEARCH AND ARREST WARRANTS

Government agents who have probable cause to believe evidence of a crime is located at a specific place or that an individual is involved in a crime must go before a neutral and detached magistrate (judge) and swear under oath who or what they are looking for and where they think it can be found.

≋ All warrants are to be based on probable cause.

In determining whether probable cause for the warrant exists, the reviewing judge must consider the totality of the circumstances. In other words, all the factors submitted are viewed as a whole in considering whether a reasonable person would believe what the officer(s) claim.

As any law enforcement officer will attest, obtaining a warrant is *not* just a matter of "walking up and getting one." Rather, it is the officer's responsibility to provide sufficient data to the judge who may sign the warrant that the facts are sufficient to provide the necessary probable cause. Because the judge determines if probable cause exists, the officer must argue the probable cause aspect of the case early on. And not every judge will sign a warrant. The officer may be directed to come back with additional information or be told that a warrant will not be issued on the facts presented.

Because an independent magistrate decides that probable cause to search or arrest exists, the defendant has to prove that the warrant was invalid. Police discretion has been removed, and thus the search or arrest with a warrant is presumed legal. The warrant must include the reasons for requesting it, the names of the officers who applied for it, names of others who have information to contribute, what or who specifically is being sought and the signature of the judge issuing it. Figure 9–1 shows a sample search warrant.

Special Conditions

Sometimes officers ask for special conditions to be attached to a warrant, including making an unannounced entrance or carrying out a search at night.

If officers want to make an unannounced entrance because they are afraid evidence might be destroyed or officer safety requires it, they can request a *no-knock* warrant. The search warrants for drug busts using bulldozers to crash through the walls of suspected crack houses would have such a provision.

Figure 9–1

Search warrant.

Source: Wayne W. Bennett and Kären M. Hess. *Criminal Investigation.* 4th ed. St. Paul: West Publishing Company, 1994, p. 126. Reprinted by permission. All rights reserved.

SEARCH WARRANT   2-1

STATE OF ANYWHERE, COUNTY OF ___Hennepin___   ___Justice___ COURT

TO: ___Edina Police Department any officer_____

_____ (A) PEACE OFFICER(S) OF THE STATE OF ANYWHERE.

WHEREAS, ___Patrick Olson___ has this day on oath, made application to the said Court applying for issuance of a search warrant to search the following described (premises) (motor vehicle) (person):

___716 Sunshine Avenue, a private residence,_____

_____

located in the city of ___Edina___ , county of ___Hennepin___ STATE OF Minn.

for the following described property and things: (attach and identify additional sheet if necessary)

    One brown, 21" Panasonic Television,
    Serial Number, 63412X

WHEREAS, the application and supporting affidavit of ___Patrick Olson_____ (was) (were) duty presented and read by the Court, and being fully advised in the premises.

NOW, THEREFORE, the Court finds that probable cause exists for the issuance of a search warrant upon the following grounds: (Strike inapplicable paragraphs)

1. The property above-described was stolen or embezzled.
2. The property above-described was used as a means of committing a crime.
3. The possession of the property above-described constitutes a crime.
4. The property above described is in the possession of a person with intent to use such property as a means of committing a crime.
5. The property above described constitutes evidence which tends to show a crime has been committed, or tends to show that a particular person has committed a crime.

The Court further finds that probable cause exists to believe that the above-described property and things (are) (will be) (at the above-described premises) (in the above-described motor vehicle) (on the person of _____).

The Court further finds that a nighttime search is necessary to prevent the loss, destruction, or removal of the objects of said search.

The Court further finds that entry without announcement of authority or purpose is necessary (to prevent the loss, destruction, or removal of the objects of said search) (and) (to protect the safety of the peace officer).

NOW, THEREFORE, YOU, ___a peace officer of the Edina Police Department_____

THE PEACE OFFICERS(S) AFORESAID, ARE HEREBY COMMANDED (TO ENTER WITH-OUT ANNOUNCEMENT OF AUTHORITY AND PURPOSE) (IN THE DAYTIME ONLY) (IN THE DAYTIME OR NIGHTTIME) TO SEARCH (THE DESCRIBED PREMISES) (THE DESCRIBED MOTOR VEHICLE) (THE PERSON OF _____) FOR THE ABOVE DESCRIBED PROPERTY AND THINGS. AND TO SEIZE SAID PROPERTY AND THINGS AND (TO RETAIN THEM IN CUSTODY SUBJECT TO COURT ORDER AND ACCORDING TO LAW) (DELIVER CUSTODY OF SAID PROPERTY AND THINGS TO _____ _____).

BY THE COURT:

___Oscar Kuntson_____
JUDGE OF   COURT

Dated ___4-14___ , 19 _96_

Justice Court

COURT-WHITE COPY •PROS. ATTY. -YELLOW COPY •PEACE OFFICER-PINK COPY•PREMISES/PERSON-GOLD COPY

In other cases, the illicit activity occurs primarily at night, illegal gambling, for example. In such cases, the officers can ask the judge to include a provision allowing them to execute the warrant at night.

Carrying out the Search Warrant

Once signed by a judge, the warrant becomes an order for the police to carry out the search or arrest. Unless special conditions have been included in the warrant, government agents must carry out the warrant during daylight hours and must also identify themselves as officers and state their purpose. The officers may use reasonable force to execute the warrant if they are denied entrance or if no one is home.

ADMINISTRATIVE WARRANTS

In some instances the Supreme Court requires a two-step warrant process. If probable cause exists that a city ordinance is being violated on private property an **administrative warrant** may be issued to check the premises for compliance. If, during this investigation, probable cause to believe a criminal offense is occurring or has occurred, a criminal warrant must be obtained to search for evidence. Any evidence so seized may then be used to establish the probable cause required to obtain a criminal search warrant. For example, to investigate a fire, the initial search may require only an administrative warrant to search the premises for the cause and origin of the fire and a criminal warrant if evidence of a crime is discovered. Both types of warrants require probable cause for issuance. As noted in *Michigan v. Clifford* (1984):

> If a warrant is necessary, the object of the search determines the type of warrant required. If the primary object is to determine the cause and origin of a fire, an administrative warrant will suffice . . . and if the primary object is to gather evidence of criminal activity, a criminal search warrant may be obtained only on a showing of probable cause to believe that the relevant evidence will be found in the place to be searched.

According to Woods and Wallace (1991, p. 80): "Administrative and criminal law overlap in arson cases due to the nature of the investigation. Administrative warrants are issued to allow civil inspections of private property to determine compliance with city ordinances such as fire codes." Administrative warrants may also be obtained for government agents to conduct a routine inspection when the occupant refuses their entry.

At times the government has a compelling interest justifying warrantless searches for the public's benefit. Certain regulated businesses may be searched during inspections without a warrant. In *United States v. Biswell* (1972), the Supreme Court reversed a court of appeals ruling that disallowed a warrantless search of a gun shop's locked storeroom, which netted illegal firearms. The Court stated that such inspections pertaining to the sale of illegal firearms is justified and that limited threat like this to the gun dealer's expectation of privacy is reasonable, adding: "When a dealer chooses to engage in this type of pervasively regulated business and to accept a federal license, he does so with the knowledge that his business records, firearms and ammunition will be subject to effective inspection."

However, in *Marshall v. Barlow's Inc.*, (1978) the Court asserted that government inspectors should not be given unlimited authority, finding that OSHA (Occupational Safety and Health Act) employees would not be permitted to simply wander within a business looking for whatever wrongs they might find because to do so would be an unreasonable intrusion into the business owner's Fourth Amendment rights.

Having looked at the requirements of the Fourth Amendment and how they are to be fulfilled, consider next just who is bound by the provisions of the Fourth Amendment.

WHO IS REGULATED BY THE FOURTH AMENDMENT

As the United States Constitution was originally drafted, the Fourth Amendment itself applies to *federal* government, but is equally applied to *state* government by the Fourteenth Amendment, as discussed previously. For all practical purposes, it is correct to say that *any* government agent (whether federal, state, county or local) is regulated by the Fourth Amendment.

When most people consider search and seizure law, they think of its impact on such agencies as the FBI or local police. But again, *any* employee of the government at any jurisdictional level is influenced by the constitutional restrictions. This would include all governmental agencies, including but not limited to the Secret Service, the Internal Revenue Service, the Immigration and Naturalization Service and the Food and Drug Administration. It also regulates state agencies such as state revenue agencies, law enforcement agencies, public schools and colleges and other regulatory bodies as well as local county and municipal bodies of government.

> If a person is an employee of any governmental agency or is an agent of the government in any capacity, that person is bound by the Fourth Amendment.

Why? Again, because the framers of the Constitution came to America to escape overzealous governmental power and control and wanted to draft a Constitution that would ensure personal freedom by restricting governmental powers. That is what the Fourth Amendment is all about—limiting government power, so as to permit it to do its job, with only truly *reasonable* power.

> The United States Constitution ensures freedom by restricting government's power.

Private individuals or agencies are *not* regulated by the Fourth Amendment. When a rebellious teenager angrily informs his parents that they can't come into his room without a warrant—this is inaccurate. Private security guards, such as store detectives, are similarly not controlled by the Fourth Amendment. Why? They are not government agents, and the Constitution was established to limit the power of *government* and its agents.

Among recent cases involving the issue of searches conducted by private individuals are the following (Carr 1995, pp. 96–97):

❖ *United States v. Parker* (1994) held that United Parcel Service employees could open packages and inspect their contents whenever a customer insured a package for more than $1,000.
❖ *United States v. Claveland* (1994) held permissible a search by an electric company employee acting on a tip that a customer was bypassing the electric meter.
❖ *United States v. Ross* (1982) held that an airline employee who inspected the defendant's luggage according to FAA regulations *was* acting in a governmental capacity.

Can a private party ever be considered a government agent? An example for discussion would involve individuals who seize evidence of a crime from the home of another—maybe because they were invited into the home, or maybe because they actually broke into the residence. Could that evidence be used in court against the homeowner, although the person who actually seized it did so without a warrant and without permission of the homeowner?

The answer is *yes,* if the person was not acting as any sort of government agent.

> The Fourth Amendment does not apply to private parties.

Similarly, a private store detective could search someone without a warrant or without the other permissible reasons the police would need because the Constitution does not regulate private police.

But what if the private party had agreed to go in and get the item from the house, or the private security guard had agreed to search the person for the police? It's arguable that this private person, while not employed by the government, has become an *agent of the government.* And then the Fourth Amendment would apply.

When Is a Private Citizen a Government Agent?

The previous discussion begs the question: *Who decides?* Our American legal system is organized so that if an obvious answer is not present, or if the parties involved do not agree that an obvious answer exists, then a court decides. To determine whether an individual is actually acting as an agent of the police, it is conceivable that the question would be presented to a judge to determine.

One aspect of our law that people find difficult to understand, if not downright frustrating, is that the law itself is anything but black and white. But it does permit the parties involved to make their positions known and to have a determination made in a legal forum.

The law becomes easier to comprehend and work with when you can accept that learning the law does not mean memorizing statutes. It means learning how the legal system works to permit the parties involved in a legal dispute (criminal or civil) to compare their circumstances to existing law and

Nonenforcement contact between police officers and citizens.

to fashion arguments as to why the law does or does not apply in this situation. This again exemplifies why the American legal system is termed a "living law"—one that works with and adapts to the facts at hand rather than just providing pigeonholes into which issues are inserted or forced.

Having discussed how the Fourth Amendment ensures individual freedom by restricting government's power to intrude, consider next when the government *is* permitted to search and seize and the broad range of contacts that exist.

THE CONTINUUM OF GOVERNMENTAL CONTACTS

To understand when government can exercise its power, which admittedly can be immense, it helps to begin by analyzing the variety of contacts people and government actually may have. This can be viewed as a *continuum of governmental contacts,* as shown in Figure 9–2.

On one end of the spectrum are the routine, day-to-day, nonenforcement contacts everyone has with government, those on the left in Figure 9–2. These could include such simple interactions as waving hello to the officers passing by in a squad car or stopping into city hall to ask a question. No one would expect to be harassed in such a situation, and normally it would not occur.

Figure 9-2
Continuum of governmental contacts.

Nonenforcement			Enforcement			
Greetings	Seeking information	Stop	Arresting of person by government agent	Handcuffing	Holding in jail	Imprisonment
		REASONABLE SUSPICION	PROBABLE CAUSE			

REASONABLE   PROBABLE CAUSE
SUSPICION

At the other extreme are the powerful and intrusive contacts, including arrest, taking into custody by force, holding in jail and imprisonment, shown on the right in Figure 9–2. Unquestionably, here government is exercising powerful controls over people and their property.

But what about the middle area when the interactions are not so clearly defined? This realm includes situations when the police or other government agencies are considering, or actually conducting, an investigation, or when an individual or business or other organization is merely *suspected* of illicit activity. Figure 9–3 illustrates the degree of intrusion on individual liberty and whether the Fourth Amendment is implicated.

Figure 9–3

Seizures and the Fourth Amendment.

Source: Joel Samaha. Criminal Procedure. 3rd ed. St. Paul: West Publishing Company, 1996, p. 109. Reprinted by permission. All rights reserved.

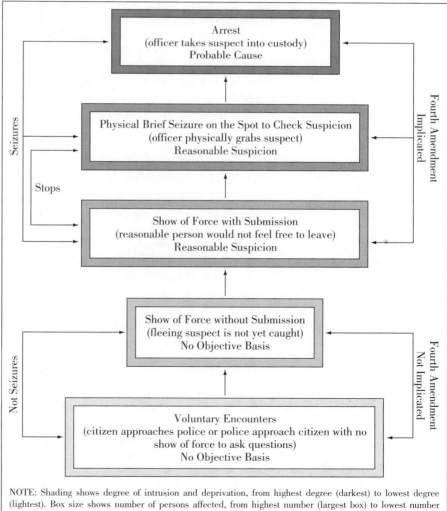

NOTE: Shading shows degree of intrusion and deprivation, from highest degree (darkest) to lowest degree (lightest). Box size shows number of persons affected, from highest number (largest box) to lowest number (smallest box).

The law of search and seizure defines what authority government has when interacting with the public and how they can follow up on their suspicions. It begins with an examination of the law of stop and frisk.

THE LAW OF STOP AND FRISK

Recognizing that government agents have absolutely no authority to interfere with people carrying out legal activity, any analysis of the law must next inquire as to what authority officers have when they develop *suspicion* that criminal activity is afoot.

This is well before what happens when one is placed in physical custody or is fully searched. The question is what power government has when officers are following up on their suspicion, but before they may legally arrest the person. As noted by Samaha (1996, p. 110): "The power to stop and question suspicious persons is at least as old as the common law of England."

> The law of stop and frisk deals with that time frame during which officers follow up on their suspicions, but before the time that the requisite probable cause is established to justify an arrest (*Terry v. Ohio,* 1968).

Police officers talk about developing a "sixth sense"—an ability to know that something is not right. What they are really talking about are observational skills officers develop. Sergeant Sylvester (Chip) Schwartz, Edina (Minnesota) Police Department, discusses the need for an officer to develop "soft vision"—surveying all that is present while on patrol, paying specific attention to those events the officer is trained to note. Tire tracks in fresh snow, furtive conduct by a pedestrian, a discarded parcel, a door ajar—to the average citizen such observations mean nothing. To the trained eye of the law enforcement professional, however, they mean an opportunity to delve further into what may be criminal activity. Just what can a government agent do in response to such suspicions?

The law of stop and frisk permits officers to act on their suspicions rather than to turn away, awaiting that infrequent, obvious crime to be committed before their eyes.

The landmark case of *Terry v. Ohio* (1968) provides both a classic example of how a stop-and-frisk situation may arise and how the law deals with it.

Terry v. Ohio

One afternoon in 1963 Detective Martin McFadden, Cleveland Police Department, saw two men standing outside a jewelry store, talking. To the casual observer, the men were simply talking. But to Detective McFadden, a 39-year veteran on the police force, with 30 years as a detective, the men looked suspicious. He watched as one man walked to the window, looked in for a while, then went to the corner, back to the store and then back to the other man. He repeated this routine several times as McFadden continued to watch. At one point a third man joined them briefly then left, and the two men began repeating their routine. McFadden suspected that they were casing the store for a robbery and was about to investigate when the two men began walking toward the store where the third man was waiting.

McFadden approached the three men, identified himself as a police officer, asked their names and then grabbed one of the men, placing the man between himself and the other two. He did a quick pat-down of the man—later identified as John Terry—and felt what could be a gun in Terry's pocket, but he couldn't remove it. He ordered the three into the store at gunpoint, removed Terry's coat and took a .38-caliber revolver from its pocket. When he patted down the other men, he found a revolver in the coat of one of them, identified as Chilton. Both were formally charged with carrying concealed weapons.

Their lawyers argued that the guns had been illegally seized and that, therefore, they could not be used as evidence. Without that evidence, there would be no case. The Ohio trial judge, however, found both guilty as charged. Chilton and Terry appealed their conviction to the United States Supreme Court, but before the case was heard, Chilton died, so the decision referred only to Terry.

When the case reached the Supreme Court, the legal issue was simply phrased "whether it is always unreasonable for a policeman to seize a person and subject him to a limited search for weapons unless there is probable cause for an arrest."

The Supreme Court upheld the Ohio verdict. The Court said McFadden had "acted reasonably" because based on his experience and training the men's actions supported McFadden's suspicion that they were planning a robbery; the robbery would probably involve weapons and nothing happened to make him think differently. He had to act quickly when he saw the three men gather at the store. The Court noted:

> Each case of this sort will, of course, have to be decided on its own facts. We merely hold today that where a police officer observed unusual conduct which leads him reasonably to conclude in light of his experience that criminal activity may be afoot and that the persons with whom he is dealing may be armed and presently dangerous, where in the course of investigating this behavior he identifies himself as a policeman and makes reasonable inquiries, and where nothing in the initial stages of the encounter serves to dispel his reasonable fear for his own or other's safety, he is entitled for the protection of himself and others in the area to conduct a carefully limited search of the outer clothing of such persons in an attempt to discover weapons which might be used to assault him.
>
> Such a search is a reasonable search under the Fourth Amendment and any weapons seized may properly be introduced in evidence against the person from whom they were taken.

The question may arise, what are reasonable inquiries? Generally this includes two specific questions: "What is your name?" and "Do you live around here?"

        The *Terry* decision established that police officers who have reasonable suspicion that someone is about to commit a crime may stop the person and possibly frisk them for weapons.

Guidelines Established by the Terry *Decision*

Guidelines established by *Terry v. Ohio* that determine if a stop and frisk is valid include the following:

❖ Suspicious circumstances, that is, conduct that leads an experienced officer to believe that a crime is about to be committed and that the person about to commit the crime may be armed and dangerous.

❖ While investigating the behavior, officers must identify themselves as police officers and make reasonable inquiries.

❖ If officers are still suspicious after reasonable inquiries, and suspect that the person may be armed and dangerous, they may conduct a limited search of the person's outer clothing to protect themselves and others in the area.

As noted by del Carmen (1987, p. 120), no "fishing expeditions" are allowed: "The frisk cannot be used to see if some type of evidence can be found on the suspect. Its only purpose is to protect the police officer and others in the area from possible harm. A frisk for any other reason is illegal and leads to the exclusion of any evidence obtained, regardless of how incriminating the evidence may be."

The Stop

As noted by Kuboviak (1995, p. 81): "The key ingredient of a lawful stop is reasonable suspicion. In *Terry* the court stated, 'A police officer may in appropriate circumstances and in an appropriate manner approach a person for the purposes of investigating possible criminal behavior even though there is no probable cause to make an arrest.'"

The purpose of a stop is to prevent crime. As stated in the *Terry* decision:

> In justifying the particular intrusion [the stop] the police officer must be able to point to specific and articulable facts which, taken together with rational inferences from all those facts, reasonably warrant that intrusion.

The *Terry* Court based such a determination on a "reasonable person" standard, stating: "Would the facts available to the officer at the moment of the seizure or the search, warrant a man of reasonable caution in the belief that the action taken was appropriate?"

In other words, a government agent may not stop people just for the sake of stopping them, or because the person is a white person in a black neighborhood, or because the agent does not like the looks of the individual. On the other hand, an officer may acquire **articulable facts**—that is, clear, distinct statements—based on observing unusual, suspicious activity; looks similar to a "wanted" poster, a known felony record and the like. Such observations may add up to provide the necessary articulable reasonable suspicion necessary for a stop.

    ≋ A **stop** is a brief detention of a person based on **specific and articulable facts** for the purpose of investigating suspicious activity.

Constitutional common law analysis will determine what rights a person will have protected when encountering the police.

The question then becomes, how long may the person be detained? The answer: however long it takes—within reason. It must be no longer than necessary for the agent to obtain the needed information. In *Florida v. Royer* (1983) the Court said: "[A]n investigative detention must be temporary and last no longer than is necessary to effectuate the purpose of the stop. Similarly, the investigative methods employed should be the least intrusive means reasonably available to verify or dispel the officer's suspicion in a short period of time."

In the 1985 case of *United States v. Sharpe*, the Court stated: "In assessing whether a detention is too long in duration to be justified as an investigative stop, we consider it appropriate to examine whether the police diligently pursued a means of investigation that was likely to confirm or dispel their suspicions quickly. . . . The question is not simply whether some other alternative was available, but whether the police acted unreasonably in failing to recognize or pursue it."

Although in *Terry* the stop was made for the purpose of preventing a crime, a stop may also be made for the purpose of crime detection. LaFave and Israel (1985, p. 176) say: "When immediately after the perpetration of a crime the police may have no more than a vague description of the possible perpetrator, it seems irrational to deprive the officer of the opportunity to 'freeze' the situation for a short time so that he may make inquiry and arrive at a considered judgment about further action to be taken." They go on to note:

> Another issue is whether an interaction would remain a "Terry Stop" if force or threat of force is used by the police. Regardless of whether the action is actually called a "stop" or an "arrest" by the police, the real question is what was done by the police. If the stop is briefly made for investigative purposes, it would remain a "stop," even if a suspect is surrounded, officers have weapons drawn, and certain force is used. The courts consider the display of weapons by police officers case by case.

As noted by Frase, et al. (1986, pp. 257–258): "*Terry* did not address the question of what happens if the police make a valid investigative stop but the suspect refuses to answer the questions or tries to leave." Justice White was of the opinion that "the person stopped is not obliged to answer, answers may not be compelled, and refusal to answer furnishes no basis for an arrest, although it may alert the officers to the need for further observation." Walker (1995, p. 44) describes two stop-related cases:

In 1989, the Supreme Court stated in *United States v. Sokolow*, that "[i]n evaluating the validity of a stop such as this, we must consider 'the totality of the circumstances'—the whole picture."

Finally, in the 1991 decision of *Florida v. Bostick*, the Supreme Court held that the state supreme court erred in concluding that police-citizen encounters occurring on a bus constitute a seizure under the Fourth Amendment.

The Frisk

A **frisk** is a reasonable search for weapons for the protection of the government agent and others and does not automatically occur with each stop.

The purpose of a frisk is protection. It does not automatically occur with every stop. Government agents should frisk an individual *only* if nothing in the initial stages of the stop reduces the reasonable suspicion that the person is about to commit a crime and the agent suspects the person may be armed and dangerous. For example, if an officer stopped a person who was running down an alley in the middle of the night carrying a paper bag and the person gave vague answers, was extremely nervous and reaching for his pocket, the officer might well conduct a frisk. If, on the other hand, the person gave straight answers—he was late to work and his lunch was in the paper bag—a frisk would *not* be reasonable and should not be performed.

Ferdico (1986, pp. 291–292) suggests a partial list of factors that might favor the decision to frisk a person: (1) the suspected crime involves a weapon (as in *Terry*), (2) the suspect is "rattled" over being stopped, (3) there is a bulge in the suspect's clothing, (4) the suspect's hand is concealed in a pocket, (5) the suspect does not have satisfactory identification or an adequate explanation for suspicious behavior, (6) the area is known to contain armed persons. The decision to frisk is also based on a combination of such factors, not on one factor alone.

As noted by the Court in the *Terry* decision: "[I]t would appear to be clearly unreasonable to deny the officer the power to take necessary measures to determine whether the person is in fact carrying a weapon and to neutralize the threat of physical harm."

Two conditions must exist for an officer to be able to frisk someone. First, that person must have been legally stopped by the officer. The mere fact that an officer sees a bulge under a pedestrian's coat will not justify a frisk. Second, the officer's observations lead to the "reasonable conclusion" that the person may be armed and presently dangerous *(Terry)*. This will always depend on the specific situation but could include such circumstances as a suspicious bulge in the suspect's clothes, the nature of the crime being investigated, suspicious activity such as reaching for a pocket or knowledge that the suspect had been armed in the past. Officers need not be in actual "fear." They need only to be able to reasonably conclude that the suspect may be armed and dangerous.

Stop-and-frisk law may be more easily understood by examining its purpose. Here, again, the purpose is to balance the rights of an individual and the rights of the people when a law enforcement official sometimes needs to act before probable cause exists. Police officers should not be expected to ignore their reasonable suspicions, nor should they be denied the right to ensure their own safety by checking for weapons. The law of stop and frisk balances the rights of the people and the individual during that "in-between time" when probable cause has not yet developed when officers should be expected to respond, at least in a limited way.

A Supreme Court ruling in June 1993 ruled that contraband discovered during a frisk *may* be seized as evidence, as discussed in Chapter 10 under the plain view doctrine.

Principles of Stop and Frisk

Wrobleski and Hess (1997, p. 419) cite seven specific principles from *Terry v. Ohio* that apply to most stop-and-frisk situations:

1. Police officers have the right and duty to approach and question people to investigate crimes.
2. Police officers may stop and make a limited search of a suspect if they observe unusual conduct that leads them to reasonably conclude, from experience, that criminal activity may be afoot and that the individual they are investigating at close range is armed and probably dangerous.
3. The test of the officers' actions is whether a reasonably prudent person in the same circumstances would believe that his or her safety or that of others was in danger.
4. Officers may proceed to stop and frisk if nothing occurs to change their theory that criminal activity may occur or that the suspect is armed.
5. The type of search in stop and frisk must be limited. It is a "protective seizure and search for weapons and must be confined to an intrusion which is reasonably designed to discover guns, knives, clubs, or other hidden instruments of assault."
6. If conditions 1–5 are met, the stop and frisk does *not* constitute an arrest.
7. Because stop and frisk actually involves a search and seizure, it must be governed by the intent of the Fourth Amendment of the Constitution that forbids indiscriminate searches and seizures.

The *Terry* case established that the authority to stop and frisk is independent of the power to arrest. A stop is not an arrest, but it is a seizure within the meaning of the Fourth Amendment and therefore requires reasonableness.

In the case of *United States v. Mendenhall* (1980), Justice Stewart wrote: "We conclude that a person has been 'seized' within the meaning of the Fourth Amendment only if, in view of all of the circumstances surrounding the incident, a reasonable person would have believed that he was not free to leave."

Leading Stop and Frisk Cases

del Carmen and Walker (1995, pp. x–xi) cite the following stop and frisk cases in addition to the landmark case of *Terry v. Ohio:*

> *Adams v. Williams* (1972): A stop and frisk may be based on information provided by another individual.
>
> *United States v. Hensley* (1985): Reasonable suspicion based on a "wanted" poster is sufficient for a valid stop.
>
> *United States v. Sharpe* (1985): There is no rigid time limit for the length of an investigatory stop; instead specific circumstances should be taken into account.
>
> *Alabama v. White* (1990): Reasonable suspicion is a less demanding standard than probable cause.
>
> *Minnesota v. Dickerson* (1993): A frisk that goes beyond that authorized in *Terry v. Ohio* is not valid.

Stop and Frisk and Vehicle Drivers

Delaware v. Prouse (1979) established that:

> . . . except in those situations in which there is at least clear articulable, reasonable suspicion that a motorist is unlicensed or that an automobile is not registered, or that either the vehicle or an occupant is otherwise subject to seizure for violation of law, stopping an automobile and detaining the driver in order to check his driver's license and the registration of the automobile are unreasonable under the Fourth Amendment.

Instances in which motorists may be stopped are summarized by Frase, et al. (1986, p. 262), who note that courts have approved stopping a car because it has expired license plates, defective turnlights, the license was tied on with baling twine or a beer can was on its roof. A vehicle may also be stopped because of erratic driving or if the vehicle matches the description of a vehicle seen at a crime or is coming from the direction of a crime scene.

> Officers may stop motorists who violate traffic laws, who appear to be driving under the influence of alcohol or who they suspect do not have a driver's license or a valid registration for the car.

The stop of a driver who appears to be driving under the influence of alcohol is fraught with hazards for the officer. Kuboviak (1995, p. 81) cautions: "Of all the issues surrounding the legalities of DUI arrests, none is more important than the initial contact made by a police officer with the suspect." He notes:

> Defense attorneys commonly attack the prosecution's case by claiming, through pretrial motions, that the initial stop of the suspect was an illegal seizure under the Fourth Amendment . . .

A good discussion of the investigatory authority contained in the *Terry* doctrine is found in the case of *State v. Whitacre*, 1992. Here, the court found that the officer had justification to stop and question a vehicle's driver based upon the officer's observations that the vehicle was being driven late at night in a rural area and came to a sliding stop behind a stationary car at a stop sign. The vehicle's occupants blew the horn and shouted at the stationary car's driver.

The court stated that the officer could temporarily detain the driver of the vehicle to investigate the officer's suspicion that the driver was drunk. The smell of alcohol upon approaching the vehicle, coupled with the occupant's answers, then gave the officer probable cause for continued investigation. The key to this holding is that the officer had articulable facts upon which he based his decision.

An opposite holding was rendered in *People v. Dionesotes*, 1992, where the court stated that the officer did not have reasonable suspicion to stop a motorist's automobile. The court stated that mere suspicion or hunch on the officer's part is insufficient to justify a *Terry* stop. In this case the motorist was driving at 10 miles per hour in a 35 mile per hour zone. The arresting officer admitted that he was not necessarily "suspicious," but found the behavior to be unusual. The officer was unable to identify a particular "crime or potential crime that prompted him to stop the defendant." The court concluded that behavior alone does not necessarily support the reasonable suspicion to establish the basis for a *Terry* stop. . . .

This legal principle was reiterated recently in *Ohio v. Wireman*, 1993. Here the court stated that: "probable cause to arrest and specific articulable facts required for an investigative stop are two separate, distinct legal burdens which are not interchangeable." The court went on to state that: "Specific and articulable facts, not probable cause, are all that is required for an officer to make a reasonable stop of a motorist in order to investigate a traffic violation."

Officers who stop motorists for traffic violations *can*, for safety, order drivers out of their vehicles. In *Pennsylvania v. Muniz* (1990), the Pennsylvania court held that without any showing that a particular suspect may be armed, an officer may order a person lawfully stopped out of the vehicle to diminish the possibility the driver could make unobserved movements. The court said: "What is at most a mere inconvenience cannot prevail when balanced against legitimate concerns for the officer's safety." If officers have reason to believe a driver may be armed and dangerous, they can legally frisk the driver for weapons.

In addition, if police officers make a stop for a traffic violation and are reasonably suspicious that the situation is dangerous, they not only can order the driver out of the car and frisk him or her, but they also can order any passengers in the car out and frisk them as well (*United States v. Tharpe*, 1976). In addition, if a frisk of at least one occupant of a car is permitted, the police may also check the passenger compartment for weapons (*Michigan v. Long*, 1983).

To fully understand the Terry decision and subsequent cases, look again at the Fourth Amendment and its underlying requirement for stop and frisk: reasonable suspicion.

THE FOURTH AMENDMENT AND STOP AND FRISK

Stop and frisk *are* forms of search and seizure. Although they fall far short of being a full-blown search or arrest, they are, nonetheless, bound by the

Fourth Amendment. As stated in the first half of that amendment, they must be reasonable.

Using the balancing approach, the *Terry* case considered the "competing interests" in the stop-and-frisk situation. On the one hand is the individual's constitutional right to be free from unreasonable searches and seizures. According to the Court: "Even a limited search of the outer clothing for weapons constitutes a severe, though brief, intrusion upon cherished personal security, and it must surely be an annoying, frightening, and perhaps humiliating experience."

On the other hand, however, is the government's duty to detect and prevent crime and to do so without endangering their own lives. The Court noted: "American criminals have a long tradition of armed violence, and every year in this country many law enforcement officers are killed in the line of duty, and thousands more are wounded." If officers reasonably suspect the person they are stopping might be armed and dangerous, they are obligated to pat down for weapons.

The right established in the *Terry* decision to stop and frisk someone based only on articulable reasonable suspicion was confirmed four years later when the Court stated (*Adams v. Williams,* 1972):

> The Fourth Amendment does not require a policeman who lacks the precise level of information necessary for probable cause to arrest to simply shrug his shoulders and allow a crime to occur or a criminal to escape. On the contrary, Terry recognizes that it may be the essence of good police work to adopt an intermediate response. . . . A brief stop of a suspicious individual, in order to determine his identity or to maintain the status quo momentarily while obtaining more information, may be most reasonable in light of the facts known to the officer of the time.

Such facts may be provided by an informant, as in *Adams v. Williams.* In this case, police were informed that Williams had a gun and was carrying drugs. Acting on this tip, a police officer stopped Williams' car and asked him to open the car door. When Williams lowered his car window, the officer reached into the car and retrieved a loaded handgun from Williams's waistband, precisely where the informant said it would be. This protective search for weapons *was* legal.

The facts known to the officer at the time may also be obtained from police in another area. The Supreme Court ruled unanimously on January 8, 1965, that police can act without a warrant to stop and briefly detain someone they know is wanted by police in another city. The stop-and-frisk rules established in *Terry* were further extended in *United States v. Hensley* (1985). In this case police officers stopped a suspect in his car based on information from a "wanted" flyer received from a neighboring police department—a very common situation. The flyer described the crime (an armed robbery) and the suspects wanted for questioning. When the officers approached the car, they saw a revolver sticking out from under the passenger's seat and arrested the driver and the passenger. The Supreme Court ruled that seizure of the handgun was legal, noting that:

> The ability to briefly stop that person, ask questions, or check identification in the absence of probable cause promotes the strong government interest in solving crimes

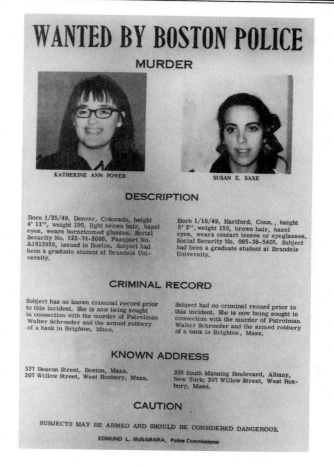

Wanted poster.
(Provided by
UPI/Corbis-Bettmann.)

and bringing offenders to justice. It also held that if a wanted flyer is issued on articulable facts supporting reasonable suspicion that the person wanted has committed an offense, the other police officers can rely on the flyer as a basis for stopping a person answering the description, for checking identification, and for posing questions about the offense, and may detain the person briefly while attempting to obtain further information from the department issuing the flyer.

In addition, the Court stressed the need for law enforcement agencies to cooperate and to communicate rapidly with each other:

In an era when criminal suspects are increasingly mobile and increasingly likely to flee across jurisdictional boundaries, this rule is a matter of common sense; it minimizes the volume of information concerning suspects that must be transmitted to other jurisdictions and enables police in one jurisdiction to act promptly in reliance on information from another jurisdiction.

Bennett and Hess (1994, p. 131) describe California's criteria for a reasonable stop and frisk: (1) furtive movements, (2) inappropriate attire, (3) carrying suspicious objects such as a TV or pillowcase, (4) vague, nonspecific answers to routine questions, (5) refusal to identify oneself and (6) appearing to be out of place.

Any one of the preceding factors may not be sufficient to establish articulable reasonable suspicion, but a combination of two or three along with the officer's experience may be justification for a stop.

Police officers must use discretion as to what is reasonable in a given situation. They are expected to act if they are reasonably suspicious of someone's actions. In a stop-and-frisk-situation, reasonable suspicion is all that is required. A full-blown search or arrest requires more than reasonable suspicion; it requires probable cause.

The severe penalty that the courts impose on police who fail to abide by the spirit of the Fourth Amendment is to declare the evidence they gathered to be inadmissible.

THE EXCLUSIONARY RULE

The role of the United States Constitution is to provide the basic rules that must be followed by the government. There are important consequences if the Constitution is not complied with by government law enforcement agents. The exclusionary rule is one of the best illustrations of common law or "judge-made" law. Simply put, judges have determined that the best way to prevent government officials from violating the constitutional rights of the public is to hit them where it hurts. The Supreme Court encourages the government to play by the rules of the Constitution by excluding from criminal trial proceedings any evidence obtained in violation of the Constitution. It is important to remember, as stressed by Ferdico (1985, p. 138):

> The most important effect of an illegal search or seizure is the exclusion of the evidence obtained from being used in court [at trial] against the person whose rights were violated by the search. . . . application of the exclusionary rule in a particular case will usually result in a lost case for the prosecution and the release of the person charged with the crime. From the law enforcement officer's standpoint, the suppression of crucial evidence[at trial] may represent a total waste of weeks or months of investigation, evidence-gathering and case evaluation. It should be clear, then, that strict compliance with all statutes, court rules, and court decisions dealing with search and seizure procedures is of the utmost importance from the first report of a possible crime through the ultimate disposition of the case.

> Evidence obtained by an illegal search or seizure will be inadmissible in court at trial under the exclusionary rule.

In some instances, however, such evidence may be used within the legal system, for example, at certain sentencing hearings, in civil suits, grand juries or probable cause hearings. It is at the criminal trial hearing that the exclusionary rule is used to prevent government misconduct.

Weeks v. United States

In this case police officers arrested Weeks for transporting lottery tickets through the mail. At the same time other officers made a warrantless search of his home without consent and seized several articles and papers, which they turned over to a United States marshal. Later that day the police and marshal returned and conducted another warrantless search without consent, again seizing papers and letters. Weeks was charged with unlawful use of the mail and convicted, but the conviction was overturned by the Supreme Court because the evidence had been illegally seized by federal government agents and therefore was inadmissible in a federal criminal prosecution. In *Weeks v. United States* (1914), the Court stated:

> If letters and private documents can thus be seized [unconstitutionally] and held and used in evidence against a citizen accused of an offense, the protection of the Fourth Amendment declaring his right to be secure against such searches and seizures is of no value, and, so far as those thus placed are concerned, might as well be stricken from the Constitution. The efforts of the courts and their officials to bring the guilty to punishment, praiseworthy as they are, are not to be aided by the sacrifice of those great principles established by years of endeavors and suffering which have resulted in their embodiment in the fundamental law of the land.

The Bill of Rights, remember, was written to limit the power of the federal government, so initially the exclusionary rule did not apply to the states. As a result, evidence that was illegally obtained at the state level was often admitted at the federal level—figuratively, handed to the federal prosecutor "on a silver platter."

The Exclusionary Rule and the States

When the Fourteenth Amendment was passed, forbidding states to "deprive any person of life, liberty, or property, without due process of law," the question arose whether the exclusionary rule should be applied at the state level. *Wolf v. Colorado* (1949) established that the exclusionary rule was not applicable at the state level. The precedent was followed for more than a decade. Some evidence was excluded for other reasons, however. For example, in *Rochin v. California* (1952) police administered an emetic by force to make a suspect vomit drugs he had swallowed. The Court disallowed the evidence saying that it was obtained by "conduct that shocks the conscience."

Another case disregarding the *Wolf* precedent was *Elkins v. United States* (1960), which disallowed the admission of evidence illegally obtained by state officials into federal trials (the silver platter doctrine): In 1961 the *Wolf* precedent was reversed in *Mapp v. Ohio.*

> ≋ *Mapp v. Ohio* made the exclusionary rule applicable at the state level.

The Supreme Court, overruling *Wolf,* held that "all evidence obtained by searches and seizures in violation of the Constitution are by the same authority inadmissible in a state court." The Court gave the following reasons:

> Since the Fourth Amendment's right of privacy has been declared enforceable against the States through the Due Process Clause of the Fourteenth, it is enforceable against them by the same sanction of exclusion as is used against the Federal Government.

Were it otherwise then just as without the *Weeks* rule the assurance against unreasonable federal searches and seizures would be "a form of words," valueless and undeserving of mention in a perpetual charter of inestimable human liberties, so too, without that rule the freedom from state invasions of privacy would be so ephemeral and so neatly severed from its conceptual nexus with the freedom from all brutish means of coercing evidence as not to merit this Court's high regard as a freedom "implicit in the concept of ordered liberty."

Excluded Evidence

Sloppy government work or inadequate knowledge of the legal rules all too frequently results in judges sustaining defense objections based on a variety of grounds. Whatever the grounds, the result is usually the same: evidence is excluded. Whether it was one crucial piece of evidence (e.g., the murder weapon or the body of the murder victim) or a series of less dramatic, circumstantial evidence obtained by the investigating officer over months, perhaps years, it is always devastating to the prosecution to hear an evidentiary objection sustained.

The case of *Brewer v. Williams* (1977) illustrates what can result from improper police investigation. In this case a crucial admission from the suspect was excluded because it was obtained in violation of the defendant's constitutional rights. The case began on Christmas Eve of 1968 when 10-year-old Pamela Powers disappeared while visiting a YMCA with her family in Des Moines, Iowa. Shortly after she was reported missing, a 14-year-old boy reported having been asked by a YMCA resident to hold several doors open for him while the man loaded a bundle from the building into a car. Within the bundle the boy reported seeing two skinny white legs.

An arrest warrant was subsequently issued for Robert Williams, a YMCA resident and an escapee from a psychiatric hospital. Williams eventually turned himself in to police in Davenport, Iowa. An agreement was reached with Williams' lawyer that the defendant would be returned by police to Des Moines.

All agreed that Williams would not be interrogated in any way during the 160-mile trip. However, during the drive, knowing that Williams was a psychiatric patient and that he possessed a strong religious faith, one officer said the following to Williams (in subsequent legal proceedings this became known as the "Christian Burial Speech"):

I want to give you something to think about while we're traveling down the road. . . . Number one, I want you to observe the weather conditions, it's raining, it's sleeting, it's freezing, driving is very treacherous, visibility is poor, it's going to be dark early this evening. They are predicting several inches of snow for tonight, and I feel that you yourself are the only person that knows where this little girl's body is, that you yourself have only been there once, and if you get a snow on top of it, you yourself may be unable to find it. And since we will be going right past the area on the way to Des Moines, I feel that we could stop and locate the body, that the parents of this little girl should be entitled to a Christian burial for the little girl who was snatched away from them on Christmas Eve and murdered. And I feel we should stop and locate it on the way rather than waiting until morning and trying to come back out after a snow storm and possibly not being able to find it at all.

The detective told Williams that he did not want an answer, but that he just wanted Williams to think about it as they drove. Williams eventually directed the officers to the little girl's body.

While the lower courts admitted Williams' damaging statements into evidence, the Supreme Court affirmed the court of appeals' decision that any statements made by Williams could not be admitted against him because the way they were elicited violated his constitutional rights. Specifically, Williams was unconstitutionally deprived of his right to counsel. The Court said:

> The pressures on state executive and judicial officers charged with the administration of the criminal law are great, especially when the crime is murder and the victim a small child. But it is precisely the predictability of those pressures that makes imperative a resolute loyalty to the guarantees that the Constitution extends to us all.

The dramatic and devastating effect of disallowing evidence is painfully clear from this particular case. Law libraries across our nation are filled with many other examples of why it is critical that police officers understand the law of evidence. (Note: Williams was eventually found guilty, with the evidence admitted for reasons to be discussed shortly.) Whitebread and Slobogin (1986, p. 16) state that:

> The exclusionary evidence rule is the result of an effort on the part of the judiciary to ensure that constitutional limitations on law enforcement are safeguarded. Simply stated, the rule prohibits the use of evidence or testimony obtained by government officials through means violative of the Fourth, Fifth, or Sixth Amendments. The rationale for the rule is that government officials, and in particular, the police, will be deterred from using illegal means to obtain evidence if such evidence may not be employed to support a conviction. A further rationale for the rule . . . is found in the sentiment that the judiciary should not be a partner to or otherwise sanction the lawlessness of a coordinate branch of government.

According to Frase, et al. (1986, p. 1):

> Most motions to exclude evidence in criminal cases are based on alleged violations of the United States Constitution, particularly the Fourth Amendment (unreasonable searches and seizures), Fifth Amendment (privilege against compelled self-incrimination), or Sixth Amendment (right to counsel and right of confrontation). It is also possible to argue that the use of particular evidence would violate due process rights, even if it does not violate a particular provision of the Bill of Rights. Thus, conduct which "shocks the conscience" of the court may be excluded (*Rochin v. California* [1952]), and any evidence—particularly confessions or identification testimony—may be excluded if it is found to be unreliable (*Stovall v. Denno* [1967]).

Underlying Rationale of the Exclusionary Rule

del Carmen (1987, p. 53) asserts: "The exclusionary rule has rested primarily on the judgment that the importance of deterring police conduct that may violate the constitutional rights of individuals throughout the community outweighs the importance of securing the conviction of the specific defendant on trial (*United States v. Caceres*, 1979)."

The purpose of the exclusionary rule is to deter police from obtaining evidence illegally and to make it clear that the court will not tolerate such illegality. This is sometimes referred to as the "judicial integrity" rationale (*Mapp v. Ohio*, 1961). Deterring police from obtaining evidence illegally is seen as one means to help protect specific constitutional rights. LaFave and Israel (1985, p. 105) cite several cases that stress the deterrent intent of the exclusionary rule:

Wolf—"the exclusion of evidence may be an effective way of deterring unreasonable searches."

Elkins—"Its purpose is to deter—to compel respect for the constitutional guarantee in the only effectively available way—by removing the incentive to disregard it."

Mapp—"a deterrent safeguard without insistence upon which the Fourth Amendment would have been reduced to 'a form of words.'"

Linkletter v. Walker (1965)—characterized the rule as "an effective deterrent to illegal police action."

Terry v. Ohio—stressed that the rule's "major thrust is a deterrent one."

The exclusionary rule serves purposes other than deterrence as well. For example, the *Elkins* Court referred to "the imperative of judicial integrity," that is, the courts should not become "accomplices in the willful disobedience of a Constitution they are sworn to uphold." This statement was later relied upon in *Mapp* and *Terry*. In addition to deterrence and preserving judicial integrity, the exclusionary rule also is a means "of assuring the people—all potential victims of unlawful government conduct—that the government would not profit from its lawless behavior, thus minimizing the risk of seriously undermining popular trust in government" (*United States v. Calandra*, 1974).

> The primary purpose underlying the exclusionary rule is deterring government misconduct. It also helps preserve judicial integrity and assures the government does not profit from lawless behavior.

The exclusionary rule is not statutory law, but is a judge-made rule of evidence, as noted in *United States v. Leon* (1984):

The Fourth Amendment contains no provision expressly precluding the use of evidence obtained in violation of its commands. . . . This rule thus operates as a judicially created remedy designed to safeguard Fourth Amendment rights generally through its deterrent effect, rather than a personal constitutional right of the person aggrieved.

The Court has held that constitutional guarantees do *not* apply to action by private citizens. If a private citizen comes by evidence illegally, for example, breaking into someone's home or car to obtain the evidence, the evidence can be used in court. This does not hold true, however, if the citizen was acting under the direction or encouragement of the government.

In *United States v. Jacobsen* (1984) the Court held that even when a private person had opened a package and then resealed it, the government agent could expose to view that which had previously been observed by the private person without it constituting an illegal search.

FRUIT OF THE POISONOUS TREE

The exclusionary rule may affect specific illegally obtained evidence as well as any other evidence obtained as a result of the originally illegally obtained evidence. Such evidence is referred to as **fruit of the poisonous tree.**

The precedent case for this extension of the exclusionary rule is *Silverthorne Lumber Co. v. United States* (1920). In this case a United States marshal unlawfully entered and searched the Silverthorne Lumber Company's offices and illegally took some books and documents. When the company demanded their return, the government did so, but not before making copies of the documents. These copies were later impounded by the district court and became the basis for a grand jury indictment. A subpoena was then served on the company to produce the originals. When the company refused, it was convicted of contempt of court. The Supreme Court, however, reversed the conviction saying: "[T]he essence of a provision forbidding the acquisition of evidence in a certain way is that not merely evidence so acquired shall not be used before the Court but that it shall not be used at all." In other words, once the primary source (the "tree") is proven to have been obtained unlawfully, any secondary evidence derived from it (the "fruit") is also inadmissible.

> The fruit of the poisonous tree doctrine states that evidence obtained as a result of an earlier illegality must be excluded from trial.

This extension of the exclusionary rule is based on the same rationale as the exclusionary rule itself, that is, to deter illegal police activity and to preserve the integrity of the court.

The Supreme Court ruled, however, that the doctrine does not apply in civil deportation proceedings or in grand jury proceedings. In *United States v. Calandra* (1974) the Court ruled that "fruits of illegally seized evidence" can be used as a basis for questions to a witness before a grand jury. In addition, some lower courts have allowed such evidence to be used in sentencing and in probation or parole revocation hearings.

EXCEPTIONS TO THE RULE

The exclusionary rule applies only in criminal trials in cases in which a constitutional right has been violated. Several important exceptions to the exclusionary rule exist.

> Among the exceptions to the exclusionary rule are existence of a valid independent source, the inevitable discovery doctrine, attenuation, harmless error and good faith.

Valid Independent Source

If similar evidence is obtained from a valid, independent source, that evidence can be admitted. In *Segura v. United States* (1984), although evidence discovered during an illegal entry into an apartment was excluded, evidence later found in the apartment while executing a warranted search was admissible *because* the warrant was obtained with information totally unconnected with the illegal entry.

The Inevitable Discovery Doctrine

This exception was established in *Nix v. Williams* (1984), the case referred to earlier, in which Detective Nix's well-known "Christian Burial Speech" caused Williams to disclose where he had hidden his victim's body. The rationale underlying the exception was that the body would "inevitably" have been discovered, even without Williams' assistance. This has also been called the "hypothetical independent source exception" because, given time, an independent source would emerge with the same evidence. In the Nix case, the Supreme Court upheld Williams' conviction.

Attenuation

Attenuation is another exception to the exclusionary rule. The word *attenuate* means "to make thin." Sometimes the link between the original illegal evidence and the related evidence is so weak that the evidence is allowed in court. As noted by Whitebread and Slobogin (1986, p. 38): "[T]he weaker the link between the initial unlawful conduct and the subsequent lawful discovery of evidence that results from the initial conduct, the less likely the poisonous tree doctrine will be invoked" (*Wong Sun v. United States,* 1963).

Harmless Error

The **harmless error** exception refers to instances in which the preponderance of evidence suggests the defendant's guilt and the "tainted" or illegal evidence is not critical to proving the case against the defendant. In *Harrington v. California* (1969) the Court ruled that the evidence should be examined as a whole, and that if overwhelming untainted evidence supported the conviction, or if the error involved a well-established element of the crime, then the error would be considered "harmless."

In *Arizona v. Fulminante* (1991) the Court ruled that the harmless error doctrine does apply to cases involving admissibility of involuntary confessions. In this case Fulminante was accused of murdering his stepdaughter, but it could not be proven. While he was in prison on an unrelated charge, he became friends with another inmate, Sarivola, who later became a paid FBI informant. Sarivola told Fulminante that Fulminante was getting hostile treatment from the other inmates because rumor had it that Fulminante was a child killer. He suggested that if Fulminante would tell him the truth, he would protect him. Fulminante confessed to him. At trial, the defense sought to suppress the confession on the grounds that it was coerced. The Court agreed. The prosecution then sought to have it admitted under the harmless error doctrine, but the Court ruled that it was *not* a harmless error because the confession was likely to contribute to his conviction. The confession was not admitted.

Good Faith

The **good faith** exception involves instances in which police officers are not aware that they are violating Fourth Amendment principles. In a dissenting opinion in *Stone v. Powell* (1976), Justice White argued that the exclusionary rule should not disqualify evidence "seized by an officer acting in the good-faith belief that his conduct comported with existing law. . . . Excluding the evidence can in no way affect his future conduct unless it is to make him less willing to do his duty."

United States v. Leon (1984) and *Massachusetts v. Sheppard* (1984), two cases decided on the same day, are, according to del Carmen and Walker (1995, p. 23): "arguably the most important cases decided on the exclusionary rule since *Mapp v. Ohio* (1961). They represent a significant, although narrow, exception to that doctrine." They explain:

> In these two cases, the Court said that there were objectively reasonable grounds for the officers' mistaken belief that the warrants authorized the searches. . . . The cases are similar . . . in that the mistakes were made by judges, not the police. The Court said that the evidence in both cases was admissible because the judge, not the police, erred and the exclusionary rule is designed to control the conduct of the police, not the conduct of judges.

Note, however, that *Leon* and *Sheppard* establish a good faith exception only if a warrant has been obtained. The onus is then on the magistrate, not the officer.

More recently, the Court in *Arizona v. Evans* (1995) continued the trend to broaden instances when objective good faith on the part of a police officer will save a constitutionally defective search.

The good faith exception often comes into play when the government is executing arrest or search warrants. If such warrants are later found to be invalid, perhaps because of a typographical error citing the wrong address or apartment number, the evidence obtained while executing the warrants is still admissible because the officers were acting in "good faith."

In *United States v. Leon* (1984) the Supreme Court specifically addressed the issue of whether the exclusionary rule should be modified so that evidence obtained by an officer with a warrant that was later found to not be based on sufficient probable cause could still be used in court against the defendant at trial. Because there is no police misconduct, which is what the exclusionary rule seeks to discourage, when an officer lawfully executes a warrant, the possibility that the warrant itself was issued without sufficient probable cause should not withhold valuable evidence from the trial.

The *Leon* case held that the exclusionary rule would be applied to only the following three situations in searches conducted pursuant to a warrant:

❖ The magistrate abandoned the prescribed detached and neutral role in issuing the warrant.

❖ The officers were dishonest or reckless in preparing their affidavit or the search warrant.

❖ The officers could not have harbored an objectively reasonable belief in the existence of probable cause.

Remember that the purpose of having a detached, neutral magistrate is to remove from the police the responsibility of determining probable cause. Obviously, if the police are acting in good faith on the validity of the warrant (which directs an officer to carry out the warrant), the motivation of the exclusionary rule no longer applies because it is not serving to prevent police misconduct.

While the Leon case is limited to searches pursuant to a warrant, the case of *Illinois v. Rodriguez* (1990) took this concept a step further by not invoking the exclusionary rule to a search based on an officer's reasonable, albeit mistaken, belief that a third party actually had authority to consent to a search.

What frequently occurs in judicial interpretation is that a court may not want the result that will occur if a direct, literal interpretation of a law is used. Therefore, rationales are stretched (sometimes to their breaking point) so as to permit the finding the court wants. In this instance, the United States Supreme Court appears to be chipping away at the exclusionary rule, and the pendulum seems to be swinging, although slowly, toward favoring the prosecution.

> ⤳ The exclusionary rule is a judge-made doctrine to enforce constitutional requirements of search and seizure: *If* search/seizure violates suspect's constitutional rights, *then* the resulting evidence may not be admitted into criminal court during trial to be used against that suspect *nor* can any evidence resulting indirectly from the unconstitutional search/seizure (fruit of the poisonous tree) *unless* the evidence would inevitably have been discovered through lawful means *or* the good faith exception allowed an error by police.

If police officers search and seize evidence legally, it will be admitted during any trial that results.

Summary

The Fourth Amendment forbids unreasonable searches and seizures and requires that any search or arrest warrant be based on probable cause. *Reasonable* means sensible, rational, justifiable. Probable cause to search means it is more likely than not that the items sought are where the officers believe them to be. Probable cause to arrest means that it is more likely than not that a crime has been committed by the person whom a law enforcement officer seeks to arrest. All warrants are to be based on probable cause.

The Fourth Amendment restricts only government agencies and their personnel. If a person is an employee of any government agency or is an agent of the government in any capacity, that person is bound by the United States

Constitution and the Fourth Amendment. In this way, freedom is assured by restricting government's power. The Fourth Amendment does not apply to private parties.

Basic to an understanding of lawful search and seizure is the law of stop and frisk, which deals with that time frame during which officers follow up on their suspicions, but before the time that the requisite probable cause is established to justify an arrest (*Terry v. Ohio*, 1968).

The *Terry* decision established that police officers who have reasonable suspicion that someone is about to commit a crime may stop the person and possibly frisk them for weapons. A stop is a brief detention of a person based on specific and articulable facts for the purpose of investigating suspicious activity. A frisk is a reasonable search for weapons to protect the government agent and others. *Terry* established that the authority to stop and frisk is independent of the power to arrest. A stop is not an arrest, but is a seizure within the meaning of the Fourth Amendment and therefore requires reasonableness.

Officers may stop motorists who violate traffic laws, who appear to be driving under the influence of alcohol or who they suspect do not have a driver's license or a valid registration for the car.

The courts assure compliance with the Fourth Amendment (and the entire Bill of Rights) by means of the exclusionary rule, which states that evidence obtained by an illegal search or seizure will be inadmissible in court during a criminal trial, with the precedent federal case being *Weeks v. United States* (1914). *Mapp v. Ohio* made the exclusionary rule applicable at the state level. The primary purpose underlying the exclusionary rule is deterring government misconduct. It also helps preserve judicial integrity and assures the government does not profit from lawless behavior.

An extension of the exclusionary rule is the fruit of the poisonous tree doctrine, which states that evidence obtained as a result of an earlier illegality must be excluded from trial.

Among the exceptions to the exclusionary rule are existence of a valid independent source, the inevitable discovery doctrine, attenuation, harmless error and good faith.

Discussion Questions

1. Explain why the Fourth Amendment applies to the federal government and also to state government.
2. Explain the meaning of search and seizure.
3. What is a stop? How does it differ from an arrest?
4. What is a frisk? How does it differ from a search?
5. Given one incident, at what point would a "stop and frisk" develop into a "search and seizure"?
6. What restrictions does the Fourth Amendment put on private security guards working at a department store?
7. In what ways can government agents be discouraged from violating the Fourth Amendment?
8. Is it fair that a case be thrown out of court because the one piece of evidence that would surely prove the defendant was guilty was not admitted just because of a police error in obtaining it?

9. To protect the public, can government ever really go "too far"?

10. Why should a government agent try to get a warrant whenever possible?

References

Bennett, Wayne W. and Kären M. Hess. *Criminal Investigation.* 4th ed. St. Paul: West Publishing Company, 1994.

Carr, James G. *Criminal Procedure Handbook.* Clark, Boardman, Callaghan, 1995.

Creamer, J. Shane. *The Law of Arrest, Search, and Seizure.* 3rd ed. New York: Holt, Rinehart & Winston, 1980.

del Carmen, Rolando V. *Criminal Procedures for Law Enforcement Personnel.* Monterey: Brooks/Cole Publishing Company, 1987.

del Carmen, Rolando V. and Jeffery T. Walker. *Briefs of Leading Cases in Law Enforcement.* 2nd ed. Cincinnati: Anderson Publishing Company, 1995.

Ferdico, John N. *Criminal Procedure for the Criminal Justice Professional.* 6th ed. St. Paul: West Publishing Company, 1986.

Frase, Richard S., Phebe Haugen and Martin J. Costello. *Minnesota Misdemeanors on Moving Traffic Violations.* St. Paul: Butterworth Legal Publishers, 1986.

Kuboviak, James. "Reasonable Suspicion: The Message of *Terry v. Ohio.*" *Law and Order.* March 1995, pp. 81–86.

LaFave, Wayne R. and Jerold Israel. *Criminal Procedure.* St. Paul: West Publishing Company, 1985.

Oran, Daniel. *Law Dictionary for Nonlawyers.* 2nd ed. St. Paul: West Publishing Company, 1985.

Samaha, Joel. *Criminal Procedure.* 3rd ed. St. Paul: West Publishing Company, 1996.

Walker, Jayne S. "Applying an Understanding of the Fourth Amendment." *The Police Chief.* July 1995, pp. 44–47.

Whitebread, Charles H. and Christopher Slobogin. *Criminal Procedure. An Analysis of Cases and Concepts.* 2nd ed. Mineola, NY: The Foundation Press, Inc., 1986.

Woods, Everett K. and Donald H. Wallace. "Investigating Arson: Coping with Constitutional Constraints." *Security Management.* November 1991, pp. 80–84.

Wrobleski, Henry M. and Kären M. Hess. *Introduction to Law Enforcement and Criminal Justice.* 5th ed. St. Paul: West Publishing Company, 1997.

Cases Cited

Adams v. Williams, 407 U.S. 143, 92 S.Ct. 1921, 32 L.Ed.2d 612 (1972).

Aguilar v. Texas, 378 U.S. 108, 84 S.Ct. 1509, 12 L.Ed.2d 723 (1964).

Alabama v. White, 496 U.S. 325, 110 S.Ct. 2412, 110 L.Ed.2d 301 (1990).

Arizona v. Evans, 56 CrL 2173 (1995).

Arizona v. Fulminante, 499 U.S. 279, 111 S.Ct. 1246, 113 L.Ed.2d 302 (1991).

Brewer v. Williams, 430 U.S. 387, 97 S.Ct. 1232, 51 L.Ed.2d 424 (1977).

Brinegar v. United States, 338 U.S. 160, 69 S.Ct. 1302, 93 L.Ed. 1879 (1948).

Delaware v. Prouse, 440 U.S. 648, 99 S.Ct. 1391, 59 L.Ed.2d 660 (1979).

Elkins v. United States, 364 U.S. 206, 80 S.Ct. 1437, 4 L.Ed.2d 1669 (1960).

Florida v. Bostick, 501 U.S. 429, 111 S.Ct. 2382, 115 L.Ed.2d 389 (1991).

Florida v. Royer, 460 U.S. 491, 103 S.Ct. 1319, 75 L.Ed.2d 229 (1983).

Harrington v. California, 395 U.S. 250, 89 S.Ct. 1726, 23 L.Ed.2d 284 (1969).

Illinois v. Gates, 462 U.S. 213, 103 S.Ct. 2317, 76 L.Ed.2d 527 (1983).

Illinois v. Rodriguez, 497 U.S. 177, 110 S.Ct. 2793, 111 L.Ed.2d 148 (1990).

Katz v. United States, 389 U.S. 347 (1967).

Linkletter v. Walker, 381 U.S. 618, 85 S. Ct. 1731, 14 L. Ed. 2d 601 (1965).

Mapp v. Ohio, 367 U.S. 643, 81 S.Ct. 1684, 6 L.Ed.2d 1081 (1961).

Marshall v. Barlow's Inc., 436 U.S. 307, 98 S.Ct. 1816 (1978).

Massachusetts v. Sheppard, 468 U.S. 981, 104 S.Ct. 3424, 82 L.Ed.2d 737 (1984).

Michigan v. Clifford (1984).

Michigan v. Long, 463 U.S. 1032, 103 S.Ct. 3469, 77 L.Ed.2d 1201 (1983).

Minnesota v. Dickerson, 508 U.S. 366, 113 S.Ct. 2130, 124 L.Ed.2d 334 (1993).

Nix v. Williams, 467 U.S. 431, 104 S.Ct. 2501, 81 L.Ed.2d 377 (1984).

Ohio v. Wireman (1993).

Pennsylvania v. Muniz, 496 U.S. 582, 110 S.Ct. 2638, 110 L.Ed.2d 528 (1990).

People v. Dionesotes, 235 Ill.App.3d 967, 177 Ill.Dec. 377, 603 N.E.2d 118 (2 Dist. 1992).

Rochin v. California, 342 U.S. 165, 72 S.Ct. 205, 96 L.Ed. 183 (1952).

Segura v. United States, 468 U.S. 796, 104 S.Ct. 3380, 82 L.Ed.2d 599 (1984).

Silverthorne Lumber Co. v. United States, 251 U.S. 385, 40 S.Ct. 182, 64 L.Ed. 319 (1920).

Smith v. United States, 337 U.S. 137, 695 S.Ct. 1000, 93 L.Ed. 1264 (1949).

Spinelli v. United States, 393 U.S. 410, 89 S.Ct. 584, 21 L.Ed.2d 637 (1969).

State v. Whitacre, 62 Ohio Misc.2d 495, 601 N.E.2d 691 (1992).

Stone v. Powell, 428 U.S. 465, 96 S.Ct. 3037, 49 L.Ed.2d 1067 (1976).

Stovall v. Denno, 388 U.S. 293, 87 S.Ct. 1967, 18 L.Ed.2d 1199 (1967).

Terry v. Ohio, 392 U.S. 1, 88 S.Ct. 1868, 20 L.Ed.2d 889 (1968).

United States v. Biswell, 406 U.S. 311, 92 S.Ct. 1593, 32 L.Ed. 2d 87 (1972).

United States v. Caceres, 440 U.S. 741, 99 S.Ct. 1465, 59 L.Ed.2d 733 (1979).

United States v. Calandra, 414 U.S. 338, 94 S.Ct. 613, 38 L.Ed.2d 561 (1974).

United States v. Claveland, 38 F.3d 1092 (9th Cir., 1994).

United States v. Hensley, 469 U.S. 221, 105 S.Ct. 675, 83 L.Ed.2d 604 (1985).

United States v. Jacobsen, 466 U.S. 109, 104 S.Ct. 1652, 80 L.Ed.2d 85 (1984).

United States v. Leon, 468 U.S. 897, 104 S.Ct. 3405, 82 L.Ed.2d 677 (1984).

United States v. Mendenhall, 446 U.S. 544, 100 S.Ct. 1870, 64 L.Ed.2d 497 (1980).

United States v. Parker, 32 F.3d 395 (8th Cir., 1994).

United States v. Ross, 456 U.S. 798, 102 S.Ct. 2157, 72 L.Ed.2d 572 (1982).

United States v. Sharpe, 470 U.S. 675, 105 S.Ct. 1568, 84 L.Ed.2d 605 (1985).

United States v. Sokolow, 490 U.S. 1, 109 S.Ct. 1581, 104 L.Ed.2d 1 (1989).

United States v. Tharpe, 536 F.2d 1098 (1976).

Weeks v. United States, 232 U.S. 383, 34 S.Ct. 341, 58 L.Ed. 652 (1914).

Wolf v. Colorado, 338 U.S. 25, 69 S.Ct. 1359, 93 L.Ed. 1782 (1949).

Wong Sun v. United States, 371 U.S. 471, 83 S.Ct. 407, 9 L.Ed.2d 441 (1963).

Chapter 10 **Conducting Constitutional Searches**

It is
unreasonable for
a police officer
to look for an
elephant in a
matchbox.

—LEGAL MAXIM

Police officers search a car.

DO YOU KNOW . . .

Why warrantless searches are presumed unreasonable?

What limitations are placed on searches with a warrant? Incident to an arrest? With consent? In a frisk?

What exceptions to the warrant requirement have been established?

What the plain view doctrine is?

How the search in a frisk is limited?

When a vehicle can be legally searched and the precedent case?

What constitutes an exigent circumstance?

How reasonable expectation of privacy relates to searches, frisks and the Fourth Amendment?

How searches at international borders and airports are viewed under the Fourth Amendment?

If electronic surveillance is governed by the Fourth Amendment?

What is required to obtain an electronic surveillance warrant?

What relationship exists between electronic surveillance and one's reasonable expectations of privacy?

What limitation is placed on *all* searches? When general searches are legal?

CAN YOU DEFINE THESE TERMS?

Contraband
Curtilage
Exigent
Plain feel
Plain view
Standing
Voluntariness test
Waiver test

INTRODUCTION

Recall that Fourth Amendment case law makes the presumption that *all* warrantless searches are unreasonable and, therefore, violative of the Constitution. This general assumption begins an analysis of Fourth Amendment search and seizure issues, but the Supreme Court has created a number of exceptions to the warrant requirement. Recall also that the Fourth Amendment is applicable to state and local government via the due process clause of the Fourteenth Amendment.

This chapter begins with the requirements for a search with a warrant. This is followed by discussions of exceptions to this requirement, including searches incident to lawful arrest, consent searches, evidence in plain view, stop and frisk, the automobile exception, exigent circumstances and the open field rule. The chapter concludes with an examination of how the Fourth Amendment affects electronic surveillance and other data gathering, an important form of search and seizure.

If evidence seized by the government is to be admissible in court, it must be legally seized; that is, it must have been obtained according to the constitutional requirements developed over the years as the legal system has struggled to determine what is and is not *reasonable* under the Fourth Amendment. A logical beginning point in any search and seizure analysis is to assume that a valid search warrant is the best way to obtain evidence that will find its way into a courtroom.

SEARCHES WITH A WARRANT

The Fourth Amendment requires that all searches conducted with a warrant be "based upon probable cause supported by oath and affirmation, and particularly describing the place to be searched and the persons or things to be seized."

The framers of the Constitution no doubt chose those words very carefully to prohibit the general searches they found so abhorrent under British rule. Although they recognized that the government would have a legitimate interest in enforcing law, including executing searches, they limited the scope of any search to only what was necessary, thus balancing the needs of society with those of the individual.

> The Fourth Amendment requires that searches conducted under authority of a search warrant be based on probable cause. Searches with a warrant are presumed to be reasonable.

The terms *probable cause* and *reasonable* have been the basis for many court decisions and remain a viable point of argument in criminal cases. The Constitution was written in general terms to permit the societies it would continue serving to determine what they consider reasonable, rather than creating a cast-in-stone definition. Such foresight enables this body of law to change along with those it serves; this is why it is called a *living law*.

Even the courts have struggled with definitions. They, too, desire to keep the door open for interpretation case by case rather than attempting to fit each case into a specific box. The guidelines provided through court opinions do not provide any more precise definitions of these terms. In *United States v. Riemer, D.C. Ohio probable cause* was defined as having more evidence for than against, or a set or probabilities grounded in the factual and practical considerations that govern the decisions of reasonable and prudent persons and is more than mere suspicion but less than the quantum of evidence required for conviction.

The term *reasonable* was defined in *Cass v. State* as that which is fair, proper, just, moderate, suitable under the circumstances, fit and appropriate to the end in view, having the faculty of reason, rational, governed by reason not immoderate or excessive, honest, equitable, tolerable.

Again, it is not the Constitution that is difficult to understand. It simply sets forth an organized government with limited powers. The efforts to *interpret* the Constitution in the context of the adversial process is what makes it seem confusing. Unlike the study of mathematics, the study of the Constitution yields few precise answers. What it does provide is a foundation on which interpretations are encouraged. And an understanding of key terms such as *probable cause* and *reasonable* are often at the heart of the interpretation.

The following simplified definitions are a compilation of previous court assertions:

❖ *Probable cause*—that which would lead a reasonable person to believe something.
❖ *Reasonable*—that which a rational person would determine to be sensible or fair by current social standards.

Probable cause is the key issue in whether a magistrate will grant officers a search warrant. Once the officers have obtained their search warrant and gained entrance, they can search only areas where it is reasonable to believe the specified items might be found.

> Searches conducted with a search warrant must be limited to the specific area and specific items described in the warrant.

Sometimes, however, government agents come across items not named in the warrant but similar to the items described. For example, officers were searching for property stolen in a burglary of an electronics store, and the warrant specified television sets, VCRs and stereos. When the officers executed the warrant, they came across a room filled with television sets, VCRs, stereos and videocameras. They could seize the videocameras as evidence, even though they were not specified in the warrant, because they were similar to the other items.

The government can also seize any **contraband** or other evidence of a crime they find during a search with a warrant, even though it was not specified. One reviewer of this text uses this definition: "Contraband is anything that advertises its own illegality." Contraband does not need to be described in the search warrant, and the lawful discovery of additional evidence could lead to additional charges. Contraband includes anything that is illegal for people to own or have in their possession, such as illegal drugs or illegal weapons. The contraband does not need to be related to the crime described in the search warrant. This is discussed further under the plain view doctrine.

In striving to limit government power, the Fourth Amendment begins with the assumption that searches should be conducted with a warrant. Subsequent decisions by the Court have developed legitimate exceptions to this general warrant requirement, but law enforcement usually prefers a search with a warrant to one without, simply because the burden is on the government agent to articulate probable cause in a warrantless search, whereas a magistrate declares within a warrant that probable cause has already been judicially acknowledged. When possible the government should obtain a search warrant. Our high-tech age is making this much easier. Car phones, for instance, can make obtaining warrants almost instantaneous.

SEARCHES WITHOUT A WARRANT

The Fourth Amendment prefers a warrant because it necessitates judicial review of government action. Therefore, the presumption exists that a warrantless search is unreasonable, thus unlawful, with the resulting evidence not permitted in court. But reasonableness itself dictates that government action may become necessary before getting a warrant signed by a judge. Such practical matters as time, emergency circumstances or the probable destruction of evidence or escape of a criminal have resulted in legitimate exceptions being made to the general requirement of a warrant. Through the development of case law, the Supreme Court has defined the following searches without a warrant to be reasonable under the Fourth Amendment guidelines.

 Exceptions to the warrant requirement include:

- ❖ Search incident to a lawful arrest.
- ❖ Consent search.
- ❖ Plain view evidence.
- ❖ Stop and frisk.
- ❖ Automobile exceptions.
- ❖ Exigent (emergency) circumstances.
- ❖ Open fields, abandoned property and public places.

Because the preceding have been recognized as lawful exceptions to the warrant requirement, evidence obtained in these circumstances is admissible in court (*Marshall v. Barlow's Inc.*, 1978; *Michigan v. Tucker*, 1974).

Searches Incident to Lawful Arrest

Once a person has lawfully been taken into custody by a police officer, our law recognizes the necessity of permitting a complete search. First, officer safety requires that any weapon on or near the defendant be located. Second, any evidence or other contraband should be recovered.

Assume during this discussion that all arrests are legal; if not, the exclusionary rule would prevent any evidence obtained during the search from being used in court. If an arrest is legal, what kind of search can be conducted? The precedent case is *Chimel v. California* (1969) in which police had an arrest warrant for Ted Chimel before they thoroughly searched his home. But the evidence found during the search was declared inadmissible. The Court said:

> When an arrest is made, it is reasonable for the arresting officer to search the person arrested to remove any weapons that the latter might seek to use to resist arrest or effect an escape.

It is entirely reasonable for the arresting officer to search for and seize any evidence on the arrestee's person in order to prevent its concealment or destruction and the area from within which the arrestee might gain possession of a weapon or destructible evidence.

The key phrases in this statement are *the arrestee's person* and *the area from within which the arrestee might gain possession.* The Court described this as *within the person's immediate control*—meaning within the person's reach (also defined as the person's "wing span"). The fact that the suspect is handcuffed does *not* restrict the scope of the search. The area remains as if the suspect was not handcuffed because it is reasonable to believe the suspect could access a weapon or hidden contraband that had been within reach.

> ➥ Searches following an arrest must be immediate and must be limited to the area within the person's reach *(Chimel).*

After the *Chimel* decision, courts generally insisted that officers making a search incidental to an arrest have a definite idea of what they were searching for, as is required by a search warrant. This knowledge should dictate the scope of the search.

In 1973, however, the Supreme Court expanded the scope of searches allowed following arrests in *United States v. Robinson.* The case involved a full-scale search of an individual arrested for a moving traffic violation. The officer inspected the contents of a cigarette package found on Robinson and discovered illegal drugs. The drugs were admitted as evidence, with the Court stating:

> It is the fact of the lawful arrest which establishes the authority to search, and we hold that in the case of a lawful custodial arrest a search of the person is not only an exception to the warrant requirement of the Fourth Amendment, but is also a "reasonable" search under that Amendment.
>
> Not all states follow this ruling, however. The Hawaiian Supreme Court, for example, limits the warrantless search following a custodial arrest to disarming the person if the officers believe him to be dangerous and searching for evidence related to the crime for which the person was arrested (*State v. Kaluna,* 1974).

Also note that in 1977 the Supreme Court severely limited the searching of luggage, briefcases or other personal property seized during an arrest. In *United States v. Chadwick* (1977) the Court said:

> Warrantless searches of luggage or other property seized at the time of an arrest cannot be justified as incident to that arrest either if the search is remote in time or place from the arrest or no exigency exists. Once law enforcement officers have reduced luggage or other personal property not immediately associated with the person of the arrestee, to their exclusive control, and there is no longer any danger that the arrestee might gain access to the property to seize a weapon or destroy evidence, a search of that property is no longer an incident of the arrest.

Cases dealing with search warrant issues have also assessed what actions *during* the execution of a warrant are acceptable. *Michigan v. Summers* (1981) established that a search with a warrant includes limited authority to detain the occupants of the premises during the search. *Illinois v. Lafayette* (1983) established that police can search the personal effects of a person under lawful arrest if it is standard procedure during booking and jailing. *Maryland v. Buie* (1990) allowed a limited sweep by the officers during an arrest in a home for the safety of the officers (to determine if anyone else was present). The Court held:

> The Fourth Amendment permits a properly limited protective sweep in conjunction with an in-home arrest when the searching officer possesses a reasonable belief based on specific and articulable facts that the area to be swept harbors an individual posing a danger to those on the arrest scene. . . .
>
> We should emphasize that such a protective sweep, aimed at protecting the arresting officers, if justified by the circumstances, is nevertheless not a full search of the premises, but may extend only to cursory inspection of those spaces where a person may be found.

USE OF FORCE IN SEARCHING AN ARRESTED PERSON   When government agents search a person incident to arrest, they may use as much force as reasonably necessary to protect themselves as well as to prevent escape or the destruction or concealment of evidence.

SEARCHING PEOPLE OTHER THAN THE ARRESTED PERSON   The Court has ruled that if an arrested person is with other people, officers can reasonably search them for weapons as well. In *United States v. Vigo* (1973), for example, officers arrested a man in the company of a woman. The officers searched the woman's purse. The Court said the search was reasonable because a purse can easily hide a weapon. It would not be reasonable, however, without other justification to search anyone not named in a search warrant if no one was actually arrested. To do so would require that they be named in the search warrant.

SEARCHING THE VEHICLE OF AN ARRESTED PERSON   The landmark case for the warrantless search of a vehicle incident to an arrest is *New York v. Belton* (1981). In this case the Supreme Court said:

> When a policeman has made a lawful custodial arrest of the occupant of an automobile, he may, as a contemporaneous incident of that arrest, search the passenger compartment of that automobile.
>
> It follows from this conclusion that the police may also examine the contents of any containers found within the passenger compartment, for if the passenger compartment is within reach of the arrestee, so also will containers in it be within his reach.

Searches with Consent

As noted by Samaha (1996, p. 243): "Consent searches definitely make the job of law enforcement easier because consent searches require neither warrants nor probable cause." He suggests that consent searches are usually sought for two reasons: convenience, to save time; or necessity, when no probable cause exists.

Government agents may conduct a search without a warrant if they are given permission by someone who has the authority to do so. Ted Chimel could have given the officers permission to search his home, but he did not. Usually the only person who can give consent is the person whose constitutional rights might be threatened by a search. This person is said to have **standing,** that is, the right to object to the unreasonableness of a search because of a reasonable expectation of privacy. Fourth Amendment rights are private and may not be raised on behalf of someone else or in some abstract, theoretical way. Standing, in constitutional law, must involve a case or controversy. As noted by Zalman and Siegel (1996, p. 73): "[T]here must be a real conflict between the parties and each party must have a real stake in the outcome of the case."

Consent to search an individual must be given by that individual. Consent to search any property must be given by the actual owner or, as set forth in *United States v. Matlock* (1974), by a person in charge of that building. If more than one person owns or occupies a building, only one needs to give permission. Thus, if two people share an apartment, all that is required is the consent from one of them (*Wright v. United States,* 1938).

In some instances, someone else can give a valid consent. For example, in *United States v. Matlock* (1974) the Supreme Court held that if a third party has common authority over the premises of items to be searched, this individual could provide government officials with a valid consent. According to Ferdico (1996, pp. 344–349), other individuals who may give consent include the following:

Host—Guest—The host or primary occupant of the premises may give a valid consent to search of the premises and any evidence found would be admissible against the guest.

Employer—Employee—In general, an employer may consent to a search of any part of the employer's premises that is used by an employee (e.g., employees' lockers can be searched with the employer's consent).

Parent—Child—A parent's consent to search premises owned by the parent will usually be effective against a child who lives on those premises. A parent may not consent to a search of an area of the parent's home occupied by the child, however, if the child uses the room exclusively, has sectioned it off, has furnished it with his own furniture, pays rent, or otherwise establishes an expectation of privacy.

Husband—Wife—If two individuals such as husband and wife have equal rights to occupying and using premises, either may give consent to a search.

The Supreme Court held in *New Jersey v. T.L.O.* (1985) that in a *public* school, education officials may search a student (including purses, backpacks or other containers) or student lockers without a warrant or probable cause if there is reasonable justification to suspect contraband exists at the point to be searched. The justification here is the responsibility of public school officials to maintain a safe environment for students. This would not apply to adult students, dorm rooms or in private schools. Remember that the Constitution applies to *government* officials, which public school personnel are, and not to private school officials.

Ferdico cites several instances of when individuals cannot give consent:

> Landlord—Tenant—A landlord has no implied authority to consent to a search of a tenant's premises or a seizure of the tenant's property during the period of the tenancy.
>
> Hotel Employee—Hotel Guest—The U.S. Supreme Court held that the principles governing a landlord's consent to a search of tenant's premises apply with equal force to consent searches of hotel (and motel) rooms allowed by hotel employees. [Only the hotel guest can give consent.]

The consent must be free and voluntary. The Supreme Court ruling in *State v. Barlow, Jr.* (1974) stated: "It is a well established rule in the federal courts that a consent search is unreasonable under the Fourth Amendment if the consent was induced by deceit, trickery, or misrepresentation of the officials making the search."

The request for permission to search must not be stated in a threatening way. It must not imply that anyone who doesn't give consent will be considered as having something to hide. No display of weapons or force should accompany a request to search. In *Weeds v. United States* (1921) police confronted the defendant with drawn guns and a riot gun and said they would get a warrant if they needed. The Court said consent given under these conditions was *not* free and voluntary. Likewise, in *People v. Loria* (1961) the police threatened to kick down the door of the defendant's apartment if he did not let them in. The court said consent was *not* free and voluntary.

Usually, the government should not request to search at night. In *Monroe v. Pape* (1961) Justice Frankfurter stated: "Modern totalitarianisms have been a stark reminder, but did not newly teach, that the kicked-in door is the symbol of a rule of fear and violence fatal to institutions founded on respect for the integrity of man. . . . Searches of the dwelling houses were the special object of this universal condemnation of officer intrusion. Nighttime search was the evil in its most obnoxious form." Again, unusual circumstances may require such a search.

Florida v. Jimeno (1991) held that consent can justify a warrantless search of a container in a car if it is reasonable for the police to believe the suspect's consent includes allowing them to open closed containers. This analysis uses the "reasonableness" line of argument, and as discussed, what one person considers reasonable may not be how another would interpret it. In a case such as *Jimeno*, it was determined that if a person gives consent to search a car, consent is being provided to search everything therein unless specifically restricted.

If the request to search is granted, it must be limited to the area specified by the person granting the permission. The consent may be limited or withdrawn at any time. Herein lies an important reason that a search with a warrant is much better for the officer than merely relying on consent.

> ➤ Consent to search must be voluntary. The search must be limited to the area specified by the person granting the permission. The person may revoke the consent at any time.

Samaha (1996, p. 244) explains that courts typically justify the consent exception by two separate theories:

> Some courts use a **voluntariness test,** based on the idea that a search following consent obtained without coercion or promises to secure it does not violate the Fourth Amendment [it is reasonable]. Others adopt a **waiver test,** based on the theory that citizens may waive their Fourth Amendment rights, but only if they do so voluntarily and intentionally. [bold added]

The voluntariness test considers the totality of circumstances involving the consent to determine if the consent was given freely and truly voluntarily. If the waiver test is used, some agencies use a waiver form such as that shown in Figure 10–1.

Consent may be revoked at any point. For example, in *State v. Lewis* (1992) a state trooper pulled a defendant over for drunk driving. The trooper offered to drive the defendant home, and the man, after accepting, went to his vehicle to retrieve a bag. The trooper asked permission to check the bag for guns, and the defendant granted it. Inside the bag the trooper found two large brown bags that smelled of marijuana so he asked permission to check the bags, but the defendant refused. The trooper opened the bags anyway and found marijuana. According to Ferdico (1996, p. 340), the court found this search to violate the defendant's Fourth Amendment right to privacy:

> Even though defendant consented to the trooper looking inside his carry-on bag, he at no time consented to the trooper looking into the brown bags contained therein. Rather, by expressly terminating his consent when the trooper requested to open the brown bags and by seeking to return them to his car, defendant most certainly manifested a subjective expectation of privacy with respect to those inside bags.

Figure 10–1

Waiver and consent to search form.

Source: Joel Samaha. *Criminal Procedure*. 3rd ed. St. Paul: West Publishing Company, 1996, p. 244. Reprinted by permission. All rights reserved.

WAIVER AND CONSENT TO SEARCH

The undersigned _____
residing at _____
_____ hereby authorizes
the following named St. Paul Police Officers_____
to search the _____
_____

(insert description of place or auto, lic. number, etc.)

owned by/or in possession of the undersigned.
I do hereby waive any and all objections that may be made by me to said search and declare that this waiver and consent is freely and voluntarily given of my own free will and accord.

Signed _____ day of _____19___ at _____ PM   AM

Signed _____

Witnessed _____

Because those bags were always closed and their contents shielded from the trooper's view, society would regard defendant's expectation of privacy in them to be reasonable.

Although consent may be revoked at any time, if contraband was found *before* the revocation of consent, probable cause to arrest that person may then exist and a search incident to arrest could ensue; or, the police might cease their search, secure the property, detain those present and seek a warrant.

PLAIN VIEW EVIDENCE

The court recognizes that it would be unreasonable to expect police officers to either ignore or to delay acting on something illegal that they see. Similar to not requiring an arrest warrant to allow officers to search someone they actually see committing a crime, a search warrant is not required for officers to seize contraband or other evidence that is in plain sight.

〰️ The **plain view** doctrine says that unconcealed evidence that officers see while engaged in a lawful activity is admissible in court.

Evidence qualifies as plain view evidence if the officers are engaged in a lawful activity when they find the evidence and the evidence is not hidden. Until 1990 it was also a requirement that the discovery of plain view evidence be "inadvertent." This requirement was overturned in *Horton v. California* (1990) in which the Court held that the inadvertence rule gave no added protection to individuals and therefore eliminated it as a requirement.

For instance, if a government official is invited into a person's home and the officer sees illegal drugs on the table, the drugs can be seized. Likewise, an officer carrying out a legal act, such as executing a traffic stop or search warrant, may seize any contraband discovered. Similarly, contraband such as marijuana fields can be legally observed from an airplane over private property without a search warrant.

However, as noted by LaFave and Israel (1985, p. 127): "If an officer standing on the public way is able to look through the window of a private residence and see contraband, he must except in extraordinary circumstances obtain a warrant before entering those premises."

Closely related to the plain view doctrine is the *plain look* situation where police observe something while in a lawful position to do so and act on that information to pursue an investigation. An example of this is *Florida v. Riley* (1989) in which a police helicopter flying over a person's backyard spotted marijuana growing and used that information as the basis for a search warrant. As noted by one reviewer of this text:

These "plain look" situations differ from plain view in that in the former, there is no triggering of the Fourth Amendment to begin with which requires that the police comply with the reasonableness or probable cause requirements of the Amendment. Much police activity is of this variety.

The plain view doctrine has been extended to include the officer's other senses in addition to sight.

Plain Feel

The plain view concept has been extended by the Supreme Court to include what searching agents *feel* as well. The Court ruled in June of 1993 that police do not need a warrant to seize narcotics detected while frisking a suspect for concealed weapons as long as the narcotics are instantly recognizable by **plain feel.** The Court's recent unanimous opinion was the first time the Court has authorized a warrantless pat-down type frisk to go beyond a protective search for weapons.

In the precedent plain feel case, *Minnesota v. Dickerson* (1993), two police officers saw Dickerson leaving a known crack house and then, upon seeing the officers, stopping abruptly and walking quickly in the opposite direction. Creamer (1994, p. 42) notes: "Based on his evasive actions and the fact that he had just exited a building known for cocaine traffic, the officers decided to stop Dickerson and investigate further." They did so, and as one officer testified later in court (Creamer, p. 42):

> As I pat-searched the front of his body, I felt a lump—a small lump—in the front pocket. I examined it with my fingers and slid it, and it felt to be a lump of crack cocaine in cellophane. I never thought the lump was a weapon."

The court upheld the seizure of the cocaine by comparing the plain touch seizure of the cocaine to the plain view doctrine allowing officers to seize drugs or contraband found in plain view during a lawful search:

> To this [c]ourt, there is no distinction as to which sensory perception the officer uses to conclude the material is contraband. An experienced officer may rely upon his sense of smell in DUI stops or in recognizing the smell of burning marijuana in an automobile. The sound of a shotgun being racked would clearly support certain reactions by an officer. The sense of touch, grounded in experience and training, is as reliable as perceptions from the other senses. "Plain feel," therefore, is no different than "plain view."

When the case was appealed to the Minnesota Supreme Court, however, the conviction was reversed. The court held that the sense of touch is much less reliable than the sense of sight and that it is far more intrusive into the personal privacy that is the core of the Fourth Amendment. The decision was granted review by the United States Supreme Court, which upheld the ruling of the Minnesota Supreme Court because the officer did not immediately recognize the object as contraband. As noted by Creamer (1994, p. 44):

> Nonetheless, the decision is significant in that it supports limited "plain touch" or "plain feel" probes in frisk situations; if contraband is plainly felt by the officer in good faith, what he finds will not be suppressed.

STOP AND FRISK

The elements of stop-and-frisk law were discussed in Chapter 9, but are important to include here as a critical exception to the warrant requirement for a legal search. Recall that if officers have a reasonable suspicion based on specific and articulable facts that an individual is involved in criminal activity, the officers may make a brief investigatory stop. If the officers reasonably suspect that the person is presently armed and dangerous, a frisk may be conducted without a warrant (*Terry v. Ohio*, 1968).

> If a frisk is authorized by the circumstances of an investigative stop, only a limited pat-down of the detainee's outer clothing for the safety of the officer is authorized.

Anything that reasonably feels like a weapon may then be removed and used as evidence against the person if it is contraband or other evidence (*Terry v. Ohio*, 1968). If an officer has specific information about where a weapon is on a person, the officer may reach directly for it (*Adams v. Williams*, 1972).

Similarly, the passenger compartment of a car can be searched if that vehicle is stopped and the person(s) are detained but not arrested. Such a search would have to remain limited to the area where a weapon could be, and it would have to be done with the belief that, as in a frisk situation, the person is presently armed and dangerous.

THE AUTOMOBILE EXCEPTION

Because of their mobility, automobiles and other vehicles may need to be searched without a warrant. This so-called "automobile exception" has arisen because it would obviously be unreasonable for law enforcement officers to expect suspects to voluntarily remain in place while the officers returned to the station to type up the warrant application and then find a judge to sign it. It would also be unreasonable for suspects to be detained that long. This exception, like the others, is not difficult to understand if the underlying reason for it is kept in mind. The automobile exception simply states that if a government agent has probable cause to believe the vehicle contains contraband or evidence of a crime, no warrant is needed. Why? Because in the time it would take to get a warrant, the car, driver and contraband or evidence could be long gone.

The precedent for a warrantless search of automobiles came from *Carroll v. United States* (1925). During Prohibition in the 1920s, among the 1,500 agents pursuing bootleggers were two federal agents posing as buyers in a Michigan honky-tonk. Two bootleggers, George Carroll and John Kiro, were somewhat suspicious. They said they had to go get the liquor and would return in about an hour. They called later to say they couldn't make it until the next day, but they never appeared.

The agents resumed surveillance of a section of road between Grand Rapids and Detroit known to be used by bootleggers. Within a week after their unsuccessful buy, the agents recognized Carroll and Kiro driving by. They gave chase, but lost them. Two months later they again recognized Carroll's car, pursued and overtook it. The agents were familiar with Carroll's car, recognized Carroll and Kiro in the automobile and believed the automobile contained bootleg liquor. A search revealed 68 bottles of whiskey and gin, most behind the upholstery of the seats where the padding had been removed. The contraband was seized and the two men arrested.

Carroll and Kiro were charged with and convicted of transporting intoxicating liquor. Carroll's appeal, taken to the United States Supreme Court, resulted in a landmark decision defining the rights and limitations for warrantless searches of vehicles.

> *Carroll v. United States* (1925) established that automobiles can be searched without a warrant provided (1) there is probable cause to believe the vehicle's contents violate the law and (2) the vehicle would be gone before a search warrant could be obtained.

Chambers v. Maroney (1970) also held that an automobile may be searched without a warrant if probable cause is present. Justifications for acting without a warrant were further specified in *Robbins v. California* (1981):

❖ The mobility of motor vehicles often produces exigent circumstances.
❖ A diminished expectation of privacy surrounds the automobile.
❖ A car is used for transportation and not as a residence or repository of personal belongings.
❖ The car's occupants and contents are in plain view.
❖ Automobiles are necessarily highly regulated by the government.

According to del Carmen (1987, p. 171): "The general rule is that a seizure occurs every time a motor vehicle is stopped; the provisions of the Fourth Amendment against unreasonable searches and seizures therefore apply. . . . There must be at least a reasonable suspicion to satisfy an investigatory stop of a motor vehicle." The leading case on this issue is *United States v. Cortez* (1981) in which the Court said: "Based upon that whole picture, the detaining officers must have a particularized and objective basis for suspecting the particular person stopped of criminal activity."

If police have legally stopped a vehicle and have probable cause to believe the vehicle contains contraband, they can conduct a thorough search of the vehicle, including the trunk and any closed packages or containers found in the car or the trunk. The Court said in *United States v. Ross* (1982): "If probable cause justifies the search of a lawfully stopped vehicle, it justifies the search of every part of the vehicle and its contents that may conceal the object of the search."

Limitations on warrantless searches of automobiles were set in *United States v. Henry* (1980), with the Court stating: "Once these items [for which a search warrant would be sought] are located, the search must terminate. If, however, while legitimately looking for such articles, the officer unexpectedly discovers evidence of another crime, he can seize that evidence as well." This is where the plain view doctrine comes into play.

Inventory Searches of Impounded Vehicles

Police officers can legally tow and impound vehicles for many reasons, including vehicles involved in accidents, parked in a tow-away zone or abandoned on a highway.

When police impound a vehicle, they may legally conduct an inventory search. This search protects both them and the vehicle owner. Rutledge (1995, p. 8) notes: "A vehicle that has been or is about to be impounded might contain valuable personal property or dangerous instruments. Therefore it's your duty to safeguard the owner's property and protect officials and the public from hazards such as weapons, explosives or toxins that might be stored in the vehicle."

The precedent case on inventory search is *South Dakota v. Opperman* (1976). Opperman's illegally parked car was towed to the city impound lot and inventoried. During the routine inventory, a bag of marijuana was found in the unlocked glove compartment. The Court concluded that the inventory was *not* unreasonable under the Fourth Amendment, noting:

> These procedures [inventory of impounded vehicles] developed in response to three distinct needs: the protection of the owner's property while it remains in police custody; the protection of the police against claims or disputes over lost or stolen property; and the protection of the police from potential danger. The practice has been viewed as essential to respond to incidents of theft or vandalism. In addition, police frequently attempt to determine whether a vehicle has been stolen and thereafter abandoned.

It is generally accepted that inventory searches are standard procedure for many departments. But if evidence from a routine inventory search is to be admissible in court, the inventory must be just that: routine. Police cannot decide that some vehicles will be searched when impounded while others are not. Routine inventory searches have been held reasonable; checking only certain vehicles has not. Officers from departments that usually do not conduct inventory searches cannot decide to inventory one particular vehicle.

Rutledge (1995, p. 9) emphasizes the importance of having standardized procedures for conducting the inventory search by citing two Supreme Court cases:

> In *Colorado v. Bertine* [1987], a lawfully impounded vehicle was thoroughly searched in conformity with the Boulder Police Department's standard inventory policy. . . . Upholding this inventory, the Supreme Court said:
>
> > We emphasize that the Police Department's procedures mandated the opening of closed containers and the listing of their contents. Our decisions have always adhered to the requirement that inventories be conducted according to standardized criteria.
>
> By contrast, the Florida Highway Patrol conducted an inventory search of a DWI arrestee's impounded vehicle. Officers found marijuana in a garbage bag hidden inside a suitcase located inside the truck. Since there was no evidence that the searching officer followed any standardized procedure for inventory searches, the Supreme Court ruled the evidence inadmissible:

The state found that the Florida Highway Patrol had no policy whatever with respect to the opening of closed containers encountered during an inventory search. We hold that absent such a policy, the instant search was not sufficiently regulated to satisfy the Fourth Amendment, and the marijuana was properly surpressed—*Florida v. Wells* [1990].

California v. Acevedo (1991) held that if police officers have probable cause to believe a container in an automobile holds contraband or evidence of a crime, a warrantless search of the container is justified even if probable cause to search the vehicle has not been established.

EXIGENT CIRCUMSTANCES

Yet another circumstance in which lawful warrantless searches can be made is if an **exigent** (emergency) situation exists. The courts have recognized that sometimes situations will arise that reasonably require immediate action or evidence may be destroyed. Police officers who have established probable cause that evidence is likely to be at a certain place and who do not have time to get a search warrant, may conduct a warrantless search. But there *must* be extenuating (exigent) circumstances.

United States v. Chadwick (1977) held that the government may not conduct a warrantless search when that search is so remote from the incident leading to it as to be considered unnecessary and, therefore, unreasonable. In this case, narcotics officers arrested Chadwick outside a train station, and over an hour later searched without a warrant luggage in a locker inside the train station. In holding that Chadwick was entitled to having the search conducted only with a warrant because there was no exigency involved, the Court added that "if officers have reason to believe that luggage contains some immediately dangerous instrumentality, such as explosives, it would be foolhardy to transport it to the station house without opening the luggage and disarming the weapon." In the case of *United States v. Johnson* (1972) the court upheld a warrantless search of a suitcase because there was probable cause to believe it contained a sawed-off shotgun. While a warrant is preferred because of the judicial decree that probable cause exists, if a genuinely exigent circumstance exists, such a search is reasonable.

> Emergency situations include danger of physical harm to the officer or others, danger of destruction of evidence, driving while intoxicated, hot-pursuit situations and individuals requiring "rescuing," for example, unconscious individuals.

Included in the "danger to life" category are individuals suspected of being armed and dangerous and those who are unconscious. If police officers come across an unconscious person, they are obligated to search the person's pockets or purse for identification and for any possible medical information. If they discover evidence of criminal activity or contraband during this search, they may seize it. For example, in *Vause v. United States* (1931) two officers came upon an unconscious man on a public street. Unable to rouse him, they called for an ambulance and then searched his pockets for identification. During this search they found 15 cellophane packets containing narcotics. The Court affirmed the reasonableness of the search: ". . . the search of one found in an unconscious condition is both legally permissible and highly necessary."

Exigent circumstances were used as a defense for the warrantless search in the O. J. Simpson murder trial. The prosecution contended that an emergency existed that needed immediate attention.

Just as a warrant may be challenged, warrantless searches may also be challenged. The most frequent challenges are that the officer did not actually establish probable cause or that there was sufficient time to obtain a warrant.

OPEN FIELDS, ABANDONED PROPERTY AND SOME PUBLIC PLACES

What about instances when someone, known or unknown, abandons property? For example, if a person throws something out of a car window while traveling on a freeway, has he or she forfeited any expectation of privacy? Or what about the tenant who abandons an apartment? And what about the garbage that is placed curbside to be transported to a dump, commingling with the trash of others throughout the process? Finally, what about something left in an open field so that it can be seen by anyone passing by?

This area of search and seizure does not neatly fit in any of the other exceptions to needing a search warrant. It might be considered a natural extension of the plain view doctrine. In effect, however, the courts have dealt with this area by extending the doctrine that anything held out to the public is not protected by the Fourth Amendment because no reasonable expectation of privacy exists.

> ➣ If there is no *reasonable* expectation of privacy, Fourth Amendment protection does not apply.

The precedent case for search and seizure of abandoned property and open fields is *Hester v. United States* (1924). In this case the police were investigating bootlegging operations and went to the home of Hester's father. As they came to the house, they saw a man identified as Henderson drive up to the house. The officers hid and saw Hester come out and give Henderson a bottle. The police sounded an alarm, and Hester ran to a car parked nearby, removed a gallon jug and he and Henderson ran across an open field.

One officer chased them. Hester dropped his jug, which broke, but retained about half its contents. Henderson threw his bottle away. Officers found another broken jar containing some liquid outside the house. The officers determined the jars contained illegal whiskey. They seized the evidence even though they had no search or arrest warrants. Hester was convicted of concealing "distilled spirits," but on appeal said the officers conducted an illegal search and seizure. The Court disagreed, stating:

> It is obvious that even if there had been a trespass, the above testimony was not obtained by an illegal search or seizure. The defendant's own acts, and those of his

associates, disclosed the jug, the jar and the bottle—and there was no seizure in the sense of the law when the officers examined the contents of each after it had been abandoned.

The Court went on to state: "The special protection accorded by the Fourth Amendment to the people in their 'persons, houses, papers, and effects,' is not extended to the open fields." This includes property disposed of in such a manner as to relinquish ordinary property rights.

The "open fields" doctrine holds that land beyond that normally associated with use of that land, that is, undeveloped land, can be searched without a warrant. In *Oliver v. United States* (1984) the Court held that "No Trespassing" signs do not bar the public from viewing open fields; therefore, the owner should have no expectation of privacy and the Fourth Amendment does not apply.

Curtilage is the term used to describe that portion of property generally associated with the common use of land, e.g., buildings, sheds, fenced-in areas and the like. The concept of curtilage evolved in the Court's attempt to ascertain just how far beyond one's house the reasonable expectation of privacy extended. Inside such areas the open fields doctrine does not apply. A warrant would be needed to search within the curtilage. In *California v. Ciraolo* (1986) the Court held that police looking from the air into the backyard of a suspect does not violate the Fourth Amendment because, although part of the curtilage, it is open to public view from the air. The following year, in *United States v. Dunn* (1987) the Court upheld the warrantless search of a barn that was not part of the curtilage on the same grounds.

Similarly, once a person has discarded or abandoned property, he or she maintains no reasonable expectation of privacy. Thus, something thrown from a car, discarded during a chase or even garbage that is disposed of (once off the curtilage) becomes abandoned property that police may inspect without a warrant. In *California v. Greenwood* (1988) the Court held that a warrantless search and seizure of trash left at curbside for collection in an area accessible by the public does not violate a person's Fourth Amendment rights as there should be no expectation of privacy. Some states, however, have declared the searching through of trash as a violation of the Fourth Amendment. In most states, garbage searches remain a standard technique for investigators, particularly narcotics investigators.

In *United States v. Diaz* (1994) a district court held that the defendant had no expectation of privacy in a motel parking lot. And in *United States v. Garcia* (1994) a district court held that using a drug-detecting dog at an Amtrak station did not violate the defendant's Fourth Amendment rights because the defendant should have no expectation of privacy in the air surrounding his bags (Carr, 1995, pp. 48–51).

In contrast to the preceding situations, *United States v. Chun* (1993) held that officers who climbed onto a garage roof so they could look into the second floor window in the defendant's building was ruled an invalid warrantless search because the occupants had a reasonable expectation of privacy in this circumstance.

BORDER SEARCHES AND SEIZURES

Border searches are perceived as vital to our national security. According to Meshbesher (1986, p. 23), at our international borders: "Generally all routine searches of persons, belongings, effects, and vehicles are presumptively reasonable under the Fourth Amendment. The Constitution does not require even a suspicion of criminal activity" (*United States v. Ramsey,* 1977; *Carroll v. United States,* 1925; *Boyd v. United States,* 1886).

The Supreme Court held in *United States v. Montoya de Hernandez* (1985) that routine searches at a United States international border require no objective justification, probable cause or warrant. More recently, in *Quinones-Ruiz v. United States* (1994) the court stated: [T]he border search exception applies equally to persons entering or exiting the country." This is another example of how *reasonableness* is determined by balancing the needs of society. People within the United States have a reasonable expectation of privacy that has been determined to be different from that at the borders of our country. The interest in national security then makes more intrusive warrantless searches reasonable.

Meshbesher (p. 34) also states: "[T]he Supreme Court has recognized that routine border searches may be carried out not only at the border itself but at its 'functional equivalents,' as well," including airports receiving nonstop flights from foreign countries.

> ⬳ The Court has ruled that routine border searches and searches at international airports are reasonable under the Fourth Amendment.

Meshbesher further notes (p. 41) that people at airports increasingly are being "subject to investigative detention" because they fit a drug courier profile. This profile, developed by drug enforcement agents, includes the following characteristics: (1) arriving from a source city, (2) little or no luggage or large quantity of empty suitcases, (3) rapid turnaround on airplane trip, (4) use of assumed name, (5) possession of large amount of cash, (6) cash purchase of ticket, (7) nervous appearance.

This is well illustrated in *United States v. Sokolow* (1989) in which the Court held that using a drug courier profile to make an investigative stop was legal. In this case officers used such a profile (developed by the Drug Enforcement Administration or DEA) to detain Sokolow. A drug-detecting dog indicated the presence of narcotics in one of Sokolow's bags. The officers arrested Sokolow and obtained a search warrant for the bag. They found no narcotics, but did find documents indicating involvement in drug trafficking. A second search with the drug-detecting dog turned up narcotics in a second bag of Sokolow.

At trial, the defense objected to the legality of the investigative stop, but the Court held that the totality of circumstances in the case, the "fit" with the numerous criteria for the drug courier profile, established a reasonable suspicion that the suspect was transporting illegal drugs, making the investigative stop without a warrant valid.

United States border inspection station. (Photo by Davie McNew. Provided by UPI/Corbis-Bettmann.)

The policy for such broad powers to search is clearly in the interest of international security. With increasing incidents of international terrorism and drug trafficking, the Court will probably continue to find such sweeping searches at our international borders sufficiently reasonable.

The farther a person gets from the border, however, the more traditional search-and-seizure requirements come back into play. Roaming border patrol agents may stop individuals or cars away from the actual border only if they have the traditional reasonable suspicion. Similar to the authorized use of roadblocks elsewhere, border agents can establish roadblocks that stop cars in a certain pattern (every car, every other car, every fifth car, etc.). But searches may only be conducted following the traditional rules applying to motor vehicles, such as probable cause to believe contraband exists and the like.

ROADBLOCKS AND CHECKPOINTS

A series of cases, including *United States v. Ortiz* (1975) and *United States v. Martinez-Fuerte* (1976), have concluded that checkpoints at or near international borders at which all vehicles are stopped to check for illegal entrants into the United States is not in violation of Fourth Amendment constitutional protections. The Supreme Court has held that the government has a genuine interest in protecting the nation's borders, and if everyone is treated similarly, the government will not be randomly selecting individuals to stop based on ethnicity, religion and the like.

However, in *United States v. Brignoni-Ponce* (1975) the Court held that roving patrols of government agents (i.e., border patrol officers) may not stop people or vehicles beyond a certain reasonable point without reasonable suspicion, adding that within 100 miles of an international border probable cause would not be necessary, but reasonable suspicion would be. Again, the Court is attempting to balance the interests of the government with personal interests. The farther away from the border one gets, the more the government is constrained by traditional search-and-seizure requirements of probable cause.

Checkpoints farther than 100 miles from an international border are sometimes also made for other reasons, stopping everyone in the name of public safety. In *Michigan Department of State Police v. Sitz* (1990) the Supreme Court held that while there is a Fourth Amendment "seizure" when a vehicle is stopped at a checkpoint, when there is a public safety justification and random stops are not being made, such a procedure does not violate the Fourth Amendment.

In this particular case the state police were challenged as to the constitutionality of their stopping every vehicle at sobriety checkpoints. In deciding this case, the Court relied on the *Martinez-Fuerte* case as well as the case of *Brown v. Texas* (1979) in balancing the state's interest in preventing accidents caused by drunk drivers, the effectiveness of sobriety checkpoints in achieving this goal and the level of intrusion on an individual's privacy caused by the checkpoint.

In the *Martinez-Fuerte* case it was held that checkpoint stops are indeed "seizures," if no discretion is exercised by the police in deciding which vehicles are stopped, a balancing of legitimate government and private interests will permit checkpoints. There were strongly worded dissenting opinions in the *Michigan* case, but as set forth in *Delaware v. Prouse* (1979) only random stops involve "the kind of standardless and unconstrained discretion which is the evil the Court has discerned when in previous cases it has insisted that the discretion of the official in the field be circumscribed."

The issue of checkpoints is one that exemplifies the analysis and balance that occurs with constitutional decisions, with an effort being made by the Court to meet the needs and interests of all. And while checkpoints have been found to be constitutional, some states have restricted their use because the idea of the police stopping everyone to check on possible violations of a few is repugnant.

ELECTRONIC SURVEILLANCE AND THE FOURTH AMENDMENT

Chapter 9 introduced the area of electronic surveillance and the issue of the expectation of privacy in the landmark case of *Katz v. United States* (1967).

 Electronic surveillance is a form of search and seizure and as such is governed by the Fourth Amendment.

While cases dating back to the 1920s may seem "old," the laws pertaining to electronic means of acquiring information are relatively young. The first

Surveillance system. (Photo by Peter Skingley. Provided by Reuters/Corbis-Bettmann.

case the United States Supreme Court considered that involved wiretapping (listening to the telephone conversations of others) occurred in 1928 *(Olmstead v. United States)*.

In *Olmstead,* the Court held that the federal agents did not need a warrant to intercept such information because the agents did not acquire any physical objects, and as LaFave and Israel (1985, p. 246) state, the thinking of the Court was that since no "things" had been seized, the Fourth Amendment did not pertain.

Olmstead has since been overturned by *Katz* for the reason that Justice Brandeis set forth in his dissenting opinion in the *Olmstead* case, that "every unjustifiable intrusion by the government upon the privacy of the individual, whatever the means employed, must be deemed a violation of the Fourth Amendment." LaFave and Israel (p. 246) add: "In an oft-quoted passage, Justice Holmes reasoned that it is 'a less evil that some criminals should escape than that the government should play an ignoble part.'"

Electronic surveillance clearly illustrates our "living law" at work. The drafters of our Constitution in their wildest fantasies could hardly have foreseen the current technology. The evolution of electronic surveillance illustrates how technology and the law become intertwined.

The use of such investigative devices must comply with the Fourth Amendment rules as much as any activity conducted 200 years ago. In other words, a balance must be struck between assuring that such intrusiveness does not become unreasonable, disturbing our right to privacy. This is precisely the equitable balance the law of criminal procedure seeks to achieve.

A series of cases and legislation evolved that sought to come to grips with this complex, powerful new area of obtaining evidence. Most place emphasis on "privacy" rather than on "property." During the 1960s case law sought to define what uses of this technology would be considered "reasonable."

In *Osborn v. United States* (1966) undercover federal agents with a warrant taped a conversation using a hidden recorder in an attempt to prove that labor leader Jimmy Hoffa's lawyer was bribing a juror. The evidence was admitted on the basis that the electronic device was used in "precise and discriminate circumstances" set forth in the warrant.

Berger v. New York (1967) held that using such devices must be limited and that a "two month surveillance period was the equivalent of a series of intrusions, searches and seizures pursuant to a single showing of probable cause" (Ferdico, 1996, p. 364). Warrants may be issued for such a redundant period, but beyond that they must be reviewed or extended.

In *Katz v. United States* (1967) the Supreme Court held that obtaining evidence by attaching an electronic device to listen on a public phone booth was an unlawful search and seizure because there was no warrant. In response, Congress enacted the Omnibus Crime Control and Safe Streets Act of 1968.

Title III of the Federal Omnibus Crime Control and Safe Streets Act of 1968 regulates the use of electronic surveillance. The act treats electronic surveillance as a "search and seizure" within the meaning of the Fourth Amendment (Ferdico, 1996, p. 362).

Other factors contributing to passage of this act included the social unrest caused by the assassinations of Martin Luther King, Jr. and Robert F. Kennedy, as well as the "law and order" presidential campaign of Richard Nixon. Title III called for judicial supervision of all aspects of electronic surveillance.

> ✑ To obtain an electronic surveillance warrant, probable cause that a person is engaging in particular communications must be established by the court and normal investigative procedures must have already been tried.

Title III established specific procedures to apply for, issue and execute court orders to intercept wire or oral communications (Ferdico, 1996, p. 367).

> ✑ Electronic surveillance is an infringement on one's privacy only when it intrudes on one's reasonable expectations of privacy.

The Supreme Court has ruled that this expectation does not exist when someone voluntarily converses with someone else—the "unreliable ear" exception. The lower courts have held that this expectation does not exist when someone converses in public because others may hear—the "uninvited ear" exception. For instance, a warrant is not required for an undercover officer to converse with suspects, using what they say in court. *United States v. Karo* (1984) established that warrantless monitoring of a beeper in a private home violates the Fourth Amendment.

Title III requires that "all nonconsensual surveillance for the purpose of investigating crime must take place pursuant to a warrant and establishes a detailed regulatory scheme for implementing this objective" (Whitebread and Slobogin, 1986, p. 320).

The government does not need a warrant to use an electronic beeper to monitor travel in public. *United States v. Knotts* (1983) held that a person traveling on a public thoroughfare has no reasonable expectation of privacy; therefore, using a beeper to track such a person cannot constitute a search. However, a warrant may be necessary to install a beeper to locate evidence or to track and monitor a person in a private residence.

Title III also regulates using electronic devices to tap or intercept wire communications. Such devices are legal under only two conditions: (1) a court order authorizes the wiretap or (2) one person consents to the wiretap. *United States v. White* (1971) held that "the Constitution does not prohibit a government agent from using an electronic device to record a telephone conversation between two parties with the consent of one party to the conversation." In some states, as long as there is one-party consent, it is not a Fourth Amendment issue.

Title III also does not require a warrant for using a device to trace telephone calls or devices that record what phone numbers were called from a specific phone. The reason is that actual conversations are not being monitored. A warrant could be required, however, to install such devices.

The federal Electronic Communication Privacy Act (ECPA) of 1986 defines an oral communication as one made by a person exhibiting a reasonable expectation of privacy and stipulates that a warrant is required only when the parties have a *reasonable* expectation of privacy (Klusmeier, 1991, p. 19).

The area of electronic surveillance and expectations of privacy offers additional support for the enduring quality of the Constitution. The explosive development of technology continues to present challenges to which the Fourth Amendment can respond. The incredible increase in the use of computers in our society will surely challenge existing law in this area. While our computer age presents search and seizure issues that Benjamin Franklin and Thomas Jefferson could never have dreamed of, the document they helped draft remains responsive. Telephones, pagers, cellular technology and the Internet all present areas that have yet to be fully addressed by constitutional interpretation and application. But undoubtedly they will be.

SCOPE OF SEARCHES

Unrestrained general searches offend our sense of justice now, just as they did when the Constitution was drafted. Limited searches conducted in accordance with established constitutional guidelines serve the needs of society while protecting the individual.

No matter under what authority a search is conducted, one general principle is critical. The search must be limited in scope. Anything beyond is unreasonable and, thus, unconstitutional as regulated by the Fourth Amendment.

> All searches must be limited. General searches are unconstitutional and never legal.

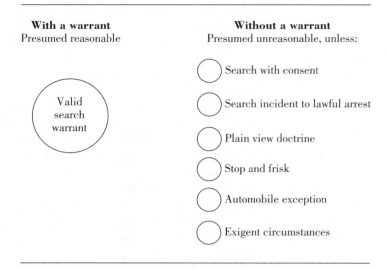

With a warrant
Presumed reasonable

Valid
search
warrant

Without a warrant
Presumed unreasonable, unless:

◯ Search with consent

◯ Search incident to lawful arrest

◯ Plain view doctrine

◯ Stop and frisk

◯ Automobile exception

◯ Exigent circumstances

Figure 10–2
Constitutional
analysis of search
and seizure.

The legal maxim at the beginning of this chapter refers to narrowing the scope of a search. Looking for "an elephant in a matchbox" suggests that it would be unreasonable to look for a stolen 24-inch television set in a dresser drawer. To avoid this problem, police officers usually include in the warrant affidavit that they wish to search for receipts as well as documents of title or ownership in addition to the actual items sought. This allows them to search in much smaller places. Figure 10–2 summaries when searches are "reasonable" and therefore constitutional.

Again, it is critical to understand that while the Fourth Amendment generally does not restrict the actions of private citizens, it does apply to all government workers. This includes federal, state, county and local governmental bodies. Just as the FBI, state police, county sheriff and local police are bound by the Fourth Amendment, so are the IRS, the postal service, fire inspectors, local building officials and code enforcement officials. It should be noted that, unlike Fifth and Sixth Amendment concerns, a government agent is *not* required to recite the Fourth Amendment protections to a suspect.

Summary

The Fourth Amendment forbids unreasonable searches and seizures and requires that any search or arrest warrant be based on probable cause. Searches with a warrant are presumed to be reasonable.

Searches conducted with a search warrant must be limited to the specific area and specific items described in the warrant. And while warrantless searches are presumed unreasonable, exceptions to the warrant requirement include the following: (1) search incident to a lawful arrest, (2) consent search, (3) plain view doctrine, (4) stop and frisk, (5) automobile exceptions, (6) exigent (emergency) circumstances and (7) open fields, abandoned property and some public places.

In the first exception, searches following an arrest, the search must be immediate and must be limited to the area within the person's reach *(Chimel).*

In the second exception, consent searches, the consent to search must be voluntary. The search must be limited to the area specified by the person granting permission. The person may revoke the consent at any time. In the third exception, plain view evidence, unconcealed evidence that officers see while engaged in a lawful activity is admissible in court.

In the fourth exception to needing a warrant, stop-and-frisk situations, if a frisk is authorized by the circumstances of an investigative stop, only a limited patdown of the detainee's outer clothing for the safety of the officer is authorized. In the fifth exception, the automobile exception, *Carroll v. United States* established that automobiles can be searched without a warrant provided there is probable cause to believe the vehicle's contents violate the law and the vehicle would be gone before a search warrant could be obtained. The sixth exception, exigent circumstances, includes danger of physical harm to officers or another person, danger of destruction of evidence, driving while intoxicated, hot-pursuit situations and individuals requiring "rescuing."

The seventh exception, open fields, abandoned property and some public places, involves the lack of expectation of privacy; therefore, the Fourth Amendment protection does not apply. The Court has ruled that routine border searches and searches at international airports are reasonable under the Fourth Amendment.

Electronic surveillance is a form of search and seizure and as such is governed by the Fourth Amendment. To obtain an electronic surveillance warrant, probable cause that a person is engaging in particular communications must be established by the court, and normal investigative procedures must have already been tried. Electronic surveillance is unconstitutional only when it intrudes on one's reasonable expectations of privacy.

All searches must be limited. General searches are unconstitutional and never legal.

Discussion
Questions

1. What are the disadvantages of a consent search?
2. Discuss the limitations of a frisk.
3. What or who determines when a search is reasonable?
4. Discuss examples of what might be considered exigent circumstances.
5. Should searches of motor vehicles differ from searches of homes? Why or why not?
6. How would you define the term *reasonable* as it relates to searches?
7. Under what circumstances would the search of a person be considered reasonable?
8. When might a person *not* have a reasonable expectation of privacy?
9. When are general searches constitutional?
10. Discuss whether Internet data is protected by the Fourth Amendment.

References

Carr, James G. *Criminal Procedure Handbook.* 1995 ed. New York: Clark Boardman Callaghan, 1995.

Creamer, J. Shane. "Understanding the 'Plain Touch' Doctrine." *The Police Chief.* August 1994, pp. 42–44.

del Carmen, Rolando V. *Criminal Procedures for Law Enforcement Personnel.* Monterey: Brooks/Cole Publishing Company, 1987.

Ferdico, John N. *Criminal Procedure for the Criminal Justice Professional.* 6th ed. St. Paul: West Publishing Company, 1996.

Klusmeier, Paul H. "The Mini-Cassette Tape Recorder: A Valuable Tool or Violation of the Law?" *The Police Chief.* August 1991, p. 19.

LaFave, Wayne R. and Jerold Israel. *Criminal Procedure.* St. Paul: West Publishing Company, 1985.

Meshbesher, Ronald I. *Minnesota Search & Seizure: What's Left of the Right to Privacy?* Eau Claire, WI: Professional Education Systems, Inc., 1986.

Rutledge, Devallis. "Taking an Inventory." *Police.* November 1995, pp. 8–9.

Samaha, Joel. *Criminal Procedure.* 3rd ed. St. Paul: West Publishing Company, 1996.

Whitebread, Charles H. and Christopher Slobogin. *Criminal Procedure. An Analysis of Cases and Concepts.* 2nd. ed. Mineola, NY: The Foundation Press, Inc., 1986.

Zalman, Marvin and Larry Siegel. *Key Cases and Comments on Criminal Procedure.* 1995 ed. St. Paul: West Publishing Company, 1996.

Cases Cited

Adams v. Williams, 407 U.S. 143, 92 S.Ct. 1921, 32 L.Ed.2d 612 (1972).
Berger v. New York, 388 U.S. 41, 87 S.Ct. 1873, 18 L.Ed.2d 1040 (1967).
Boyd v. United States, 116 U.S. 616, 6 S.Ct. 524, 29 L.Ed. 746 (1886).
Brown v. Texas, 443 U.S. 47, 99 S.Ct. 2637, 61 L.Ed.2d 357 (1979).
California v. Acevedo, 500 U.S. 565, 111 S.Ct. 1982, 114 L.Ed.2d 619 (1991).
California v. Ciraolo, 476 U.S. 207, 106 S.Ct. 1809, 90 L.Ed.2d 210 (1986).
California v. Greenwood, 486 U.S. 35, 108 S.Ct. 1625, 100 L.Ed.2d 30 (1988).
Carroll v. United States, 267 U.S. 132, 45 S.Ct. 280, 69 L.Ed. 543 (1925).
Cass v. State, 124 Tex. Cr. R. 208, 61 W.W.2d 500.
Chambers v. Maroney, 399 U.S. 42, 90 S.Ct. 1975, 26 L.Ed.2d 419 (1970).
Chimel v. California, 395 U.S. 752, 89 S.Ct. 2034, 23 L.Ed.2d 685 (1969).
Colorado v. Bertine, 479 U.S. 367, 107 S.Ct. 738, 93 L.Ed.2d 739 (1987).
Delaware v. Prouse, 440 U.S. 648, 99 S.Ct. 1391, 59 L.Ed.2d 660 (1979).
Florida v. Jimeno, 499 U.S. 934, 111 S.Ct. 1385, 113 L.Ed.2d 442 (1991).
Florida v. Riley, 488 U.S. 445, 109 S.Ct. 693, 102 L.Ed.2d 835 (1989).
Florida v. Wells, 495 U.S. 1, 110 S.Ct. 1632, 109 L.Ed.2d 1 (1990).
Hester v. United States, 265 U.S. 57, 44 S.Ct. 445, 68 L.Ed. 898 (1924).
Horton v. California, 496 U.S. 128, 110 S.Ct. 2301, 110 L.Ed.2d 112 (1990).
Illinois v. Lafayette, 462 U.S. 640, 103 S.Ct. 2605, 77 L.Ed.2d 65 (1983).
Katz v. United States, 389 U.S. 347, 88 S.Ct. 507, 19 L.Ed.2d 576 (1967).
Marshall v. Barlow's Inc., 436 U.S. 307, 98 S.Ct. 1816, 56 L.Ed.2d 305 (1978).
Maryland v. Buie, 494 U.S. 325, 110 S.Ct. 1093, 108 L.Ed.2d 276 (1990).
Michigan v. Summers, 452 U.S. 692, 101 S.Ct. 2587, 69 L.Ed.2d 340 (1981).
Michigan v. Tucker, 417 U.S. 433, 94 S.Ct. 2357, 41 L.Ed.2d 182 (1974).
Michigan Department of State Police v. Sitz, 496 U.S. 444, 110 S.Ct. 2481, 110 L.Ed.2d 412 (1990).
Minnesota v. Dickerson, 508 U.S. 336 (1993).
Monroe v. Pape, 365 U.S. 167, 81 S.Ct. 473, 5 L.Ed.2d 492 (1961).
New Jersey v. T.L.O., 469 U.S. 325, 105 S.Ct. 733, 83 L.Ed.2d 720 (1985).
New York v. Belton, 453 U.S. 454, 101 S. Ct. 2860, 69 L.Ed.2d 768 (1981).
Oliver v. United States, 466 U.S. 170, 104 S.Ct. 1735, 80 L.Ed.2d 214 (1984).

Olmstead v. United States, 277 U.S. 438, 48 S.Ct. 564, 72 L.Ed. 944 (1928).

Osborn v. United States, 385 U.S. 323, 87 S.Ct. 429, 17 L.Ed.2d 394 (1966).

People v. Loria, 10 N.Y.2d 368, 223 N.Y.S.2d 462, 179 N.E.2d 478 (1961).

Quinones-Ruiz v. United States, 864 F.Supp. 983, 986 (S.D.Cal., 1994).

Robbins v. California, 453 U.S. 420, 101 S.Ct. 2841, 69 L.Ed.2d 744 (1981).

South Dakota v. Opperman, 428 U.S. 364, 96 S.Ct. 3092, 49 L.Ed.2d 1000 (1976).

State v. Barlow, Jr., 320 A.2d 895 (ME, 1974).

State v. Kaluna, 55 Hawaii 361, 520 P.2d 51 (1974).

State v. Lewis, 611 A.2d 69 (ME, 1992).

Terry v. Ohio, 392 U.S. 1, 88 S.Ct. 1868, 20 L.Ed.2d 889 (1968).

United States v. Brignoni-Ponce, 422 U.S. 873, 95 S.Ct. 2574, 45 L.Ed.2d 607 (1975).

United States v. Chadwick, 433 U.S. 1, 97 S.Ct. 2476, 53 L.Ed.2d 538 (1977).

United States v. Chun, 857 F.Supp. 353 (D.N.J., 1993).

United States v. Cortez, 449 U.S. 411, 101 S.Ct. 690, 66 L.Ed.2d 621 (1981).

United States v. Diaz, 25 F.3d 392 (6th Cir., 1994).

United States v. Dunn (1987).

United States v. Garcia, 42 F.3d 604 (10th Cir., 1994).

United States v. Henry, 447 U.S. 264, 100 S.Ct. 2183, 65 L.Ed.2d 115 (1980).

United States v. Johnson, 467 F.2d 630 (2d Cir., 1972).

United States v. Karo, 468 U.S. 705, 104 S.Ct. 3296, 82 L.Ed.2d 530 (1984).

United States v. Knotts, 460 U.S. 276, 103 S.Ct. 1081, 75 L.Ed.2d 55 (1983).

United States v. Martinez-Fuerte, 428 U.S. 543, 96 S.Ct. 3074, 49 L.Ed.2d 1116 (1976).

United States v. Matlock, 415 U.S. 164, 94 S.Ct. 988, 39 L.Ed.2d 242 (1974).

United States v. Montoya de Hernandez, 473 U.S. 531, 105 S.Ct. 3304, 87 L.Ed.2d 381 (1985).

United States v. Ortiz, 422 U.S. 891, 95 S.Ct. 2585, 45 L.Ed.2d 623 (1975).

United States v. Ramsey, 431 U.S. 606, 97 S.Ct. 1972, 52 L.Ed.2d 617 (1977).

United States v. Riemer, D.C. Ohio, 392 F.Supp. 1291, 1294.

United States v. Robinson, 414 U.S. 218, 97 S.Ct. 1972, 52 L.Ed.2d 617 (1973).

United States v. Ross, 456 U.S. 798, 102 S.Ct. 2157, 72 L.Ed.2d 570 (1982).

United States v. Sokolow, 490 U.S. 1 (1989).

United States v. Vigo, 487 F.2d 295 (1973).

United States v. White, 401 U.S. 745, 91 S.Ct. 1122, 28 L.Ed.2d 453 (1971).

Vause v. United States, 284 U.S. 661, 52 S.Ct. 37, 76 L.Ed. 560 (1931).

Weeds v. United States, 255 U.S. 109, 41 S.Ct. 306, 65 L.Ed. 537 (1921).

Wright v. United States, 302 U.S. 583, 58 S.Ct. 395, 82 L.Ed. 439 (1938).

Chapter 11 The Law of Arrest

The Constitution does not guarantee that only the guilty will be arrested. If it did, § 1983 would provide a cause of action for every defendant acquitted— indeed, for every suspect released.

—UNITED STATES SUPREME COURT

The Rock—Alcatraz.

How to define the term *arrest*?

When a person is actually under arrest?

What the elements of an arrest are?

When an arrest can legally be made?

Where an arrest can be made?

How much force can be used in making an arrest?

What the only justification for use of deadly force is?

Who has immunity from arrests?

CAN YOU DEFINE THESE TERMS?

Arrest
Fresh pursuit
Hot pursuit

INTRODUCTION*

Chapter 9 discussed how the Fourth Amendment influences searches and seizures. This chapter looks at the requirements for the *ultimate seizure,* a lawful arrest. Perhaps one of the most intrusive and powerful of all government actions is the actual taking into physical custody, or the arresting, of an individual. This is the unique power that the police have, setting them apart from all other professions. It is also the power that our Constitution seeks to control through a variety of rules and the courts. And while an area of extreme concern for champions of our Constitution, the necessity for the power to arrest is recognized as a power that government requires.

Arrest is included under the Fourth Amendment because an arrest is, indeed, a seizure—of the person. The power of arrest is discussed by Ferdico (1996, p. 108):

> The power of arrest is the most important power that law enforcement officers possess. It enables them to deprive a person of the freedom to carry out daily personal and business affairs, and it initiates against a person the process of criminal justice, which may ultimately result in that person being fined or imprisoned. Since an arrest has a potentially great detrimental effect upon a person's life, the law provides severe limitations and restrictions on the law enforcement officer's exercise of the power of arrest.

This chapter begins with some definitions of arrest and an overview of when arrests may generally be lawfully made. This is followed by a discussion of the elements of an arrest, when an arrest has occurred and where arrests

---

*Much of this chapter's material is adapted from *Criminal Procedure,* Harr and Hess, West Publishing Company, 1990.

may be made. Next, issues arising from an arrest are presented, including searches incident to arrests, fresh pursuit, use of force and use of deadly force. The chapter concludes with a brief discussion of the citizen arrest and of who is immune from arrest in this country.

ARREST DEFINED

According to Bennett and Hess (1994, p. 260): "Most state laws define an **arrest** in general terms as: The taking of a person into custody, in the manner authorized by law for the purpose of presenting that person before a magistrate to answer for the commission of a crime." *Black's Law Dictionary* defines *arrest* as follows:

> To arrest is "to deprive a person of his liberty by legal authority. Taking under real or assumed authority, custody of another for the purpose of holding or detaining him to answer a criminal charge or civil demand."

The Maine Supreme Court has said: "An arrest in criminal law signifies the apprehension or detention of the person of another in order that he may be forthcoming to answer for an alleged or supposed crime" (*State v. MacKenzie*, 1965). The general guideline is that a person is indeed under arrest if a reasonable person would believe that under the existing circumstances, they were, in fact, being detained by the police and not free to go.

As noted by *Black's* (p. 110), *Com. v. Brown* established that "all that is required for an 'arrest' is some act by an officer indicating his intention to detain or take the person into custody and thereby subject that person to the actual control and will of the officer; no formal declaration of arrest is required."

A suspect under arrest.

An arrest may involve actual physical detention or a command, verbal or otherwise, by the officer requiring the suspect to not leave. If the person reasonably believes he or she is not free to go, he or she is under arrest. Often this results from what began as a simple stop based on reasonable suspicion.

AN ARREST AND A STOP COMPARED

Law enforcement involves decisions and discretion. Police officers are charged with investigating suspicious circumstances. What begins as a simple stop of a person merely to investigate the possibility of crime may progress to a frisk and then to an arrest and full-body search. The reasonableness of this progression was established in the landmark *Terry* case. The basic differences between a stop and an arrest are summarized in Table 11–1.

AN ARREST OR NOT?

As noted, a simple stop can escalate to become an arrest. There is a middle ground that is technically short of an arrest, but more than a simple stop. Ferdico (1996, p. 71) notes:

> At a still higher level of intensity [than a stop] are police contacts with members of the public involving a detention or temporary seizure of a person that is more intrusive on a person's freedom of action than a brief investigatory "stop." . . . In such instances, courts often hold that, despite the lack of a technical arrest, the seizure is so similar to an arrest in important respects that it should be allowed only if supported by probable cause to believe a crime has been or is being committed.

The leading case in this area is *Dunaway v. New York* (1979). In this case police picked up the defendant based on information implicating him in a murder. They took him to the police station for questioning. He was never told that he was under arrest, but he was not free to leave. Even though he was not booked and, therefore, would have no arrest record, the Supreme Court ruled that the seizure was illegal because the defendant was not free to leave. The "seizure" was much more than a simple stop and frisk and, as such, should have been based on probable cause. In its ruling, the Court declared: "Hostility to seizures based on mere suspicion was a prime motivation for the adoption of the Fourth Amendment."

"It does not matter," asserts del Carmen (1987, p. 94), "whether the act is termed an 'arrest' or a mere 'stop' or 'detention' under state law. When a person has been taken into custody against their will for purposes of criminal

Table 11–1   Stop versus arrest.

	Stop	Arrest
Justification	Reasonable suspicion	Probable cause
Warrant	None	Preferable
Officer's intent	Investigate suspicious activity	Make a formal charge
Search	Pat-down for weapons	Full search for weapons and evidence
Scope	Outer clothing	Area within suspect's immediate control
Record	Minimal (field notes)	Fingerprints, photographs and booking

prosecution or interrogation, there is an arrest under the Fourth Amendment, regardless of what state law says."

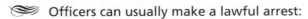 Individuals are under arrest if they reasonably believe they are not free to go.

This contention is echoed in *Cupp v. Murphy* (1973): "The detention of the respondent against his will constituted a seizure of his person, and the Fourth Amendment guarantees of freedom from unreasonable searches and seizures is clearly implicated."

WHAT CONSTITUTES AN ARREST?

At what point does an arrest actually occur? Ferdico (1996, p. 107) lists four basic elements necessary to constitute an arrest:

❖ A purpose or intention of a law enforcement officer to take a person into the custody of the law.
❖ Exercise of real or pretended authority.
❖ Detention or restraint of the person to be arrested, whether by physical force or by submission to assertion of authority.
❖ An understanding by the person to be arrested that it is the intention of the arresting officer then and there to arrest and detain him or her.

The elements of an arrest are (1) an intent to take a person into custody, (2) exercise of authority to do so, (3) a detention or restraint of the person to be arrested and (4) an understanding of what is happening by the arrestee.

WHEN ARRESTS MAY BE LAWFULLY MADE

Generally, lawful arrests can be made in one of three ways.

Officers can usually make a lawful arrest:

❖ For any crime committed in their presence.
❖ For any felony if they have probable cause.
❖ With an arrest warrant.

In the first two instances a warrant is not required. In fact, according to del Carmen (1987, p. 103): "Although arrest warrants are preferred by the courts and desirable for purposes of police protection from liability lawsuits, they are in fact seldom used in police work and are not constitutionally required, except in home arrests. About 95 percent of all arrests are made without a warrant."

Warrantless Arrests for Crimes Committed in the Presence of an Officer

If police officers observe a crime being committed, they have the authority to arrest the individual(s) involved in committing the crime. "In the presence of" includes any of the officer's senses, for example, hearing a drug buy going down, or smelling the odor of marijuana. The information the officer obtains becomes the probable cause for arrest.

As noted in *State v. Pluth* (1923), the officers must know that a crime is being committed before making the arrest. They cannot merely suspect that someone is about to commit a crime. The crime or the attempt must actually take place in the officer's presence.

> Police may arrest for any crime committed in their presence.

Some laws of arrest depend on whether the violation constitutes a misdemeanor or a felony level crime. The difference, specifically defined within a state's criminal code, is a mathematical one: How much *time* would a person be sentenced to if convicted of that particular offense? Generally speaking, a felony is a crime carrying a minimum prison sentence of one year.

Officers who come to the crime scene of a misdemeanor after it has been committed usually cannot make an arrest even though the suspect is still at the scene. State criminal procedure statutes define such limitations. In many states officers must obtain an arrest warrant to make an arrest for a misdemeanor not committed in their presence.

In some states, however, exceptions exist. For example, officers may arrest for misdemeanors not committed in their presence if the suspect might flee or might conceal or destroy evidence or if the incident involves a traffic accident. In other states, such as Minnesota, officers may arrest for some unwitnessed misdemeanors such as domestic assault, driving under the influence of drugs or alcohol and shoplifting. In fact, in the case of domestic assault, police in Minnesota are *mandated* to make an arrest if there is probable cause to believe an assault was committed by that person.

In some states, officers may not only be granted statutory *permission* to arrest for certain unwitnessed misdemeanors such as driving under the influence or shoplifting, but there is a trend to *direct* law enforcement officers to arrest in situations such as domestic assault. This is referred to as a *legislatively required arrest*. Of course, any specific arrest laws permitted by a state must comply with United States constitutional requirements.

While some states have permitted arrests to be made for certain offenses not committed in the presence of the officer, other states have held that they consider issuing a traffic ticket as an arrest, but with an immediate release of the violator on his or her own recognizance.

Warrantless Arrests Based on Probable Cause

The second type of lawful warrantless arrest is an arrest based on probable cause that the suspect has committed a felony. According to Creamer (1980, p. 9): "Probable cause for an arrest is defined as a combination of facts or apparent facts, viewed through the eyes of an experienced police officer, which would lead a man of reasonable caution to believe that a crime is being [or is about to be] or has been committed."

> ⌇ Police may arrest for an unwitnessed felony based on probable cause.

United States v. Watson (1976) established that an arrest without a warrant made in a public place is valid if it is based on probable cause, even if there was time to obtain an arrest warrant. Recall that probable cause can be based on anything an officer becomes aware of through the senses—observational probable cause, or on information provided by others.

In contrast to warrantless arrests for misdemeanors, which must be made as soon as practical, warrantless arrests for felonies based on probable cause do *not* need to be made immediately. This differentiation is made based on the severity of the felony and society's interest in expediting the arrest of a felon so long as sufficient probable cause exists.

Arrests with a Warrant

A conventional interpretation of the Fourth Amendment requires that to be reasonable all arrests be made with a warrant based on probable cause. The warrant must name the person making the complaint, the specific offense being charged, the name of the accused and the basis for the probable cause.

The person making the complaint must swear the facts given are true and sign the complaint. Usually the complaint is made by the investigating police officer.

WHERE ARRESTS MAY BE MADE

Arrests may be made in public places without a warrant if probable cause exists, as established in *United States v. Watson* (1976). Even if a person retreats to a private place, the warrantless arrest based on probable cause is valid, as established in *United States v. Santana* (1975).

Payton v. New York (1980) established that police may not enter a private home to make a routine felony arrest unless exigent circumstances exist, as in hot pursuit to be discussed shortly. In this case police gathered evidence sufficient to establish probable cause that Payton had murdered a gas station manager. Without a warrant, they went to his apartment to arrest him. When no one answered the door, they forced it open. Payton was not there, but the police found a .30-caliber shell casing that was used as evidence in Payton's murder conviction. On appeal, the evidence was excluded, with the Court holding: "In terms that apply equally to seizures of property and to seizures of persons, the Fourth Amendment has drawn a firm line at the entrance to the house. Absent exigent circumstances, that threshold may not reasonably be crossed without a warrant."

A similar ruling was handed down in *Minnesota v. Olson* (1990) regarding warrantless, nonconsensual entrance into a private home to arrest a guest within. This case involved a tip that a robbery-murder suspect was staying at the home of two women. A police officer telephoned the home and asked the woman who answered to tell Olson to step outside. The officer overheard Olson tell her to say that he had left, so the officer ordered the police to enter, service revolvers drawn. They found Olson hiding in a closet and arrested him. The Court held this arrest to be illegal, stating that a houseguest "seeks shelter in another's home precisely because it provides him with privacy, a place where he and his possessions will not be disturbed by anyone except his host and those his host allows inside."

The Court held that guests "are entitled to a legitimate expectation of privacy despite the fact that they have no legal interest in the premises and do not have the legal authority to determine who may or may not enter the household." It also held that a person's "status as to an overnight guest is alone enough to show that he had an expectation of privacy in the home that society is prepared to recognize as reasonable."

As recently as 1990, the Supreme Court has changed its earlier position so that now one may have a legitimate expectation of privacy for standing purposes, even without the "right to exclude other persons from access to" the premises in question.

> Police may make a warrantless arrest based on probable cause in a public place or in a private place that a suspect has retreated to from a public place. They may not make a nonconsensual, warrantless arrest inside a person's home or arrest a guest within that home without exigent circumstances.

Indeed, the founding fathers wanted to assure that a person's home was free from unreasonable searches or seizures, and the courts have upheld this basic freedom.

SEARCH INCIDENT TO ARREST

Once a person is under arrest, that person may be searched. Recall that *Chimel v. California* (1969) provides that it is legal for police officers to search an arrested person and the area within his or her immediate control (reach) for weapons and destructible evidence, as discussed in the previous chapter. This search should normally be done as soon as possible for the officers' safety and to locate any contraband.

Inventory Searching

As discussed in Chapter 10, prisoners who are to be jailed are subject to search. This serves two purposes. First, it protects the prisoner's personal property in that it is all listed and then held in a safe place until the prisoner is released. Second, it protects the officers and other prisoners and helps assure that no weapons or illegal drugs will be taken into the jail.

Chief Justice Burger wrote in *Illinois v. Lafayette* (1983): "It is entirely proper for police to remove and list or inventory property found on the person or in the possession of an arrested person who is to be jailed. A range of governmental interests supports an inventory process."

Similarly, an impounded vehicle can be inventoried for the same reasons as long as there exists a routine practice of the police agency doing the inventory searches so as to protect the interests of both the vehicle owner and the police (*South Dakota v. Opperman,* 1976). But, according to *Florida v. Wells* (1990), an inventory search "must not be a ruse for general rummaging in order to discover incriminating evidence."

PURSUIT

Three relevant cases have been previously discussed. First, *Payton v. New York* (1980) clearly established the sanctity of the home and the illegality of a warrantless, nonconsensual entrance to make a routine arrest—with no exigent circumstances. The second case, *United States v. Santana* (1975), however, established that a hot pursuit justifies forcible entry into an offender's home without a warrant. In this case the police attempted to arrest the defendant in her doorway when she fled into her house and the police followed. The Court found: "We thus conclude that a suspect may not defeat an arrest that has been set in motion in a public place, . . . by the expedient of escaping to a private place."

The third case, *Minnesota v. Olson* (1989), held that "a warrantless intrusion may be justified by hot pursuit of a fleeing felon, or imminent destruction of evidence . . . or the need to prevent a suspect's escape, or the risk of danger to the police or to other persons inside or outside the dwelling." The Court went on to state: "In the absence of hot pursuit there must be at least probable cause to believe that one or more of the other factors justifying the entry were present and that in assessing the risk of danger, the gravity of the crime and likelihood that the suspect is armed should be considered."

The pursuit of a suspect does not necessarily end at the border as often portrayed in the movies. The terms **fresh pursuit** and **hot pursuit** are used to establish this distinction. The term *fresh pursuit* explains the circumstances in which officers can cross state jurisdictional lines to make an arrest of a felon who committed the felony in the officers' state and then crossed the border into another state. *Hot pursuit* refers to the exigent conditions that a pursuit creates, permitting warrantless searches and arrests.

Stuckey (1986, p. 44) states: "Today most states have adopted what is known as the Uniform Act of Fresh Pursuit. This act provides that a peace officer of one state may enter another state in fresh pursuit to arrest one who has committed a felony in the state from which the offender fled." He goes on to explain what constitutes fresh pursuit: "It is generally held today that if a pursuit is uninterrupted and continuous, it is a fresh pursuit," and the police may continue after their suspect.

Some states require that anyone so arrested be brought before the nearest court. Other states allow the arresting officers to return with their prisoner to their own state. Often the result of the pursuit will be that the suspect will be charged with crimes in all jurisdictions involved.

USE OF FORCE IN MAKING AN ARREST

The landmark case in use of force is *Graham v. Connor* (1989). In this case, Graham, a diabetic, asked a friend to take him to a convenience store to get some orange juice to counteract an oncoming insulin reaction. He went in and upon seeing the long line at the checkout, he hurried back to the car and asked his friend to take him to another friend's house instead. Police observing his actions became suspicious, followed the car and made an investigatory stop. Officers ignored Graham's attempts to explain the situation and his condition and during the ensuing encounter, Graham sustained multiple injuries.

He sued the police for excessive force under Section 1983. As noted by Thomas and Means (1990, p. 45), the district court considered four factors in ruling on the defendant's motion:

> The factors to be considered in determining when the excessive use of force gives rise to a cause of action under § 1983: (1) the need for the application of force, (2) the relationship between that need and the amount of force that was used, (3) the extent of the injury inflicted; and (4) whether the force was applied in good faith effort to maintain and restore discipline or maliciously and sadistically for the very purpose of causing harm.

The Court replaced the "substantive due process test" of whether the officer acted "in good faith" or "maliciously and sadistically" with a new test: "objective reasonableness." The reasonableness of force used must be judged "from the perspective of the officer on the scene rather than with the 20/20 vision of hindsight." In finding against Graham, the Court showed that it will support police officers when they properly and reasonably do their jobs.

≈ When making an arrest, police officers can use only as much force as is needed to overcome resistance. If the suspect does not resist arrest, *no* force can be used. Excessive force may cause the officer to be sued.

The Rodney King incident provides an opportunity to examine the excessive force issue in depth. No case in recent history has put the police more in the spotlight when considering improper behavior than the Rodney King episode in California. Americans watched with horror a videotape of the defendant repeatedly struck with police batons and subjected to electrical jolts. While everyone had opinions, the police were held accountable, although not to the extent many thought would have been more appropriate.

Attorney Steven Lerman displays a photo of Rodney King. (Photo by Lee Celano. Provided by Reuters/Corbis-Bettmann.)

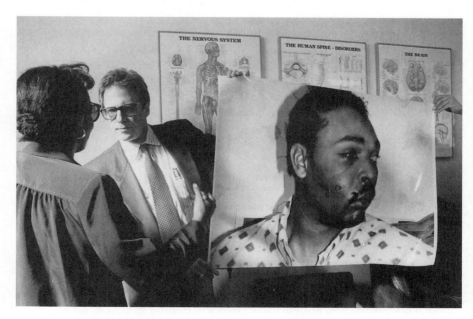

While on the other hand, most law enforcement professionals fully understand that there was more to the story than what the media chose to air.

Our electronic age has made video recorders accessible to many people, and police are finding more than ever that their actions are being watched with strict scrutiny. We are presently experiencing a technological phenomenon whereby Americans in their own homes are developing their personal opinions as to just what "reasonable force" means based on what they can immediately see on the TV news.

Officers can break a door or window or break a car window to make an arrest if necessary. This can be done only after officers have announced themselves, stating the purpose of entry and demanding to be let in. Exceptions may be made if the officers fear the suspect may harm them or others or may destroy evidence. In such cases they may request a "no-knock arrest warrant" to permit them to enter without first announcing themselves, as discussed in Chapter 7.

A warrant with a no-knock provision authorizes the police to enter premises unannounced. They can, for example, break down a door or enter through a window to force entry into fortified crack houses that have barricaded doors and windows, alarms and other protection. A no-knock warrant affords officers the element of surprise and is justified when either officer or citizen safety or the destruction of evidence is a concern. A safety trend is the development of specially trained "entry teams" to assist in executing such dangerous warrant services.

Use of Deadly Force

Use of deadly force is restricted to cases of self-defense or the public safety. In the past this was not the case. The "fleeing felon" rule allowed police officers to shoot to kill any felon who fled to escape arrest. This is no longer true. In *Tennessee v. Garner* (1985) the Court ruled that law enforcement officers cannot shoot "fleeing felons" unless they present an "imminent danger to life."

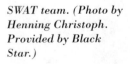

SWAT team. (Photo by Henning Christoph. Provided by Black Star.)

As Justice White set forth, even deadly force can be exercised in preventing the escape (i.e., "arresting") of an individual, but "only if the officer has probable cause to believe that the suspect poses a significant threat of death or serious physical injury to the officer or others." Thus, no longer can one be shot with justification merely because he or she is a fleeing felon.

> The only justification for use of deadly force is self-defense or protecting the lives of others.

As noted by Roberts (1992, p. 16), in 1989 the Supreme Court extended the *Garner* analysis, stating:

> Today we make explicit what was implicit in Garner's analysis and hold that all claims that law enforcement officers have used excessive force—deadly or not—in the course of an arrest, investigatory stop or other "seizure" of a free citizen should be analyzed under the Fourth Amendment and its "reasonableness" standard.

RIGHTS OF THOSE IN CUSTODY

People who are arrested usually have the right to know the charges against them, make a phone call and appear before a magistrate without "undue delay."

CITIZEN'S ARREST

Not all arrests are made by government agents. Individuals not associated with the government may also make arrests if they see a crime being committed. This includes ordinary people who witness a crime as well as private security officers. They must then immediately turn the arrested person over to law enforcement officers. Stuckey (1986, p. 42) clarifies:

> The arrest by a private person is sometimes referred to as a "citizen's arrest," but the private person does not have to be a citizen to make an arrest. The private person may make arrests under certain conditions. These conditions are restrictive to discourage the private person from making arrests. . . . A private person arrest generally requires that the crime for which the arrest is made must have been committed, or attempted, in the presence of the arresting person.

Most state statutes do not specify if a private person making an arrest can use force. Nor do most state statutes specify if a private person making an arrest can call for assistance from others as the police can.

IMMUNITY FROM ARREST

Certain classifications of people have immunity from arrest because of federal or state statutes.

> Foreign diplomats, including ambassadors, ministers, their assistants and attaches and their families and servants have complete immunity from arrest. Foreign consuls and their deputies as well as some legislators and out-of-state witnesses also have limited immunity.

Many states have granted their legislators immunity from civil lawsuits. Some states even give legislators immunity from traffic arrests on their way to sessions, as is the case with federal legislators as well. However, a legislator facing criminal charges has no such immunity.

Finally, out-of-state witnesses may also be granted immunity, as noted by Stuckey (1986, p. 51):

> The Uniform Act to Secure the Attendance of Witnesses from Without the State in Criminal Cases has been adopted by most of the states. This act provides that if a person goes into a state in obedience of a subpoena to testify in that state, he shall not be subject to arrest in connection with any crime committed in the state prior to his entrance into the state to testify. He is also granted a reasonable time to leave the state after testifying without being subject to such an arrest. He is not, however, granted any immunity from arrest for a crime that he may commit while in the state to testify.

The reason for such immunity is to permit individuals carrying out important legal functions to be free to do so.

Summary

An arrest is the official taking of a person to answer criminal charges, depriving him or her of liberty by legal authority. To arrest is "to deprive a person of his liberty by legal authority. Taking under real or assumed authority, custody of another for the purpose of holding or detaining him to answer a criminal charge or civil demand" *(Black's Law Dictionary)*. A person is under arrest if he or she reasonably believes he or she is not free to go.

The elements of an arrest are (1) an intent to take a person into custody, (2) exercise of authority to do so, (3) a detention or restraint of the person to be arrested and (4) an understanding of what is happening by the arrestee. Officers can usually make a lawful arrest for any crime committed in their presence, for any felony if they have probable cause and with an arrest warrant.

A warrantless arrest that begins in a public place may be carried out, even if the person being arrested retreats to a private place. Police may not enter a private home to make a warrantless felony arrest unless exigent circumstances exist. Likewise, police cannot enter a residence to arrest a guest without a warrant or consent.

When making an arrest, police officers can use only as much force as is needed to overcome resistance. If the suspect does not resist arrest, *no* force can be used. Excessive force may classify the officer as a criminal. The only justification for use of deadly force is self-defense or protecting the lives of others.

Foreign diplomats, including ambassadors, ministers, their assistants and attaches and their families and servants have complete immunity from arrest. Foreign consuls and their deputies as well as some legislators and out-of-state witnesses also have limited immunity.

Discussion Questions

1. Explain at what point a person is considered to be "under arrest."
2. Explain the difference between a stop and an arrest.

3. Why might states authorize probable cause arrests for certain unwitnessed misdemeanors?

4. How much force can be used by an officer when executing an arrest? How is it determined?

5. When determining whether a stop or an arrest is lawful, how is the term *reasonable* determined?

6. How does the entertainment industry portray arrest situations? Do you feel this is generally realistic?

7. Do you know anyone who has been arrested? If so, what did they have to say about it?

8. Should anyone be immune from arrest, for example foreign diplomats?

9. Should police officers who are doing their best to enforce the law ever be punished in any way if they are acting in "good faith"?

10. Under what circumstances is someone other than a law enforcement official authorized to make an arrest?

References

Bennett, Wayne W. and Kären M. Hess. *Criminal Investigation.* 4th ed. St. Paul: West Publishing Company, 1994.

Black, Henry Campbell. *Black's Law Dictionary.* 6th ed. St. Paul: West Publishing Company, 1990.

Creamer, J. S. *The Law of Arrest, Search, and Seizure.* 3rd ed. New York: Holt, Rinehart & Winston, 1980.

del Carmen, Rolando V. *Criminal Procedure for Law Enforcement Personnel.* Monterey: Brooks/Cole Publishing Company, 1987.

Ferdico, John N. *Criminal Procedure for the Criminal Justice Professional.* 6th ed. St. Paul: West Publishing Company, 1996.

Roberts, Barbara E. "Legal Issues in Use-of-Force Claims." *The Police Chief.* February 1992, pp. 16–29.

Stuckey, Gilbert B. *Procedures in the Justice System.* 3rd ed. Columbus: Charles E. Merrill Publishing Company, 1986.

Thomas, Bob and Randy Means. "Objective Reasonableness Standard for Use of Non-Deadly Force Established." *The Police Chief.* July 1990, pp. 45–46.

Cases Cited

Chimel v. California, 395 U.S. 752, 89 S.Ct. 2034, 23 L.Ed.2d 685 (1969).

Com. v. Brown

Cupp v. Murphy, 412 U.S. 291, 93 S.Ct. 2000, 36 L.Ed.2d 900 (1973).

Dunaway v. New York, 442 U.S. 200, 99 S.Ct. 2248, 60 L.Ed.2d 824 (1979).

Florida v. Wells, 495 U.S. 1, 110 S.Ct. 1632, 109 L.Ed.2d 1 (1990).

Graham v. Connor, 490 U.S. 386, 109 S.Ct. 1865, 104 L.Ed.2d 443 (1989).

Illinois v. Lafayette, 462 U.S. 640, 103 S.Ct. 2605, 77 L.Ed.2d 65 (1983).

Minnesota v. Olson, 495 U.S. 91, 110 S.Ct. 1684, 109 L.Ed.2d 85 (1990).

Payton v. New York, 445 U.S. 573, 100 S.Ct. 1371, 63 L.Ed.2d 634 (1980).

South Dakota v. Opperman, 428 U.S. 364, 96 S.Ct. 3092, 49 L.Ed.2d 1000 (1976).

State v. MacKenzie, 161 Me. 123, 210 A.2d 24 (1965).

State v. Pluth, 157 Minn. 145, 195 N.W. 789 (1923).

Tennessee v. Garner, 471 U.S. 1, 105 S.Ct. 1694, 85 L.Ed.2d 1 (1985).

Terry v. Ohio, 392 U.S. 1, 88 S.Ct. 1868, 20 L.Ed.2d 889 (1968).

United States v. Santana (1975).

United States v. Watson, 423 U.S. 411, 96 S.Ct. 820, 46 L.Ed.2d 598 (1976).

Chapter 12   The Fifth Amendment: Obtaining Information Legally and Due Process

*No person . . .
shall be
compelled in any
criminal case to
be a witness
against himself;
nor be deprived
of life, liberty, or
property,
without due
process of law
. . .*

—FIFTH
AMENDMENT OF
THE UNITED
STATES
CONSTITUTION

A trial in progress. (Photo by Michelle Bogre. Provided by Black Star.)

DO YOU KNOW . . .

What amendment protects citizens against self-incrimination and guarantees them due process of law?

How the voluntariness of a confession is determined?

The primary modern case for analyzing confession cases?

When the *Miranda* warning must be given?

What constitutes a valid waiver of the rights guaranteed by the *Miranda* decision?

Whether the *Miranda* warning is required during a stop?

Whether private security officers need to recite the *Miranda* warning before interrogating suspects?

What the public safety exception allows police officers to do?

How expectations of privacy are related to statements, including confessions?

What the historical two-pronged test for establishing probable cause based on an informant's information consisted of? The modern day precedent?

What *entrapment* means and how the government can entrap one into committing a crime?

CAN YOU DEFINE THESE TERMS?

Admission
Confession
Entrapment
Informant
Public safety exception
Statement
Waiver

INTRODUCTION*

Our world revolves around communication. But as the electronic and technological advancements continue to defy the imagination, most of the work the government does is communicating with people the old fashioned way—by talking with them. Interviewing remains an important skill for investigators.

What the government can do with the information they acquire usually is determined by *who* acquired the data, and if it was the government, *how* they obtained the information.

---

*Portions of this chapter are adapted from *Criminal Procedure*, Harr and Hess, West Publishing Company, 1990.

The Constitution recognized that government is capable of letting the ends justify the means. This is not to imply that government will stop at nothing to obtain what they want. While there have been reprehensible examples of governmental misconduct, the majority of governmental agents strive to do the best they can with what they have.

The framers of our Constitution, after all, had seen confessions forced through abhorrent means. Keep in mind that this sort of excessive and intensive government action is what compelled the people to forge both a new government and its framework, which continues to define the basics of today's governmental authority. Their goal was to limit government power to ensure freedom for the people. Those who put so much careful thought into developing a document capable of lasting as the world around it changed, could have had absolutely no idea how complex crime would become.

Imagine a discussion around 1787 between the likes of James Madison, Thomas Jefferson, George Washington and Benjamin Franklin anticipating the types of crimes that would occur in the future and the means government might use to investigate them. Technology, the education of government officials *and* criminals, combined with the amount of legal development over the past 200 years have created a legal milieu that would be unimaginable to the framers of our Constitution; and yet, their document continues to work, as well as, if not better than, when they provided their final draft. Simply amazing.

Technological developments have only increased the challenges of determining how and when government agents can obtain information. And while technology has been addressed elsewhere in this text, the acquisition of information is an important means by which the Constitution may control potential government misconduct.

It was never the intent of those who developed the Constitution to anticipate *what* the government would use to collect data. It was, however, their intent to limit overzealous governmental efforts to acquire this data. For this they had experienced firsthand, and each of them knew too well that an equitable and kind government, whose job it was to serve the people rather than a person, needed definite restrictions on what . . . and how . . . information was acquired by its agents.

This chapter introduces the different means by which the government acquires information and the laws that apply. This area of law is not to be taken lightly. Because a confession by the accused provides the prosecution with powerful evidence, it can be devastating when such an admission is rejected by the court for failing to meet the necessary legal requirements. What other proof can be as damning as an accused proclaiming, "I did it!"? While this area of law is admittedly complex, the basic guidelines are consistent with the spirit of the Constitution and are based on fairness.

This chapter begins with a discussion of the government's need to know certain information and how the Fifth Amendment governs this need to know and promises due process. Next, the law surrounding confessions and the well-known *Miranda* decision are explored. This is followed by discussions of the expectation of privacy and of using informants to obtain information. The chapter concludes with a discussion of entrapment as police overreach.

Figure 12-1
Individual rights versus societal needs.

Judicial interpretations of the Constitution seek to balance all needs to ultimately make a better nation based on the idea of fairness.

Individual rights   Societal needs

GOVERNMENT'S NEED TO KNOW

Much of what government can do *for* people is based on what that government knows about them. After all, the services that federal, state and local governments are expected to provide are the result of listening to and studying the needs and desires of those it serves. A debate as old as any government has been "What does the government need to know, and what are the limits by which it is acquired?" In 1790 George Washington's friend and contributor to *The Federalist Papers,* John Jay, wrote: "Let it be remembered that civil liberty consists not in a right to every man to do just what he pleases, but it consists in an equal right to all citizens to have, enjoy, and do, in peace, security and without molestation, whatever the equal and constitutional laws of the country admit to be consistent with the public good."

The enforcement of laws depends to a great degree on government agents' ability to obtain confessions from those suspected of committing crimes or knowing who did. The balance lies in having this done within the boundaries of the Constitution.

DUE PROCESS OF LAW AND CONFESSIONS

The Fifth Amendment states that "No person shall . . . be compelled in any criminal case to be witness against himself; nor be deprived of life, liberty, or property, without due process of law." The guarantees in the Fifth Amendment were incorporated under the Fourteenth Amendment and held applicable to the states in *Malloy v. Hogan* (1964) because it is one of those amendments determined to be fundamental to our concept of ordered liberty.

The Due Process Model

Bacigal (1996, p. 149) explains the due process model as follows:

> The Due Process Model derives its name from, and is based on, the Due Process clause of the Fourteenth Amendment: "nor shall any state deprive any person of life, liberty, or property, without due process of law." In the case of *Rochin v. California,* Justice Frankfurter states, "Due process of law, as a historic and generative principle, precludes defining, and thereby confining these standards of conduct more precisely than to say that convictions cannot be brought about by methods that offend 'a sense of justice.'"

In *Rochin v. California* (1952), three deputy sheriffs, acting on a tip, entered the defendant's unlocked front door and then forced open the second floor bedroom door. They saw two capsules on the nightstand and asked whose they were. The defendant grabbed and put them in his mouth. After the deputies were unable to extract them from his mouth before he swallowed them, they took him to the hospital and had his stomach pumped. Two capsules containing morphine were recovered and used as evidence against him. In overturning his conviction, Justice Frankfurter wrote:

> The proceedings by which this conviction was obtained do more than offend some fastidious squeamishness or private sentimentalism about combatting crime too energetically. This is conduct that shocks the conscience. . . . This court of proceeding by agents of government to obtain evidence is bound to offend even hardened sensibilities. They are methods too close to the rack and the screw to permit constitutional differentiation.

Bacigal also suggests that the: "Due Process Model recognizes that determination of factual guilt may be subordinated to other goals, such as controlling and correcting misconduct by government officials."

> ≈≋ The Fifth Amendment provides for protection against self-incrimination and guarantees citizens due process of law by limiting the federal government. The Fourteenth Amendment made this applicable to the states.

Whether you look at this area from a due process model or as a strict Fifth Amendment interpretation, this has been a significant area of judicial examination and has produced a great deal of litigation in an effort to apply constitutional limits. The Supreme Court has taken several paths to reach an answer over the years, but questions remain. The primary question that concerns government agents is "When will confessions be admissible as evidence in court?" Justice Frankfurter, in *Culombe v. Connecticut* (1961), stated:

> Despite modern advances in the technology of crime detection, offenses frequently occur about which things cannot be made to speak. And where there cannot be found innocent human witnesses to such offenses, nothing remains—if police investigation is not to be balked before it has fairly begun—but to seek out possibly guilty witnesses and ask them questions, witnesses, that is, who are suspected of knowing something about the offense precisely because they are suspected of implication in it.

The Need for Interrogation

Early common law permitted confessions to be obtained by any manner, including force or the threat of force. For obvious reasons, the reliability of such admissions is to be questioned. By the middle of the eighteenth century, English courts began to limit the admissibility of confessions. The courts increasingly questioned whether the confession was voluntary and not provided under improper pressure by the authorities. And so, while the need for interrogations by law enforcement is acknowledged, not all confessions will be admissible in court. According to Whitebread and Slobogin (1986, p. 357): "The Supreme Court has excluded confessions which are considered the product of 'compulsion' by the state, in part because it may not be reliable as evidence, but primarily because society should not sanction coercive techniques, regardless of the importance of the information they may produce."

Statements, Admissions and Confessions

Ferdico (1996, p. 438) provides the following definitions:

Statement is a broad term meaning simply any oral or written declaration or assertion. *Admission* means a statement or acknowledgement of facts by a person tending to incriminate that person, but not sufficient of itself to establish guilt of a crime. An admission, alone or in connection with other facts, tends to show the existence of one or more, but not all, elements of a crime. *Confession* means a statement or acknowledgement of facts by a person establishing that person's guilt of all elements of a crime [bold added].

Voluntariness of Confessions

The exclusionary rule prohibits using confessions obtained in violation of a person's constitutional rights and those that are otherwise coerced and, thus, inherently unreliable. Recalling that the judge-made common law exclusionary rule seeks to hold government misconduct accountable by prohibiting illegally obtained evidence from being admitted into evidence, it is critical that there be an understanding of what is legally or illegally obtained data.

The first confession case decided by the Supreme Court was *Brown v. Mississippi* (1936). In this case, Brown was accused of murder, and when he denied the accusation, a deputy sheriff and another hung him from a tree, but he insisted on his innocence. He was then tied to the tree and whipped, but still he maintained his innocence, so he was released. Several days later, Brown was again beaten by the deputy and was told he would continue to receive beatings until he confessed. Finally, Brown did confess and was taken to jail.

Two other suspects were also taken to that jail and accused of the murder. They were made to strip, were laid over chairs and were beaten with a leather strap with a buckle on it. They also finally confessed. The next day, the three were taken to the sheriff where they confessed to the murder. At the trial, which began the next day, the defendants said their confessions were false, obtained through torture. And although rope marks were clearly visible and although none of the participants denied that beatings had taken place, the defendants were convicted and sentenced to death.

The Court held the confessions inadmissible, finding the convictions void for violating the Fourteenth Amendment due process rights of the defendants and noting that coerced confessions are simply not reliable.

In the case of *Fikes v. Alabama* (1957), the Supreme Court summarized the standard of that time as "whether the totality of the circumstances that preceded the confessions deprived the defendant of his power of resistance." This has been termed the *due process voluntariness test*. This is to say, for there to be the required constitutional element of due process in such an occurrence, the suspect must be making any admission *voluntarily*. A coerced confession, obviously, has little credibility.

Whitebread and Slobogin (1986, p. 358) state: "Determining such a standard required a specific case-by-case analysis. But the factors that the courts have identified in assessing the voluntariness of a confession can be broken down into three broad categories."

 Voluntariness of a confession is determined by (1) the police conduct involved, (2) the characteristics of the accused and (3) the timing of the confession.

THE POLICE CONDUCT INVOLVED   In the case of *Rogers v. Richmond* (1961), Justice Frankfurter stated that involuntary confessions are "excluded not because such confessions are unlikely to be true, but because the methods used to extract them offend an underlying principle in the enforcement of our criminal law; that ours is an accusatorial and not an inquisitorial system—a system in which the state must establish guilt by evidence independently and freely secured and may not by coercion prove its charge against an accused out of his own mouth."

Government conduct found to extract confessions in ways inconsistent with due process include:

❖ Physical force or the threat of force (*State v. Jennings*, 1979).
❖ Promises of any kind (*Bram v. United States*, 1897).
❖ Unfair and manipulative questioning by a state-employed psychiatrist (*Leyra v. Denno*, 1954).
❖ Confinement in a small place (*United States v. Koch*, 1977).
❖ Isolation from family, friends or lawyer (*Davis v. North Carolina*, 1966).
❖ Deprivation of basic needs such as food, drink and sleep (*Robinson v. Smith*, 1978).
❖ Unreasonably long interrogations (*Ashcraft v. Tennessee*, 1944; *Davis v. North Carolina*, 1966).
❖ Trickery or deception (*Spano v. New York*, 1959).

Recall that *Arizona v. Fulminante* (1991) established that cases involving the admissibility of involuntary confessions could apply the harmless error doctrine. If no harm resulted, the confession should be admissible. A key question in this case was whether Fulminante's confession was coerced. In this case, Fulminante was in prison for one crime, but was also suspected of having committed murder. A fellow inmate offered to protect Fulminante if he would tell him the truth about the murder, which he did. This inmate later became a state's witness and disclosed Fulminante's confession. The Court ruled that the confession was, indeed, coerced, and therefore involuntary. Since it was a key factor in his conviction, the error was not harmless, and the conviction was reversed.

CHARACTERISTICS OF THE ACCUSED   In this area, the court needs to ask whether any special characteristics of the accused might cause the reliability of the information to be questioned. Factors considered here include:

❖ Age of the accused.
❖ Level of intelligence and education.
❖ Mental illness or other emotional problems.
❖ Physical condition.
❖ Drug or alcohol influence.

Each of the preceding must be considered when an admission or confession is obtained. In addition, *Mincey v. Arizona* (1978) held that continued interrogation of an injured, depressed suspect in a hospital intensive care unit was violative of due process.

TIMING OF THE CONFESSION   This refers to the stage of the legal action at which the confession is obtained. If the accused has, in fact, already been indicted for a crime, criminal procedure dictates that at such a critical stage in the process the lawyer for the accused must be in attendance. This may prohibit certain attempts by law enforcement to obtain admissions unless this right is properly waived by the defendant. Jayne and Buckley (1992, p. 70) caution that often the defense will hire a psychologist to evaluate the interrogation used on a defendant:

> The psychologist's description of the interrogation frequently includes a variety of adjectives that are intended to convince the judge that the confession was involuntary. The interrogation is commonly characterized as involving brainwashing, hypnosis, coercion, compulsive tactics, or undue duress.
> According to defense counsel, if an interrogation fits any of these descriptions, the logical conclusion must be that the suspect's free will was removed and, therefore, the confession was involuntary.

An effective interrogation is able to accomplish two things: (1) reduce the suspect's self-preserving resistance to confessing and (2) increase the suspect's desire to tell the truth. Jayne and Buckley (1992, p. 72) note that although effective interrogators use psychologically sophisticated techniques, they do so from necessity:

> They involve persuasion, insincerity, potential trickery, and deceit, but they do not involve coercion, compulsion, brainwashing, or hypnosis. And they do not remove a suspect's free will.
> Proper interrogation techniques allow the suspect to terminate an interrogation at any time by either leaving the interrogation room in a noncustodial situation or by respecting the custodial suspect's invocation of [their] *Miranda* rights.

What the Supreme Court in *Haynes v. Washington* (1963) held was that the Fourteenth Amendment due process voluntariness test requires that the totality of the circumstances surrounding each confession be examined. Was the admission truly voluntary? Were the individual's constitutional guarantees protected? Was the good of the people balanced with the needs of their government and the freedoms of the accused? As with all constitutional cases, the balance being considered is delicate, for the final result will vitally affect all concerned, not only in the case at hand, but in all future matters that will depend on the outcome.

The first step away from the case-by-case voluntariness analysis occurred in *Massiah v. United States* (1964), followed by *Escobedo v. Illinois* (1964) in which the Supreme Court emphasized the defendant's Sixth Amendment right to counsel, to be discussed in Chapter 13.

In *Escobedo v. Illinois* the Court moved from evaluating the voluntariness of a statement or confession on the "totality of the circumstances," and shifted instead to a single circumstance: "When the process shifts from investigatory to accusatory—when its focus is on the accused and its purpose is to elicit a confession . . . the accused must be permitted to consult with his lawyer." This shift from the Fifth Amendment to the Sixth Amendment is discussed in the next chapter.

Two years after *Massiah* and *Escobedo,* the Supreme Court decided the landmark case of *Miranda v. Arizona* (1966).

MIRANDA

The *Miranda* case is perhaps the best known case and has been said to be the most significant law enforcement case ever decided. Actually, the *Miranda* case, because of its notoriety, has arguably done more to teach constitutional law to the masses than any other source. Most television and movie watchers can recite the requirements set forth in this pivotal case by Chief Justice Warren and understand that the purpose of the warning is to let the accused know that they do have rights and to protect themselves. This is a basic understanding of justice.

In applying the basic idea of *fairness* to this famous case, the issue was whether the suspect actually waived his constitutional rights. While a seemingly simple question, the case is full of intriguing legal issues, and some controversial scholars believe the *Miranda* case to have been the most famous and controversial of the Warren Court. Because of the notoriety of the basic requirements arising from the *Miranda* decision, many people have a much greater concept of constitutional law than may be aware of it!

Miranda served to extend the *Escobedo* decision and to shift the area of inquiry to the Fifth Amendment.

> *Miranda* remains the precedent case referred to by courts analyzing confession issues.

The Case

Ernesto Miranda was a poor 23 year old with only a ninth-grade education. He was arrested at his home for rape and was taken to the police station where he was identified by the complaining witness. Within two hours he signed a written confession. Miranda was never informed of his right to consult with an attorney, to have an attorney present during questioning or of his right not to be compelled to incriminate himself.

The legal issue in the *Miranda* case was whether the police must inform a suspect who is the subject of custodial interrogation of his constitutional rights concerning self-incrimination and counsel before questioning. Chief Justice Warren wrote:

We hold that when an individual is taken into custody or otherwise deprived of his freedom by the authorities and is subject to questioning, the privilege against self-incrimination is jeopardized. Procedural safeguards must be employed. . . . He must be warned prior to any questioning that he has a right to remain silent, that anything he says can be used against him in a court of law, that he has the right to the presence of an attorney, and that if he cannot afford an attorney one will be appointed for him prior to any questioning if he so desires.

Opportunities to exercise those rights must be offered to him throughout the interrogation. According to del Carmen (1987, pp. 256–257):

Miranda v. Arizona has had the deepest impact on the day-to-day crime investigation phase of police work. Miranda is significant in that seldom does the Court tell police exactly what to do. The Court literally told the police what warnings ought to be given if the evidence attained from the interrogation will be admitted in court. Miranda also clarified some of the ambiguous terms used in Escobedo. "By custodial interrogation," said the Court, "we mean questioning initiated by law enforcement officers after a person has been taken into custody or otherwise deprived of his freedom of action in any significant way." It added, "This is what we meant in Escobedo when we spoke of an investigation which had focused on an accused." The Escobedo case brought the right to counsel to the police station prior to trial; the Miranda case went beyond the police station and brought the right to counsel out into the street if an interrogation is to take place.

LaFave and Israel (1985, pp. 284–285) stress:

Miranda thus represents a striking contrast to both *Escobedo v. Illinois,* decided two years earlier, and the Court's usual "totality of circumstances" approach to the due process voluntariness issue. While the holding in *Escobedo* had been cautiously limited to the facts of the particular case before the Court, the *Miranda* holding most certainly was not, for it contained a set of rules to be followed by police in all future custodial interrogations. And while "totality of circumstances" holdings were not easily applied to other cases with somewhat different pressures or defendants of somewhat different susceptibilities, the nature of the *Miranda* rule was such that this was not true of this landmark decision.

The Miranda *Warning*

The *Miranda* warning itself may be read from a printed card as shown in Figure 12-2, or recited from memory and must include the following:

The Constitution requires that I inform you that:

❖ You have the right to remain silent.
❖ Anything you say can and will be used against you in court.
❖ You have the right to talk to a lawyer now and have him present now or at any time during questioning.
❖ If you cannot afford a lawyer, one will be appointed for you without cost.

Duckworth v. Eagan (1989) held that the *Miranda* warning does not need to be given verbatim—word for word—as stated in *Miranda v. Arizona.* What is required is that suspects' rights as set forth in the *Miranda* case are clearly

---

MIRANDA WARNING/WAIVER

You have the right to remain silent.
Tiene el derecho a permanecer callado(a).

Anything you say can and will be used against you in a court of law.
Todo lo que diga puede y será usado en su contra en una corte legal.

You have the right to consult an attorney and to have that attorney present during questioning by police.
Tiene el derecho a consultar a un abogado y a tener a su abogado presente durante la interrogación de la policía.

If you decide to talk without an attorney present, you may request an attorney at any time during questioning.
Si decide hablar sin un abogado presente, puede pedir un abogado cuando quiera durante la interrogación.

If you are unable to afford an attorney, one will be appointed to represent you without charge.
Si no puede pagarle a un abogado, uno le será asignado para que lo/la represente sin cargo.

Do you understand?	**Do you want an attorney?**
¿Entiende usted?	¿Quiere a un abogado?
Do you wish to remain silent?	**Do you wish to talk?**
¿Quiere permanecer callado(a)?	¿Quiere hablar?

Figure 12–2
Miranda card in English and Spanish.

conveyed. As stated in *Anderson v. State* (1969), the question is "whether the words used by the officer, in view of the age, intelligence, and demeanor of the individual being interrogated, convey a clear understanding of all *Miranda* rights."

Some officers refer to a "soft *Miranda* warning," which is recited in a less harsh and direct manner than that imprinted on most *Miranda* cards. This is permissible as long as all elements of the warning are present. But unless the warning is read from a card, a defense attorney is sure to press the issue of whether the officer might not have forgotten any portion of the warning.

When the Miranda Warning Must Be Given

Circumstances surrounding an interrogation and whether the situation requires a *Miranda* warning were expanded on in *Oregon v. Mathiason* (1977) when the Court said:

Any interview of one suspected of a crime by a police officer will have coercive aspects to it, simply by virtue of the fact that the police officer is part of a law enforcement system which may ultimately cause the suspect to be charged with a crime. But police officers are not required to administer *Miranda* warnings to everyone whom they question. Nor is the requirement of warnings to be imposed simply because the questioning takes place in the station house, or because the questioned person is one whom the police suspect. *Miranda* warnings are required only where there has been such a restriction on a person's freedom as to render him "in custody." It was that sort of coercive environment which *Miranda* by its terms was made applicable, and to which it is limited.

> The *Miranda* warning must be given to a suspect who is interrogated in the custody of the police, that is, when the suspect is not free to leave.

According to Ferdico (1996, p. 314): "Law enforcement officers often have difficulty determining when a person is in 'custody' or is 'deprived of his freedom of action in any significant way' so as to entitle the person to the *Miranda* warnings. One of the reasons for this difficulty is that the meaning of the word custody depends upon a consideration of a variety of circumstances. A safe policy to follow is to give the warnings whenever there is any doubt whether or not they apply."

And del Carmen (1987, p. 263) gives this advice: "A lot of confusion can be avoided if the officer simply remembers that 'custodial interrogation' takes

Agents use force to subdue a suspect.

place in two general situations: (1) when the suspect is under arrest and (2) when the suspect is not under arrest, but is 'deprived of his freedom in a significant way.'"

While confusion continues to exist over just exactly when a person is "in custody," you can make two basic inquiries to answer the questions:

1. Has the person been told by the police that he or she is under arrest?
2. Has the person been deprived of his or her freedom in a significant way so that he or she does not feel reasonably free to leave the situation, based on a totality of the circumstances?

In regard to the second question, if the police won't allow the person to leave on his or her own, and if the person tries he or she will be detained by the police, other than in a stop situation during a brief investigatory stop, that person is under arrest, even if the police haven't said, "You're under arrest."

This echoes the statement of the court in *California v. Bakeler* (1983) that, for the purpose of *Miranda*, the ultimate determinant of whether a person is "in custody" is "whether the suspect has been subjected to a formal arrest or to equivalent restraints on his freedom of movement."

No *Miranda* warning is required if there is no seizure of the person as long as the police do not convey the message that compliance is required. An arrest situation is a much clearer type of encounter.

SUSPECT UNDER ARREST   Clearly, an arrested person is in custody and must be given the *Miranda* warning *if* he or she is to be questioned by police. Mere detention does not by itself require the *Miranda* warning.

Even if a person is the suspect of a crime and being questioned, unless the interrogation is done while the suspect is in custody or deprived of freedom in any significant way, the *Miranda* warning need not be given (*Beckwith v. United States*, 1976).

SUSPECT AT THE POLICE STATION   If police direct a suspect to come to the police station for questioning or take the suspect there, this is a coercive atmosphere and the *Miranda* warning is required. If, however, the suspect voluntarily comes to the station, no warning is required. As noted in *Miranda*: "There is no requirement that police stop a person who enters a police station and states that he wishes to confess to a crime, or a person who calls the police to offer a confession or any other statement he desires to make. Volunteered statements of any kind are not barred by the Fifth Amendment and their admissibility is not affected by our holding today."

The same is usually true of questioning a suspect in a police car. If the suspect is asked to get into the car, it is usually a custodial situation, especially if the person can't get out of the car.

If, on the other hand, someone flags down a police car and makes a voluntary confession of a crime the suspect just committed, no *Miranda* warning is required. If the officer did not ask any questions of the suspect, no *Miranda* is necessary, nor is the warning required if the person just walks up to the cer and is not in custody and confesses (*United States v. Jones,* 1986; *United States v. Wright,* 1993).

SUSPECT IS IN CUSTODY FOR ANOTHER OFFENSE   Since the suspect is obviously in custody, it is imperative that the *Miranda* warning be given before any questioning begins. All that is required is that a custodial situation exist. It does not matter what the person is in custody for.

OTHER FACTORS INDICATING A CUSTODIAL SITUATION   Any kind of physical restraint places the situation within the *Miranda* requirement. As found in *People v. Shivers* (1967), if a police officer holds a gun on a person, that person is in custody and not free to leave. If, however, the suspect also has a gun, it is unlikely he would be considered in custody (*Yates v. United States,* 1967). Ferdico (1996, p. 320) stresses: "This is a potentially important situation because armed offenders often make damaging admissions while holding off the police."

Waiving the Rights

A **waiver** is a purposeful, voluntary giving up of a known right. Suspects must know and understand their constitutional rights to legally waive them. The Court in *Miranda* set forth that a statement will be admissible only if the government meets its "heavy burden" of demonstrating "that the defendant knowingly and intelligently waived his privilege against self-incrimination and his right to retained or appointed counsel." Further, at any time during questioning the defendant may choose to exercise the right to remain silent.

> If after hearing a police officer read the *Miranda* warning, suspects remain silent, this is not a waiver. To waive their rights, suspects must state, orally or in writing, that (1) they understand their rights and (2) they will voluntarily answer questions without a lawyer present.

The competency of suspects to understand and waive their rights should always be considered. People who are under the influence of alcohol or other drugs, who are physically injured, who are in shock or who are very young or very old may have difficulty understanding the situation. As noted, suspects may rescind the waiver at any point in the interrogation. It is only common sense that people must possess sufficient competence to understand that they are waiving a critical constitutional right that they have. And while television may have exposed many to such rights, the Court in *Tague v. Louisiana* (1980) reemphasized that the government has the "heavy burden" of showing that the person was competent to relinquish these rights.

Oregon v. Elstad (1985) established that if police obtain a voluntary admission from the suspect without first being advised of his right to remain silent, a confession made after the *Miranda* warning is given will be admissible.

Colorado v. Spring (1987) established that a waiver of *Miranda* rights is valid even though the suspect thought the questioning was going to be about a minor crime, but the police change their line of questioning to inquire about a more serious crime. At this point the suspect could recant the waiver.

Connecticut v. Barrett (1987) established that if a suspect refuses to make a written statement without a lawyer present but does make an oral confession, that confession is admissible.

Finally, *Patterson v. Illinois* (1988) established that a waiver includes waiving the right to counsel in addition to the right against self-incrimination.

There is often confusion as to what constitutes a valid waiver and what constitutes an invocation of those rights. According to some, this is where the real battle is being fought.

When Miranda *Warnings Generally Are Not Required*

Vaughn (1992, p. 71) notes: "Over the years and through exceptions, however, the Court systematically has blurred the bright-line rule of *Miranda*, thus changing its original impact and meaning." del Carmen (1987, pp. 266–268) lists nine instances in which *Miranda* warnings are not normally required:

❖ No questions asked [not an interrogation].
❖ General questioning at the crime scene.
❖ Questioning witnesses.
❖ Volunteered statements.
❖ Statements made to private persons, e.g., friends, cellmates.
❖ Questioning in an office or place of business [if the person is free to go].
❖ Stop-and-frisk cases.
❖ Before a grand jury.
❖ Noncustodial interrogations by a probation officer.

Brief questioning in stores, restaurants, parks, hospitals and other public places is generally considered noncustodial unless the subject is not free to leave. If the suspect is not being detained by the police, it is not a custodial situation. The question is: "If the person tried to leave, would the police stop them?"

Likewise, very brief questioning such as in the stop-and-frisk cases and general questioning at a crime scene mentioned above are not custodial situations. Ferdico (1996, p. 318) notes: "It is likely that a law enforcement officer would be allowed to briefly detain all potential witnesses at the scene of a crime for questioning without triggering *Miranda*. Innocent citizen witnesses directed by an officer not to leave the scene of a crime are not likely to consider themselves in custody or under arrest and it is unlikely that a court would so consider them" (*Arnold v. United States,* 1967).

Another question that arises is whether the *Miranda* warning needs to be given to individuals who are temporarily detained by the police. Ferdico (1996, p. 292) describes a case in which this question arose:

Police officers had been alerted via radio to be on the lookout for a white Mustang with California license plates believed to be driven by a person involved in a robbery in a nearby town. When the officers spotted a car fitting that description, they stopped the defendant, asked him for identification, and asked if he had been in the town where the robbery occurred. Defendant replied that he had. No *Miranda* warnings had been given prior to the questions. Defendant was convicted of robbery and appealed.

The court found nothing in the questioning that amounted to an in-custody interrogation calling for *Miranda* warnings:

Miranda does not bar all inquiry by authorities without previous warnings. . . . In our opinion *Miranda* was not intended to prohibit police officers from asking suspicious persons such things as their names and recent whereabouts without fully informing them of their constitutional rights" (*Utsler v. South Dakota*, 1969).

> The *Miranda* warning need not be given during a stop, as compared to an arrest.

The Supreme Court of Washington agreed in *State v. Lane* (1970) when it stated: "We hold that it is not a violation of either the letter or the spirit of *Miranda* for police to ask questions which are strictly limited to protecting the immediate physical safety of the police themselves and which could not reasonably be delayed until after warnings are given."

The same is true of routine traffic stops; questioning a driver who has committed a traffic violation is not considered custodial. It is similar to the brief, on-the-street stop-and-frisk encounter. *Berkemer v. McCarty* (1984) established that the *Miranda* rule does not apply to roadside questioning of a motorist who has been detained during a routine traffic stop. In addition, *Pennsylvania v. Muniz* (1990) established that police may ask routine questions of individuals suspected of driving under the influence of alcohol or drugs without giving them the *Miranda* warning. They may also videotape the responses given.

Another exception to interrogation in the absence of a *Miranda* warning is questioning done by a private security officer.

> Private security officers are not required to advise suspects of their *Miranda* rights.

The rule from *Miranda* applies only to public police officers or other government agents or personnel. Case law continues to recognize the clear differentiation between public police and private security.

In 1990 the Supreme Court made another decision related to *Miranda* in *Illinois v. Perkins*. In this case the Court held that undercover police agents do not have to administer *Miranda* warnings to incarcerated suspects before soliciting incriminating information from them. The Court decided that *Miranda* did not apply because there was no custodial interrogation (not a police dominated atmosphere) that would necessitate reading the warnings. As noted by Vaughn (1992, p. 72): "The 1990 Court appears to condone police deception in eliciting incriminating remarks from criminal suspects."

He also notes (p. 75): "As a general rule these cases [lower court interpretations of *Perkins*] demonstrate that governmental trickery and deception are acceptable law enforcement practices." Vaughn suggests a four-part "ends-justifies-the-means" test to the Court's reasoning in *Perkins* and argues that a new "crime-control bright-line test" is replacing the original due process-oriented *Miranda* rule.

❖ The end must itself be good.
❖ The means must be a plausible way to achieve the end.
❖ There must be no alternative, better, means to achieve the same end.
❖ The means must not undermine some other equal or greater end (Cohen, 1991, p. 87).

The Public Safety Exception

An important exception to the *Miranda* requirement involves the safety of the public. The precedent case occurred in 1984 in *New York v. Quarles* when the Supreme Court ruled on the **public safety exception** to the *Miranda* warning requirement.

In this case a young woman stopped two police officers and told them she had been raped. She described the rapist and said he had just entered a nearby supermarket, armed with a gun. The officers located the suspect, Benjamin Quarles, and ordered him to stop. Quarles ran, and the officers momentarily lost sight of him. When Quarles was apprehended and frisked, he was wearing an empty shoulder holster. One officer asked Quarles where the gun was, and Quarles nodded toward some cartons, saying, "The gun is over there." The officer retrieved the gun, arrested Quarles and read him his rights. Quarles waived his rights to an attorney and answered questions.

At the trial, the court ruled pursuant to *Miranda* that the statement "The gun is over there" and the discovery of the gun as a result were inadmissible.

The United States Supreme Court, in reviewing the case, ruled that if *Miranda* warnings had deterred the response to the officer's question, the result would have been more than the loss of evidence. As long as the gun was concealed in the store, it was a danger to the public safety.

> The public safety exception allows police officers to question suspects without first giving the *Miranda* warning if the information sought sufficiently affects the officers' and the public's safety.

The Court ruled that in this case the need to have the suspect talk took precedence over the requirement to read the defendant his rights. As the Court noted, the material factor in applying this public safety exception is whether a public threat could be removed by the suspect's statement. In this case, the officer asked the question only to ensure his and the public safety. He then gave the *Miranda* warning before continuing questioning.

FOURTH AMENDMENT VIOLATIONS OF EXPECTATIONS OF PRIVACY

Another important consideration in whether information obtained will be admitted in court is whether it violates a person's Fourth Amendment right to a reasonable expectation of privacy. The precedent landmark case, *Katz v. United States* (1967), recall, involved such an issue. Recordings of phone calls placed from a public telephone booth were used in obtaining the defendant's conviction. The Supreme Court reversed the California decision, saying: ". . . the Fourth Amendment protects people not places. . . . Wherever a man may be, he is entitled to know that he will remain free from unreasonable searches and seizures." The investigators had probable cause, but erred in not obtaining prior approval for their actions in the form of a warrant.

> ⪜ Statements, including confessions, will not be admissible in court if obtained while violating a person's Fourth Amendment right to a reasonable expectation of privacy.

Sometimes this reasonable expectation of privacy involves someone conversing with an informant.

USING INFORMANTS

Many crimes are solved not because officers stumble on crimes in progress, but because they get information from a number of sources that help them learn who may have been involved. Informants remain an important source of information. An **informant** is any person who gives government agencies information on criminal activity.

According to Ferdico (1996, p. 230): "The method of establishing probable cause through the use of an informant's information is sometimes referred to as the 'hearsay method,' as opposed to the direct observation method."

Officers who use informants to establish probable cause must follow specific legal procedures established by case law. Recall that two Supreme Court decisions, *Aguilar v. Texas* (1964) and *Spinelli v. United States* (1969), formerly established specific requirements for officers who use informants' information to prepare complaints or affidavits. These two cases were considered separate and independent of each other.

The *Aguilar* case applied a two-pronged test to determine probable cause. The first prong tested the informant's basis of knowledge. Was the information accurate? Did the informant personally witness the information given? If not, did the information come from another source? Is there still reason to believe it?

The second prong tested the informant's credibility. Was the person reliable? Was the informant's identity known? Was the informant an ordinary citizen or a criminal?

〜 The historical two-pronged test for establishing probable cause using information obtained from an informant looked at (1) the basis of knowledge and (2) the informant's credibility.

Ordinary citizens are presumed credible when they claim to be victims of or witnesses to a crime, or when they express concern for their own safety and do not expect anything in return for the information. It is also presumed that citizen informants would probably fear the consequences of committing perjury and would, therefore, be truthful.

When informants are criminals, they seldom will identify themselves. This poses a problem in determining credibility. One way to establish the credibility of criminal informants is to show that they have given accurate information in the past. Another way is to show that they made admissions or produced evidence against their own interest. A third way is to show they have been informants for a period of time. A fourth way to establish criminal informant credibility is to conduct the investigation with the informant supervised by a law enforcement officer.

The two-pronged test to establish probable cause was abandoned in 1983 in the landmark case *Illinois v. Gates.* Here the Supreme Court said that in the future they would rely upon the totality of the circumstances in judging the trustworthiness of informant information.

〜 The current precedent case in most states for determining probable cause based on an informant's information is the totality of the circumstances as established in *Illinois v. Gates* (1983). In other words, is the information reliable?

Nonetheless, an understanding of the historic two-pronged test is important because, as noted by Ferdico (p. 230):

> [T]he underlying rationales of these decisions and other cases interpreting them retain their vitality and help in analyzing the totality of the circumstances under Gates. Second, several states have rejected the Gates decision based on their state constitutions or statutes. These states still require complaints and affidavits to be prepared according to the Aguilar and Spinelli requirements.

The law dealing with information obtained from informants is on the move.

POLICE OVERREACH

The due process issue of police overreach and unconscionable law enforcement practices does implicate the Constitution. One form of such overreach is entrapment, a common law and statutory defense to a crime.

Entrapment is discussed here because, while it can be included in any chapter concerning people's rights, the concept of government going "too far" is what the study of entrapment is about. And like the issues raised in the *Miranda* case, government going "too far" is not good for either the government or those it serves.

Entrapment, like the *Miranda* rule, is a subject the public believes it is well versed on because of a heavy diet of television police shows. These "dramas" often depict officers setting up radar in obviously inconspicuous locations and then being assertively informed by the citizens tagged that the police method is a clear case of entrapment. If only it were so easy. . . . According to LaFave and Israel (1985, p. 369):

> It is everywhere agreed that the agents of the government, in combatting crime, may properly employ some subterfuge and deception to obtain evidence of crime. A policeman may properly pretend to be drunk, lie in the gutter with his wallet protruding from his hip pocket and await the coming of the thief who is ready and willing to "roll" the drunk . . . there is no entrapment if the policeman merely furnishes an opportunity for the commission of the crime by one ready and willing to commit it.

Entrapment is often used as a defense. Just what is entrapment? One definition was provided in *Sorrells v. United States* (1932): "Entrapment is the conception and planning of an offense by an officer and his procurement of its commission by one who would not have perpetrated it except for the trickery, persuasion, or fraud of the officer." At the same time, however, the Court noted: "Society is at war with the criminal classes, and the courts have uniformly held that in waging this warfare the forces of prevention and detection may use traps, decoys, and deception to obtain evidence of the commission of crime. Nonetheless, when police officers encourage others to engage in criminal activity, this should not be viewed lightly. Such encouragement might, in fact, cause normally lawabiding citizens to commit crime." Oran (1985, p. 111) says:

> ⟫ *Entrapment* is the act of government officials or agents (usually police) inducing a person to commit a crime that the person probably would not have otherwise committed.

According to Whitebread and Slobogin (1986, p. 443): "The defense of entrapment arises when a defendant, who has admittedly committed a crime, can prove that the actions of law enforcement authorities caused him to commit the crime. . . . The defense of entrapment is grounded in the belief that the government should not be able to accuse a person of a crime when the government itself is the instigator of the conduct." As noted by Justice Frankfurter in *Sherman v. United States* (1958):

> The power of government is abused and directed to an end for which it was not constituted when employed to promote rather than detect crime and bring about the downfall of those who, left to themselves, might well have obeyed the law. Human nature is weak enough and sufficiently beset by temptations without government adding to them and generating crime.

If a private person not connected with law enforcement induces someone to commit a crime, no defense of entrapment can be used.

More recently, *Jacobson v. United States* (1992) held that: "Government entrapment exists if government agents originate a criminal design, implant in an innocent person's mind the disposition to commit a criminal act, and then induce the commission of the crime so that the government can prosecute" (del Carmen and Walker, 1995, p. 235). They also cite cases in which no entrapment was found when government agents:

❖ Supplied one of the necessary ingredients for the manufacture of a prohibited drug. (*United States v. Russell,* 1973).

❖ Supplied heroin to a suspect predisposed to commit the crime of selling heroin. (*Hampton v. United States,* 1976).

Summary

The Fifth Amendment provides protection against self-incrimination and guarantees citizens due process of law by limiting the actions of the federal government. The Fourteenth Amendment made this applicable to the states. This protection applies to confessions, which must be voluntary. Voluntariness of a confession is determined by (1) the police conduct involved, (2) the characteristics of the accused and (3) the timing of the confession.

Miranda remains the precedent case referred to by courts analyzing confession issues. The *Miranda* warning must be given to a suspect who is interrogated in the custody of the police, that is, when the suspect is not free to leave. If after hearing a police officer read the *Miranda* warning, suspects remain silent, that is *not* a waiver. To waive their rights, suspects must state, orally or in writing, that (1) they understand their rights and (2) they will voluntarily answer questions without a lawyer present.

Private security officers are not required to advise suspects of their *Miranda* rights. The public safety exception allows police officers to question suspects without first giving the *Miranda* warning if the information sought sufficiently affects the officers' and the public's safety.

Further, statements, including confessions, will not be admissible in court if they were obtained while violating a person's Fourth Amendment right to a reasonable expectation of privacy.

Information provided by informants also sometimes involves questions associated with due process. The historical two-pronged test for establishing probable cause based on information obtained from an informant looked at (1) the informant's basis of knowledge and (2) the informant's credibility (*Aguilar* and *Spinelli*). This two-pronged test was overturned by *Illinois v. Gates,* which relies on the totality of the circumstances in determining probable cause.

Entrapment is the act of government officials or agents (usually police) inducing a person to commit a crime that the person would not have otherwise committed.

Discussion Questions

1. Why should government be limited on how and when they ask questions?

2. How do you feel about police "encouraging" suspects to talk by threatening, using physical force or otherwise intimidating them?

3. Do you think the *Miranda* decision impedes police work?

4. Do you think a different result would occur given exactly the same circumstances of an interrogation for what a private security officer could do as opposed to what a city police officer had to?

5. Why shouldn't a stop require *Miranda?*

6. Referencing Justice Holmes' proposition that it is better that some criminals escape rather than to have the government involved in playing an ignoble part, what logic can you see in releasing a suspect who has confessed to a crime under circumstances that prohibit use of that admission, when the police *know* that person committed the crime? Where is the fairness here?

7. What do you think motivates informants, and should their information be considered reliable?

8. Discuss why it would be wise for an officer to read the *Miranda* rights from a card.

9. Why might trickery, innuendo or even falsehoods asserted by police during questioning not be Fifth Amendment violations?

10. How do you feel about allowing people to not have to incriminate themselves? What response do you have when you hear individuals on the witness stand invoke their Fifth Amendment right to remain silent?

References

Bacigal, Ronald J. *Criminal Law and Procedure: An Introduction.* St. Paul: West Publishing Company, 1996.

Cohen, H. "Overstepping Police Authority." In M. Braswell and B. McCarthy, eds. *Justice, Crime and Ethics.* Cincinnati: Anderson Publishing Co., 1991.

del Carmen, Rolando V. *Criminal Procedure for Law Enforcement Personnel.* Monterey, CA: Brooks/Cole Publishing Company, 1987.

del Carmen, Rolando V. and Jeffery T. Walker. *Briefs of Leading Cases in Law Enforcement.* 2nd ed. Cincinnati: Anderson Publishing Co., 1995.

Ferdico, John N. *Criminal Procedure for the Criminal Justice Professional.* 6th ed. St. Paul: West Publishing Company, 1996.

Jayne, Brian C. and Joseph P. Buckley III. "Criminal Interrogation Techniques on Trial." *Security Management.* October 1992, pp. 64–72.

LaFave, Wayne R. and Jerold Israel. *Criminal Procedure.* St. Paul: West Publishing Company, 1985.

Oran, D. *Law Dictionary for Nonlawyers.* 2nd ed. St. Paul: West Publishing Company, 1985.

Vaughn, Michael S. "The Parameters of Trickery As an Acceptable Police Practice." *American Journal of Police*, 1992, vol. XI, no. 4, pp. 71–95.

Whitebread, Charles H. and Christoper Slobogin. *Criminal Procedure. An Analysis of Cases and Concepts.* 2nd ed. Mineola, NY: The Foundation Press, Inc., 1986.

Cases Cited

Aguilar v. Texas, 378 U.S. 108, 84 S.Ct. 1509, 12 L.Ed.2d 723 (1964).

Anderson v. State, 6 Md.App. 688, 253 A.2d 387 (Md.Spec.App. 1969).

Arizona v. Fulminante, 499 U.S. 279 (1991).

Arnold v. United States, 382 F.2d 4 (9th Cir. 1967).

Ashcraft v. Tennessee, 322 U.S. 143, 64 S.Ct. 921, 88 L.Ed. 1192 (1944).

Beckwith v. United States, 425 U.S. 341, 96 S.Ct. 1612, 48 L.Ed. 2d 1 (1976).

Berkemer v. McCarty, 468 U.S. 420, 104 S.Ct. 3138, 82 L.Ed.2d 317 (1984).

Bram v. United States, 168 U.S. 532, 18 S.Ct. 183, 42 L.Ed. 568 (1897).

Brown v. Mississippi, 297 U.S. 278, 56 S.Ct. 461, 80 L.Ed. 682 (1936).

California v. Bakeler, 33 CrL 4108 (1983).

Colorado v. Spring, 479 U.S. 564, 107 S.Ct. 851, 93 L.Ed.2d 954 (1987).

Connecticut v. Barrett, 479 U.S. 523, 107 S.Ct. 828, 93 L.Ed.2d 920 (1987).

Culombe v. Connecticut, 367 U.S. 568, 81 S.Ct. 1860, 6 L.Ed.2d 1037 (1961).

Davis v. North Carolina, 384 U.S. 737, 86 S.Ct. 1761, 16 L.Ed.2d 895 (1966).

Duckworth v. Eagan, 492 U.S. 195, 109 S.Ct. 2875, 106 L.Ed.2d 166 (1989).

Escobedo v. Illinois, 378 U.S. 478, 84 S.Ct. 1758, 12 L.Ed.2d 977 (1964).

Fikes v. Alabama, 352 U.S. 191, 77 S.Ct. 281, 1 L.Ed.2d 246 (1957).

Haynes v. Washington, 373 U.S. 503, 83 S.Ct. 1336, 10 L.Ed.2d 513 (1963).

Illinois v. Gates, 462 U.S. 213, 103 S.Ct. 2317, 76 L.Ed.2d 527 (1983).

Illinois v. Perkins, 496 U.S. 292, 110 S.Ct. 2394, 110 L.Ed.2d 243 (1990).

Jacobson v. United States, 503 U.S. 540, 112 S.Ct. 1535 118 L.Ed.2d 174, (1992).

Katz v. United States, 389 U.S. 347 (1967).

Leyra v. Denno, 347 U.S. 556, 74 S.Ct. 716, 98 L.Ed. 948 (1954).

Malloy v. Hogan, 378 U.S. 1, 84 S.Ct. 1489, 12 L.Ed.2d 653 (1964).

Massiah v. United States, 377 U.S. 201, 84 S.Ct. 1199, 12 L.Ed.2d 246 (1964).

Mincey v. Arizona, 437 U.S. 385, 98 S.Ct. 2408, 57 L.Ed.2d 290 (1978).

Miranda v. Arizona, 384 U.S. 436, 86 S.Ct. 1602, 16 L.Ed.2d 694 (1966).

New York v. Quarles, 467 U.S. 649, 104 S.Ct. 2626, 81 L.Ed.2d 550 (1984).

Oregon v. Elstad, 470 U.S. 298, 105 S.Ct. 1285, 84 L.Ed.2d 222 (1985).

Oregon v. Mathiason, 429 U.S. 492, 97 S.Ct. 711, 50 L.Ed.2d 714 (1977).

Patterson v. Illinois, 487 U.S. 285, 108 S.Ct. 2389, 101 L.Ed.2d 261 (1988).

Pennsylvania v. Muniz, 496 U.S. 582, 110 S.Ct. 2638, 110 L.Ed.2d 528 (1990).

People v. Shivers, 21 N.Y.2d 188, 286 N.Y.S.2d 827, 233 N.E.2d 836 (N.Y. Court of Appeals 1967).

Robinson v. Smith, 451 F. Supp. 1278 (W.D.N.Y. 1978).

Rochin v. California, 342 U.S. 165 (1952).

Rogers v. Richmond, 365 U.S. 534, 540-41, 81 S.Ct. 735, 739, 5 L.Ed.2d 760 (1961).

Sherman v. United States, 356 U.S. 369, 78 S.Ct. 819, 2 L.Ed.2d 848 (1958).

Sorrells v. United States, 287 U.S. 435, 53 S.Ct. 210, 77 L.Ed. 413 (1932).

Spano v. New York, 360 U.S. 315, 79 S.Ct. 1202, 3 L.Ed.2d 1265 (1959).

Spinelli v. United States, 393 U.S. 410, 89 S.Ct. 584, 21 L.Ed.2d 637 (1969).

State v. Jennings, 367 So.2d 357 (La. 1979).

State v. Lane.

Tague v. Louisiana, 444 U.S. 469, 100 S.Ct. 652, 62 L.Ed.2d 622 (1980).

United States v. Jones, 786 F.2d 1019 (11th Cir. 1986).

United States v. Koch, 552 F.2d 1216 (7th Cir. 1977).

United States v. Russell, 411 U.S. 423 (1973).

United States v. Wright, 991 F.2d 1182 (4th Cir. 1993).

Utsler v. South Dakota, 171 N.W.2d 739 (1969).

Yates v. United States, 384 F.2d 586 (5th Cir. 1967).

Chapter 13 # The Sixth Amendment: Right to Counsel and a Fair Trial

In all criminal prosecutions, the accused shall enjoy the right to a speedy and public trial, by an impartial jury of the state and district wherein the crime shall have been committed . . . and to be informed of the nature and cause of the accusation; to be confronted with the witnesses against him; to have compulsory process for obtaining witnesses in his favor, and to have the assistance of counsel for his defense.

—SIXTH AMENDMENT OF THE UNITED STATES CONSTITUTION

O. J. Simpson—on trial for murder—and attorney Robert Shapiro. (Photo by Blake Sell. Provided by Reuters/Corbis-Bettmann.)

DO YOU KNOW . . .

Which amendment guarantees citizens' right to counsel in criminal proceedings?

What precedent case supports the right to have an attorney present during interrogation?

How all American law is developed?

What happens if a defendant cannot afford to hire an attorney? The precedent case?

How the *Miranda* case interacts with the Sixth Amendment right to counsel?

When a Sixth Amendment right to counsel exists?

How the right to counsel can be waived?

What is meant by a person appearing pro se during a trial?

What the Sixth Amendment right to counsel presumes about the attorneys?

What the Sixth Amendment requires of trials?

What the Sixth Amendment requires of adverse witnesses?

CAN YOU DEFINE THESE TERMS?

Case law
Court trial
Indigent
Pro se

INTRODUCTION

While not one of the best known amendments, the Sixth Amendment plays a very important role in ensuring the basic fairness that our Constitution guarantees. It does this by setting forth basic requirements for a fair trial and the events leading up to it.

By this point, it should be obvious that it is *freedom* that has the most important role in how and why the United States Constitution was developed. Thinking back as to why the framers of the document felt it necessary to flee their homeland and develop an entirely new government helps one comprehend just how important freedom is to Americans.

This concept is not just historical trivia. True, it helps put our constitutional studies into a proper perspective, but keep in mind that this desire for freedom continues today and will, no doubt, continue well into the future. The concept of freedom is emphasized because of its importance in truly understanding the Constitution.

No matter where or when one studies constitutional law, someone somewhere is putting his or her life on the line to get freedom or to keep it. And when one boils down the meaning of freedom, it can be considered to a great degree simple fairness. It is rather amazing that Americans are willing to support our national military organizations as well as our domestic legal system to uphold the simple concept of *fairness*. But it is that important and is, in a word, what America is about. The price remains high, but the benefits worthy.

It is actually difficult to isolate one amendment to discuss because the Constitution is an integral document that interacts with its own different components. For example, several key constitutional provisions work jointly to ensure fair criminal proceedings.

The framers of the United States Constitution, through the Sixth Amendment, set forth the basic requirements necessary for a fair day in court, including the right to counsel.

This chapter begins with an in-depth look at the Sixth Amendment right to counsel, including its historical development, its role in the adversarial system and its development to the present day. Discussed next are instances in which the right can be invoked and how it can be waived. This is followed by examples of violations of the Sixth Amendment and a discussion of the assumption of competence on the part of the lawyer. The chapter concludes with other important rights guaranteed by the Sixth Amendment: the right to a speedy and public trial by a jury of one's peers and the right to confront witnesses, including the implied right to cross-examine such witnesses.

RIGHT TO COUNSEL

Much has been written about the constitutionally guaranteed right to have the assistance of legal counsel for one's defense when charged through the legal system. This, too, has been held applicable to state and local governments through the Fourteenth Amendment. What is meant by right to counsel is the right to have the qualified representation of an attorney. This is such an important right that in the case of *Geders v. United States* (1976) the Court held that a defendant must have adequate opportunities to consult with legal counsel, and "ineffective assistance of counsel," meaning receiving inept work from a defense lawyer also can be a defense if the attorney made such serious errors that the attorney was, in effect, not acting as a lawyer (*Strickland v. Washington,* 1984). By guaranteeing this, one is assured of having a knowledgeable person watching over the system as a whole.

Recall that the first step away from the case-by-case voluntariness analysis occurred in *Massiah v. United States* (1964), in which the Supreme Court emphasized the defendant's Sixth Amendment right to counsel.

 The Sixth Amendment guarantees citizens the right to counsel.

The Court held that incriminating statements obtained by the government from a radio transmitter voluntarily installed in a car belonging to a friend of the defendant violated the defendant's Sixth Amendment rights. Government agents had deliberately elicited the statement after he had been indicted and in the absence of retained counsel.

The case of *Escobedo v. Illinois* (1964) was decided in the same year as *Messiah* and also dealt with the defendant's Sixth Amendment right to counsel. After being arrested, Escobedo was released on a writ of habeas corpus. He was rearrested 10 days later and questioned. His requests to see his lawyer were ignored. Eventually Escobedo provided a statement and was subsequently convicted of murder. In holding the statement inadmissible, Justice Goldberg stated:

> We hold . . . that whereas here the investigation is no longer a general inquiry into an unsolved crime but has begun to focus on a particular suspect, the suspect has been taken into police custody, the police carry out a process of interrogations that leads itself to eliciting incriminating statements, the suspect has requested and been denied an opportunity to consult with his lawyer, and the police have not effectively warned him of his constitutional right to remain silent, the accused has been denied the assistance of counsel in violation of the Sixth Amendment . . . and that no statements elicited by the police during the interrogation may be used against him at a criminal trial.

~ *Escobedo* established the Sixth Amendment right of a defendant to have a lawyer present during interrogation.

Whitebread and Slobogin (1986, p. 365) expand on this case:

> *Escobedo* held that once an individual is the focus of investigation by the police, he may not be denied access to his attorney—if he has one and if he asks for him. But it still did not define precisely when a suspect becomes the accused. More importantly, the decision did not state what rights accrue to a person who does not have, and cannot afford, an attorney, or to a person who has an attorney and does not ask to see him. In *Miranda*, the Court took a significant step toward resolving those questions, effectively limiting the *Escobedo* holding to its facts.

HISTORICAL DEVELOPMENT OF THE RIGHT-TO-COUNSEL PROTECTION

Laws relating to counsel for criminal defendants developed over several centuries. According to Zalman and Siegel (1991, p. 406): "From the misty beginnings of the common law jury trial in thirteenth century England to mid-nineteenth-century America, the assistance of counsel was virtually unknown; in some instances, the presence of defense counsel was forbidden by law."

In fact, the legal system in England saw the assistance of legal counsel as such a benefit, that to give the government a stronger likelihood of winning a case involving felonies, no lawyer was allowed to defend persons charged with a felony. It was not until 1695 that defendants charged with treason, for example, were permitted to be represented. And only in 1836 did Parliament formally allow other felons to be represented by legal counsel. The evolution of the right to counsel in the United States is described by Zalman and Siegel (1991, p. 407):

In contrast [to England], Colonial America embraced the use of attorneys in criminal trials. Several of the colonies specifically allowed the right to counsel, as exemplified by the career of John Adams as a criminal defense lawyer in the celebrated Boston Massacre case. Adams, although a member of the pro-liberty party, vigorously defended and won acquittals for the British soldiers who fired in self-defense on a large, stone-throwing mob of zealous patriots. This historical precedent helps explain that the Sixth Amendment provision of counsel (1791) was not at first intended to provide free lawyers for indigent defendants but to insure that a defendant who could afford a lawyer would not have the counsel barred from the trial.

Throughout the nineteenth and into the twentieth centuries, defendants with sufficient means could hire lawyers for their defense if they wished. Poor defendants had to defend themselves, with the judge taking special care to insure that they did not completely ruin their defense, or, in cases involving the death penalty, the judge could order a lawyer to donate his services free of charge as a professional obligation. . . . [A study of] the Old Bailey criminal court in London at the beginning of the eighteenth century gives some insight into the development of the legal profession and the adversary process. In these early trials, a jury of "regulars" would sit for several weeks, hear up to twenty cases in a day, and openly comment on the cases. Judges would overtly attempt to sway the jury. There was no plea bargaining and confessions were rare. Justice in this system was very swift, with cases heard within a month after arrest and examination by a justice of the peace. There were no strict rules of evidence, and witnesses simply told their stories, with the defendant being allowed to question them and present his or her own version and defense. These informal procedures were employed in all criminal trials, even those involving persons charged with capital crimes. When lawyers became more common, the rules of evidence were formalized. The pace of trials slowed down, and closer attention was paid to each case.

After the Declaration of Independence in 1776, several of the 13 original states' constitutions had provisions guaranteeing the right to counsel. In addition, this right was built into the federal level by the Sixth Amendment.

Insistence on the right to counsel was partially the result of abuses to human rights that occurred in England and other countries before the Revolution. The Star Chamber, for example, was an English court that tried political criminals in secret with no regard for due process. Likewise, during the Spanish Inquisition trials were conducted with no regard for the defendant's rights. To avoid a recurrence of such unfairness the Sixth Amendment was written.

According to Zalman and Siegel (1991, p. 407): "Throughout the nineteenth and into the twentieth centuries, defendants with sufficient means could hire lawyers for their defense if they wished. Poor defendants had to defend themselves."

In 1932, however, this changed as a result of *Powell v. Alabama*, growing out of the infamous "Scottsboro Boys" case. This case involved seven black teenagers who allegedly threw seven white youths off a train. Two of the white girls claimed to have been raped by the black teenagers. As noted by Zalman and Siegel (1991, p. 408), the youths were arrested by a sheriff's posse in Scottsboro, Alabama, "in an atmosphere of such hostility that the militia was called out to guard the defendants and maintain order." Zalman and Siegel also noted: "The defendants, young, ignorant, illiterate, surrounded by hostile sentiment, hauled back and forth under guard of soldiers, charged with an atrocious crime" were indicted within a week. As a result of this case, the Supreme Court established the right to counsel for indigent offenders facing the death penalty.

According to Bacigal (1996, p. 153): "The purpose of the Sixth Amendment right to counsel is to protect an accused during critical confrontations with the government. The right to counsel attaches at the commencement of adversary judicial proceedings, which signal that the government has committed itself to prosecution of the defendant, and that the adverse positions of government and defendant have solidified."

THE UNITED STATES ADVERSARIAL COURT SYSTEM

The American legal system is an adversarial system; that is, one side is challenged by the other. The prosecution challenges the defense, with both sides rigorously seeking a final determination in their favor. It is believed that such a system will have the most likelihood of producing an accurate outcome. Whether it be the lawyer representing the government (prosecution) or representing the defendant (defense), each is expected to do everything legally permissible to win in court.

This concept offends many onlookers to legal proceedings. The question is frequently heard, "How can that lawyer defend a person charged with such a heinous crime?" The answer is that not only is it the job of the defense lawyer, but that our Constitution demands it.

Criminal trial proceedings. (Photo by John J. Lopinot. Provided by Black Star.)

According to Zalman and Siegel (1991, p. 406): "Despite the criticisms that are made of the excesses and weaknesses of the adversary system, it is not likely to undergo fundamental change. If anything, improvement should come not in the structure of the trial process but in the competence of those to which it is entrusted."

Imagine how terrifying it must be to find oneself immersed in the system—particularly being challenged by the government, perhaps in jail, and with few financial resources. It is, to be sure, overwhelming, and given a moment to think about it, anyone charged with a crime would want nothing less than a vigorous defense.

DEVELOPMENT OF PRESENT-DAY RIGHT TO COUNSEL

Recall how laws develop in general, whether a particular law is specifically defined in a statute (referred to as "codified" law because it is presented within a code or the result of holdings within a case—case law or common law), all law is developed through the common law system. Common law, also known as **case law,** uses the decisions reached in previous cases to decide similar current cases, so that predictability remains a part of the system.

> All American law is developed through the common law system.

Also recall that our common law developed in England as cases were decided based on how previous cases were decided. So, how your own case would be decided depends on how a previous court determined similar cases, even though your case may differ to some degree from previous cases. The idea is that people can best determine what the law is by looking at how courts decided things in the past. This common law approach continued to more precisely mold, shape and define the law, which although quite specific, relies on case law to address specific issues as they arise.

- ❖ CODIFIED LAW = law set forth by law-making bodies such as legislatures (for example, state statutes).
- ❖ COMMON LAW = law set forth in previous cases.

This has been so with the development of the Sixth Amendment right to assistance of counsel as well. While the constitutional amendment itself does say what is expected to ensure fairness, all the amendment can really be expected to do is provide the conceptual basis for this particular law. It may help to recall the general discussion of how the Constitution is meant to serve as a framework for all other law, to be built within and upon. So, while the Sixth Amendment says that assistance of counsel is a right, case law must be examined as it has developed to fully understand what right to counsel is all about.

A series of cases served to mold the right to counsel. In cases such as *Harris v. South Carolina* (1949), the Supreme Court began to recognize that if a defendant was denied access to an attorney that his confession may not have been voluntary. Remember that in determining whether a confession was, indeed, given voluntarily, the court considers the totality of the circumstances to make sure that there was due process. In *Spano v. New York* (1959) it was held that there was an absolute right for a defendant to be represented and that a confession was not voluntary if the police ignored a defendant's "reasonable request to contact the attorney he had already retained." As cases continued to reinforce the right to counsel, it was the case of *Gideon v. Wainwright* (1963) that firmly held that not only was it an absolute right, but, in all serious cases, **indigent** (poor, unable to afford a lawyer) defendants were to be provided with legal counsel.

This case, as well as others cited, caused an explosion in the size and importance of the public defender's office nationwide. Figure 13–1 is a sample form that determines eligibility for indigent defense services. A criminal defendant completes this form to allow the court to determine if the defendant qualifies for a court-appointed attorney.

> *Gideon v. Wainwright* established that indigent defendants are to be provided lawyers in serious cases.

In 1972, in *Argersinger v. Hamlin,* the Court held that any time the penalty could include prison, the defendant must have access to a lawyer. This was later modified by *Scott v. Illinois* (1979), which made actual, not potential, punishment the trigger for the right to counsel.

WHEN THE RIGHT TO COUNSEL MAY BE INVOKED

The question of just when someone has the right to legal counsel was addressed in the case of *Massiah v. United States* (1964), which held that a defendant's right to be represented attaches once he is indicted and therefore considered an "accused" rather than merely a "suspect."

In the case of *Escobedo v. Illinois* (1964), which occurred five weeks after *Massiah,* the Court held that a defendant has the right to legal counsel when being interrogated while in the custody of the police and that this Sixth Amendment right has been violated if he requests a lawyer and is refused the opportunity.

It is important to note here that it was also the *Escobedo* case that definitively applied the Sixth Amendment to the states as well by virtue of the Fourteenth Amendment. Remember, the amendments themselves were drafted to specifically apply to the federal government, but that most of the Bill of Rights have been applied to the states as well (so that neither the federal government nor the state or local government can violate these rights).

The well-known case of *Miranda v. Arizona* (1966), discussed in the preceding chapter, further clarified the question of when a person had the right to counsel. In this case the Supreme Court created the *Miranda* warning that most TV watchers and moviegoers know by heart: "You have the right to remain silent . . ." The Court made it clear what rights a defendant has when being questioned by the police while in custody. The *Miranda* warning was

FINANCIAL STATEMENT–
ELIGIBILITY DETERMINATION FOR INDIGENT DEFENSE SERVICES

Case No. . . . .

Presumptive Eligibility:

☐ I currently receive the following type(s) of public assistance in _____

City/County

☐ AFDC $ _____   ☐ Food Stamps $ _____   ☐ Medicaid _____

☐ Supplemental Security Income $ _____   ☐ Other (specify type and amount) _____

☐ I currently do not receive public assistance.

Names and addresses of employer(s) for defendant and spouse:

Self _____

Spouse _____

NET INCOME: Self   Spouse

Pay period (weekly, every second week, twice monthly, monthly) . . . . _____ _____

Net take home pay (salary/wages, minus deductions required by law) . . . . . $_____ _____

Other income sources (please specify)—see reverse

_____ . . . . $_____ _____

TOTAL INCOME $_____ + _____ = [COURT USE ONLY _____] A

ASSETS:

Cash on hand . . . . $_____ _____

Bank accounts at: . . . . $_____ _____

Any other assests: (please specify)

_____ with a value of . . . . . . $_____ _____

Real estate - $ _____ with net value of . . . . . $_____ _____
            Net Value

Motor Vehicles { _____ with net value of. . . . . . $_____ _____
                      Year and Make

_____ with net value of . . . . . . $_____ _____
                      Year and Make

Other Personal Property: (describe)

_____ . . . . $_____ _____

TOTAL ASSETS $_____ + _____ = [COURT USE ONLY _____] A

| Number in household _____ |
| Number of dependents (spouse/children) |
| whom you support: _____ |

EXCEPTIONAL EXPENSES (Total Exceptional Expenses of Family)

Medical Expenses (list only unusual and continuing expenses) . . . . $_____

Court-ordered support payments/alimony. . . . . $_____

Child-care payments (e.g. day care) . . . . $_____

Other (describe): _____

} $_____ [COURT USE ONLY _____]

TOTAL EXPENSES $_____ = [COURT USE ONLY _____] C

COLUMN "A" plus COLUMN "B" minus COLUMN "C" equals available funds = [_____]

THIS STATEMENT IS MADE UNDER OATH: ANY FALSE STATEMENT OF A MATERIAL FACT TO ANY QUESTION CONTAINED HEREIN SHALL CONSTITUTE PERJURY UNDER THE PROVISIONS OF §19.2-161 OF THE CODE OF VIRGINIA. THE MAXIMUM PENALTY FOR PERJURY IS CONFINEMENT IN THE PENITENTIARY FOR A PERIOD OF TEN YEARS.

I hereby state that the above information is correct to the best of my knowledge.

Name of defendant (type or print) _____

_____   _____
      Date   Signature

Sworn/affirmed and signed before me this day.

_____   _____   _____
      Date   Signature   Title

**FINANCIAL STATEMENT—ELIGIBILITY DETERMINATION
FOR INDIGENT DEFENSE SERVICES**

FORM DC-333 4/93 (1143-021 5/94)

Figure 13-1

Statement of indigency.

Source: Ronald J. Bacigal. *Criminal Law and Procedure: An Introduction.* St. Paul: West Publishing Company, 1996, p. 155. Reprinted by permission. All rights reserved.

meant to both safeguard the Fifth Amendment right against self-incrimination and to declare that when a person is questioned while in custody of the police they have the right to counsel.

While addressed in detail in Chapter 12, it is important to review the requirements established in the *Miranda* case. Suspects being interrogated while in custody must be told that anything they say could be used against them in court, that if they cannot afford a lawyer, one will be appointed without cost, and that any waiver to these rights must be made knowingly and voluntarily.

> The *Miranda* case requires suspects to be told of their right to an attorney. The exclusionary rule will prohibit confessions obtained in violation of a person's constitutional rights from being used in court.

In 1977, in *Brewer v. Williams,* the right to counsel was again reinforced by the Supreme Court declaring that once a person has the right to legal counsel (in this case because adversarial proceedings had been initiated against the defendant—he was under arrest), he must make a knowing and voluntary waiver to legally give up his rights.

Brewer v. Williams is called the "Christian Burial Speech" case because of the facts that included police detectives telling the defendant, arguably of limited intellectual capacity to begin with, and fancying himself somewhat of a preacher, that the murdered child he was suspected of killing "should be entitled to a Christian burial" in a manner that the Court said was "deliberately and designedly set out to elicit information." Williams responded to this speech (although he was not actually questioned by the detectives) and the girl's body was found, after his lawyer had been appointed and after the police agreed to not question Williams. The Court held that in these circumstances, the defendant had not adequately waived his right to legal counsel.

While more of an evidentiary issue, it is noteworthy that in spite of the Supreme Court holding that Williams' statements and the subsequent evidence obtained as a result of them (the body, clothing, etc.) were inadmissable, they did not let Williams go. Rather, the Court held that "if the prosecution can establish by a preponderance of the evidence that the information ultimately or inevitably would have been discovered by lawful means, the fact that the defendant made a statement to the officers in the absence of counsel should not contaminate the evidence."

Thus, the inevitable discovery doctrine was developed to permit the evidence in this case (because the girl's body was about to be found anyway by a group of Iowa's finest converging on the site, unrelated to Williams' statement), with the Court concluding that "anything less would reject logic, experience, and common sense."

The Court seeks to balance justice with emerging law. While the *Williams* case provided fertile ground to address the issue of, among other things, right to counsel—with a most intriguing set of facts—was the Court going to let the murderer of a child go free if they could "have their cake and eat it too"? No.

They very skillfully succeeded in clarifying the Sixth Amendment while permitting the evidence to be retained.

From the cases to this point, it can be seen that, as the Court stated in *Brewer v. Williams:* "[T]he right to counsel granted by the Sixth and Fourteenth Amendments means at least that a person is entitled to the help of a lawyer at or after the time that judicial proceedings have been initiated against him—whether by way of formal charges, during the preliminary hearing, at the indictment, or upon arraignment." As noted by Senna and Siegel (1987, p. 153):

> The right of the individual to be represented by an attorney has been extended to numerous stages of the criminal justice process, including pretrial custody, identification and lineup procedures, the preliminary hearing, the submission of a guilty plea, the trial, sentencing, and postconviction appeal.

The various stages at which the right to counsel might be invoked are also delineated by Zalman and Siegel (1991, p. 404):

> [T]he right to counsel is an issue not only in the criminal trial itself but also in a large number of ancillary proceedings, including pretrial identification procedures, station house questioning, post-arrest probable cause hearings, preliminary examinations, plea bargaining, sentencing, probation and parole revocation hearings, in-prison legal activity, criminal appeals, and habeas corpus hearings.

Zalman and Siegel (p. 405) also suggest: "The right to counsel has played a central role in the development of modern criminal procedure law. The current law of confessions, although focusing primarily on the Fifth Amendment right against self-incrimination, rests on special protections generated by access to a lawyer."

Merely being the focus of an investigation does not alone invoke the Sixth Amendment right to counsel. Cases are split as to whether merely having a complaint filed is sufficient to determine that "judicial proceedings" have been initiated. In the *Brewer v. Williams* case the defendant had already been arrested and arraigned and, as the Court properly held, he had the right to a lawyer.

From examining cases in point, LaFave and Israel (1985, p. 307) suggest that "at least from the time the defendant is brought into court and arraigned on a warrant, the Sixth Amendment right to counsel applies." It should also be noted that the Supreme Court considers whether the defendant has yet retained a lawyer (*McLeod v. Ohio*, 1965).

The question of when a suspect has a right to legal counsel is complex. The following summarizes some of the instances when the right to counsel exists.

Sixth Amendment Right to Legal Counsel

❖ At trial in federal courts in felony cases (*Johnson v. Zerbst*, 1938).
❖ At trial in state courts in felony cases (*Powell v. Alabama*, 1932; *Gideon v. Wainwright*, 1963).

❖ At the arraignment. The Court's position is that an arraignment, because it is the last official step before a trial itself, is a critical stage of the proceeding and thus the right to counsel attaches (*Hamilton v. Alabama,* 1961).

❖ At a preliminary hearing. It is a critical stage when the accused can enter a plea (*White v. Maryland,* 1963).

❖ During an investigation *after* an indictment (*Massiah v. United States,* 1964).

❖ During an investigation *before* an indictment. *Miranda* (1966) and *Escobedo* (1964) taken together mean that when a person is taken into custody and questioned, he must be advised of his right to counsel when questioned. With a view to obtaining incriminating statements although not in custody, suspects must be permitted to consult with counsel.

❖ In cases involving misdemeanors. Historically the Sixth Amendment applied only to capital cases and then felonies, but this was expanded to apply to any case in which imprisonment could occur (*Argersinger v. Hamlin,* 1972).

❖ In cases involving juveniles (*In re Gault,* 1967).

❖ During a postcharge lineup. The role of counsel is limited to that of an observer (*United States v. Wade,* 1967).

The vast number of precharge investigatory lineups or identification procedures need not have appointed counsel as a constitutional requirement (*Kirby v. Illinois,* 1972).

United States v. Henry (1980) established that a defendant's Sixth Amendment right to counsel is violated if police intentionally create a situation likely to result in incriminating statements.

Although this may appear confusing, these cases must be considered in context and viewed in the manner in which they were intended: as refining steps in the scheme of common law. Each separate case does not necessarily make a separate and different law. Each case expands upon the general Sixth Amendment right to counsel.

The Supreme Court has interpreted the Sixth Amendment to mean that an accused has the constitutional right to counsel at any *critical stage* of a proceeding.

> ⤳ The Sixth Amendment right to counsel is required at any critical stage during a criminal proceeding.

All of the Sixth Amendment cases merely serve to define what is and isn't a critical stage. A common sense or logical approach could be taken by assuming that beyond a point where the police are merely investigating a crime, and where the suspect is being put in a position whereby anything he or she says could be used against him or her (including formal judicial proceedings), a Sixth Amendment right to counsel attaches.

Table 13–1 shows the progression of the particularly noteworthy Sixth Amendment cases. A review of these cases should help clarify when the right to counsel is present. And, if all the courts involved had this much trouble defining when the Sixth Amendment right to counsel exists, it's understandable that you might have questions, too.

Table 13–1 **Major United States Supreme Court cases granting right to counsel throughout pretrial, trial and posttrial stages of criminal justice process.**

Case	Stage and ruling
Escobedo v. Illinois 378 U.S. 478 (1964)	The defendant has the right to counsel during the course of any police interrogation.
Miranda v. Arizona 384 U.S. 694 (1966)	Procedural safeguards, including the right to counsel, must be followed at custodial interrogation to secure the privilege against self-incrimination.
Brewer v. Williams 430 U.S. 387 (1977) (see also *Massiah v. United States* 377 U.S. 201 [1961])	Once adversary proceedings have begun against the defendant, he or she has a right to the assistance of counsel.
Hamilton v. Alabama 368 U.S. 52 (1961)	The arraignment is a critical stage in the criminal process, so that denial of the right to counsel is a violation of due process of law.
Coleman v. Alabama 399 U.S. 1 (1970)	The preliminary hearing is a critical stage in a criminal prosecution requiring the state to provide the indigent defendant with counsel.
Moore v. Illinois 434 U.S. 220 (1977)	An in-court identification at a preliminary hearing after a criminal complaint has been initiated requires counsel to protect the defendant's interests.
United States v. Wade 388 U.S. 218 (1967)	A defendant in a pretrial postindictment lineup for identification purposes has the right to assistance of counsel.
Moore v. Michigan 355 U.S. 155 (1957)	The defendant has the right to counsel when submitting a guilty plea to the court.
Powell v. Alabama 287 U.S. 45 (1932)	Defendants have the right to counsel at their trial in a state capital case.
Gideon v. Wainwright 372 U.S. 335 (1963)	An indigent defendant charged in a state court with a noncapital felony has the right to the assistance of counsel at trial under the due process clause of the Fourteenth Amendment.
Argersinger v. Hamlin 407 U.S. 25 (1972)	A defendant has the right to counsel at trial whenever a person may be imprisoned for any offense, even one day, whether classified as a misdemeanor or felony.
Scott v. Illinois 440 U.S. 367 (1979)	A criminal defendant charged with a statutory offense for which imprisonment on conviction is authorized but not imposed does not have the right to appointed counsel.
In re Gault 387 U.S. 1 (1967)	Procedural due process, including the right to counsel, applies to juvenile delinquency adjudication that may lead to a child's commitment to a state institution.
Faretta v. California 422 U.S. 806 (1975)	A defendant in a state criminal trial has a constitutional right to proceed without counsel when he voluntarily and intelligently elects to do so.
Townsend v. Burke 334 U.S. 736 (1948)	A convicted offender has a right to counsel at the time of sentencing.
Douglas v. California 372 U.S. 353 (1963)	An indigent defendant granted a first appeal from a criminal conviction has the right to be represented by counsel on appeal.
Mempa v. Rhay 389 U.S. 128 (1967)	A convicted offender has the right to assistance of counsel at probation revocation hearings in which the sentence has been deferred.
Gagnon v. Scarpelli 411 U.S. 778 (1973)	Probationers and parolees have a constitutionally limited right to counsel on a case-by-case basis at revocation proceedings.
Johnson v. Zerbst 304 U.S. 458 (1938)	A defendant charged with a crime of a serious nature in federal court must be provided with legal counsel, provided by the government if the defendant is indigent.
White v. Maryland 373 U.S. 59 (1963)	A defendant is entitled to a lawyer at a preliminary hearing.

Source: Adapted from Joseph J. Senna and Larry J. Siegel. *Introduction to Criminal Justice.* 4th ed. St. Paul: West Publishing Company, 1987, p. 285.

WAIVER OF THE RIGHT TO BE REPRESENTED BY COUNSEL

It should be noted that although everyone has the right to counsel, this does not mean they have to have an attorney. In *Brewer v. Williams* the Court set out the requirements for a lawfully acceptable waiver of one's rights. In *Johnson v. Zerbst* (1938) the Court held that the burden would be on the prosecution to show that there was "an intentional relinquishment or abandonment of a known right." In *Williams* the Court held that a valid waiver "requires not merely comprehension [of the rights], but relinquishment as well." So, as stated in *Estelle v. Smith* (1981), "a waiver is a possibility only when the defendant makes a statement to one known to be in a position adverse to him, such as a police officer." A shake of the head, a wave of the hand or anything else that is short of the accused making a knowing and voluntary waiver of the rights guaranteed by the Constitution is unacceptable. Figure 13–2 shows a sample waiver form.

> A waiver of one's Sixth Amendment right to counsel must be knowing and voluntary.

Some people represent themselves in court **pro se,** which is Latin, meaning "for himself." These individuals act as their own lawyers.

> Individuals can appear in court without an attorney, representing themselves. This is said to be appearing pro se.

While it is difficult to fully understand just why a person would feel more comfortable without a lawyer present, particularly considering how terribly complex the legal system is, it is nonetheless an option that some select. One reason seems to be a mistrust some have of anyone involved in the system, even when that individual is representing them. Others just assume they can do better, or some feel that even though they may not qualify for a public defender, they still are not in a position to afford legal counsel.

VIOLATIONS OF THE SIXTH AMENDMENT RIGHT TO COUNSEL

The judge-made exclusionary rule will prevent the use of *any* evidence obtained in violation of one's constitutional rights. This rule applies to Sixth Amendment violations as well. It is not only the evidence that was obtained that is excluded, but the fruit of the poisonous tree doctrine will exclude any evidence obtained as the result of the tainted evidence. It is particularly important to realize that should a Sixth Amendment violation occur, an entire stream of subsequent evidence, including any statements, could be excluded as evidence. As noted by Klotter and Kanovitz (1991, p. 422):

> [I]f counsel is denied at the post-indictment lineup or in certain other confrontation-for-identification situations, such denial could contaminate the in-court identification of the accused by the witness.

TRIAL WITHOUT A LAWYER
Va. Code § 19.2-160

CASE NO. . . . .

- -

☐ General District Court
☐ Juvenile and Domestic Relations District Court
☐ Circuit Court

- v. -

WAIVER OF RIGHT TO BE REPRESENTED BY A LAWYER (CRIMINAL CASE)

I have been advised by a judge of this court of the nature of the charges in the cases pending against me and the potential punishment for the offenses, which includes imprisonment in the penitentiary or confinement in jail. I understand the nature of these charges and the potential punishment for them if I am found to be guilty.

I have been further advised by a judge of this court that I have the following rights to be represented by a lawyer in these cases:

a. I have a right to be represented by a lawyer.

b. If I choose to hire my own lawyer, I will be given a reasonable opportunity to hire, at my expense, a lawyer selected by me. The judge will decide what is a reasonable opportunity to hire a lawyer. If I have not hired a lawyer after such reasonable opportunity, the judge may try the case even though I do not have a lawyer to represent me.

c. If I ask the judge for a lawyer to represent me and the judge decides, after reviewing my sworn financial statement that I am indigent, the judge will select and appoint a lawyer to represent me. However, if I am found to be guilty of an offense, the lawyer's fee as set by the judge within statutory limits will be assessed against me as court costs and I will be required to pay it.

I understand these rights to be represented by a lawyer. I understand the manner in which a lawyer can be of assistance and I understand that, in proceeding without a lawyer, I may be confronted with complicated legal issues. I also understand that I may waive (give up) my rights to be represented by a lawyer.

Understanding my rights to be represented by a lawyer as described above and further understanding the nature of the case and the potential punishment if I am found to be guilty. I waive all of my rights to be represented by a lawyer in these cases, with the further understanding that the cases will be tried without a lawyer either being hired by me or being appointed by the judge for me. I waive these rights of my own choice, voluntarily, of my own free will, without any threats, promises, force or coercion.

_____
ADULT

Upon oral examination, the undersigned judge of this Court finds that the Adult, having been advised of the rights and matters stated above and having understood these rights and matters, thereafter has knowingly, voluntarily and intelligently waived his rights to be represented by a lawyer.

-          _____
DATE   JUDGE

CASE NO. . . . .

TRIAL WITHOUT A LAWYER

Figure 13–2
Waiver of right to counsel.
Source: Ronald J. Bacigal. *Criminal Law and Procedure: An Introduction.* St. Paul: West Publishing Company, 1996, p. 157. Reprinted by permission. All rights reserved.

If, at the preliminary hearing, the accused is not afforded the right to counsel when this is a "critical stage" of the proceeding, a plea of guilty will not be accepted at a future trial of the case. The same reasoning applies where the right-to-counsel requirements are not complied with at the arraignment. The right to assistance of counsel at the criminal trial itself is deemed so fundamental that failure properly to observe that right automatically vitiates any conviction resulting from that trial. This is true even though there is no showing of prejudicial unfairness.

Legally, a conviction obtained without the proper representation by counsel is totally void.

COMPETENCE OF COUNSEL

While the right to counsel is not the only aspect of the Sixth Amendment worth considering, it has been deemed one of the most important. Another issue that the Supreme Court has addressed is that the Sixth Amendment presumes that one's legal counsel is effective counsel.

The case of *Strickland v. Washington* (1984) held that the basic issue as to whether one's counsel was ineffective is "whether the counsel's conduct so undermined the proper functioning of the adversarial process that the trial cannot be relied on as having produced a just result." The Court went on to state: "The proper measure of attorney performance remains simply reasonableness under prevailing professional norms."

What is, in effect, "legal malpractice" is obviously a very involved area of law that seems to be emerging at an increased rate in the 1990s. Much of it is based on identifiable professional standards and abilities rather than whether the outcome was not what the client wanted (remember that in 50% of cases one party isn't pleased with the outcome) or whether the client didn't like his lawyer (probably half of all clients don't like their lawyers).

> The Sixth Amendment right to counsel presumes counsel is effective.

As noted by Klotter and Kanovitz (1991, pp. 453–454):

> Although the Supreme Court has never enunciated any clear standards for courts to follow on claims of ineffectiveness of counsel . . . over a period of time the courts have generally accepted a formula which came to be known as the "mockery of justice" standard:
> "[A] charge of inadequate representation can prevail only if it can be said that what was or was not done by the defendant's attorney for his client made the proceedings a farce and a mockery of justice, shocking to the conscience of the Court [*Cardarell v. United States* (1967), quoting *O'Malley v. United States* (1961)].

According to Klotter and Kanovitz (1991, p. 456), in 1985 the Supreme Court "recognized for the first time a constitutional right to have effective counsel on appeal where the appeal is a matter of right."

The Sixth Amendment also outlines other rights of those accused of crimes, including the right to a speedy and public trial.

THE RIGHT TO A SPEEDY AND PUBLIC TRIAL

〰️ The right to a speedy and public trial is also established in the Sixth Amendment.

In the 1990s, even in the justice system where things seem anything but speedy, timeliness *is* expected. *Barker v. Wingo* (1972) was one of the Supreme Court's first attempts at determining what is or is not a speedy trial. *Barker v. Wingo* also included a number of continuances by the defense and failed to draw a "bright line" on the right to a speedy trial, setting up the four-pronged balancing test. As a result, the factors to be considered are (1) the length of the delay, (2) the reasons for the delay, (3) a timely assertion of this right by the defendant and (4) whether the defendant was harmed by the delay.

In the *Barker* case, the defendant was charged with murder and tried five years later after numerous continuances by the prosecution. The Court admitted that it is a "balancing act" in ascertaining whether a trial failed to be "speedy enough" to meet the requirement of the Sixth Amendment. Perhaps the most important issue is whether the defendant was unduly harmed because of the delay. The wheels of justice do move slowly.

A speedy trial is necessary in a system that places fairness above all else; and, indeed, an expeditious trial does promote fairness. Not only does a system that fails to provide a speedy trial encourage prolonged imprisonment for the accused, but the defendant's ability to acquire accurate information lessens as time goes on. The system, too, suffers because of the additional expenses incurred by the government. And their case does not necessarily improve with time. The Supreme Court, in such cases as *Smith v. Hooey* (1969), which dealt with the negative effects of a delayed trial for the defendant, and *Barker v. Wingo* (1972), just discussed, dealing with the negative effects of a delayed trial for the government, has continued to emphasize why this Sixth Amendment right benefits both the accused and the prosecution.

America prides itself on having the justice system open to public scrutiny. In the case of *Press-Enterprise Co. v. Superior Court* (1984), elaborated upon by Klotter and Kanovitz (1991, p. 499), it is said that "open trials enhance both the basic fairness of the criminal trial and the appearance of fairness so essential to public confidence in the system."

Exceptions to the Requirement for a Public Trial

In rare instances, the court has been allowed to bar the public from a trial for a limited time. Before a judge can do so, however, four limitations specified in the Sixth Amendment must be met (Klotter and Kanovitz, 1991, p. 499):

> First, before ordering closure, the trial judge must weigh the Sixth Amendment interests of the accused against the opposing claimed need for closure. He may close the courtroom only when closure is essential to preserve higher values. Second, the duration and scope of the closure order may be no broader than necessary to protect

the interests that create the need for this order. Third, before ordering closure, the court must explore reasonable alternatives to this action. Finally, the judge must make written findings adequate to support his closure order.

Closing a trial to the public is often challenged as violating the public's First Amendment rights. However, as ruled in *Estes v. Texas* (1965), if a trial turns into a three-ring circus, losing the dignified atmosphere expected in a trial, the defendant can claim a deprivation of his due process rights.

Although the Sixth Amendment specifies the defendant's right to a public trial, this does *not* require that the trial be taped or broadcast live. The Sixth Amendment requirement is met as long as members of the press are allowed into the courtroom. A current struggle is being waged by the media in demanding that television cameras be permitted in courtrooms. At this time, this decision has been left to the states.

THE RIGHT TO BE TRIED BY A JURY OF ONE'S PEERS

While there is an emphasis on trials, it is important to bear in mind that the majority of cases are disposed of prior to trial. However, the American jury system is an important aspect of our criminal justice system, and understanding it is an important part of understanding constitutional law. The Magna Carta provided the right to some basic forms of jury trials, which were greatly superior to trials by ordeal used before that time.

The framers of our Constitution felt so strongly about a right to be tried by their peers that they included it in Article 3, Section 2 of the Constitution for most criminal trials. In addition, the Sixth Amendment provides that: "In all criminal prosecutions, the accused shall enjoy the right to a speedy and public trial, by an impartial jury." The other important aspects of jury trials have been left to common law to develop a system of fairness according to constitutional guidelines. A jury composed of government officials, for example, or those selected only by the prosecution would provide little fairness.

Not everyone wants to have his or her case heard by a jury. For various tactical reasons, defendants may prefer to have their case heard by only a judge, called a **court trial.** *Codispoti v. Pennsylvania* (1974) supports the Sixth Amendment guarantee that a criminal defendant has a right to a jury trial whenever a penalty of incarceration of more than six months is a possibility. The Supreme Court has held that a jury trial is not guaranteed when jail time of less than six months is the maximum possibility (*Baldwin v. New York*, 1970). States may assure a jury trial for offenses that may result in jail time less than six months, but they would not be constitutionally mandated to do so.

The number of jurors required in particular crimes is generally left up to each state to determine, although the Federal Rules of Civil Procedure do require a 12-member jury in criminal cases in federal court. Most states direct that 12 jurors be used for felony-level trials.

It has been held a denial of equal protection to try defendants before juries unfairly comprised of a group likely to hold against them. For example, in *Strauder v. West Virginia* (1880), the Court held that a black defendant could not be tried before a jury from which all members of his race were purposely excluded. This was also established in *Swain v. Alabama* (1865).

Taylor v. Louisiana (1975) held that women cannot be excluded from serving as jurors, and a series of cases at the Supreme Court level have held that excluding anyone as a juror based on his or her profession is unconstitutional (*Rawlins v. Georgia,* 1906). Further, in *Glasser v. United States* (1942), the Court stated that "the proper functioning of the jury system and, indeed, our democracy itself, requires that the jury be a 'body truly representative of the community,' and not the organ of any special group or class."

Federal and state courts have a system in place to enable them to randomly compile lists of potential jurors. *Taylor v. Louisiana* established that the jury panel (those considered eligible to serve on a jury) may not be determined so as to systematically exclude any class of persons, since selection of a jury from a cross-section of the community is an important component of the Sixth Amendment.

THE RIGHT TO CONFRONT AND CROSS-EXAMINE ADVERSE WITNESSES

The Sixth Amendment also requires that the accused has the right to confront his accusers and, by implication, to cross-examine them. This is in keeping with the adversarial nature of our criminal justice system.

> The Sixth Amendment further establishes the right of defendants to confront adverse witnesses.

Although the Sixth Amendment does not specifically mention cross-examination, it is common sense that to simply confront an adverse witness would serve little purpose. As noted by Klotter and Kanovitz (1991, p. 522): "Cross-examination is so central to the constitutional right of confrontation that the Supreme Court, in references to the confrontation clause, has repeatedly alluded to it as assuring the 'right to confront and *cross-examine*' as if the latter term appeared in the constitutional text." According to Schmalleger (1993, p. 643):

> Some courts now permit only an indirect confrontation, through the use of television, videotapes, and the like. Abused juveniles, for example, appear to jurors in some jurisdictions only on television screens to spare them the trauma and embarrassment of the courtroom. Although such strategies may appear to be an "end run" around the Sixth Amendment, they are complicated by claims that justice is better served by an articulate witness rather than a frightened one and by the fact that most such testimonial strategies involve juveniles as witnesses.

The confrontation clause has been modified as it applies to child victim witnesses in *Maryland v. Craig* (1990). This case held that the testimony of a young child in a sex abuse case can be conducted via a one-way closed-circuit television as an example of when a right to confront witnesses may be amended to protect the witness.

Summary

The Sixth Amendment guarantees defendants the right to counsel during criminal proceedings. Like most other amendments contained within the Bill of Rights, this amendment also has been held to apply to state and local government. *Escobedo* established the Sixth Amendment right of a defendant to have a lawyer present during interrogation.

The right to counsel, like all American law, was developed through the common law system. *Gideon v. Wainwright* established that indigent defendants are to be provided lawyers in serious cases. The *Miranda* case required suspects to be told of their Sixth Amendment right to an attorney. The exclusionary rule will prohibit confessions obtained in violation of a person's constitutional rights from being used in court.

The Sixth Amendment right to counsel is required at any critical stage during a criminal proceeding. A waiver of one's Sixth Amendment right to counsel must be knowing and voluntary. Individuals can appear in court without an attorney, representing themselves. This is said to be appearing pro se. The Sixth Amendment right to counsel presumes counsel is effective.

The right to a speedy and public trial is also established in the Sixth Amendment, as is the right of defendants to confront adverse witnesses.

Discussion Questions

1. Do you think having a lawyer present during a trial ensures fairness?
2. Why would people want to represent themselves in court pro se? Would you think more or less of those representing themselves pro se? Why?
3. Should there be a right to self-representation?
4. Explain your understanding of the "common law" system?
5. Why do you think someone would choose to be a defense attorney? A prosecutor?
6. Some believe that public defenders provide less of a defense than would a private attorney. What do you think?
7. Does money buy justice? Consider the "dream team" in the O.J. Simpson trial.
8. Why do you think one government attorney couldn't represent *both* sides in a trial by providing objective facts?
9. Does the adversary system encourage, or even demand, that attorneys represent their clients "too vigorously"?
10. If you were a lawyer, would you prefer to represent the prosecution or the defense? Why? Could a person effectively prosecute for, as an example, a city part-time and defend people in other jurisdictions as well?

References

Bacigal, Ronald J. *Criminal Law and Procedure: An Introduction.* St. Paul: West Publishing Company, 1996.

Klotter, John C. and Jacqueline R. Kanovitz. *Constitutional Law.* 6th ed. Cincinnati: Anderson Publishing Company, 1991.

LaFave, Wayne R. and Jerold Israel. *Criminal Procedure.* St. Paul: West Publishing Company, 1985.

Schmalleger, Frank. *Criminal Justice Today.* 2nd ed. Englewood Cliffs, NJ: Prentice-Hall, 1993.

Senna, Joseph J. and Larry J. Siegel. *Introduction to Criminal Justice.* 4th ed. St. Paul: West Publishing Company, 1987.

Whitebread, Charles H. and Christoper Slobogin. *Criminal Procedure. An Analysis of Cases and Concepts.* 2nd ed. Mineola, NY: The Foundation Press, Inc., 1986.

Zalman, Marvin and Larry J. Siegel. *Criminal Procedure: Constitution and Society.* St. Paul: West Publishing Company, 1991.

Cases Cited

Argersinger v. Hamlin, 407 U.S. 25, 92 S.Ct. 2006, 32 L.Ed.2d 530 (1972).
Baldwin v. New York, 399 U.S. 66, 90 S.Ct. 1886, 26 L.Ed.2d 437 (1970).
Barker v. Wingo, 407 U.S. 514, 92 S.Ct. 2182, 33 L.Ed.2d 101 (1972).
Brewer v. Williams, 430 U.S. 387, 97 S.Ct. 1232, 51 L.Ed.2d 424 (1977).
Cardarell v. United States, 375 F.2d 222 (8th Cir. 1967).
Codispoti v. Pennsylvania, 418 U.S. 506, 94 S.Ct. 2687, 41 L.Ed.2d 912 (1974).
Coleman v. Alabama, 399 U.S. 1 (1970).
Douglas v. California, 372 U.S. 353, 83 S.Ct. 814, 9 L.Ed.2d 811 (1963).
Escobedo v. Illinois, 378 U.S. 478, 84 S.Ct. 1758, 12 L.Ed.2d 977 (1964).
Estelle v. Smith, 451 U.S. 454, 101 S.Ct. 1866, 68 L.Ed.2d 359 (1981).
Estes v. Texas, 381 U.S. 532, 85 S.Ct. 1628, 14 L.Ed.2d 543 (1965).
Faretta v. California, 422 U.S. 806 (1975).
Gagnon v. Scarpelli, 411 U.S. 778 (1973).
Geders v. United States, 425 U.S. 80, 96 S.Ct. 1330, 47 L.Ed.2d 592 (1976).
Gideon v. Wainwright, 372 U.S. 335, 83 S.Ct. 792, 9 L.Ed.2d 799 (1963).
Glasser v. United States, 315 U.S. 60, 62 S.Ct. 457 (1942).
Hamilton v. Alabama, 368 U.S. 52, 82 S.Ct. 157, 7 L.Ed.2d 114 (1961).
Harris v. South Carolina, 338 U.S. 68, 69 S.Ct. 1354, 93 L.Ed. 1815 (1949).
In re Gault, 387 U.S. 1, 87 S.Ct. 1428, 18 L.Ed.2d 527 (1967).
Johnson v. Zerbst, 304 U.S. 458, 58 S.Ct. 1019, 82 L.Ed. 1461 (1938).
Kirby v. Illinois, 406 U.S. 682, 92 S.Ct. 1877, 32 L.Ed.2d 411 (1972).
Maryland v. Craig, 497 U.S. 836, 110 S.Ct. 3157, 111 L.Ed.2d 666 (1990).
Massiah v. United States, 377 U.S. 201, 84 S.Ct. 1199, 12 L.Ed.2d. 246 (1964).
McLeod v. Ohio, 381 U.S. 356, 85 S.Ct. 1556, 14 L.Ed.2d 682 (1965).
Mempa v. Rhay, 389 U.S. 128 (1967).
Miranda v. Arizona, 384 U.S. 436, 86 S.Ct. 1602 (1966).
Moore v. Illinois, 434 U.S. 220 (1977).
Moore v. Michigan, 355 U.S. 155 (1957).
O'Malley v. United States, 285 F.2d 733, 734 (6th Cir. 1961).
Powell v. Alabama, 287 U.S. 45, 53 S.Ct. 55, 77 L.Ed. 158 (1932).
Press-Enterprise Co. v. Superior Court, 464 U.S. 501, 104 S.Ct. 819, 78 L.Ed.2d 629 (1984).
Rawlins v. Georgia, 201 U.S. 638, 26 S.Ct. 560, 50 L.Ed.2d 899 (1906).
Scott v. Illinois, 440 U.S. 367, 99 S.Ct. 1158, 59 L.Ed.2d 383 (1979).

Smith v. Hooey, 393 U.S. 374, 89 S.Ct. 575, 21 L.Ed.2d 607 (1969).

Spano v. New York, 360 U.S. 315, 79 S.Ct. 1202, 3 L.Ed.2d 1265 (1959).

Strauder v. West Virginia, 100 U.S. (10 Otto.) 303, 25 L.Ed. 664 (1880).

Strickland v. Washington, 466 U.S. 668, 104 S.Ct. 2052, 80 L.Ed.2d 674 (1984).

Swain v. Alabama, 380 U.S. 202, 85 S.Ct. 824, 13 L.Ed.2d 759 (1865).

Taylor v. Louisiana, 419 U.S. 522, 95 S.Ct. 692, 42 L.Ed.2d 690 (1975).

Townsend v. Burke, 334 U.S. 736 (1948).

United States v. Henry, 447 U.S. 264, 100 S.Ct. 2183, 65 L.Ed.2d 115 (1980).

United States v. Wade, 388 U.S. 218, 87 S.Ct. 1926, 18 L.Ed.2d 1149 (1967).

White v. Maryland, 373 U.S. 59, 83 S.Ct. 1050, 10 L.Ed.2d 193 (1963).

Chapter 14 The Eighth Amendment: Bail, Fines and Punishment

Excessive bail shall not be required, nor excessive fines imposed, nor cruel and unusual punishment inflicted.

—EIGHTH AMENDMENT OF THE UNITED STATES CONSTITUTION

ELDER ANDERSON IN THE PILLORY.

The pillory. (Provided by Corbis-Bettmann.)

INTRODUCTION

The Eighth Amendment protects three rights, one which applies before trial, the other two after a person has been convicted of a crime. Bail allows the accused to be freed from jail pending trial by putting up either a money bond or property as security for the court. If the accused does not appear in court on the scheduled date, he or she forfeits the bail. Bail prevents a person from remaining in jail before actually being convicted of a crime. The Eighth Amendment says that bail shall not be "excessive."

After trial, if the accused is found guilty, the Eighth Amendment also forbids "excessive fines" as punishment. Furthermore, the Eighth Amendment prohibits "cruel and unusual punishment." Note that a brief amendment allows for significant controversy over interpretation. How should "cruel and unusual" be defined? What is "excessive"? Does the Eighth Amendment ban only those punishments that were "cruel and unusual" in 1791, such as drawing and quartering (disemboweling and cutting the body into four parts), but allow those that were not considered quite so bad back then, such as cutting off ears and death by hanging? The Eighth Amendment must be interpreted by evolving standards of decency. Do current standards of decency prohibit the death penalty in all its forms, or is capital punishment necessary for justice? These questions of life or death are dealt with in the very meaning of the Eighth Amendment.

HISTORY BEFORE THE EIGHTH AMENDMENT

The language of the Eighth Amendment came almost verbatim from the Virginia Declaration of Rights of 1776, which was virtually identical to a provision in the English Bill of Rights of 1689. Even before these documents, the Massachusetts Body of Liberties, enacted in 1641, provided a right to bail and prohibited cruel and inhumane punishment. The idea of being held in prison for an indefinite time without any opportunity for even temporary release was an abhorrent thought to those who knew how restrictive government could be.

The Massachusetts Bay Colony, founded by the Puritans, sought to eliminate such English punishments as cutting off hands and burning at the stake. The Body of Liberties allowed the death penalty for religious offenses such as blasphemy, but not for burglary and robbery, which were capital crimes in England. Society itself was, and continues, to determine what is a reasonable punishment, and what is unreasonable.

Nonetheless, the Puritans allowed many punishments that would seem cruel and unusual today. Physical punishments included piercing the tongue with a hot iron, cutting off body parts, branding and whipping. The Puritans also shamed offenders by public punishment in which the law breakers were confined to the stocks and pillory while townspeople hurled garbage at them. Some adulterers were required to wear the letter "A" on their clothing and were forced to wear signs. For example, in 1675 one Salem sex offender wore the following sign: "This person is convicted for speaking words in a boasting manner of his lascivious and unclean practices." The ultimate punishment, besides hanging, was banishment from the colony.

BAIL

The use of **bail** dates back at least as far as the Greek philosopher Plato, who wrote:

> Prosecutors must demand bail from the defendant [who] shall provide three substantial securities who guarantee to produce him at the trial, and if a man be unable or unwilling to provide these securities, the court must take, bind and keep him, and produce him at the trial of the case (Samaha, 1994, p. 335).

The first part of the Eighth Amendment deals with the granting of bail to individuals accused of crimes.

Bail serves two purposes. First, it helps to assure the appearance of the accused at the time of the trial. Second, it avoids continued incarceration of individuals not yet convicted of a crime. Bail also allows the individual time to prepare a defense and to continue earning income if employed.

> ⋙ Bail is money or property pledged by a defendant for pretrial release from custody that would be forfeited should the defendant fail to appear at subsequent court proceedings.

Bail is based on the principle that a person is "innocent until proven guilty." Keeping accused people in jail while awaiting trial before they actually have been convicted of a crime would violate this principle. And while the Eighth Amendment does not state that there is an absolute right to bail in every case, in *Stack v. Boyle* (1951), the Supreme Court ruled that bail was excessive when set higher than necessary to guarantee the accused's appearance at trial. In other words, bail is excessive if set at a figure higher than an amount reasonably calculated to fulfill the purpose of the Eighth Amendment. The right to bail has historically been assumed through case law and statutory law rather than constitutionally guaranteed.

> ◿ The Eighth Amendment prohibits "excessive bail," but it does not define what this is, nor does the amendment guarantee a right to bail in general. It says only that where bail is available, the amount shall not be excessive. The conditions under which bail may be granted are set forth in federal and state laws and by case law (common law).

Bail may be denied in capital cases, those involving the death penalty and when the accused has threatened possible trial witnesses. Also, the amount of bail does not have to be something the accused can pay. Some poor people cannot afford bail at all and must stay in jail, thus generating debate over whether the system caters to those with money while discriminating against those without.

Some individuals use the services of a bail bondsman, called **commercial bail.** The bail bondsman will post a person's bond for a fee, in effect making a loan, but in a situation in which traditional financial institutions may well fear to tread. If the accused skips bail (fails to appear in court as ordered), the bail bondsman will often help the police catch the person because the bond company would lose their money. In some states, in fact, bail bondsman have significant authority to locate "bail jumpers" and bring them before the court. Several objections have been raised to bail, as noted by Samaha (1994, pp. 335–336):

❖ It discriminates against poor defendants.
❖ It is impossible to translate the risk of flight and/or danger into money values.
❖ The premise that money will secure appearance is questionable because bondsmen keep the money paid.
❖ Judges may set bail high in order to punish defendants prior to conviction.
❖ It transfers the release decision from judges to bail bondsmen.
❖ It provides for little or no supervision of defendants.
❖ It fosters corrupt and abusive practices.
❖ Pretrial detention informally punishes poor defendants prior to legal proof of guilt.

The preceding objections to bail are valid, except that courts have usually, at least within the last 40 years, been able to add additional requirements for release.

Perhaps in response to such objections, several states have eliminated for-profit bail bond businesses and have replaced them with state-operated pretrial service resources.

Another alternative to bail originated in the 1960s when two New Yorkers conducted an experimental pretrial release agency known as the Manhattan Bail Project. After a year of the experiment, the results provided "overwhelming and persuasive evidence" that pretrial release was a viable option. In fact, the default rate was less than seven tenths of 1% (Senna and Siegel, 1993, p. 426). The success of this project was partially responsible for congressional passage of the Bail Reform Act of 1966. This act allowed judges to consider the defendant's background, family ties and prior record in setting bail. Under this comprehensive statute, the primary bail condition was for defendants to be released on their own recognizance, or **ROR,** which means that the court trusts them to show up in court when required. No bail money is required. Criteria for ROR varies from state to state, but usually includes the person's residential stability, a good employment record and no previous convictions. A 1986 survey of bail reform found that ROR does not discriminate against the poor, does not expose defendants to the legal, social and economic hardships of jail and has outperformed the traditional bond system (Samaha, 1994, p. 344).

Schmalleger (1993, p. 281) lists the following available alternatives to a cash bond in addition to ROR:

❖ Conditional release.
❖ Third-party custody.
❖ Attorney affidavit.
❖ Unsecured or signature bond.
❖ Property bond.
❖ Deposit bail.

As noted by Samaha (1994, p. 341): "The preference for nonmonetary bail arose in the 1960s heyday of criminal justice reform when activists favored individual rights. During the 1970s the pendulum swung in the other direction, and concern for public safety came to the fore." One result was the Bail Reform Act of 1984 which significantly departed from the philosophy underlying the Bail Reform Act of 1966.

The Bail Reform Act of 1984

The Bail Reform Act of 1984, allowed the Federal Courts for the first time to deny bail on the basis of danger to the community or of risk to not appear at trial. Known as **preventive detention,** this practice authorized judges to predict the future criminal conduct of those accused of serious offenses and deny bail on those grounds. According to Ferdico (1996, p. 25):

> Most significantly . . . the 1984 act allowed an authorized judicial officer to detain an arrested person pending trial if the government demonstrates by clear and convincing evidence after an adversary hearing that no release conditions "will reasonably assure . . . the safety of any other person and the community."

≈ The Bail Reform Act of 1984 established the practice of preventive detention for individuals deemed a threat to society or likely to flee.

Opponents of preventive detention argued that the accused was being punished without trial, and that protecting the community was the job of the police, not the purpose of bail. A few months after passage of the Bail Reform Act, in *United States v. Hazzard* (1984), the Supreme Court held that Congress was justified in denying bail to offenders who represented a danger to the community. The Supreme Court also upheld preventive detention in *United States v. Salerno* (1987), stating that pretrial detention under this act did not violate due process or the Eighth Amendment. In this case the government charged Salerno with 29 counts of racketeering and conspiracy to commit murder. The Court ruled that since the Bail Reform Act contained many procedural safeguards, the government's interest in protecting the community outweighed the individual's liberty.

According to Senna and Siegel (1993, p. 432):

> *Salerno* legitimizes the use of preventive detention as a crime control method. . . . *Salerno* further illustrates the concern for community protection that has developed in the past decade. It is a good example of the recent efforts by the Court to give the justice system greater control over criminal defendants.

Strongly dissenting to the *Salerno* majority opinion was Justice Marshall who said:

> It is a fair summary of history to say that the safeguards of liberty have frequently been forged in controversies involving not very nice people. Honoring the presumption of innocence is often difficult; sometimes we must pay substantial social costs as a result of our commitment to the values we espouse. But at the end of the day the presumption of innocence protects the innocent; the shortcuts we take with those whom we believe to be guilty injure only those wrongfully accused and, ultimately, ourselves.
>
> Throughout the world today there are men, women, and children interned indefinitely, awaiting trials which may never come or which may be a mockery of the word, because their governments believe them to be "dangerous." Our Constitution, whose construction began two centuries ago, can shelter us forever from the evils of such unchecked power. Over two hundred years it has slowly, through our efforts, grown more durable, more expansive, and more just. But it cannot protect us if we lack the courage, and the self-restraint to protect ourselves.

Nonetheless, several states have incorporated elements of preventive detention into their bail systems, as summarized in Table 14–1.

≈ The Eighth Amendment's prohibition against excessive bail does not apply to the states.

Therefore, even after *Salerno,* state courts are free to forbid preventive detention of state and local prisoners based on excessive bail provisions in the state constitution.

Table 14–1   Legislative provisions to assure community safety.

Type of provision	States that have enacted the provision
Exclusion of certain crimes from automatic bail eligibility	Colorado, District of Columbia, Florida, Georgia, Michigan, Nebraska, Wisconsin
Definition of the purpose of bail to ensure appearance and safety	Alaska, Arizona, California, Delaware, District of Columbia, Florida, Hawaii, Minnesota, South Carolina, South Dakota, Vermont, Virginia, Wisconsin
Inclusion of crime control factors in the release decision	Alabama, California, Florida, Georgia, Minnesota, South Dakota, Wisconsin
Inclusion of release conditions related to crime control	Alaska, Arkansas, Delaware, District of Columbia, Florida, Hawaii, Illinois, Minnesota, New Mexico, North Carolina, South Carolina, Vermont, Virginia, Washington, Wisconsin
Limitations on the right to bail for those previously convicted	Colorado, District of Columbia, Florida, Georgia, Hawaii, Michigan, New Mexico, Texas, Wisconsin
Revocation of pretrial release when there is evidence that the accused committed a new crime	Arkansas, Colorado, Illinois, Indiana, Massachusetts, Nevada, New York, Rhode Island, Virginia, Wisconsin
Limitations on the right to bail for crimes alleged to have been committed while on release	Colorado, District of Columbia, Florida, Maryland, Michigan, Nevada, Tennessee, Texas, Utah
Provisions for pretrial detention to ensure safety	Arizona, California, District of Columbia, Florida, Georgia, Hawaii, Michigan, Wisconsin

Source: Bureau of Justice Statistics. *Report to the Nation on Crime and Justice.* 2nd ed. Washington: U.S. Government Printing Office, 1988, p. 59.

EXCESSIVE FINES

After the accused is convicted of a crime, the Eighth Amendment also prohibits punishment by excessive fines. Like the prohibition of excessive bail, the excessive fines clause has not been incorporated to apply to the states.

Very few Supreme Court cases have dealt with the issue of excessive fines. One recent case, *Browning-Ferris Industries v. Kelco Disposal, Inc.* (1989), presented the question whether the Eighth Amendment applied to civil punishments as well as criminal punishments. In criminal law, the government is always involved as a party to the case. Civil law, however, addresses disputes between private parties, not crimes against the government.

In civil lawsuits between private parties, the plaintiff usually seeks monetary damages from the defendant to right an alleged wrong. **Compensatory damages** reimburse the plaintiff for actual harm done, such as medical expenses or lost business. **Punitive damages** above and beyond the actual economic loss can be awarded to punish the defendant and to warn others not to engage in similar conduct.

Private individuals who bring lawsuits have been called "private attorneys general" because they help enforce acceptable standards of societal behavior beyond what the law defines as a crime. For instance, if a manufacturer produces a faulty product, an injured consumer can sue for punitive damages, which would discourage the defendant from making other harmful products even though the criminal law might not apply. Consumer advocates argue that punitive damages help protect the public from harmful actions of major industries. Businesses counter by saying that huge punitive damage awards raise the cost of liability insurance, thus driving up prices for current products and potentially delaying the development of new ones.

In *Browning-Ferris Industries,* the Supreme Court ruled that the Eighth Amendment applied not only to criminal cases, but also to "direct actions initiated by the government to inflict punishment." Punitive damages in civil cases did not involve government actions, said the Court, so the Eighth Amendment did not apply. The Court noted that while it agreed that punitive damages advance the interest of punishment and deterrents, which are also among the interest advanced by criminal law, it failed to see how this overlap required that the excessive fines clause be applied in cases between private parties.

Asset Forfeiture and the Prohibition against Excessive Fines

In *Austin v. United States* (1993), the Supreme Court unanimously ruled that the Eighth Amendment prohibition against excessive fines applies to civil forfeiture proceedings against property connected to drug trafficking. They held that the amount seized by the forfeiture must bear some relationship to the value of the illegal enterprise, under the Eighth Amendment prohibition on excessive fines. This is the first constitutional limitation on the government's power to seize property connected with illegal activity and could result in challenges to seizures related to criminal activity.

CRUEL AND UNUSUAL PUNISHMENT

The final clause of the Eighth Amendment forbids punishments that are "cruel and unusual," but it does not say what those punishments are. The Supreme Court, in *Trop v. Dulles* (1958), said that the Eighth Amendment "must draw its meaning from the evolving standards of decency that mark the progress of a maturing society." Therefore, as Justice Thurgood Marshall noted in a later case: "[A] penalty that was permissible at one time in our nation's history is not necessarily permissible today." Thus, common punishments in the 1790s, such as whippings and pillories, are not constitutional in the 1990s.

While this text emphasizes American law and the events leading to the formation of current law, it is interesting to observe the determination of punishment by other countries and cultures, both past and present. Because law in any society seeks to respond to the present needs of that society, which are always in flux, the punishments considered appropriate also change. Perhaps it is the "extremity" of the available punishment forms that tends to change as does the society's overall social feelings.

For example, while Americans are steadfast in their belief that crime must be curtailed "at any price," the recent caning (whipping) of a young American adult in Singapore, who was found guilty of damage to property, was considered an outrage by many. Yet the crime rate in Singapore is consider-

American teenager Michael Fay convicted of vandalism in a Singapore court and sentenced to imprisonment, a fine and six strokes of the cane. (Photo by Jonathan Drake. Provided by Reuters/Corbis-Bettmann.)

ably lower than that in the United States. So what *is* appropriate punishment? What a society defines it as. Ferdico (p. 26) notes:

> The cruel and unusual punishment clause of the Eighth Amendment limits the punishment that may be imposed upon conviction of a crime in three ways. First, the clause "imposes substantive limits on what can be made criminal and punished as such. . . ." Also, a person may not be punished in retaliation for exercising a constitutional right (*United States v. Heubel*, 1989). Second, the cruel and unusual punishment clause proscribes certain kinds of punishment such as torture and divestiture of citizenship. Third, the clause prohibits punishment that is excessive in relation to the crime committed.

In *Coker v. Georgia* (1977) the Court held that a "punishment is 'excessive' and unconstitutional if it (1) makes no measurable contribution to acceptable goals of punishment and hence is nothing more than the purposeless and needless imposition of pain and suffering; or (2) is grossly out of proportion to the severity of the crime" (Ferdico, p. 26).

The Supreme Court established three criteria for **proportionality analysis** of sentences in *Solem v. Helm* (1983):

> [A] court's proportionality analysis under the Eighth Amendment should be guided by objective criteria, including (i) the gravity of the offense and the harshness of the penalty; (ii) the sentences imposed on other criminals in the same jurisdiction; and (iii) the sentences imposed for the commission of the same crime in other jurisdictions.

 The general rule under the Eighth Amendment is that punishments must be proportional or directly related to the crime committed.

For example, in *Robinson v. California* (1962), the Supreme Court found "excessive" a 90-day jail term for the crime of being "addicted to the use of narcotics." Robinson was not under the influence of drugs when arrested, and the only evidence against him were the scars and needle marks on his arms. The Court believed that the defendant was being punished for the mere status of being an addict, not for actual criminal behavior. On the other hand, in *Harmelin v. Michigan* (1991), the Supreme Court upheld a mandatory life sentence without parole for a first-time cocaine conviction.

The Supreme Court tackled the issue of **corporal punishment** (causing bodily harm) in *Ingraham v. Wright* (1978). James Ingraham, a junior high school student, had been hit more than 20 times with a paddle for disobeying a teacher's order. He required medical attention and missed 11 days of school. The Court held: "[T]he state itself may impose such corporal punishment as is necessary for the proper education of the child for the maintenance of group discipline." Furthermore, the Court stated: "[T]he school child has little need for protection of the Eighth Amendment because the openness of the public school and its supervision by the community affords significant safeguards against the kinds of abuses from which the Eighth Amendment protects the prisoner." This case is included as an example of the controversy over which there continues to be significant debate, both in the courtroom and elsewhere, as to what consequences are appropriate in the home, school and court.

Modern technology presents the possibility of several treatments for criminals, including Antabuse, a drug used in treating alcoholics by causing nausea and vomiting when alcohol is ingested. Sex offenders have been treated with Depo-Provera, a drug which reduces the sex drive. Schmalleger (1993, p. 644) cautions: "Drugs such as Antabuse and Depo-Provera, and surgical procedures like castration and lobotomy, may run afoul of the Eighth Amendment's ban on cruel and unusual punishment." He also notes: "The American Civil Liberties Union . . . has argued that the use of Depo-Provera and other drugs in the treatment of criminal offenders is a form of coercion."

Although other forms of bodily punishment for criminals have disappeared, the death penalty remains a controversial issue. The Supreme Court has decided many cases on the constitutionality of capital punishment. It has also defined the nature of cruel and unusual punishment in noncapital cases. But the death penalty remains the most debated issue under the Eighth Amendment, probably because it concerns the ultimate issue: life or death.

CAPITAL PUNISHMENT

The death penalty dates back centuries. History records many brutal methods of execution, including being buried alive, flayed alive, thrown to wild animals, drawn and quartered, boiled in oil, burned, stoned, drowned, impaled, crucified, pressed to death, smothered, stretched on a rack, disemboweled, beheaded, hanged and shot.

In biblical times criminals were stoned to death or crucified. The Ancient Greeks, in a much more humane fashion, administered poison from the hem-

Electric chair. (Photo by Chip Mitchell. Provided by UPI/Corbis-Bettmann.)

lock tree to execute criminals. The Romans, in contrast, used beheading, clubbing, strangling, drawing and quartering, and being fed to the lions.

During the Dark Ages ordeals were devised to serve as both judgment and punishment. These ordeals included being submerged in water or in boiling oil, crushed under huge boulders or forced to do battle with skilled swordsmen. It was presumed the innocent would survive the ordeal; the guilty would be killed by it. Later, in France, the guillotine was the preferred means of execution. Societies have always struggled with the challenge of seeking to balance societal needs with socially accepted means of punishment.

Although there is hope that today's methods are more civilized, accounts of witnesses to executions raise doubts as to whether progress has been made. The death penalty has been an established feature of the American criminal justice system since Colonial times, with hanging often the preferred execution, especially on the frontier. Executions evolved as states sought more humane ways of killing its condemned—from hangings to the first electrocution in 1890, the invention of the gas chamber in 1923, the use of the firing squad and finally the addition of lethal injection, now the predominant method of execution in the United States. Figure 14–1 shows the various methods of execution used by states that have the death penalty (Stephan and Brien, 1994, p. 6). (Kansas has since enacted a death penalty statute.)

Until the mid-nineteenth century, the death penalty was the automatic sentence for a convicted murderer. State laws began to draw distinctions between degrees of murder, but the death penalty was still automatic for first-degree murderers. By the early twentieth century, however, state legislatures

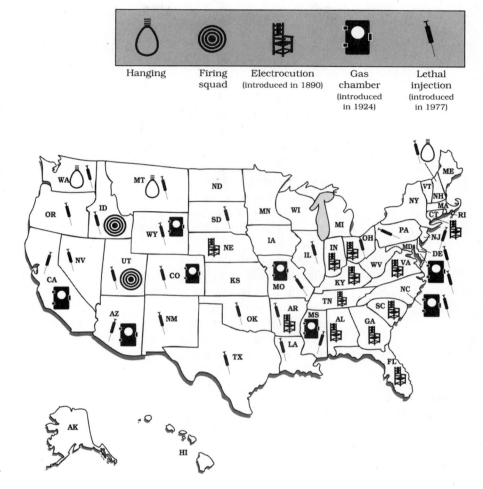

Figure 14–1
U.S. methods of execution.
Source: Death Row. Carlsbad, CA: Glenn Hare Publications, 1995, p. 88. Reprinted by permission.

had given jurors more discretion in sentencing. The jurors were given no guidance by state law in choosing between life and death sentences. Jurors had total discretion in this decision that could not be reviewed upon appeal.

Murderers and rapists were quite often executed in the United States during the 1930s, with the rate of execution peaking at 200 per year during the Depression. But in the 1960s, the death penalty faced increased opposition. Some social scientists argued that the death penalty did not achieve its major purpose, deterrence of other murders. Studies of execution patterns also indicated that the juries did not treat like cases alike, instead acting randomly and unreasonably. Furthermore, research would indicate that there was a pattern to death penalty sentencing based on race. Blacks were executed far more often than whites for murder, and almost all those executed for rape were black men convicted of raping white women.

Support for capital punishment reached an all-time low in 1966, when a Gallup Poll reported only 42% of Americans favored the death penalty. However, a Gallup Poll conducted in 1988 showed a significant shift in attitude, with 79% of Americans in favor of capital punishment (Dionne, 1990, p. 181). Many criminal justice scholars believe increased support for the death penalty is a result of the public's *perception* that violent crime is increasing (even though data indicate a decline in the overall crime index), their disgust with the legal system and their belief that criminals don't serve long enough sentences (Dionne, 1990, p. 182).

Figure 14–2 shows the number of persons under sentence of death from 1953 to 1993. Figure 14–3 shows the number of people executed between 1930 and 1993. Table 14–2 provides a profile of prisoners under sentence of death. Table 14–3 illustrates the time between sentencing and execution.

As of July 1994, 2,870 inmates were under sentence of death in the United States (Wunder, 1994, p. 9). In 1993, 282 inmates were sentenced to death, but only 38 inmates on death row were executed (Stephan and Brien, 1994, p. 1). In other words, death sentences are being handed down more frequently than they are being carried out, resulting in our country's death rows filling up.

Most criminals were sentenced under state law, not federal law. Thus, the Eighth Amendment's prohibition against cruel and unusual punishment was not relevant to the overwhelming majority of death penalty cases until the Supreme Court incorporated it to apply to the states in *Robinson v. California* (1962). The issue of cruel and unusual punishment has a long history, but has given the courts great difficulty in defining it. In *Furman v. Georgia* (1972), the Court's opinion was more than 230 pages long—the longest in Supreme

Figure 14–2

Persons under sentence of death, 1953–1993.

Source: James Stephan and Peter Brien. *Capital punishment 1993: Bureau of Justice Statistics Bulletin.* Washington: U.S. Department of Justice, December 1994, p. 12.

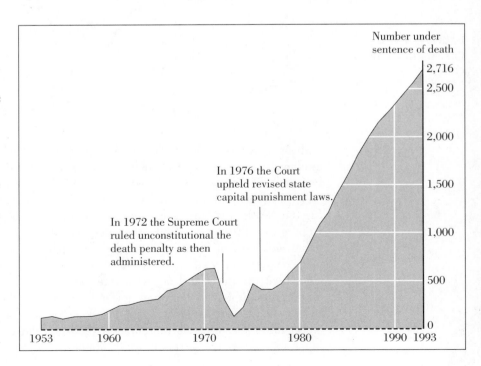

Number under sentence of death

In 1976 the Court upheld revised state capital punishment laws.

In 1972 the Supreme Court ruled unconstitutional the death penalty as then administered.

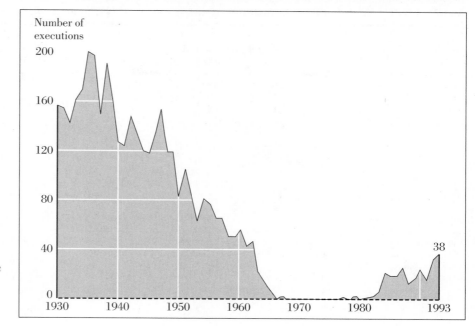

Figure 14–3

Persons executed, 1930–1993.

Source: James Stephan and Peter Brien. *Capital punishment 1993: Bureau of Justice Statistics Bulletin.* Washington: U.S. Department of Justice, December 1994, p. 12.

Table 14–2   Criminal-history profile of prisoners under sentence of death.

	Number				Percent[a]			
	All races[b]	White	Black	Hispanic	All races[b]	White	Black	Hispanic
U.S. total (1993)	2,716	1,566	1,109	206	100%	100%	100%	100%
Prior felony convictions								
Yes	1,740	963	760	120	67.9%	64.8%	73.2%	60.9%
No	822	522	278	77	32.1	35.2	26.8	39.1
Not reported	154	81	71	9				
Prior homicide convictions								
Yes	240	128	110	18	9.1%	8.4%	10.2%	9.0%
No	2,403	1,399	966	183	90.9	91.6	89.8	91.0
Not reported	73	39	33	5				
Legal status at time of capital offense								
Charges pending	167	101	61	10	6.9%	7.3%	6.3%	5.5%
Probation	230	130	98	16	9.5	9.2	10.1	8.8
Parole	491	255	232	51	20.3	18.1	23.7	28.0
Prison escapes	42	28	13	3	1.7	2.0	1.3	1.6
Prison inmate	60	33	27	4	2.5	2.3	2.8	2.2
Other status[c]	33	17	15	1	1.4	1.2	1.5	.6
None	1,395	841	529	97	57.7	59.9	54.3	53.3
Not reported	298	161	134	24				

[a]Percentages are based on those offenders for whom data were reported.

[b]Includes whites, blacks, Hispanics and persons of other races.

[c]Includes 9 persons on work release, 4 persons on mandatory conditional release, 4 persons on bail, 1 person on temporary leave, 2 persons in a halfway house, 1 absconder from bail, 1 person on accelerated rehabilitation, 1 person AWOL from the U.S. Army, 1 person on work furlough, 2 persons in jail, 1 person under house arrest, 1 person in a pre-release treatment center, 1 person in a community diversion program, 1 person in a supervised road gang, 2 persons in a community diversion program and 1 person on conditional release.

Source: Death Row. Carlsbad, CA: Glenn Hare Publications, 1995, p. 89. Reprinted by permission.

Table 14–3   **Time between imposition of death sentence and execution, by race, 1977–1993.**

Year of execution	Number executed			Average elapsed time from sentence to execution for:		
	All races*	White	Black	All races*	White	Black
Total	226	135	88	94 mos	88 mos	103 mos
1977–83	11	9	2	51	49	58
1984	21	13	8	74	76	71
1985	18	11	7	71	65	80
1986	18	11	7	87	78	102
1987	25	13	12	86	78	96
1988	11	6	5	80	72	89
1989	16	8	8	95	78	112
1990	23	16	7	95	97	91
1991	14	7	7	116	124	107
1992	31	19	11	114	104	135
1993	38	23	14	113	112	121

Note: Average time was calculated from the most recent sentencing date. The range for elapsed time for the 226 executions was 3 months to 212 months. Some numbers have been revised from those previously reported.

*Includes Native Americans

Source: Death Row. Carlsbad, CA: Glenn Hare Publications, 1995, p. 89. Reprinted by permission.

Court history. All nine justices wrote separate opinions trying to define the meaning of four words: *cruel and unusual punishment.*

In the *Furman* case, the court ruled five to four that the death penalty as then administered in the United States was cruel and unusual punishment because it was "wantonly and freakishly" imposed. Judges and juries had far too much unguided discretion under current state laws, and the Court held this led to arbitrary and capricious or random and unreasonable death sentences.

In this case, Furman had broken into a private home in the middle of the night, intending only to burglarize it, although he was carrying a gun. Furman attempted to escape when the owner of the house awoke. But Furman tripped and his gun discharged, hitting and killing the owner through a closed door. Furman was black and the owner was white.

In *Furman,* the Supreme Court did not rule that the death penalty was unconstitutional in all circumstances. Rather, the Court held that the states had to give judges and juries more guidance in capital sentencing to prevent discretionary use of the death penalty. In effect, the *Furman* case struck down capital punishment statutes in 37 states. Executions across the country were suspended as a result. In response, about three fourths of the states and the federal government passed new death penalty laws. In most a two-step trial procedure was instituted: the first step a determination of innocence or guilt and the second step a determination of whether to seek the death penalty. Such a two-stage trial is often referred to as a **bifurcated trial.** While reviewing these laws, the Supreme Court finally decided whether the death penalty was inherently cruel and unusual punishment.

Just four years later, however, in the 1976 case of *Gregg v. Georgia,* the Court overturned its previous decision by a seven to two margin, once again granting constitutionality to the death penalty by stating:

A punishment is unconstitutionally cruel and unusual only if it violates the evolving levels of decency that define a civilized society. The death penalty today in the United States does not do that—as is proved by public opinion substantially favoring executions, by legislatures enacting death penalty statutes or refusing to repeal them, and by courts willing to sentence hundreds of murderers to death every year (Ecenbarger, 1994, p. A12).

> *Furman v. Georgia* (1972) was the landmark case in which the Supreme Court called for a ban on the death penalty, ruling such practice as "cruel and unusual punishment." In *Gregg v. Georgia* (1976) the Supreme Court reversed, reinstating the death penalty.

In rendering its opinion, the Court recognized the significance of public opinion, citing strong public support for the death penalty. The Court noted that three fourths of state legislatures reenacted the death penalty after *Furman;* therefore, the death penalty was not "unusual" punishment. In a strong dissent, Justice William Brennan repeated the arguments he had made against the death penalty in *Furman.* Brennan questioned "whether a society for which the dignity of the individual is the supreme value can, without a fundamental inconsistency, follow the practice of deliberately putting some of its members to death. . . . Even the most vile criminal remains a human being possessed of common human dignity."

Brennan argued that the law has progressed to the point where we should declare that, like the punishments on the rack, the screw and the wheel, the punishment of death is no longer morally tolerable in our civilized society. As a general rule, the Supreme Court has upheld the death penalty for the crime of murder, but not for other crimes. Under the Eighth Amendment, the punishment must be related to the crime, so execution is appropriate only in cases of murder—a life for a life.

Since the Supreme Court reinstated the death penalty in *Gregg v. Georgia* (1976), only 143 of the approximately 2,400 prisoners on death row had been executed as of 1990. In 1993, 10 states executed 38 prisoners, seven more than in 1992 and the largest annual number since the Supreme Court upheld the constitutionality of revised state capital punishment laws in 1976 (Stephan and Brien, 1994, p. 1). Table 14–4 shows the status of the death penalty in December 1994. Table 14–5 illustrates executions by state and method. Figure 14–4 shows executions from 1977 to 1994.

According to Stephan and Brien (1994, p. 4), in 1993, 12 states revised their death penalty statutes, most involving additional aggravating circumstances, additional categories of victims permitting application of the death penalty and a broadening of the law to allow defendants a choice between two methods of execution. Table 14–6 summarizes these statutory changes.

One reason for this small percentage of executions is the number of court appeals made in death penalty cases. Most capital cases originate in the states and can be filed directly through the state court system, but in addition, the defendants may make indirect or collateral appeals of their sentences through the federal court system by arguing that their constitutional rights

Table 14–4 Status of the death penalty, December 31, 1994.

Executions during 1994		Number of prisoners under sentence of death		Jurisdictions without a death penalty
Texas	14	Texas	394	Alaska
Arkansas	5	California	381	District of Columbia
Virginia	2	Florida	342	Hawaii
Delaware	1	Pennsylvania	182	Iowa
Florida	1	Illinois	155	Maine
Georgia	1	Ohio	140	Massachusetts
Idaho	1	Alabama	135	Michigan
Illinois	1	Oklahoma	129	Minnesota
Indiana	1	Arizona	121	New York
Maryland	1	North Carolina	111	North Dakota
Nebraska	1	Tennessee	100	Rhode Island
North Carolina	1	Georgia	96	Vermont
Washington	1	23 other jurisdictions	604	West Virginia
				Wisconsin
Total	31	Total	2,890	

Source: James J. Stephan and Tracy L. Snell. *Capital Punishment 1994. Bureau of Justice Statistics Bulletin.* Washington: U.S. Department of Justice, February 1996, p. 1.

Table 14–5 Execution by state and method, 1977–1994.

State	Electrocution	Firing squad	Gas chamber	Hanging	Lethal injection	Number executed
Texas					85	85
Florida	32				1	33
Louisiana	20				1	21
Virginia	24					24
Georgia	18					18
Missouri					11	11
Alabama	10					10
Nevada			1		4	5
North Carolina			1		5	6
Arkansas	1				8	9
South Carolina	4					4
Utah		1			3	4
Mississippi			4			4
Arizona			1		2	3
Delaware					4	4
Oklahoma					3	3
California			2			2
Indiana	3					3
Illinois					2	2
Washington				2		2
Wyoming					1	1
Maryland					1	1
Nebraska	1					1
Idaho					1	1
Total count	113	1	9	2	132	257

Note: This table shows the frequency of execution methods used since 1977. Until recently, the most frequently used method of execution was electrocution; however, lethal injection is now more common. Statistics from 1991 show executions by electrocution outnumbering those by lethal injection by a margin of 90 to 61. Statistics from mid-1993 demonstrate the trend toward lethal injection.
Source: Death Row. Carlsbad, CA: Glenn Hare Publications, 1995, p. 93. Reprinted by permission.

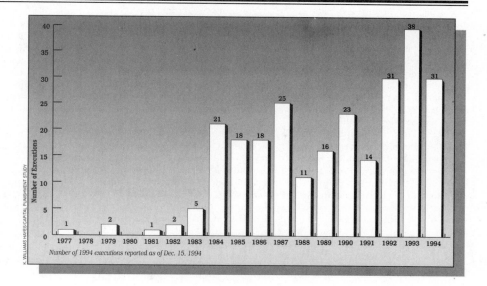

Figure 14–4
**Executions,
1977–1994.**
Source: Death Row. Carlsbad,
CA: Glenn Hare Publications,
1995, p. 93. Reprinted by permission.

have been violated. These federal appeals, known as **petitions for the writ of habeas corpus,** can last many years, long after state appeals have been exhausted.

The Issues in the Controversy Surrounding Capital Punishment

The debate between those who support and those who oppose capital punishment centers on several issues: deterrence, retribution, life imprisonment, the loopholes, cost-effectiveness, disparity, the nature of the punishment as cruel and unusual and the potential for error.

DETERRENCE   Supporters of capital punishment argue that it is a strong deterrent to potential murders. Their justification is that state-sanctioned killings prevent homicides because the state makes it clear that the punishment for homicide is death. However, data indicate the deterrent value is overestimated, and that, as a crime fighting tool, capital punishment is relatively useless.

In a recent poll of police chiefs and sheriffs, most stated that capital punishment was a hollow deterrent and an ineffective law enforcement tool (Murphy, 1995, p. 11A). According to the poll, most police chiefs and sheriffs (82%) believed killers did not weigh the possible penalties before committing the crime. The probability that a murderer will receive a death sentence is low, and the probability of being executed even smaller. Further, according to Wunder (1994, p. 9): "A prisoner sentenced to death who leaves death row has only an 11 percent likelihood of leaving death row for the death chamber." The remaining 89% have their sentences commuted to life imprisonment, are given a new trial and resentenced, die before the execution or have their charges dropped.

No proof exists that capital punishment will deter potential murders. In fact, some suggest that the opposite occurs, that execution may actually

Table 14–6 Statutory changes in capital punishment laws by state, 1993.

Alabama. Murder during kidnaping, robbery, rape, sodomy, burglary, sexual assault, or arson; murder of a peace officer, correctional officer, or public official; murder while under a life sentence; murder for pecuniary gain or contract; aircraft piracy; murder by a defendant with a previous murder conviction; murder of a witness to a crime; murder when a victim is subpoenaed in a criminal proceeding, when the murder is related to the role of the victim as a witness; murder when a victim is less than 14 years old; murder in which a victim is killed while in a dwelling by a deadly weapon fired from outside the dwelling; murder in which a victim is killed while in a motor vehicle by a deadly weapon fired from outside that vehicle; murder in which a victim is killed by a deadly weapon fired from a motor vehicle (13A-5-40).

Arizona. First-degree murder accompanied by at least 1 of 10 aggravating factors.

Arkansas. Capital murder as defined by Arkansas statute (5-10-101). Felony murder; arson causing death; intentional murder of a law enforcement officer, teacher or school employee; murder of prison, jail, court, or correctional personnel or of military personnel acting in line of duty; multiple murders; intentional murder of a public officeholder or candidate; intentional murder while under life sentence; contract murder.

California. Treason; homicide by a prisoner serving a life term; first-degree murder with special circumstances; train wrecking; perjury causing execution.

Colorado. First-degree murder; kidnaping with death of victim; felony murder. Capital sentencing excludes persons determined to be mentally retarded.

Connecticut. Murder of a public safety or correctional officer; murder for pecuniary gain; murder in the course of a felony; murder by a defendant with a previous conviction for intentional murder; murder while under a life sentence; murder during a kidnaping; illegal sale of cocaine, methadone, or heroin to a person who dies from using these drugs; murder during first-degree sexual assault; multiple murders; the defendant committed the offense(s) with an assault weapon.

Delaware. First-degree murder with

aggravating circumstances.

Florida. First-degree murder; capital felonies (FS 921.141); capital drug trafficking felonies (FS 921.142).

Georgia. Murder; kidnaping with bodily injury when the victim dies; aircraft hijacking; treason; kidnaping for ransom when the victim dies.

Idaho. First-degree murder; aggravated kidnaping.

Illinois. First-degree murder accompanied by at least 1 of 12 aggravating factors.

Indiana. Murder with 13 aggravating circumstances.

Kentucky. Aggravated murder; kidnaping when victim is killed.

Louisiana. First-degree murder; treason (La. R.S. 14:30 and 14:113).

Maryland. First-degree murder, either premeditated or during the commission of a felony.

Mississippi. Capital murder includes murder of a peace officer or correctional officer, murder while under a life sentence, murder by bomb or explosive, contract murder, murder committed during specific felonies (rape, burglary, kidnaping, arson, robbery, sexual battery, unnatural intercourse with a child, nonconsensual unnatural intercourse), and murder of an elected official. Capital rape is the forcible rape of a child under 14 years old by a person 18 years or older. Aircraft piracy.

Missouri. First-degree murder (565.020 RSMO).

Montana. Deliberate homicide; aggravated kidnaping when victim or rescuer dies; attempted deliberate homicide, aggravated assault, or aggravated kidnaping by a State prison inmate who has a prior conviction for deliberate homicide or who has been previously declared a persistent felony offender (46-18-303, MCA).

Nebraska. First-degree murder.

Nevada. First-degree murder with 9 aggravating circumstances.

New Hampshire. Contract murder; murder of a law enforcement officer; murder of a kidnaping victim; killing another after being sentenced to life imprisonment without parole.

New Jersey. Purposeful or knowing murder; contract murder.

New Mexico. First-degree murder; felony murder with aggravating circumstances.

North Carolina. First-degree murder

(N.C.G.S. 14-17).

Ohio. Assassination; contract murder; murder during escape; murder while in a correctional facility; murder after conviction for a prior purposeful killing or prior attempted murder; murder of a peace officer; murder arising from specified felonies (rape, kidnaping, arson, robbery, burglary); murder of a witness to prevent testimony in a criminal proceeding or in retaliation (O.R.C. secs. 2929.02, 2903.01, 2929.04).

Oklahoma. Murder with malice aforethought; murder arising from specified felonies (forcible rape, robbery with a dangerous weapon, kidnaping, escape from lawful custody, first-degree burglary, arson); murder when the victim is a child who has been injured, tortured, or maimed.

Oregon. Aggravated murder.

Pennsylvania. First-degree murder.

South Carolina. Murder with statutory aggravating circumstances.

South Dakota. First-degree murder; kidnaping with gross permanent physical injury inflicted on the victim; felony murder.

Tennessee. First-degree murder.

Texas. Murder of a public safety officer, fireman, or correctional employee; murder during the commission of specified felonies (kidnaping, burglary, robbery, aggravated rape, arson); murder for remuneration; multiple murders; murder during prison escape; murder by a State prison inmate; murder of an individual under 6 years of age.

Utah. Aggravated murder (76-5-202, Utah Code annotated).

Virginia. Murder during the commission or attempts to commit specified felonies (abduction, armed robbery, rape, sodomy); contract murder; murder by a prisoner while in custody; murder of a law enforcement officer; multiple murders; murder of a child under 12 years during an abduction; murder arising from drug violations (18.2-31, Virginia Code as amended).

Washington. Aggravated first-degree premeditated murder.

Wyoming. First-degree murder, including both premeditated and felony murder.

Source: James Stephan and Peter Brien. *Capital Punishment 1993: Bureau of Justice Statistics Bulletin.* Washington: U.S. Department of Justice, December 1994, p. 5.

arouse the urge to kill. Others argue that state-sanctioned killings cheapen the value of human life. Still others fear the death penalty may be interpreted by some as a "green light" to put to death those they feel have wronged them, a phenomenon identified as "villain identification" or "lethal vengeance" (Hawkins and Alpert, 1989, p. 173).

Finally, some question if the person executed five or ten years after the fact is the "same" person who committed the crime. These opponents argue that people *do* change and can make positive contributions to society if given the chance through life imprisonment without parole. On the other hand, supporters of the death penalty ask, "What chance did the victim have? Why should the killer be allowed to live?"

Faced with data that the death penalty does not deter killing, capital punishment supporters have turned to retribution to justify the execution of convicted murderers.

RETRIBUTION   Those who use retribution to justify the death penalty state that murderers *deserve* to be killed, an argument that cannot be confirmed or denied scientifically. Murphy (1995, p. 11A) notes: "While a majority of the police chiefs surveyed support the death penalty philosophically . . . they are also keenly aware that government spending is being cut and budgets are tight. Support must be given to programs that work."

LIFE IMPRISONMENT, THE LOOPHOLES AND COST-EFFECTIVENESS Many capital punishment opponents argue that life imprisonment with no chance of parole is a suitable alternative to execution. The inmate might provide restitution to the victim's family and participate in rehabilitating other inmates.

Death penalty supporters argue, however, that a such a sentence does not guarantee a life behind bars. Many prisoners serving time for murder are eligible for parole after 13 or 14 years (Bartollas and Conrad, 1992, p. 169). Only when the guarantee of no parole is given do many people side with the life imprisonment alternative.

Because many murderers are young and are likely to spend many years behind bars if given a life sentence without parole, the cost to "warehouse" these criminals is another issue. Murphy (1995, p. 11A) reports: "The death penalty was rated as the least cost-effective method for controlling crime. Police chiefs would rather spend their limited crime-fighting dollars on such proven measures as community policing, more police training, neighborhood watch programs and longer prison sentences."

The data is conflicting as to which is more expensive: housing an inmate for 20 or more years or covering the expenses that accompany the death penalty, e.g., longer investigations, additional expert testimony, and postconviction appeals. Cook and Slawson ("Death Penalty . . . ," 1994, p. 23) have found: "[I]n North Carolina, it costs taxpayers $329,000 more to convict and execute a murderer than it does to convict the same person and give him or her a 20-year prison term." However, many life sentences extend well beyond 20 years. According to Schmickle and Christensen (1994, pp. A19, A22): "California spends $600,000 on each prisoner it executes, much more than those it locks up for life." Bartollas and Conrad (1992, p. 169) claim, however: "[P]roponents of the death penalty estimate that at a cost of $10,000 to $20,000 a year, a 20-year-old who lives 60 years in prison would cost society more than $1 million."

DISPARITY   Another criticism of the death penalty is that it is often applied arbitrarily and unfairly, that is, death sentences are not handed down equitably. These statistics focus on the race of the offender and victim, as well as the offender's socioeconomic status, where the offense occurred and the sex of the offender.

RACE OF THE OFFENDER   Bureau of Justice Statistics (BJS) data indicate that of the 38 prisoners executed in 1993, 54% were white, 40% were black and 6% were Hispanic (Proband, 1994, p. 1). This seems unequitable because 1990 census information reports that whites represented 80.3% of the total United States population, whereas only 12.1% were black.

Additional BJS data, however, indicate that of persons convicted of violent offenses by state courts in 1990, 50% were white, 48% black. When murder is separated from the other violent offenses of rape, robbery and aggravated assault, whites account for only 42% of the convictions, while blacks constitute 56%. From these statistics, blacks are *not* receiving more than their share of executions.

RACE OF THE VICTIM   Many studies show that the victim's race is more influential than the offender's in determining who receives a death sentence. One study of capital punishment indicated a black offender was eight times more likely to receive the death penalty if the victim was white than if the victim was black (Paternoster and Kazyaka, 1988). The Baldus study, a study of murder cases in Georgia, reported a black offender convicted of murdering a white person was 22 times more likely to receive the death penalty than if the victim was black (Baldus, et al., 1986). The Baldus study also found that blacks who killed whites received the death penalty seven times more often than whites who killed blacks. Trumbo (1995, p. 10) provides the following statistics:

> The Death Penalty Information Center in Washington, D.C. reports that 65 blacks have been executed for murders of whites since 1976, compared to one white person executed for the death of a black victim. However, a look at the race of victims for capital cases shows whites are way ahead of blacks—85 percent to 11 percent. Hispanic victims make up 2 percent and Asians represent 1 percent. . . .
>
> From 1976 to 1991, there were 157 executions in the United States. Ninety-four of them were Caucasians and 63 were African-Americans. That is 59.9 percent white and 40.1 percent black, which is almost a perfect match to the ratio of white and black people who occupy the nearly 2,500 death row cells in this country.

Figure 14–5 illustrates the race of death row inmates, race of those executed and race of the victims.

FINANCIAL STATUS   The offender's financial status may also affect whether a death sentence is imposed. Some studies show that offenders who can afford

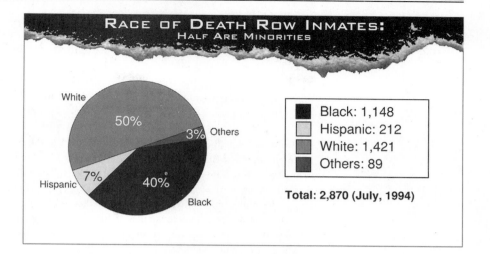

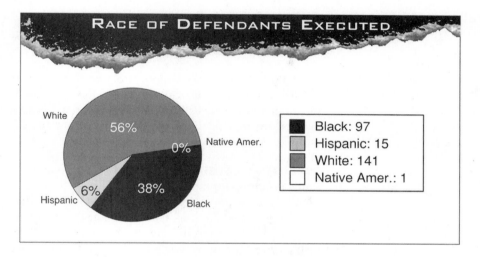

Figure 14–5
Race of death row inmates, race of defendants executed and race of victims.
Source: Death Row. Carlsbad, CA: Glenn Hare Publications, 1995, p. 12. Reprinted by permission.

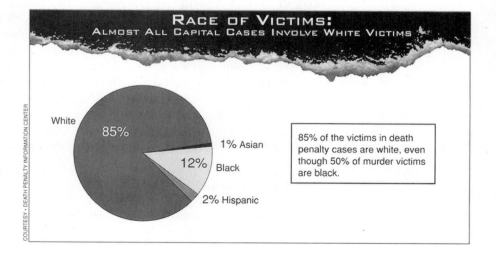

private attorneys are less likely to be sentenced to death than offenders having court-appointed representation. Hawkins and Alpert (1989, p. 181) state: "The correlation of income and race compounds the injustice of the death penalty."

Trumbo (p. 10) cites the reaction of Clive Stafford Smith of the Louisiana Crisis Assistance Center in New Orleans to the Los Angeles District Attorney's Office not seeking the death penalty in the O.J. Simpson case:

> Smith was not surprised when the Los Angeles District Attorney's Office choose not to pursue the death penalty with O.J. Simpson.
>
> Even though he is black, Simpson is also rich—and that is a different kind of color issue. Some would call it green.
>
> It's simple, Smith says. Prosecutors are less inclined to press for capital punishment when the defense is well-financed. "They (Simpson's prosecutors) aren't charging the death penalty because they won't get it. His defense is too well equipped," Smith said.

LOCATION   Yet another variable influencing sentencing is the location of the crime. Courts in large cities tend to impose capital punishment less often than courts in rural and suburban regions.

GENDER   An obvious disparity related to the death penalty centers on the gender of the offender. Only 1.3% of the inmates on death row are women (Stephan and Brien, 1994, p. 1), although roughly 15% of persons arrested for murder are women. By 1993 the number of women on death row had risen to 35.

CRUEL AND UNUSUAL PUNISHMENT   Executions in America evolved as states sought more humane ways of killing its condemned, as noted earlier— from hangings, to electrocution, the gas chamber, the firing squad and finally lethal injections. And, as noted previously, in *Furman v. Georgia* (1972) the Supreme Court ruled that the death penalty was "cruel and unusual punishment," reversing itself four years later in *Gregg v. Georgia* (1976), reinstating the death penalty.

POTENTIAL FOR ERROR   Opponents state that innocent people may be executed. Studies have reported over 100 instances where innocent people were mistakenly convicted of murder. At least 31 of those wrongful convictions resulted in imposing the death penalty and at least eight innocent people were executed (Zimring and Laurence, no date, p. 3). To many the potential for even one mistake is enough reason to abolish capital punishment.

After looking at the issues involved in the controversy swirling around capital punishment, consider now the arguments set forth by each side.

Arguments in Favor of the Death Penalty

Several arguments have been made in support of the death penalty, including the following:

❖ It acts as a deterrent to future murders by serving as an example.
❖ It certainly incapacitates murderers.

❖ It is deserved and morally correct. As the ancient Code of Hammurabi and the Bible stress: "An eye for an eye."
❖ It is also proportional, with the punishment fitting the crime as required by the Eighth Amendment.
❖ It is supported by public opinion.
❖ Sufficient checks and appeal possibilities make the chance of error extremely unlikely.

〜 Among the arguments in favor of the death penalty are that it is a deterrent, it incapacitates, it is deserved and morally correct, it is proportional, it is supported by public opinion and errors are unlikely.

Arguments against the Death Penalty

Several arguments have also been made in opposition to the death penalty, including the following:

❖ No proof exists that it serves as a deterrent.
❖ It is inhumane, uncivilized and brutal.
❖ It is fallible—innocent people may be executed.
❖ The most serious criminals will be spared as they are more likely to plea bargain rather than face execution.
❖ It is racially biased with a disproportionate number of minorities being executed.
❖ It is more costly than life imprisonment.

〜 Arguments against the death penalty are that it does not deter; it is inhumane, uncivilized and brutal; it is fallible; it spares the most serious criminals; it is racially biased and it is costly.

In regard to the final argument involving cost, according to Samaha (1994, p. 439):

It takes about seven-and-one-half years between the trial and the execution of a death-row prisoner, a cost to the taxpayers of about $2.3 million for every capital case. To imprison someone in a single cell at the highest security level in a Texas prison for forty years costs $750,000.

Continuing Contoversy

The cruel and unusual punishment clause may well stand at a constitutional crossroads. It has enjoyed a brief period of prominence, although this prominence may have been achieved at some cost in terms of public perception of the legitimacy of the court's decision-making process. In any event, the court's recent concern with the clause is now seriously threatened by attempts to adopt a more traditional authoritarian approach toward interpreting the clause's language. The death penalty has been and remains extremely controversial.

As this text was being prepared, two executions were carried out in different states. In one, the defendant was shot, the process consisting of five law enforcement volunteers shooting with one blank cartridge among their weapons, aiming at a target pinned over the sentenced person's heart. In the other case the individual was hanged so as to break his neck.

How you personally respond to such circumstances indicates the emotion that goes into determining what sentences are within our legal confines, with the logical question being whether any particular method serves its purpose. To be sure, debate will continue. The death penalty will be an issue for years to come, with strong advocates and opponents because at the core of the issue is the question of values.

Summary

The Eighth Amendment prohibits "excessive bail," but it does not define what this is, nor does the amendment guarantee a right to bail in general. It says only that where bail is available, the amount shall not be excessive. The conditions under which bail may be granted are set forth in federal and state laws.

The Bail Reform Act of 1984 established the practice of preventive detention for individuals deemed a threat to society or likely to flee. The Eighth Amendment's prohibition against excessive bail does not apply to the states.

The general rule for punishment under the Eighth Amendment is that punishments must be proportional or directly related to the crime committed. In *Gregg v. Georgia* (1976), the Supreme Court held that "the punishment of death does not invariably violate the Constitution."

Among the arguments in favor of the death penalty are that it is a deterrent, it incapacitates, it is deserved and morally correct, it is proportional, it is supported by public opinion and errors are unlikely. Arguments against the death penalty are that it does not deter; it is inhumane, uncivilized and brutal; it is fallible; it spares the most serious criminals; it is racially biased and it is costly.

Discussion Questions

1. What historical background do you suspect led to the Eighth Amendment being included in the Bill of Rights?

2. Explain how the Eighth Amendment applies to the states as well as to the federal government.

3. If the Bill of Rights does not guarantee the right to bail, how can bail be assured to those accused of crimes?

4. Explain the basic need(s) for bail.

5. Does the bail system discriminate against the poor?

6. How would you define "cruel and unusual punishment"?

7. Do you support the death penalty? Why or why not?

8. Could you be an executioner or witness to an execution?

9. Why don't we carry out death sentences in public as prior generations did?

10. Do you think the death penalty serves as a deterrent to murder or rape? Why or why not?

References

Baldus, David C., Charles A. Pulaski Jr. and George Woodworth. "Arbitrariness and Discrimination in the Administration of the Death Penalty: A Challenge to State Supreme Courts." *Stetson Law Review.* Spring 1986, vol. XV, no. 2, pp. 146–149.

Bartollas, Clemens and John P. Conrad. *Introduction to Corrections.* 2nd ed. New York: Harper Collins Publishers, 1992.

Dionne, E. J., Jr. "Capital Punishment Gaining Favor as Public Seeks Retribution." *Corrections Today.* August 1990, pp. 178, 180–182.

Ecenbarger, William. "A Good Kill Is Gruesomely Hard to Find." (Minneapolis/St. Paul) *Star Tribune.* July 15, 1994, p. A12.

Ferdico, John N. *Criminal Procedure for the Criminal Justice Professional.* 6th ed. St. Paul: West Publishing Company, 1996.

Hawkins, Richard and Geoffrey P. Alpert. *American Prison Systems: Punishment and Justice.* Englewood Cliffs, NJ: Prentice Hall, 1989.

Murphy, Patrick V. "Death Penalty Useless: Poll of Police Chiefs Finds That Most Say Capital Punishment Is a Hollow Deterrent; They'd Choose Other Methods to Reduce Crime." *USA Today.* February 23, 1995, p. 11A.

Paternoster, Raymond and Ann Marie Kazyaka. "The Administration of the Death Penalty in South Carolina: Experience over the First Few Years." *South Carolina Law Review 39.* 1988, pp. 245–411.

Proband, Stan C. "38 Executions in 1993, 31 in '92." *Overcrowded Times.* February 1994, pp. 1–2.

Samaha, Joel. *Criminal Justice.* 3rd ed. St. Paul: West Publishing Company, 1994.

Schmalleger, Frank. *Criminal Justice Today.* 2nd ed. Englewood Cliffs, NJ: Prentice-Hall, 1993.

Schmickle, Sharon and Jean Christensen. "Death Row: A House Divided." (Minneapolis/St. Paul) *Star Tribune.* April 17, 1994, pp. A19, A22.

Senna, Joseph J. and Larry J. Siegel. *Introduction to Criminal Justice.* 6th ed. St. Paul: West Publishing Company, 1993.

Stephan, James and Peter Brien. *Capital Punishment 1993: Bureau of Justice Statistics Bulletin.* Washington: U.S. Department of Justice, December 1994.

Trumbo, John H. "The Color of Justice." In Gerald Mortimer, ed. *Death Row.* Carlsbad, CA: Glenn Hare Publications, 1995.

Wunder, Amanda. "Capital Punishment 1994." *Corrections Compendium.* November 1994, pp. 8–16.

Zimring, Franklin E. and Michael Laurence. "Death Penalty." Crime File Study Guide. National Institute of Justice (no date).

Cases Cited

Austin v. United States, 509 U.S. 602, 113 S.Ct. 2801, 125 L.Ed.2d 488 (1993).

Browning-Ferris Industries v. Kelco Disposal, Inc., 472 U.S. 257, 109 S.Ct. 2909, 106 L.Ed.2d 219 (1989).

Coker v. Georgia, 433 U.S. 584, 592, 97 S.Ct. 2861, 2866, 53 L.Ed.2d 982, 989 (1977).

Furman v. Georgia, 408 U.S. 238, 92 S.Ct. 2726, 33 L.Ed.2d 346 (1972).

Gregg v. Georgia, 428 U.S. 153, 96 S.Ct. 2909, 49 L.Ed.2d 859 (1976).

Harmelin v. Michigan, 501 U.S. 957, 111 S.Ct. 2680, 115 L.Ed.2d 836 (1991).

Ingraham v. Wright, 430 U.S. 651, 667, 97 S.Ct. 1401, 1410, 51 L.Ed.2d 711, 728 (1977).

Robinson v. California, 370 U.S. 660, 82 S.Ct. 1417, 8 L.Ed.2d 758 (1962).

Solem v. Helm, 463 U.S. 277, 103 S.Ct. 3001, 77 L.Ed.2d 637 (1983).

Stack v. Boyle, 342 U.S. 1, 72 S.Ct. 1, 96 L.Ed. 3 (1951).

Trop v. Dulles, 356 U.S. 86, 78 S.Ct. 590, 2 L.Ed.2d 630 (1958).

United States v. Hazzard, 598 F. Supp. 1442 (1984).

United States v. Heubel, 864 F.2d 1104 (3d Cir. 1989).

United States v. Salerno, 481 U.S. 739, 107 S.Ct. 2095, 95 L.Ed.2d 697 (1987).

Section Five

Coming Full Circle

The Bill of Rights on display. (Provided by UPI/Corbis-Bettmann.)

THIS FINAL SECTION rounds out the discussion of the United States Constitution by examining the remaining amendments to it (Chapter 15) and by taking a brief look at what might be anticipated for the future of constitutional law in America (Epilogue).

The Remaining Amendments of the United States Constitution

We justices read the Constitution the only way we can: as 20th century Americans. The genius of the Constitution rests not in any static meaning it might have had in a world that is dead and gone, but in the adaptability of its great principles to cope with current problems.

—WILLIAM BRENNAN, former Supreme Court justice

The United States Constitution—featuring Articles V–VII and the signatures. (Provided by Corbis-Bettmann.)

CAN YOU DEFINE THESE TERMS?

Caption
Delegated powers
Penumbra
Reserve powers
Selective incorporation
Unenumerated rights
Zones of privacy

INTRODUCTION

The amount of material generated by constitutional cases, analysis and research is astounding. Of course, since it affects every American's daily life, it should come as no surprise that so many are intrigued by it. While several amendments have generated the majority of attention, it is important in your examination of the Constitution to look at the other amendments as well.

The amendments discussed so far are probably the best known amendments in the Bill of Rights and those best suited for students beginning their study of this area of law. To complete your understanding of the Constitution and its amendments, turn your attention to the four remaining amendments of the Bill of Rights. That discussion will be followed by a brief look at the other amendments that have been made to the United States Constitution.

As you read, keep in mind the analogy of the United States Constitution as a framework that serves to provide the basis on which all American law is to be built. There are many, many subareas of the Constitution that can be examined. Those selected for inclusion in this text should help you tie together your studies at the basic level, as they themselves serve to help tie together this workable, complex document. But remember, there is much more to this fascinating document than time and space allow in this introductory text.

THE REMAINING AMENDMENTS OF THE BILL OF RIGHTS

Four amendments in the Bill of Rights remain to be discussed: the Third, Seventh, Ninth and Tenth.

The Third Amendment

No soldier shall, in time of peace, be quartered in any house, without the consent of the owner, nor in time of war, but in a manner to be prescribed by law.

 ⁓ The Third Amendment prohibited housing soldiers in
private homes without the owner's consent during peacetime.

This amendment illustrates the founding fathers' dislike of England's military rule and the practice of soldiers of the king forcing their presence upon landowners and their possessions.

Because of the history and foundation of our country, there has been no need to challenge this matter in the United States. According to Nowak and Rotunda (1991, p. 334): "The third amendment . . . has not been interpreted or applied by the Supreme Court." The amendment does, however, show that the founding fathers wanted to establish a nation that gave preference to the civilian over the military.

The Seventh Amendment

In suits at common law, where the value in controversy shall exceed twenty dollars, the right of trial by jury shall be preserved, and no fact tried by a jury, shall be otherwise re-examined in any Court of the United States, than according to the rules of the common law.

 ⁓ The Seventh Amendment establishes the right to a jury
trial for all "suits at common law" if the value is over twenty
dollars.

Recall that the Sixth Amendment guaranteed a jury trial for all criminal proceedings. The Seventh Amendment extends this right to civil proceedings involving more than twenty dollars, a large sum in 1791 when the Bill of Rights was passed.

By civil it is meant a legal controversy between two individuals (or it could be an organization, group or corporation) arising out of civil law as opposed to criminal law. The difference is easiest to observe in the **caption** (or title) of the case, which, at the trial court level, would always be the government (e.g., the city, county or state *v.* or the United States *v.* the specific defendant in a criminal case.) In a civil case the caption would have the name of one party *v.* the name of the other party. The caption of a case indicates the parties involved. The citation of the case indicates where the judicial opinion could be located.

The criminal system ensures the protection of rights everyone enjoys, while the civil system ensures rights that one person has against another.

The issues involved in civil cases become as complex as those for criminal matters and because of the complexity of our emerging society, maybe are more complex. While the importance of the outcome in criminal cases is obvious, civil disputes can often involve large sums of money, contracts, the ownership of land or other property, the rights to patents, the custody of children and an almost endless list of other issues that have great impact on those involved.

The Seventh Amendment is seeking to address the question of when an individual (as opposed to the government or a criminal defendant) is entitled to a jury trial at the federal level (as opposed to bringing the case before a local or state court). The reasons that a party would prefer having his or her case heard before one court or another or before a jury or just a judge are basically tactical, in that different procedures can apply at the different levels of courts, and it may be believed that a court at a federal level would be more impartial and, thus, more fair than at a local or state level. Some feel that a jury would help or hinder their cause. Where and how a case is handled is one example of the many decisions an attorney faces in best representing the client.

With this said, the history and historical effects on the Seventh Amendment are complex and for the most part beyond the scope of the basic goals of this text. But to provide you with some basic understanding of why this amendment was important enough to have been included, you need only recall that the basic premise of the Constitution was *fairness.*

The reference in this amendment to *suits at common law* indicates by historical terminology that at issue was the distinction between types of cases in England, which were brought along with most of the rest of developmental American law. This has to do with the differentiation between the types of cases that might have been pursued in actions at law or in equity, affecting which court would have jurisdiction over what type of case. These terms should sound awkward as they, for all practical purposes, have not been used since 1791. However, our Constitution is based on the legal history of those who brought their new ideas to America and because the tendency has been for subsequent courts to not change the basic legal concepts of our legal history too drastically in most cases, it has remained. The challenge has been for the courts to interpret this amendment into something that serves both a practical purpose while maintaining its historical significance.

The Supreme Court, along with numerous others who have reflected on these issues, has acknowledged that Seventh Amendment analysis is mostly historical. Today, the practical approach to determining if there is a Seventh Amendment right to a jury trial is based on whether "a suit raises factual disputes over legal issues or claims for legal relief such that the suit or issue is a type for which a jury trial should be required because it is similar to the types of claims for which jury trials were guaranteed by common law" (Nowak and Rotunda, 1991, p. 527). Most issues can be solved by examination of the history of common law jury trials and the Supreme Court decisions on point. Whether there is a Seventh Amendment right to a jury trial is based mainly on historical analysis.

This analysis is included because the Seventh Amendment is important enough to be included in the Bill of Rights, and so an awareness of it is called for. But also because it serves as an excellent example of how the framers of the Constitution included both what they considered important to them at that time in American history, as well as what they thought would be important in the future of this country. As stated earlier, while some amendments have come and gone, it has been a difficult process to excise portions of the Constitution that were not done so with the mass support of the American people. In this area, the matter has basically been determined by courts at all levels looking at prior cases to help them determine which cases may be decided in front of a federal jury. And so, one answer to the question of where a case can most fairly be tried can be found in where earlier cases have been fairly tried. This is what the *common law* provides—answers by examining previous cases. To assist in such determinations, many such questions of jurisdiction are most easily answered by referring to federal or state rules of civil procedure.

     ≫ Which cases involve issues that justify a Seventh Amendment right to a federal jury trial are determined by examining the types of cases heard previously or by a common law analysis.

The Ninth Amendment

The enumeration in the Constitution of certain rights shall not be construed to deny or disparage others retained by the people.

     ≫ The Ninth Amendment says that simply because certain rights are listed in the Constitution, that does not mean those are the only rights the people have.

The Ninth Amendment highlights the founders' belief that government's powers are limited by the rights of the people, not the other way around. The government does not have unlimited power to invade specific rights of the people.

The Ninth Amendment states that the people keep other rights not listed in the Bill of Rights. The question is, who determines what those rights "retained by the people" are, and who protects such rights?

Some believe that the Ninth Amendment was designed only to limit the power of the federal government and should not be used by the courts to expand the individual rights guaranteed by the Bill of Rights. Others have argued that unless the courts interpret the Ninth Amendment to protect rights not listed in the Bill of Rights, the very purpose of the amendment is defeated. Consequently, the Ninth Amendment has generated significant controversy among courts and scholars of the Bill of Rights and serves as an example of how the Constitution does not always provide specific or easy answers.

HISTORY OF THE NINTH AMENDMENT   One argument against adding the Bill of Rights to the original Constitution was that any listing of rights would, by its very nature, be incomplete. Such a list could imply that American people had only those rights included in the list. Or the Bill of Rights could arguably give the federal government extra powers by implying that government could do all the things not expressly forbidden in the list. A concern could be that the Bill of Rights would end up limiting Americans' freedom, not protecting it, as was the original intent.

It was for these very reasons James Madison had initially opposed the Bill of Rights. To avoid misunderstandings, Madison included the words of the Ninth Amendment in his proposal to Congress. His original language addressed both concerns: that the Bill of Rights would not deny other rights not listed, and that it would not expand the powers of the federal government. In the final version, however, the Ninth Amendment did not refer to the expanded powers of the federal government, although the Tenth Amendment did.

Scholars disagree about the historical meanings of the changed language in the Ninth Amendment. Some argue that the Ninth and Tenth Amendments mean virtually the same thing—that the federal government has limited powers. It has been maintained that the Ninth Amendment does not protect extra rights beyond those listed in the Constitution. The rights "retained by the people," they argue, are rights that must be protected by the states, not by the federal courts.

Other constitutional experts believe that Madison was trying to prevent two problems. One, the Ninth Amendment protects all the rights not listed in the Bill of Rights, and two, the Tenth Amendment specifically restricts the powers of the federal government. Some argue that the Ninth Amendment means exactly what it says—that federal courts have an obligation to protect those "unenumerated" or unlisted rights just as they protect other rights specifically listed. After all, it has been argued, James Madison intended that the Courts would "consider themselves in a peculiar manner the guardians of those rights," including Ninth Amendment rights.

The Ninth Amendment has been referred to on occasion as the forgotten amendment in the Bill of Rights because it has almost never been used as a basis for a Supreme Court decision. Some believe that judges have been reluctant to rely on the Ninth Amendment because its language is vague, mentioning no specific rights. Legal scholar Robert Bork, nominated for the Supreme Court in 1987 but rejected by the Senate, gave the following analysis of the Ninth Amendment at his confirmation hearing:

> I do not think you can use the Ninth Amendment unless you know something of what it means. For example, if you had an amendment that says "Congress shall make no" and there is an ink blot, and you cannot read the rest of it, and that is the only copy you have, I do not think the Court can make up what might be under the ink blot."

Bork and others who agree with him believe the Ninth Amendment gives judges too much power. Its vague language, they say, invites judges to rely on their own ideas of fairness rather than the law to decide cases. These experts argue that such a role for judges would destroy democracy, because unelected federal court judges, based only on their personal opinions would be overruling the laws passed by the people's elected representatives.

Other scholars take exception to Bork's comparison of the Ninth Amendment to an ink blot. They argue that the Ninth Amendment is no more vague than other phrases in the Bill of Rights that judges frequently rely on, such as "due process of law." Judges, they say, must always interpret the law. Judges play an important part in the constitutional system, these scholars maintain, and judges have an obligation to enforce all amendments in the Bill of Rights, including the Ninth Amendment. The Supreme Court, however, has never defined what rights are protected by the Ninth Amendment. The Court has referred to the Ninth Amendment in a handful of cases, but the Amendment has never been the basis of a decision by a majority of the justices. Although the Supreme Court has protected rights not listed in the Bill of Rights, it has not used the Ninth Amendment to do so. The Ninth and Tenth Amendments, again, serve as examples of the discussion and interpretations that the Constitution continues to generate, particularly by those asserting that the interpretation be made in their own favor.

UNENUMERATED RIGHTS   Rights not specifically listed in the Bill of Rights are known as **unenumerated rights.** These are the type of rights to which the Ninth Amendment refers. They are no less important than specified rights, but have been left to develop with our society. According to Nowak and Rotunda (p. 389):

> [T]he Ninth Amendment gave textual recognition to the fact that there were other values of equal importance to the specific provisions to the Bill of Rights even though they were not mentioned in the first eight amendments. While the ninth amendment did not directly create those rights, it authorized the Court to identify them and protect them against the acts of the other branches of government.

Among the unenumerated rights, the Supreme Court has recognized the right to privacy, the right to interstate and international travel, the right to vote and freedom of association. But the Supreme Court has used other ways, besides the Ninth Amendment, to protect these rights. Sometimes the Supreme Court decides that a right not listed in the Bill of Rights is implied by other rights that are listed. For example, the Court ruled that freedom of association is protected because it is implied by other rights in the First Amendment. The Court also has ruled that some aspects of the right to privacy are implied by rights listed in the Third, Fourth and Fifth Amendments. Again, specific or exact answers are not always forthcoming from the Constitution, leaving much room for interpretation.

Just as some Constitutional law experts object to Ninth Amendment rights, they also criticize the Supreme Court for recognizing unenumerated rights using other amendments in the Constitution. The critics argue that the Court relies on its own subjective standards of justice to find "fundamental" rights, which they believe is inappropriate for nonelected judiciary. These critics say that if the American people want to recognize such rights, they should amend the Constitution.

Still others say that the federal courts, including the Supreme Court, have a special role in protecting individual rights against majority rule. The very reason Supreme Court justices are not elected, these scholars argue, is so they may protect unpopular rights without worrying about being reelected. The Constitution created by "we the people" gives the Supreme Court such power in the first place that for them to refuse this power by not making decisions would violate the Constitution itself.

RIGHT TO PRIVACY   An important right not specifically listed in the Constitution is a right to privacy. Many parts of a right to privacy have been recognized by the Supreme Court, including the right to marry, to have children, have an abortion and the right of parents to send their children to private schools. By referring to a right of privacy, it is being said that the government should not interfere.

The Supreme Court had never directly examined rights protected by the Ninth Amendment, but in 1965 the Court heard a case challenging an 1879 Connecticut law that prohibited the use of "any drug, medicinal article or instrument for the purpose of preventing conception." In that case, *Griswold v. Connecticut* (1965), three of the justices finally agreed on a right protected by the Ninth Amendment, the right to marital privacy or privacy within the marriage relationship. Justice Arthur Goldberg devoted several pages to the Ninth Amendment in rendering the decision in this case (Killian, 1987, pp. 1412-1413):

> The language and history of the Ninth Amendment reveal that the framers of the Constitution believed that there are additional fundamental rights, *protected from governmental infringement,* which exist alongside those fundamental rights specifically mentioned in the first eight constitutional amendments. . . . To hold that a right so basic and fundamental and so deep-rooted in our society as the right of privacy in marriage may be infringed because that right is not guaranteed in so many words by the first eight amendments to the Constitution is to ignore the Ninth Amendment and to give it no effect whatsoever.

Most of the Court, however, did not rely on the Ninth Amendment. Justice William O. Douglas, in his opinion for the Court, held that "specific guarantees in the Bill of Rights have penumbras, formed by emanations from those guarantees that help give them life and substance." In astronomy, a **penumbra** is a type of shadow. Douglas used astronomy as an example to show how certain rights in the Bill of Rights have other rights implied in or along with them, which "give them life and substance." Justice Douglas went on to write that various guarantees in the Bill of Rights, among them the Third, Fourth and Fifth Amendments, created **zones of privacy,** safe from governmental intrusion. The intimacy of the marriage relationship, said Douglas, involved a "right of privacy older than the Bill of Rights." The Connecticut law was struck down as unconstitutional.

Not all the justices agreed with Douglas' reasoning, however, even though they agreed with the Court's ruling. Some justices believed that marital privacy was protected by the due process clause of the Fourteenth Amendment, not "penumbras formed by emanations." Other justices argued that the Ninth Amendment was more relevant. Justice Goldberg wrote a concurring opinion on that basis, joined by Justice William Brennan and Chief Justice Earl Warren. The Ninth Amendment, Justice Goldberg wrote, was not intended to be ignored. It gave support, he argued, to the Courts protection of unenumerated rights through the due process clause of the Fourteenth Amendment.

Justice Hugo Black, however, vehemently disagreed. Black argued that the Ninth Amendment was virtually identical to the Tenth Amendment, which reserves certain powers to the states. Black said unenumerated rights should be protected by the states, not by the federal courts. That was why the Ninth Amendment had been forgotten as a source of individual rights for the past

150 years. As an unenumerated right, the Supreme Court has relied on varied justifications to maintain its existence.

Griswold led to other cases in which the Supreme Court upheld privacy rights and issues pertaining to sexual relations for unmarried as well as married individuals, with an increasing number of cases concerning homosexual relations being considered by the Court. Also, the Supreme Court referenced the right to privacy, supporting a woman's right to an abortion in *Roe v. Wade* (1973).

The Supreme Court's decisions, whether under the Ninth or the Fourteenth Amendment, continually upheld the right to sexual privacy until the case of *Bowers v. Hardwick* (1986). Michael Hardwick was arrested in his bedroom for engaging in sodomy with a consenting male adult by an Atlanta police officer with an expired warrant for a minor offense. Hardwick challenged the Georgia sodomy law on the grounds that, among other things, it violated his rights under the Ninth Amendment.

The Supreme Court, however, upheld the Georgia law, saying that Hardwick was asking the Court to recognize "a fundamental right to engage in homosexual sodomy." Justice Harry Blackmun dissented, pointing out the Georgia law applied to heterosexuals as well as homosexuals. Under the Court's current rulings on sexual privacy, the law would not be constitutional as applied to heterosexuals, argued Blackmun, so it should not be constitutional when applied to homosexuals. Justice Lewis Powell, the crucial swing vote in the 5 to 4 decision, later commented that he believed his decision may have been a mistake. Change remains a strong possibility even at the level of the United States Supreme Court.

The Tenth Amendment

The powers not delegated to the United States by the Constitution, nor prohibited by it to the states, are reserved to the states respectively, or to the people.

The Tenth Amendment embodies the principle of federalism, reserving for the states those powers not granted to the federal government or withheld from the states.

Although the Tenth Amendment is part of the Bill of Rights, it does not refer to individual rights specifically as do the first nine amendments. Rather, it focuses on limiting the general powers of the national government and in that way protecting individual freedom. Many Americans of the Revolutionary period thought the greatest threat to liberty was a national government with too much power. The Tenth Amendment was designed in response to such a threat.

However, a national government with too little power cannot govern effectively, as Americans discovered with the Articles of Confederation. Therefore, the United States Constitution gave the federal government more power while still being restrained. The Tenth Amendment was an attempt to strike a balance between the power of the federal government and the power of the states, while all the time maintaining freedom for the individual. That balance has not always been easy to maintain throughout American history. During one

The capture of Roanoke Island during the Civil War. (Provided by Corbis-Bettmann.)

such very difficult period, only a bloody Civil War finally resolved the question of federal versus state power. Since the Civil War, the Supreme Court has worked hard to find the proper balance of the Tenth Amendment.

HISTORY OF THE TENTH AMENDMENT   All eight states that proposed amendments to the Constitution included some version of the Tenth Amendment, the only item in the Bill of Rights proposed by every state. The issue of state versus federal power was critical in ratifying the Constitution and the Bill of Rights. James Madison included the Tenth Amendment in his original draft of the Bill of Rights to satisfy those who feared the Bill of Rights could imply additional federal power. One of the Federalist arguments against adding a Bill of Rights to the Constitution was that it was dangerous. In limiting the powers of the national government to deny specific rights, the Federalists argued, the Bill of Rights could also be interpreted to mean that the government had power in all the areas not specifically denied.

Madison's version of the Tenth Amendment made it clear that any powers not delegated to the federal government belonged to the states or to the people. However, some members of Congress wanted the Tenth Amendment to limit the federal government to those powers specifically listed in the Constitution, just as the Articles of Confederation had done. They wanted the Tenth Amendment to say that powers not expressly delegated to the United States government were reserved to the states. Madison felt that it was impossible to confine a government to the exercise of expressed powers. There must necessarily be powers by implication.

By proposing that the Tenth Amendment limit the federal government to expressed powers, some Anti-Federalists in Congress were arguing to weaken the strong national government created by the Constitutional Convention in 1787. One of the Anti-Federalists' primary objections to the Constitution was that it simply gave the national government too much power. Having lost the battle over the ratification of the Constitution, Anti-Federalists tried to resurrect the issue of federal power via the Tenth Amendment. Attempts to add more to the Tenth Amendment failed in both the House and the Senate.

The history of the Tenth Amendment indicates that it was not intended to restrict the federal government only to those powers specifically listed in the Constitution. The question remained then, however, just what powers were reserved to the states under the Tenth Amendment?

Some Americans have asserted that the Tenth Amendment recognized states' rights and the powers of the states as sovereign governments with authority equal to the federal government. This position held that the Supreme Court should protect state rights no less than individual rights. Others have supported nationalism—the view that the national government is supreme over the states. Nationalists say the Tenth Amendment was meant only to state the obvious, and that powers not delegated were not to be considered an independent source of power for the states. For over 200 years the issue has remained one for debate.

FEDERALISM REVIEWED   The Tenth Amendment reflects the basic principle of American government: federalism. (Recall the discussion of this concept in Chapter 1.) Under federalism, power is shared by the national government and the states. The United States Constitution established a federal system to preserve the existing state governments, while at the same time creating a new national government strong enough to deal with the country's problems. The nation's first form of government under the Articles of Confederation had been a confederation, an alliance of independent states that created a central government with very limited power. This form of government proved ineffective, leading to the Constitutional Convention, as described in Chapter 1.

A controversial question at the Constitutional Convention was just how much power the national government should have. A primary limit was that the government was one of enumerated powers, powers specifically listed in the Constitution. But the Constitution also included an elastic clause stating that congress had the power to make all laws "necessary and proper" to carry out its enumerated powers. The necessary and proper clause became the basis for the implied powers, those powers not specifically listed in the Constitution that are implied by the enumerated powers.

The powers of the national government, both enumerated and implied, are known as the **delegated powers,** because they were delegated or entrusted to the national government by the states and the people. The powers kept by the states are known as the **reserve powers.** The Tenth Amendment refers to both types of powers. A primary reserve power is police power, which enables the state to pass laws and regulations involving the public health, safety, morals and welfare.

While the Constitution recognizes the powers of both the states and the federal government, it contains the supremacy clause in Article 6 stating that the Constitution of the United States is "the supreme law of the land."

The critical issue of federalism was addressed in *United States v. Lopez* (1995) in which the Court invalidated an act of Congress for the first time in 50 years, raising important issues of federal versus states' rights.

NOT ALL AMENDMENTS APPLY TO THE STATES

It could be an easy assumption to think that the entire Bill of Rights would apply to the state governments as well as the federal government. And while some have argued that this is naturally the case, the majority disagree.

The history of the Constitution continues to bear repeating. Why was it drafted? To limit a federal government's power to keep it from being too controlling. The idea was to let the various states regulate themselves as they saw fit, but for the basic rights set forth in the Bill of Rights that the United States Supreme Court held are "fundamental to the American system of law (*Duncan v. Louisiana*, 1968). While the Constitution was devised to control federal power, and most of the Bill of Rights has been applied to state government as well, not all of these amendments are applicable to both levels of government.

Selective Incorporation and the Ninth and Tenth Amendments

The term **selective incorporation** refers to the idea that the Supreme Court has chosen, through case law and common law, to selectively apply certain amendments to both federal and state governments. Since the Ninth and Tenth Amendments, according to Nowak and Rotunda (p. 331), are usually not considered specific guarantees of individual liberties, the first eight amendments are the ones traditionally considered to be the Bill of Rights.

In review, the Ninth Amendment says: "The enumeration in the Constitution of certain rights, shall not be construed to deny or disparage others retained by the people." And the Tenth Amendment says: "The powers not delegated to the United States by the Constitution, nor prohibited by it to the states, are reserved to the states respectively, or to the people." In other words, the Ninth Amendment is about the balance between individual, state and federal rights and powers. While the first ten amendments are most often referred to as the Bill of Rights, sometimes people include only the first eight. This is because the Ninth and Tenth Amendments have not been viewed as specifically guaranteeing *individual rights*.

ADDITIONAL AMENDMENTS THROUGH THE YEARS

From 1791, when the first ten amendments were ratified, until the present, our Constitution continues to evolve in a glorious example of how ink on paper is alive. The Eleventh Amendment (1798) dealt with the extent of the judicial power of the United States:

> *The Judicial power of the United States shall not be construed to extend to any suit in law or equity, commenced or prosecuted against one of the United States by Citizens of another State, or by Citizens or Subjects of any Foreign State.*

This amendment serves as an administrative directive. The Eleventh Amendment is the only amendment that concerns the judicial branch of the federal government. It was a strictly political amendment introduced a day after the Court ruled that a citizen of one state had the right to sue another state.

A key amendment to the Constitution is the Thirteenth Amendment (1865), which abolished slavery, as previously discussed:

> *Neither slavery nor involuntary servitude, except as a punishment for crime whereof the party shall have been duly convicted, shall exist within the United States, or any place subject to their jurisdiction.*
> *Congress shall have power to enforce this article by appropriate legislation.*

The Thirteenth Amendment overturned the Supreme Court's *Dred Scott* decision (1857). Using an amendment to overturn a specific Supreme Court decision is rare, dramatic and a good illustration of the checks and balances in our government.

Closely related to this amendment was the Fourteenth Amendment (1868), which asserted:

> *All persons born or naturalized in the United States, and subject to the jurisdiction thereof, are citizens of the United States and of the State wherein they reside. No state shall make or enforce any law which shall abridge the privileges or immunities of citizens of the United States; nor shall any State deprive any person of life, liberty, or property, without due process of law; nor deny to any person within its jurisdiction the equal protection of the laws.*

This powerful amendment brought a closure to a controversy that seriously disrupted this nation's growth, while reasserting basic tenets that America was built upon.

Amendments Related to Elections and Structure of Congress

Not all amendments and other portions of the Constitution deal directly with specific rights and liberties. It is necessary for any successful entity to have basic administrative guidelines to function properly, and these are found in the Constitution as well.

Seven amendments deal in detail with numerous matters related to how our federal government is to be structured and its officials elected. Following is a brief summary of these amendments. The full text of each is presented in Appendix D.

The *Twelfth Amendment* (1804) established the elector system by which our president and vice president are chosen.

The *Fourteenth Amendment* (1868) established how representatives should be apportioned and what their qualifications should be.

The *Seventeenth Amendment* (1913) described how the United States Senate was to be composed, the qualifications required and how vacancies were to be filled.

The *Twentieth Amendment* (1933) established that the terms of the president and vice president end at noon on the 20th day of January and that the terms of senators and representatives end at noon on the 3rd day of January. It also established how often Congress should meet and what the chain of succession would be if the president is no longer able to carry out the responsibilities of the office.

The *Twenty-second Amendment* (1951) restricted the term of presidency to two terms.

The *Twenty-third Amendment* (1961) gave representation to the district constituting the seat of government of the United States, that is to the District of Columbia.

The *Twenty-fifth Amendment* (1967) established procedures for filling vacancies and for actions to take should the president be unable to "discharge the powers and duties" of the office.

The preceding amendments, along with portions of the Constitution, are important in that they provide the basic administrative and operational bases through which an orderly government will operate. Above all, it remains important to understand that, like a set of directions for any piece of complex machinery, these guidelines provide people with the ability to make something work that would not be possible without such a reference.

Voting Rights

The ability of the Constitution to reflect the changing needs of the society it serves are well illustrated in the amendments broadening the right to vote, which, initially, was reserved for males over age 21.

The *Fifteenth Amendment* (1870) required that the right to vote shall not be denied or abridged because of race, color or previous condition of servitude. In other words, blacks (males) were given the vote.

The *Nineteenth Amendment* (1920) required that the right to vote shall not be denied on account of sex. Women finally got the vote, 50 years after black males.

The *Twenty-fourth Amendment* (1964) required that the right to vote shall not be denied or abridged by reason of failure to pay any poll tax or other tax.

The *Twenty-sixth Amendment* (1971) lowered the voting age, giving the vote to United States citizens 18 years old and older.

Taxes

The Sixteenth Amendment (1913) established the federal income tax: "The Congress shall have power to lay and collect taxes on incomes, from whatever source derived, without apportionment among the several States, and without regard to any census or enumeration."

Prohibition

An excellent example of how the Constitution, through the amendment process, can adjust and change to reflect society's wishes, the Eighteenth

Federal agents conduct a raid during Prohibition. (Provided by UPI/Corbis-Bettmann.)

Amendment (1919), ratified by the states, prohibited the sale and purchase of "intoxicating liquors." This prohibition was ignored by many, with speakeasies opening and gangsters profiting from the illegal sale of liquor. Hundreds of thousands of law enforcement hours and dollars were spent trying to enforce this amendment, but in the end, it was seen as hopeless, because it was not what the people wanted. Therefore, the Twenty-first Amendment (1933) was ratified, repealing the "eighteenth article of amendment to the Constitution."

Other Attempts at Amendments

Over the years, various amendments have been proposed espousing different thoughts considered to be important. For example, Congress has considered an amendment prohibiting the burning of the American flag. Although it was narrowly defeated, it is likely to be brought up again and serves as yet another example of how change in constitutional law comes about.

However, because of the extraordinary importance a basic document such as our Constitution has, Congress has been, and continues to be, reluctant to make significant changes by adding amendments.

The life of the law has not been logic; it has been experience. The felt necessities of the time, the prevalent moral and political theories . . . even the prejudices which judges share with their fellow men . . . have a good deal in determining the rules by which men should be governed.

Chief Justice Oliver Wendell Holmes Jr.
United States Supreme Court

Summary

You should be familiar with four additional important amendments of the Bill of Rights: the Third, Seventh, Ninth and Tenth Amendments.

The Third Amendment prohibited housing soldiers in private homes without the owner's consent during peacetime. The Seventh Amendment established the right to a jury trial for all suits at common law if the value was over twenty dollars. The Ninth Amendment said that simply because certain rights are listed in the Constitution, that does not mean those are the only rights the people have. The Tenth Amendment embodied the principle of federalism, reserving for the states those powers not granted to the federal government or withheld from the states.

Discussion Questions

1. Discuss why the framers of the Constitution probably thought it necessary to include the Ninth *and* Tenth Amendments.

2. With reference to question #1, could only one or the other have been sufficient?

3. If you were to eliminate the Ninth or Tenth Amendment, which would it be and why?

4. Having come this far in your study of constitutional law, do you think the United States could ever get along without a written Constitution? Discuss.

5. Do you think the Constitution works as well as it was meant to? Why or why not?

6. Do you think there is any way a military dictatorship could take over the present government in America and be successful? Discuss.

7. Discuss whether federalism is as important now as it was to the framers of the Constitution.

8. If you were to eliminate any portions of the Constitution, which would they be? Why?

9. If you were to propose any new amendments, what would they be?

10. Let your imagination wander and imagine that a time machine would permit those who conceived the Constitution to be present today. What would they think about how their prescription for freedom has endured the challenges of time?

References

Killian, Johnny H., ed. *The Constitution of the United States of America: Analysis and Interpretation.* Washington: U.S. Government Printing Office, 1987.

Nowak, John E. and Ronald D. Rotunda. *Constitutional Law.* 4th ed. St. Paul: West Publishing Company, 1991.

Cases Cited

Bowers v. Hardwick, 478 U.S. 186, 106 S.Ct. 2841, 92 L.Ed.2d 140 (1986).

Duncan v. Louisiana, 391 U.S. 145, 88 S.Ct. 1444, 20 L.Ed.2d 491 (1968).

Griswold v. Connecticut, 381 U.S. 479, 85 S.Ct. 1678, 14 L.Ed.2d 510 (1965).

Roe v. Wade, 410 U.S. 113, 93 S.Ct. 705, 35 L.Ed.2d 147 (1973).

Scott v. Sandford, 60 U.S. 393 (1857).

United States v. Lopez, ___ U.S. ___, 115 S.Ct. 1624, 131 L.Ed.2d 626 (1995).

Epilogue
A Look toward the Future

Our Constitution is in active operation, everything appears to promise that it will last, but in this world, nothing is certain but death and taxes.

—BENJAMIN FRANKLIN, 1789

The future of the United States depends on the Constitution. (Photo by Keith Piaseczny. Provided by Corbis-Bettmann.)

T HE ONLY CONCLUSION one can draw from the study of the history of our Constitution is that it will not remain static. The American people would not stand for that. Americans are demanding of their law, and the fact that their Constitution has the built-in ability to change as demanded by its people reflects this very important component of our law.

The basic freedoms set forth in the amazing document known as the United States Constitution shall remain, for they are the cornerstones on which America was built. Freedom of speech and religion, the right to assemble and speak up, and the freedom to not be subjected to unreasonable governmental intrusions will maintain the tests of time. But change itself will continue. It has to. As our country and the needs of its people have changed with time, so will the laws that support this society.

However, the basic premise on which law can change will be maintained. That's what our Constitution is all about—providing the predictability that ensures a continuation of America's ideals, but including the ability to permit law to flow with natural changes brought on by society. But as those who have tried have learned, changing the Constitution is not easy. Nor should it be. Anything as powerful as this document should be altered only when intense scrutiny, evaluation and input from every side have been used to weigh the need for change. While politicians speak of constitutional change as part of their platforms, true scholars understand the importance of maintaining it apolitically. Should the Constitution cater to one side, its effectiveness is lost. *Its goal is to serve everyone.*

Consider societal desires as a whole to be a pendulum of sorts. On one end of the arc is a conservative perspective and the other liberal. Such perspectives influence how society perceives its country. It answers such questions as "Why do people act the way they do?" and "How should society respond?" The perspective a society responds from says a lot about how that society views life at any point in time.

For example, there are two primary schools of thought on the causes of delinquency. While the classical theory as developed by Cesare Beccaria sets forth the concept that people are responsible for their own behavior because they act on their own free will, the positivist theory as developed by Cesare Lombroso operates on the premise that people's personal and background characteristics are to answer for their behavior, suggesting that these individuals are, in effect, "victims of their society." Depending on how one perceives the issues will influence how one will respond. Classicalists would argue for accountability for delinquent behavior, while positivists would argue treatment. Delinquency trends in society reflect whether society is leaning more toward a conservative or liberal trend at the time.

Similarly, the various laws of governments in America (be they municipal, county, state or federal) will surely reflect whether society at that point in time sees itself as being more toward the liberal or conservative side of the pendulum's arc. Prohibition. Marijuana. Flag desecration. Women voting. Slavery. Abortion. Guns. Religion. The laws addressing important societal issues reflect how American society sees itself and reflect what society thinks is important at that time, all the while looking to the future. Change is inevitable, but it seems that the changes reflect the pendulum's position between conservative and liberal notions for our society at any given moment in history. And it seems that the pendulum does indeed have a tendency to go back and forth, back and forth, back and forth . . . and this is all the more reason that changes to the Constitution come about only after sincere debate.

What can be drawn from this analysis of change? Simply that change will continue. The fact that the premise for change is exactly what has kept American law so viable is an amazing thing to contemplate. This is what the study of the United States Constitution is all about. We began by stating: the complex simpleness on which the Constitution is conceived is so astounding because it has continued to provide stability for one of the most complicated societies to ever develop on the face of the earth.

Could we, as a society, operate without a written constitution as some other societies have? Doubtful. Why can the United Kingdom, for example, operate so efficiently simply on tradition, when Americans demand a written document? It is the very nature of the American people. It was the questioning and demanding nature of those who left England that lead to the Constitution. Americans want to know *why* things are the way they are and to know exactly what is expected of them and what can be expected of others. "Because your government knows best" would never be an acceptable answer here. The only answer that appeases the critical nature of the American people is that an approach, an issue or a law is constitutionally permissible.

Not everyone agrees with the Constitution in full or in part, and people will continue to challenge it and consider changing it. The document can be changed, but because of the importance of maintaining the premises on which subsequent law will be built, changes to the Constitution itself will continue to come with great debate and consideration. This is the way it should be. But remember, as history has proven, even this great document can change when the people it serves so demand. Fairness. Justice. Due process. Freedom. These words are what our Constitution is about.

Appendix A The Declaration of Independence

July 4, 1776

(F. N. Thorpe, ed. *Federal and State Constitutions,* Vol. I, p. 3 ff. The text is taken from the version in the Revised Statutes of the United States, 1878 ed., and has been collated with the facsimile of the original as printed in the original Journal of the old Congress.)

On June 7, 1776, Richard Henry Lee of Virginia introduced three resolutions one of which stated that the "colonies are, and of right ought to be, free and independent States." On the 10th a committee was appointed to prepare a declaration of independence; the committee consisted of Jefferson, John Adams, Franklin, Sherman and R. R. Livingston. This committee brought in its draft on the 28th of June, and on the 2nd of July a resolution declaring independence was adopted. July 4 the Declaration of Independence was agreed to, engrossed, signed by Hancock, and sent to the legislatures of the States. The engrossed copy of the Declaration was signed by all but one signer on August 2. On the Declaration, see C. L. Becker, *The Declaration of Independence,* esp. ch. v with its analysis of Jefferson's draft; H. Friedenwald, *The Declaration of Independence;* J. H. Hazelton, *Declaration of Independence;* J. Sanderson, *Lives of the Signers to the Declaration;* R. Frothingham, *Rise of the Republic,* ch. xi.; C. H. Van Tyne, *The War of Independence, American Phase.*

In Congress, July 4, 1776,

THE UNANIMOUS DECLARATION OF THE THIRTEEN UNITED STATES OF AMERICA,

When in the Course of human events, it becomes necessary for one people to dissolve the political bands which have connected them with another, and to assume among the Powers of the earth, the separate and equal station to which the Laws of Nature and of Nature's God entitle them, a decent respect to the opinions of mankind requires that they should declare the causes which impel them to the separation.

We hold these truths to be self-evident, that all men are created equal, that they are endowed by their Creator with certain unalienable Rights, that among these are Life, Liberty and the pursuit of Happiness. That to secure these rights, Governments are instituted among Men, deriving their just powers from the consent of the governed. That whenever any Form of Government becomes destructive of these ends, it is the Right of the People to alter or to abolish it, and to institute new Government, laying its foundation on such principles and organizing its powers in such form, as to them shall seem most likely to effect their Safety and Happiness. Prudence, indeed, will dictate that Governments long established should not be changed for light and transient causes; and accordingly all experience hath shown, that mankind are more disposed to suffer, while evils are sufferable, than to right themselves by abolishing the forms to which they are accustomed. But when a long train of abuses and usurpations, pursuing invariably the same Object evinces a design to reduce them under absolute Despotism, it is their right, it is their duty, to throw off such Government, and to provide new Guards for their future security.—Such has been the patient sufferance of these Colonies; and such is now the necessity which constrains them to alter their former Systems of Government. The history of the present King of Great Britain is a history of repeated injuries and usurpations, all having in direct object the establishment of an absolute Tyranny over these States. To prove this, let Facts be submitted to a candid world.

He has refused his Assent to Laws, the most wholesome and necessary for the public good.

He has forbidden his Governors to pass Laws of immediate and pressing importance, unless suspended in their operation till his Assent should be obtained; and when so suspended, he has utterly neglected to attend to them.

He has refused to pass other Laws for the accommodation of large districts of people, unless those people would relinquish the right of Representation in the Legislature, a right inestimable to them and formidable to tyrants only.

He has called together legislative bodies at places unusual, uncomfortable, and distant from the depository of their Public Records, for the sole purpose of fatiguing them into compliance with his measures.

He has dissolved Representative Houses repeatedly, for opposing with manly firmness his invasions on the rights of the people.

He has refused for a long time, after such dissolutions, to cause others to be elected; whereby the Legislative Powers, incapable of Annihilation, have returned to the People at large for their exercise; the State remaining in the mean time exposed to all the dangers of invasion from without, and convulsions within.

He has endeavoured to prevent the population of these States; for that purpose obstructing the Laws of Naturalization of Foreigners; refusing to pass others to encourage their migration hither, and raising the conditions of new Appropriations of Lands.

He has obstructed the Administration of Justice, by refusing his Assent to Laws for establishing Judiciary Powers.

He has made Judges dependent on his Will alone, for the tenure of their offices, and the amount and payment of their salaries.

He has erected a multitude of New Offices, and sent hither swarms of Officers to harass our People, and eat out their substance.

He has kept among us, in times of peace, Standing Armies without the Consent of our legislature.

He has affected to render the Military independent of and superior to the Civil Power.

He has combined with others to subject us to a jurisdiction foreign to our constitution, and unacknowledged by our laws; giving his Assent to their acts of pretended legislation:

For quartering large bodies of armed troops among us:

For protecting them, by a mock Trial, from Punishment for any Murders which they should commit on the Inhabitants of these States:

For cutting off our Trade with all parts of the world:

For imposing taxes on us without our Consent:

For depriving us in many cases, of the benefits of Trial by Jury:

For transporting us beyond Seas to be tried for pretended offences:

For abolishing the free System of English Laws in a neighbouring Province, establishing therein an Arbitrary government, and enlarging its Boundaries so as to render it at once an example and fit instrument for introducing the same absolute rule into these Colonies:

For taking away our Charters, abolishing our most valuable Laws, and altering fundamentally the Forms of our Governments:

For suspending our own Legislature, and declaring themselves invested with Power to legislate for us in all cases whatsoever.

He has abdicated Government here, by declaring us out of his Protection and waging War against us.

He has plundered our seas, ravaged our Coasts, burnt our towns, and destroyed the lives of our people.

He is at this time transporting large armies of foreign mercenaries to compleat the works of death, desolation and tyranny, already begun with circumstances of Cruelty & perfidy scarcely paralleled in the most barbarous ages, and totally unworthy the Head of a civilized nation.

He has constrained our fellow Citizens taken Captive on the high Seas to bear Arms against their Country, to become the executioners of their friends and Brethren, or to fall themselves by their Hands.

He has excited domestic insurrections amongst us, and has endeavoured to bring on the inhabitants of our frontiers, the merciless Indian Savages, whose known rule of warfare, is an undistinguished destruction of all ages, sexes and conditions.

In every stage of these Oppressions We have Petitioned for Redress in the most humble terms: Our repeated Petitions have been answered only by repeated injury. A Prince, whose character is thus marked by every act which may define a Tyrant, is unfit to be the ruler of a free People.

Nor have We been wanting in attention to our Brittish brethren. We have warned them from time to time of attempts by their legislature to extend an unwarrantable jurisdiction over us. We have reminded them of the circumstances of our emigration and settlement here. We have appealed to their native justice and magnanimity, and we have conjured them by the ties of our common kindred to disavow these usurpations, which, would inevitably interrupt our connections and correspondence. They too have been deaf to the voice of justice and of consanguinity. We must, therefore, acquiesce in the necessity, which denounces our Separation, and hold them, as we hold the rest of mankind, Enemies in War, in Peace Friends.

We, therefore, the Representatives of the United States of America, in General Congress, Assembled, appealing to the Supreme Judge of the world for the rectitude of our intentions, do, in the Name, and by Authority of the good People of these Colonies, solemnly publish and declare, That these

United Colonies are, and of Right ought to be Free and Independent States; that they are Absolved from all Allegiance to the British Crown, and that all political connection between them and the State of Great Britain, is and ought to be totally dissolved; and that as Free and Independent States, they have full Power to levy War, conclude Peace, contract Alliances, establish Commerce, and to do all other Acts and Things which Independent States may of right do. And for the support of this Declaration, with a firm reliance on the Protection of Divine Providence, we mutually pledge to each other our Lives, our Fortunes and our sacred Honor.

JOHN HANCOCK.

New Hampshire
JOSIAH BARTLETT,
WM. WHIPPLE,
MATTHEW THORNTON.

Massachusetts-Bay
SAML. ADAMS,
JOHN ADAMS,
ROBT. TREAT PAINE,
ELBRIDGE GERRY.

Rhode Island
STEP. HOPKINS,
WILLIAM ELLERY.

Connecticut
ROGER SHERMAN,
SAM'EL HUNTINGTON,
WM. WILLIAMS,
OLIVER WOLCOTT.

New York
WM. FLOYD,
PHIL. LIVINGSTON,
FRANS. LEWIS,
LEWIS MORRIS.

Pennsylvania
ROBT. MORRIS,
BENJAMIN RUSH,
BENJA. FRANKLIN,
JOHN MORTON,
GEO. CLYMER,
JAS. SMITH,
GEO. TAYLOR,
JAMES WILSON,
GEO. ROSS.

Delaware
CAESAR RODNEY,
GEO. READ,
THO. M'KEAN.

Georgia
BUTTON GWINNETT,
LYMAN HALL,
GEO. WALTON.

Maryland
SAMUEL CHASE,
WM. PACA,
THOS. STONE,
CHARLES CARROLL of
  CARROLLTON.

Virginia
GEORGE WYTHE,
RICHARD HENRY LEE,
TH. JEFFERSON,
BENJA. HARRISON,
THS. NELSON, JR.,
FRANCIS LIGHTFOOT LEE,
CARTER BRAXTON.

North Carolina
WM. HOOPER,
JOSPH HEWES,
JOHN PENN.

South Carolina
EDWARD RUTLEDGE,
THOS. HEYWARD, JUNR.,
THOMAS LYNCH, JUNR.,
ARTHUR MIDDLETON.

New Jersey
RICHD. STOCKTON,
JNO. WITHERSPOON,
FRAS. HOPKINSON,
JOHN HART,
ABRA. CLARK.

Appendix B

Characteristics of presidential appointees to the United States Supreme Court by presidential administration, 1930–1993

Presidential administration and justice	Political party	Home state	Years on Court	Age at nomination	Number of years of previous judicial experience
Hoover appointees					
Charles E. Hughes	Republican	New York	1930–1941	67	0
Owens J. Roberts	Republican	Pennsylvania	1930–1945	55	0
Benjamin N. Cardozo	Democrat	New York	1932–1938[a]	61	18
F. Roosevelt appointees					
Hugo L. Black	Democrat	Alabama	1937–1971[a]	51	1.5
Stanley F. Reed	Democrat	Kentucky	1938–1957	53	0
Felix Frankfurter	Independent	Massachusetts	1939–1962	56	0
William O. Douglas	Democrat	Connecticut	1939–1975	40	0
Frank Murphy	Democrat	Michigan	1940–1949[a]	49	7
James F. Byrnes	Democrat	South Carolina	1941–1942	62	0
Harlan Fiske Stone	Republican	New York	1941–1946[a]	68	0[b]
Robert H. Jackson	Democrat	New York	1941–1954[a]	49	0
Wiley B. Rutledge	Democrat	Iowa	1943–1949[a]	48	4
Truman appointees					
Harold H. Burton	Republican	Ohio	1945–1958	57	0
Fred M. Vinson	Democrat	Kentucky	1946–1953[a]	56	5
Tom C. Clark	Democrat	Texas	1949–1967	49	0
Sherman Minton	Democrat	Indiana	1949–1956	58	8
Eisenhower appointees					
Earl Warren	Republican	California	1953–1969	62	0
John M. Harlan	Republican	New York	1955–1971	55	1
William J. Brennan	Democrat	New Jersey	1956–1990	50	7
Charles E. Whittaker	Republican	Missouri	1957–1962	56	3
Potter Stewart	Republican	Ohio	1958–1981	43	4
Kennedy appointees					
Byron R. White	Democrat	Colorado	1962–present	44	0
Arthur J. Goldberg	Democrat	Illinois	1962–1965	54	0
Johnson appointees					
Abe Fortas	Democrat	Tennessee	1965–1969	55	0
Thurgood Marshall	Democrat	New York	1967–1991	59	4
Nixon appointees					
Warren E. Burger	Republican	Minnesota	1969–1986	61	13
Harry A. Blackmun	Republican	Minnesota	1970–present	61	11
Lewis F. Powell Jr.	Democrat	Virginia	1971–1987	64	0
William H. Rehnquist	Republican	Arizona	1971–1986	47	0
Ford appointee					
John Paul Stevens	Republican	Illinois	1976-present	55	5
Reagan appointees					
Sandra Day O'Connor	Republican	Arizona	1981–present	51	6.5
William H. Rehnquist	Republican	Arizona	1986–present	61	0[b]
Antonin Scalia	Republican	Illinois	1986–present	50	4
Anthony Kennedy	Republican	California	1988–present	51	12
Bush appointees					
David H. Souter	Republican	New Hampshire	1990–present	50	13
Clarence Thomas	Republican	Georgia	1991–present	43	1
Clinton appointee					
Ruth Bader Ginsburg	Democrat	New York	1993–present	60	13

[a]Died in office.
[b]Prior to appointment to associate justice.
Source: Harold W. Stanley and Richard G. Niemi, *Vital Statistics on American Politics.* Washington, CQ Press, 1994, pp. 294–299. Table adapted by SOURCEBOOK staff. Reprinted by permission.

Appendix C Members of the Supreme Court of the United States

Name	State appointed from	Appointed by President	(B) Judicial oath taken	Date service terminated
Chief justices				
Jay, John	New York	Washington	(a) October 19, 1789	June 29, 1795
Rutledge, John	S. Carolina	Washington	August 12, 1795	December 15, 1795
Ellsworth, Oliver	Connecticut	Washington	March 8, 1796	December 15, 1800
Marshall, John	Virginia	Adams, John	February 4, 1801	July 6, 1835
Taney, Roger Brooke	Maryland	Jackson	March 28, 1836	October 12, 1864
Chase, Salmon Portland	Ohio	Lincoln	December 15, 1864	May 7, 1873
Waite, Morrison Remick	Ohio	Grant	March 4, 1874	March 23, 1888
Fuller, Melville Weston	Illinois	Cleveland	October 8, 1888	July 4, 1910
White, Edward Douglas	Louisiana	Taft	December 19, 1910	May 19, 1921
Taft, William Howard	Connecticut	Harding	July 11, 1921	February 3, 1930
Hughes, Charles Evans	New York	Hoover	February 24, 1930	June 30, 1941
Stone, Harlan Fiske	New York	Roosevelt, F.	July 3, 1941	April 22, 1946
Vinson, Fred Moore	Kentucky	Truman	June 24, 1946	September 8, 1953
Warren, Earl	California	Eisenhower	October 5, 1953	June 23, 1969
Burger, Warren Earl	Virginia	Nixon	June 23, 1969	September 26, 1986
Rehnquist, William H.	Virginia	Reagan	September 26, 1986	
Associate justices				
Rutledge, John	S. Carolina	Washington	(a) February 15, 1790	March 5, 1791
Cushing, William	Massachusetts	Washington	(c) February 2, 1790	September 13, 1810
Wilson, James	Pennsylvania	Washington	(b) October 5, 1789	August 21, 1798
Blair, John	Virginia	Washington	(c) February 2, 1790	October 25, 1795
Iredell, James	N. Carolina	Washington	(b) May 12, 1790	October 20, 1799
Johnson, Thomas	Maryland	Washington	(a) August 6, 1792	January 16, 1793
Paterson, William	New Jersey	Washington	(a) March 11, 1793	September 9, 1806
Chase, Samuel	Maryland	Washington	February 4, 1796	June 19, 1811
Washington, Bushrod	Virginia	Adams, John	(c) February 4, 1799	November 26, 1829
Moore, Alfred	N. Carolina	Adams, John	(a) April 21, 1800	January 26, 1804
Johnson, William	S. Carolina	Jefferson	May 7, 1804	August 4, 1834
Livingston, Henry Brockholst	New York	Jefferson	January 20, 1807	March 18, 1823
Todd, Thomas	Kentucky	Jefferson	(a) May 4, 1807	February 7, 1826
Duvall, Gabriel	Maryland	Madison	(a) November 23, 1811	January 14, 1835
Story, Joseph	Massachusetts	Madison	(c) February 3, 1812	September 10, 1845
Thompson, Smith	New York	Monroe	(b) September 1, 1823	December 18, 1843
Trimble, Robert	Kentucky	Adams, J. Q.	(a) June 16, 1826	August 25, 1828
McLean, John	Ohio	Jackson	(c) January 11, 1830	April 4, 1861
Baldwin, Henry	Pennsylvania	Jackson	January 18, 1830	April 21, 1844
Wayne, James Moore	Georgia	Jackson	January 14, 1835	July 5, 1867
Barbour, Philip Pendleton	Virginia	Jackson	May 12, 1836	February 25, 1841
Catron, John	Tennessee	Van Buren	May 1, 1837	May 30, 1865
McKinley, John	Alabama	Van Buren	(c) January 9, 1838	July 19, 1852
Daniel, Peter Vivian	Virginia	Van Buren	(c) January 10, 1842	May 31, 1860
Nelson, Samuel	New York	Tyler	February 27, 1845	November 28, 1872
Woodbury, Levi	New Hampshire	Polk	(b) September 23, 1845	September 4, 1851
Grier, Robert Cooper	Pennsylvania	Polk	August 10, 1846	January 31, 1870
Curtis, Benjamin Robbins	Massachusetts	Fillmore	(b) October 10, 1851	September 30, 1857
Campbell, John Archibald	Alabama	Pierce	(c) April 11, 1853	April 30, 1861
Clifford, Nathan	Maine	Buchanan	January 21, 1858	July 25, 1881
Swayne, Noah Haynes	Ohio	Lincoln	January 27, 1862	January 24, 1881
Miller, Samuel Freeman	Iowa	Lincoln	July 21, 1862	October 13, 1890
Davis, David	Illinois	Lincoln	December 10, 1862	March 4, 1877
Field, Stephen Johnson	California	Lincoln	May 20, 1863	December 1, 1897
Strong, William	Pennsylvania	Grant	March 14, 1870	December 14, 1880
Bradley, Joseph P.	New Jersey	Grant	March 23, 1870	January 22, 1892
Hunt, Ward	New York	Grant	January 9, 1873	January 27, 1882
Harlan, John Marshall	Kentucky	Hayes	December 10, 1877	October 14, 1911
Woods, William Burnham	Georgia	Hayes	January 5, 1881	May 14, 1887

Name	State appointed from	Appointed by President	(B) Judicial oath taken	Date service terminated
Matthews, Stanley	Ohio	Garfield	May 17, 1881	March 22, 1889
Gray, Horace	Massachusetts	Arthur	January 9, 1882	September 15, 1902
Blatchford, Samuel	New York	Arthur	April 3, 1882	July 7, 1893
Lamar, Lucius Quintus C.	Mississippi	Cleveland	January 18, 1888	January 23, 1893
Brewer, David Josiah	Kansas	Harrison	January 6, 1890	March 28, 1910
Brown, Henry Billings	Michigan	Harrison	January 5, 1891	May 28, 1906
Shiras, George, Jr.	Pennsylvania	Harrison	October 10, 1892	February 23, 1903
Jackson, Howell Edmunds	Tennessee	Harrison	March 4, 1893	August 8, 1895
White, Edward Douglass	Louisiana	Cleveland	March 12, 1894	December 18, 1910*
Peckham, Rufus Wheeler	New York	Cleveland	January 6, 1896	October 24, 1909
McKenna, Joseph	California	McKinley	January 26, 1898	January 5, 1925
Holmes, Oliver Wendell	Massachusetts	Roosevelt, T.	December 8, 1902	January 12, 1932
Day, William Rufus	Ohio	Roosevelt, T.	March 2, 1903	November 13, 1922
Moody, William Henry	Massachusetts	Roosevelt, T.	December 17, 1906	November 20, 1910
Lurton, Horace Harmon	Tennessee	Taft	January 3, 1910	July 12, 1914
Hughes, Charles Evans	New York	Taft	October 10, 1910	June 10, 1916
Van Devanter, Willis	Wyoming	Taft	January 3, 1911	June 2, 1937
Lamar, Joseph Rucker	Georgia	Taft	January 3, 1911	January 2, 1916
Pitney, Mahlon	New Jersey	Taft	March 18, 1912	December 31, 1922
McReynolds, James Clark	Tennessee	Wilson	October 12, 1914	January 31, 1941
Brandeis, Louis Dembitz	Massachusetts	Wilson	June 5, 1916	February 13, 1939
Clarke, John Hessin	Ohio	Wilson	October 9, 1916	September 18, 1922
Sutherland, George	Utah	Harding	October 2, 1922	January 17, 1938
Butler, Pierce	Minnesota	Harding	January 2, 1923	November 16, 1939
Sanford, Edward Terry	Tennessee	Harding	February 19, 1923	March 8, 1930
Stone, Harlan Fiske	New York	Coolidge	March 2, 1925	July 2, 1941*
Roberts, Owen Josephus	Pennsylvania	Hoover	June 2, 1930	July 31, 1945
Cardozo, Benjamin Nathan	New York	Hoover	March 14, 1932	July 9, 1938
Black, Hugo Lafayette	Alabama	Roosevelt, F.	August 19, 1937	September 17, 1971
Reed, Stanley Forman	Kentucky	Roosevelt, F.	January 31, 1938	February 25, 1957
Frankfurter, Felix	Massachusetts	Roosevelt, F.	January 30, 1939	August 28, 1962
Douglas, William Orville	Connecticut	Roosevelt, F.	April 17, 1939	November 12, 1975
Murphy, Frank	Michigan	Roosevelt, F.	February 5, 1940	July 19, 1949
Byrnes, James Francis	S. Carolina	Roosevelt, F.	July 8, 1941	October 3, 1942
Jackson, Robert Houghwout	New York	Roosevelt, F.	July 11, 1941	October 9, 1954
Rutledge, Wiley Blount	Iowa	Roosevelt, F.	February 15, 1943	September 10, 1949
Burton, Harold Hitz	Ohio	Truman	October 1, 1945	October 13, 1958
Clark, Tom Campbell	Texas	Truman	August 24, 1949	June 12, 1967
Minton, Sherman	Indiana	Truman	October 12, 1949	October 15, 1956
Harlan, John Marshall	New York	Eisenhower	March 28, 1955	September 23, 1971
Brennan, William J., Jr.	New Jersey	Eisenhower	October 16, 1956	July 20, 1990
Whittaker, Charles Evans	Missouri	Eisenhower	March 25, 1957	March 31, 1962
Stewart, Potter	Ohio	Eisenhower	October 14, 1958	July 3, 1981
White, Byron Raymond	Colorado	Kennedy	April 16, 1962	June 28, 1993
Goldberg, Arthur Joseph	Illinois	Kennedy	October 1, 1962	July 25, 1965
Fortas, Abe	Tennessee	Johnson, L.	October 4, 1965	May 14, 1969
Marshall, Thurgood	New York	Johnson, L.	October 2, 1967	October 1, 1991
Blackmun, Harry A.	Minnesota	Nixon	June 9, 1970	
Powell, Lewis F., Jr.	Virginia	Nixon	January 7, 1972	June 26, 1987
Rehnquist, William H.	Arizona	Nixon	January 7, 1972	September 26, 1986*
Stevens, John Paul	Illinois	Ford	December 19, 1975	
O'Connor, Sandra Day	Arizona	Reagan	September 25, 1981	
Scalia, Antonin	Virginia	Reagan	September 26, 1986	
Kennedy, Anthony M.	California	Reagan	February 18, 1988	
Souter, David H.	New Hampshire	Bush	October 9, 1990	
Thomas, Clarence	Georgia	Bush	October 23, 1991	
Ginsburg, Ruth Bader	New York	Clinton	August 10, 1993	

Notes: The acceptance of the appointment and commission by the appointee, as evidenced by the taking of the prescribed oaths, is here implied; otherwise the individual is not carried on this list of the members of the Court. Examples: Robert Hanson Harrison is not carried, as a letter from President Washington of February 9, 1790, states Harrison declined to serve. Neither is Edwin M. Stanton, who died before he could take the necessary steps toward becoming a member of the Court. Chief Justice Rutledge is included because he took his oaths, presided over the August term of 1795, and his name appears on two opinions of the Court for that term.

The date a member of the Court took his/her judicial oath (the Judiciary Act provided "That the Justice of the Supreme Court, and the district judges, before they proceed to execute the duties of their respective offices, shall take the following oath . . .") is here used as the date of the beginning of his/her service, for until that oath is taken he/she is not vested with the prerogatives of the office. The dates given in this column are for the oaths taken following the receipt of the commissions. Dates without small-letter references are taken from the minutes of the Court or from the original oath which are in the Curator's collection. The small letter (a) denotes the date is from the minutes of some other court; (b) from some other unquestionable authority; (c) from authority that is questionable, and better authority would be appreciated.

*Promoted

Appendix D The United States Constitution and Amendments

CONSTITUTION OF THE UNITED STATES

We the People of the United States, in Order to form a more perfect Union, establish Justice, insure domestic Tranquility, provide for the common defence, promote the general Welfare, and secure the Blessings of Liberty to ourselves and our Posterity, do ordain and establish this Constitution for the United States of America.

Article I

SECTION 1.   All legislative Powers herein granted shall be vested in a Congress of the United States, which shall consist of a Senate and House of Representatives.

SECTION 2.   The House of Representatives shall be composed of Members chosen every second Year by the People of the several States, and the Electors in each State shall have the Qualifications requisite for Electors of the most numerous Branch of the State Legislature.

No Person shall be a Representative who shall not have attained to the Age of twenty five Years, and been seven Years a Citizen of the United States, and who shall not, when elected, be an Inhabitant of that State in which he shall be chosen.

[Representatives and direct Taxes shall be apportioned among the several States which may be included within this Union, according to their respective Numbers, which shall be determined by adding to the whole Number of free Persons, including those bound to Service for a Term of Years, and excluding Indians not taxed, three fifths of all other Persons.]* The actual Enumeration shall be made within three Years after the first Meeting of the Congress of the United States, and within every subsequent Term of ten Years, in such Manner as they shall by Law direct. The number of Representatives shall not exceed one for every thirty Thousand, but each State shall have at Least one Representative; and until such enumeration shall be made, the State of New Hampshire shall be entitled to chuse three, Massachusetts eight, Rhode-Island and Providence Plantations one, Connecticut five, New-York six, New Jersey four, Pennsylvania eight, Delaware one, Maryland six, Virginia ten, North Carolina five, South Carolina five, and Georgia three.

---

*Changed by section 2 of the Fourteenth Amendment.

When vacancies happen in the Representation from any State, the Executive Authority thereof shall issue Writs of Election to fill such Vacancies.

The House of Representatives shall chuse their Speaker and other Officers; and shall have the sole Power of Impeachment.

SECTION 3. The Senate of the United States shall be composed of two Senators from each State, [chosen by the Legislature thereof,]* for six Years; and each Senator shall have one Vote.

Immediately after they shall be assembled in Consequence of the first Election, they shall be divided as equally as may be into three Classes. The Seats of the Senators of the first Class shall be vacated at the Expiration of the second Year, of the second Class at the Expiration of the fourth Year, and of the third Class at the Expiration of the sixth Year, so that one third may be chosen every second Year; [and if Vacancies happen by Resignation, or otherwise, during the Recess of the Legislature of any State, the Executive thereof may make temporary Appointments until the next Meeting of the Legislature, which shall then fill such Vacancies.]*

No Person shall be a Senator who shall not have attained to the Age of thirty Years, and been nine Years a Citizen of the United States, and who shall not, when elected, be an Inhabitant of that State for which he shall be chosen.

The Vice President of the United States shall be President of the Senate, but shall have no Vote, unless they be equally divided.

The Senate shall chuse their other Officers, and also a President por tempore, in the Absence of the Vice President, or when he shall exercise the Office of President of the United States.

The Senate shall have the sole Power to try all Impeachments. When sitting for that Purpose, they shall be on Oath or Affirmation. When the President of the United States is tried, the Chief Justice shall preside: And no Person shall be convicted without the Concurrence of two thirds of the Members present.

Judgment in Cases of Impeachment shall not extend further than to removal from Office, and disqualification to hold and enjoy any Office of honor, Trust or Profit under the United States: but the Party convicted shall nevertheless be liable and subject to Indictment, Trial, Judgment and Punishment, according to Law.

SECTION 4. The Times, Places and Manner of holding Elections for Senators and Representatives, shall be prescribed in each State by the Legislature thereof; but the Congress may at any time by Law make or alter such Regulations, except as to the Places of chusing Senators.

The Congress shall assemble at least once in every Year, and such Meeting shall be [on the first Monday in December,]† unless they shall by Law appoint a different Day.

---

*Changed by the Seventeenth Amendment.

†Changed by section 2 of the Twentieth Amendment.

SECTION 5.　Each House shall be the Judge of the Elections, Returns and Qualifications of its own Members, and a Majority of each shall constitute a Quorum to do Business; but a smaller Number may adjourn from day to day, and may be authorized to compel the Attendance of absent Members, in such Manner, and under such Penalties as each House may provide.

Each House may determine the Rules of its Proceedings, punish its Members for disorderly Behaviour, and, with the Concurrence of two thirds, expel a Member.

Each House shall keep a Journal of its Proceedings, and from time to time publish the same, excepting such Parts as may in their Judgment require Secrecy; and the Yeas and Nays of the Members of either House on any question shall, at the Desire of one fifth of those Present, be entered on the Journal.

Neither House, during the Session of Congress, shall, without the Consent of the other, adjourn for more than three days, nor to any other Place than that in which the two Houses shall be sitting.

SECTION 6.　The Senators and Representatives shall receive a Compensation for their Services, to be ascertained by Law, and paid out of the Treasury of the United States. They shall in all Cases, except Treason, Felony and Breach of the Peace, be privileged from Arrest during their Attendance at the Session of their respective Houses, and in going to and returning from the same; and for any Speech or Debate in either House, they shall not be questioned in any other Place.

No Senator or Representative shall, during the Time for which he was elected, be appointed to any civil Office under the Authority of the United States, which shall have been created, or the Emoluments whereof shall have been encreased during such time; and no Person Holding any Office under the United States, shall be a Member of either House during his Continuance in Office.

SECTION 7.　All Bills for raising Revenue shall originate in the House of Representatives; but the Senate may propose or concur with Amendments as on other Bills.

Every Bill which shall have passed the House of Representatives and the Senate, shall, before it becomes a Law, be presented to the President of the United States; If he approve he shall sign it, but if not he shall return it, with his Objections to that House in which it shall have originated, who shall enter the Objections at large on their Journal, and proceed to reconsider it. If after such Reconsideration two thirds of that House shall agree to pass the Bill, it shall be sent, together with the Objections, to the other House, by which it shall likewise be reconsidered, and if approved by two thirds of that House, it shall become a Law. But in all Cases the Votes of both Houses shall be determined by yeas and Nays, and the Names of the Persons voting for against the Bill shall be entered on the Journal of each House respectively. If any Bill shall not be returned by the President within ten Days (Sundays excepted) after it shall have been presented to him, the Same shall be a Law, in like Manner as if he had signed it, unless the Congress by their Adjournment prevent its Return, in which Case it shall not be a Law.

Every Order, Resolution, or Vote to which the Concurrence of the Senate and House of Representatives may be necessary (except on a question of Adjournment) shall be presented to the President of the United States; and before the Same shall take Effect, shall be approved by him, or being disapproved by him, shall be repassed by two thirds of the Senate and House of Representatives, according to the Rules and Limitations prescribed in the Case of a Bill.

SECTION 8.   The Congress shall have Power To lay and collect Taxes, Duties, Imposts and Excises, to pay the Debts and provide for the common Defence and general Welfare of the United States; but all Duties, Imposts and Excises shall be uniform throughout the United States;

To borrow Money on the credit of the United States;

To regulate Commerce with foreign Nations, and among the several States, and with Indian Tribes;

To establish an uniform Rule of Naturalization, and uniform Laws on the subject of Bankruptcies throughout the United States;

To coin Money, regulate the Value thereof, and of foreign Coin, and fix the Standard of Weights and Measures;

To provide for the Punishment of counterfeiting the Securities and current Coin of the United States;

To establish Post Offices and post Roads;

To promote the Progress of Science and useful Arts, by securing for limited Times to Authors and Inventors the exclusive Right to their respective Writings and Discoveries;

To constitute Tribunals inferior to the supreme Court;

To define and punish Piracies and Felonies committed on the high Seas, and Offenses against the Law of Nations;

To declare War, grant Letters of Marque and Reprisal, and make Rules concerning Captures on Land and Water;

To raise and support Armies, but no Appropriation of Money to that Use shall be for a longer Term than two Years;

To provide and maintain a Navy;

To make Rules for the Government and Regulation of the land and naval Forces;

To provide for calling forth the Militia to execute the Laws of the Union, suppress Insurrections and repel Invasions;

To provide for organizing, arming, and disciplining, the Militia, and for governing such Part of them as may be employed in the Service of the United States, reserving to the States respectively, the Appointment of the Officers, and the Authority of training the Militia according to the discipline prescribed by Congress;

To exercise exclusive Legislation in all Cases whatsoever, over such District (not exceeding ten Miles square) as may, by Cession of particular States, and the Acceptance of Congress, become the Seat of the Government of the United States, and to exercise like Authority over all Places purchased by the Consent of the Legislature of the State in which the Same shall be, for the Erection of Forts, Magazines, Arsenals, dock-Yards and other needful Buildings;—And

To make all Laws which shall be necessary and proper for carrying into Execution the foregoing Powers, and all other Powers vested by this Constitution in the Government of the United States, or in any Department or Officer thereof.

SECTION 9. The Migration or Importation of such Persons as any of the States now existing shall think proper to admit, shall not be prohibited by the Congress prior to the Year one thousand eight hundred and eight, but a Tax or duty may be imposed on such Importation, not exceeding ten dollars for each Person.

The Privilege of the Writ of Habeas Corpus shall not be suspended, unless when in Cases of Rebellion or Invasion the public Safety may require it.

No Bill of Attainder or ex post facto Law shall be passed.

[No Capitation, or other direct, Tax shall be laid, unless in Proportion to the Census or Enumeration herein before directed to be taken.]*

No Tax or Duty shall be laid on Articles exported from any State.

No Preference shall be given by any Regulation of Commerce or Revenue to the Ports of one State over those of another: nor shall Vessels bound to, or from, one State, be obliged to enter, clear, or pay Duties in another.

No Money shall be drawn from the Treasury, but in Consequence of Appropriations made by Law; and a regular Statement and Account of the Receipts and Expenditures of all public Money shall be published from time to time.

No Title of Nobility shall be granted by the United States: And no Person holding any Office of Profit or Trust under them, shall, without the Consent of the Congress, accept of any present, Emolument, Office, or Title, of any kind whatever, from any King, Prince, or foreign State.

SECTION 10. No State shall enter into any Treaty, Alliance, or Confederation; grant Letters of Marque and Reprisal; coin Money; emit Bills of Credit; make any Thing but gold and silver Coin a Tender in Payment of Debts; pass any Bill of Attainder, ex post facto Law, or Law impairing the Obligation of Contracts, or grant any Title of Nobility.

No State shall, without the Consent of the Congress, lay any Imposts or Duties on Imports or Exports, except what may be absolutely necessary for executing it's inspection Laws: and the net Produce of the Duties and Imposts, laid by any State on Imports or Exports, shall be for the Use of the Treasury of the United States; and all such Laws shall be subject to the Revision and Control of the Congress.

No State shall, without the Consent of Congress, lay any Duty of Tonnage, keep Troops, or Ships of War in time of Peace, enter into any Agreement or Compact with another State, or with a foreign Power, or engage in War, unless actually invaded, or in such imminent Danger as will not admit of delay.

Article II

SECTION 1. The executive Power shall be vested in a President of the United States of America. He shall hold his Office during their Term of four Years, and, together with the Vice President, chosen for the same Term, be elected, as follows

Each State shall appoint, in such Manner as the Legislature thereof may direct, a Number of Electors, equal to the whole Number of Senators and Rep-

---

*Changed by the Sixteenth Amendment.

resentatives to which the State may be entitled in the Congress: but no Senator or Representative, or Person holding an Office of Trust or Profit under the United States shall be appointed an Elector.

[The Electors shall meet in their respective States, and vote by Ballot for two Persons, of whom one at least shall not be an Inhabitant of the same State with themselves. And they shall make a List of all the Persons voted for, and of the Number of Votes for each; which List they shall sign and certify, and transmit sealed to the Seat of the Government of the United States, directed to the President of the Senate. The President of the Senate shall, in the Presence of the Senate and House of Representatives, open all the Certificates, and the Votes shall then be counted. The Person having the greatest Number of Votes shall be the President, if such Number be a Majority of the whole Number of Electors appointed; and if there be more than one who have such Majority, and have an equal Number of Votes, then the House of Representatives shall immediately chuse by Ballot one of them for President, and if no Person have a Majority, then from the five highest on the List the said House shall in like Manner chuse the President. But in chusing the President, the Votes shall be taken by States, the Representation from each State having one Vote; A quorum for this Purpose shall consist of a Member or Members from two thirds of the States, and a Majority of all the States shall be necessary to a Choice. In every Case, after the Choice of the President, the Person having the greatest Number of Votes of the Electors shall be the Vice President. But if there should remain two or more who have equal Votes, the Senate shall chuse from them by Ballot the Vice President.]*

The Congress may determine the Time of chusing the Electors, and the Day on which they shall give their Votes; which Day shall be the same throughout the United States.

No Person except a natural born Citizen, or a Citizen of the United States, at the time of the Adoption of this Constitution, shall be eligible to the Office of the President; neither shall any person be eligible to that Office who shall not have attained to the Age of thirty five Years, and been fourteen Years a Resident within the United States.

[In Case of the Removal of the President from Office, or of his Death, Resignation, or Inability to discharge the Powers and Duties of the said Office, the Same shall devolve on the Vice President, and the Congress may by Law provide for the Case of Removal, Death, Resignation or Inability, both of the President and Vice President, declaring what Officer shall then act as President, and such Officer shall act accordingly, until the Disability be removed, or a President shall be elected.]†

The President shall, at stated Times, receive for his Services, a Compensation which shall neither be increased nor diminished during the Period for which he shall have been elected, and he shall not receive within that Period any other Emolument from the United States, or any of them.

---

*Changed by the Twelfth Amendment.

†Changed by the Twenty-Fifth Amendment.

Before he enter on the Execution of his Office, he shall take the following Oath or Affirmation:—"I do solemnly swear (or affirm) that I will faithfully execute the Office of President of the United States, and will to the best of my Ability, preserve, protect and defend the Constitution of the United States."

SECTION 2. The President shall be Commander in Chief of the Army and Navy of the United States, and of the Militia of the several States, when called into the actual Service of the United States; he may require the Opinion, in writing, of the principal Officer in each of the executive Departments, upon any Subject relating to the Duties of their respective Offices, and he shall have Power to grant Reprieves and Pardons for Offenses against the United States, except in Cases of Impeachment.

He shall have Power, by and with the Advice and Consent of the Senate, to make Treaties, provided two thirds of the Senators present concur; and he shall nominate, and by and with the Advice and Consent of the Senate, shall appoint Ambassadors, other public Ministers and Consuls, Judges of the supreme Court, and all other Officers of the United States, whose Appointments are not herein otherwise provided for, and which shall be established by Law: but the Congress may by Law vest the Appointment of such inferior Officers, as they think proper, in the President alone, in the Courts of Law, or in the Heads of Departments.

The President shall have Power to fill up all Vacancies that may happen during the Recess of the Senate, by granting Commissions which shall expire at the End of their next Session.

SECTION 3. He shall from time to time give to the Congress Information of the State of the Union, and recommend to their Consideration such Measures as he shall judge necessary and expedient; he may, on extraordinary Occasions, convene both Houses, or either of them, and in Case of Disagreement between them, with Respect to the Time of Adjournment, he may adjourn them to such Time as he shall think proper; he shall receive Ambassadors and other public Ministers; he shall take Care that the Laws be faithfully executed, and shall Commission all the Officers of the United States.

SECTION 4. The President, Vice President and all civil Officers of the United States, shall be removed from Office on Impeachment for, and Conviction of, Treason, Bribery, or other high Crimes and Misdemeanors.

Article III

SECTION 1. The judicial Power of the United States, shall be vested in one supreme Court, and in such interior Courts as the Congress may from time to time ordain and establish. The Judges, both of the supreme and inferior Courts, shall hold their Offices during good Behaviour, and shall, at stated Times, receive for their Services, a Compensation, which shall not be diminished during their Continuance in Office.

SECTION 2. The judicial Power shall extend to all Cases, in Law and Equity, arising under this Constitution, the Laws of the United States, and Treaties made, or which shall be made, under their Authority;—to all Cases affecting Ambassadors, other public Ministers and Consuls:—to all Cases of admiralty and maritime Jurisdiction;—to Controversies to which the United States shall be a Party;—to Controversies between two or more States; [between a State and Citizens of another State;—]* between Citizens of different States—between Citizens of the same State claiming Lands under Grants of different States, [and between a State, or the Citizens thereof, and foreign States, Citizens or Subjects.]*

In all Cases affecting Ambassadors, other public Ministers and Consuls, and those in which a State shall be Party, the supreme Court shall have original Jurisdiction. In all the other Cases before mentioned, the supreme Court shall have appellate Jurisdiction, both as to Law and Fact, with such Exceptions, and under such Regulations as the Congress shall make.

The Trial of the Crimes, except in Cases of Impeachment; shall be by Jury; and such Trial shall be held in the State where the said Crimes shall have been committed; but when not committed within any State, the Trial shall be at such Place or Places as the Congress may by Law have directed.

SECTION 3.   Treason against the United States, shall consist only in levying War against them, or in adhering to their Enemies, giving them Aid and Comfort. No Person shall be convicted of Treason unless on the Testimony of two Witnesses to the same overt Act, or on Confession in open Court.

The Congress shall have Power to declare the Punishment of Treason, but no Attainder of Treason shall work Corruption of Blood, or Forfeiture except during the Life of the Person attained.

Article IV

SECTION 1.   Full Faith and Credit shall be given in each State to the public Acts, Records, and judicial Proceedings of every other State, And the Congress may by general Laws prescribe the Manner in which such Acts, Records and Proceedings shall be proved, and the Effect thereof.

SECTION 2.   The Citizens of each State shall be entitled to all Privileges and Immunities of Citizens in the several States.

A Person charged in any State with Treason, Felony, or other Crime, who shall flee from Justice, and be found in another State, shall on Demand of the executive Authority of the State from which he fled, be delivered up, to be removed to the State having Jurisdiction of the Crime.

[No Person held to Service or Labour in one State, under the Laws thereof, escaping into another, shall, in Consequence of any Law or Regulation therein, be discharged from such Service or Labour, but shall be delivered up on Claim of the Party to whom such Service or Labour may be due.]†

---

*Changed by the Eleventh Amendment.
†Changed by the Thirteenth Amendment.

SECTION 3. New States may be admitted by the Congress into this Union; but no new State shall be formed or erected within the Jurisdiction of any other State; nor any State be formed by the Junction of two or more States, or Parts of States, without the Consent of the Legislatures of the States concerned as well as of the Congress.

The Congress shall have Power to dispose of and make all needful Rules and Republican respecting the Territory or other Property belonging to the United States; and nothing in this Constitution shall be so construed as to Prejudice any Claims of the United States, or of any particular State.

SECTION 4. The United States shall guarantee to every State in this Union a Republican Form of Government, and shall protect each of them against Invasion; and on Application of the Legislature, or of the Executive (when the Legislature cannot be convened) against domestic Violence.

Article V

The Congress, whenever two thirds of both Houses shall deem it necessary, shall propose Amendments to this Constitution, or, on the Application of the Legislatures of two thirds of the several States, shall call a Convention for proposing Amendments, which, in either Case, shall be valid to all Intents and Purposes, as Part of this Constitution, when ratified by the Legislatures of three fourths of the several States, or by Conventions in three fourths thereof, as the one or the other Mode of Ratification may be proposed by the Congress; Provided that no Amendment which may be made prior to the Year one thousand eight hundred and eight shall in any Manner affect the first and fourth Clauses in the Ninth Section of the first Article; and the no State, without its Consent, shall be deprived of it's [*sic*] equal Suffrage in the Senate.

Article VI

All Debts contracted and Engagements entered into, before the Adoption of this Constitution, shall be as valid against the United States under this Constitution, as under the Confederation.

This Constitution, and the Laws of the United States which shall be made in Pursuance thereof; and all Treaties made, or which shall be made, under the Authority of the United States, shall be the supreme Law of the Land; and the Judges in every State shall be bound thereby, any Thing in the Constitution or Laws of any State to the Contrary nowithstanding.

The Senators and Representatives before mentioned, and the Members of the several State Legislatures, and all executive and judicial Officers, both of the United States and of the several States, shall be bound by Oath or Affirmation, to support this Constitution; but no religious Test shall ever be required as a Qualification to any Office or public Trust under the United States.

Article VII

The Ratification of the Conventions of nine States, shall be sufficient for the Establishment of this Constitution between the States so ratifying the Same.

done in Convention by the Unanimous Consent of the States present the Seventeenth Day of September in the Year of our Lord one thousand seven hundred and Eighty seven and of the Independence of the United States of America the Twelfth In Witness whereof We have hereunto subscribed our Names,

G?: Washington—Presid!
and deputy from Virginia

New Hampshire	John Langdon Nicholas Gilman
Massachusetts	Nathaniel Gorham Rufus King
Connecticut	Wm. Saml. Johnson Roger Sherman
New York	Alexander Hamilton
New Jersey	Wil: Livingston David Brearley Wm. Paterson Jona: Dayton
Pennsylvania	B Franklin Thomas Mifflin Robt Morris Geo. Clymer Thos. FitzSimons Jared Ingersoll James Wilson Gouv Morris
Delaware	Geo: Read Gunning Bedford jun John Dickinson Richard Bassett Jaco: Broom
Maryland	James McHenry Dan of St Thos. Jenifer Danl Carroll
Virgina	John Blair— James Madison Jr.
North Carolina	Wm. Blount Richd. Dobbs Spaight Hu Williamson
South Carolina	J. Rutledge Charles Cotesworth Pinckney Charles Pinckney Pierce Butler
Georgia	William Few Abr Baldwin

Attest William Jackson Secretary

IN CONVENTION MONDAY SEPTEMBER 17TH 1787

PRESENT
THE STATES OF

New Hampshire, Massachusetts, Connecticut, Mr. Hamilton from New York, New Jersey, Pennsylvania, Delaware, Maryland, Virginia, North Carolina, South Carolina and Georgia.

Resolved,

That the preceeding Constitution be laid before the United States in Congress assembled, and that it is the Opinion of this Convention, that it should afterwards be submitted to a Convention of Delegates, chosen in each State by the People thereof, under the Recommendation of its Legislature, for their Assent and Ratification; and that each Convention assenting to, and ratifying the Same, should give Notice thereof to the United States in Congress assembled. Resolved, That it is the Opinion of this Convention, that as soon as the Conventions of nine States shall have ratified this Constitution, the United States in Congress assembled should fix a Day on which Electors should be appointed by the States which shall have ratified the same, and a Day on which the Electors should assemble to vote for the President, and the Time and Place for commencing Proceedings under this Constitution.

That after such Publication the Electors should be appointed, and the Senators and Representatives elected: That the Electors should meet on the Day fixed for the Election of the President, and should transmit their Votes certified, signed, sealed and directed, as the Constitution requires, to the Secretary of the United States in Congress assembled, that the Senators and Representatives should convene at the Time and Place assigned; that the Senators should appoint a President of the Senate, for the sole Purpose of receiving, opening and counting the Votes for President; and, that after he shall be chosen, the Congress, together with the President, should, without Delay, proceed to execute this Constitution.

By the unanimous Order of the Convention

G? WASHINGTON–Presid!

W. JACKSON Secretary.

AMENDMENTS TO THE CONSITUTION OF THE UNITED STATES

Amendment I [1791]

Congress shall make no law respecting an establishment of religion, or prohibiting the free exercise thereof; or abridging the freedom of speech, or of the press; or the right of the people peaceably to assembly, and to petition the Government for a redress of grievances.

Amendment II [1791]

A well regulated Militia, being necessary to the security of a free State, the right of the people to keep and bear Arms, shall not be infringed.

Amendment III [1791]

No Soldier shall, in time of peace be quartered in any house, without the consent of the Owner, nor in time of war, but in a manner to be prescribed by law.

Amendment IV [1791]

The right of the people to be secure in their persons, houses, papers, and effects, against unreasonable searches and seizures, shall not be violated, and no Warrants shall issue, but upon probable cause, supported by Oath or affirmation, and particularly describing the place to be searched, and the persons or things to be seized.

Amendment V [1791]

No person shall be held to answer for a capital, or otherwise infamous crime, unless on a presentment or indictment of a Grand Jury, except in cases arising in the land or naval forces, or in the Militia, when in actual service in time of War or public danger; nor shall any person be subject for the same offence to be twice put in jeopardy of life or limb; nor shall be compelled in any criminal case to be a witness against himself, nor be deprived of life, liberty, or property, without due process of law; nor shall private property be taken for public use, without just compensation.

Amendment VI [1791]

In all criminal prosecutions, the accused shall enjoy the right to a speedy and public trial, by an impartial jury of the State and district wherein the crime shall have been committed, which district shall have been previously ascertained by law, and to be informed of the nature and cause of accusation; to be confronted with the witnesses against him; to have compulsory process for obtaining witnesses in his favor, and to have the Assistance of Counsel for his defence.

Amendment VII [1791]

In Suits at common law, where the value in controversy shall exceed twenty dollars, the right of trial by jury shall be preserved, and no fact tried by jury, shall be otherwise re-examined in any Court of the United States, than according to the rules of the common law.

Amendment VIII [1791]

Excessive bail shall not be required, nor excessive fines imposed, nor cruel and unusual punishments inflicted.

Amendment IX [1791]

The enumeration in the Constitution, of certain rights, shall not be construed to deny or disparage others retained by the people.

Amendment X [1791]

The powers not delegated to the United States by the Constitution, nor prohibited by it to the States, are reserved to the States respectively, or to the people.

Amendment XI [1798]

The Judicial power of the United States shall not be construed to extend to any suit in law or equity, commenced or prosecuted against one of the United States by Citizens of another State, or by Citizens or Subjects of any Foreign State.

Amendment XII [1804]

The Electors shall meet in their respective states, and vote by ballot for President and Vice-President, one of whom, at least, shall not be an inhabitant of the same state with themselves; they shall name in their ballots the person voted for as President, and in distinct ballots the person voted for as Vice-President, and they shall make distinct lists of all persons voted for as President, and of all persons voted for as Vice-President, and of the number of votes for each, which lists they shall sign and certify, and transmit sealed to the seat of the government of the United States, directed to the President of the Senate;—The President of the Senate shall, in the presence of the Senate and House of Representatives, open all the certificates and the votes shall then be counted;—The person having the greatest number of votes for President, shall be the President, if such number be a majority of the whole number of Electors appointed; and if no person have such majority, then from the persons having the highest numbers not exceeding three on the list of those voted for as President, the House of Representatives shall choose immediately, by ballot, the President. But in choosing the President, the votes shall be taken by states, the representation from each state having one vote; a quorum for this purpose shall consist of a member or members from two-thirds of the states, and a majority of all states shall be necessary to a choice. And if the House of Representatives shall not choose a President whenever the right of choice shall devolve upon them, before the fourth day of March next following, then the Vice-President shall act as President, as in the case of the death or other constitutional disability of the President.—The person having the greatest number of votes as Vice-President, shall be the Vice-President, if such number be a majority of the whole number of Electors appointed, and if no person have a majority, then from the two highest numbers on the list, the Senate shall choose the Vice-President; a quorum for the purpose shall consist of two-thirds of the whole number of Senators, and a majority of the whole number shall be necessary to a choice. But no person constitutionally ineligible to the office of President shall be eligible to that of Vice-President of the United States.

Amendment XIII [1865]

SECTION 1.   Neither slavery nor involuntary servitude, except as a punishment for crime whereof the party shall have been duly convicted, shall exist within the United States, or any place subject to their jurisdiction.

SECTION 2.   Congress shall have power to enforce this article by appropriate legislation.

Amendment XIV [1868]

SECTION 1.   All persons born or naturalized in the United States, and subject to the jurisdiction thereof, are citizens of the United States and of the State wherein they reside. No State shall make or enforce any law which shall abridge the privileges or immunities of citizens of the United States; nor shall any State deprive any person of life, liberty, or property, without due process of law; nor deny to any person within its jurisdiction the equal protection of the laws.

SECTION 2.   Representatives shall be apportioned among the several States according to their respective numbers, counting the whole number of persons in each State, excluding Indians not taxed. But when the right to vote at any election for the choice of electors for President and Vice President of the United States, Representatives in Congress, the Executive and Judicial officers of a State, or the members of the Legislature thereof, is denied to any of the male inhabitants of such State, being twenty-one years of age, and citizens of the United States, or in any way abridged, except for participation in rebellion, or other crime, the basis of representation therein shall be reduced in the proportion which the number of such male citizens shall bear to the whole number of male citizens twenty-one years of age in such State.

SECTION 3.   No person shall be a Senator or Representative in Congress, or elector of President and Vice President, or hold any office, civil or military, under the United States, or under any State, who having previously taken an oath, as a member of Congress, or as an officer of the United States, or as a member of any State legislature, or as an executive or judicial officer of any State, to support the Constitution of the United States, shall have engaged in insurrection or rebellion against the same, or given aid or comfort to the enemies thereof. But Congress may by a vote of two-thirds of each House, remove such disability.

SECTION 4.   The validity of the public debt of the United States, authorized by law, including debts incurred for payment of pensions and bounties for services in suppressing insurrection or rebellion, shall not be questioned. But neither the United States nor any State shall assume or pay any debt or obligation incurred in aid of insurrection or rebellion against the United States, or any claim for the loss or emancipation of any slave; but all such debts, obligations and claims shall be held illegal and void.

SECTION 5.   The Congress shall have power to enforce, by appropriate legislation, the provisions of this article.

Amendment XV [1870]

SECTION 1.   The right of citizens of the United States to vote shall not be denied or abridged by the United States or by any State on account of race, color, or previous condition of servitude.

SECTION 2.   The Congress shall have power to enforce this article by appropriate legislation.

Amendment XVI [1913]

The Congress shall have power to lay and collect taxes on incomes, from whatever source derived, without apportionment among the several States, and without regard to any census or enumeration.

Amendment XVII [1913]

SECTION 1.   The Senate of the United States shall be composed of two Senators from each State, elected by the people thereof, for six years; and each Senator shall have one vote. The electors in each State shall have the qualifications requisite for electors of the most numerous branch of the State legislatures.

SECTION 2.   When vacancies happen in the representation of any State in the Senate, the executive authority of such State shall issue writs of election to fill such vacancies: Provided, That the legislature of any State may empower the executive thereof to make temporary appointments until the people fill the vacancies by election as the legislature may direct.

SECTION 3.   This amendment shall not be so construed as to affect the election or term of any Senator chosen before it becomes valid as part of the Constitution.

Amendment XVIII [1919]

SECTION 1.   After one year from the ratification of this article the manufacture, sale, or transportation of intoxicating liquors within, the importation thereof into, or the exportation thereof from the United States and all territory subject to the jurisdiction thereof for beverage purposes is hereby prohibited.

SECTION 2.   The Congress and the several States shall have concurrent power to enforce this article by appropriate legislation.

SECTION 3.   This article shall be inoperative unless it shall have been ratified as an amendment to the Constitution by the legislatures of the several States, as provided in the Constitution, within seven years from the date of the submission hereof to the States by the Congress.

Amendment XIX [1920]

SECTION 1.   The right of citizens of the United States to vote shall not be denied or abridged by the United States or by any State on account of sex.

SECTION 2.   Congress shall have power to enforce this article by appropriate legislation.

Amendment XX [1933]

SECTION 1.   The terms of the President and Vice President shall end at noon on the 20th day of January, and the terms of Senators and Representatives at noon on the 3d day of January, of the years in which such terms would have ended if this article had not been ratified; and the terms of their successors shall then begin.

SECTION 2.   The Congress shall assemble at least once in every year, and such meeting shall begin at noon on the 3d day of January, unless they shall by law appoint a different day.

SECTION 3.   If, at the time fixed for the beginning of the term of the President, the President elect shall have died, the Vice President elect shall become President. If the President shall not have been chosen before the time fixed for the beginning of his term, or if the President elect shall have failed to qualify, then the Vice President elect shall act as President until a President shall have qualified; and the Congress may by law provide for the case wherein neither a President elect nor a Vice President elect shall have qualified, declaring who shall then act as President, or the manner in which one who is to act shall be selected, and such person shall act accordingly until a President or Vice President shall have qualified.

SECTION 4.   The Congress may by law provide for the case of the death of any of the persons from whom the House of Representatives may choose a President whenever the right of choice shall have devolved upon them, and for the case of the death of any of the persons from whom the Senate may choose a Vice President whenever the right of choice shall have devolved upon them.

SECTION 5.   Sections 1 and 2 shall take effect on the 15th day of October following the ratification of this article.

SECTION 6.   This article shall be inoperative unless it shall have been ratified as an amendment to the Constitution by the legislatures of three-fourths of the several States within seven years from the date of its submission.

Amendment XXI [1933]

SECTION 1.   The eighteenth article of amendment to the Constitution of the United States is hereby repealed.

SECTION 2.   The transportation or importation into any State, Territory, or possession of the United States for delivery or use therein of intoxicating liquors, in violation of the laws thereof, is hereby prohibited.

SECTION 3.   This article shall be inoperative unless it shall have been ratified as an amendment to the Constitution by conventions in the several States, as provided in the Constitution, within seven years from the date of the submission hereof to the States by the Congress.

Amendment XXII [1951]

SECTION 1.   No person shall be elected to the office of the President more than twice, and no person who has held the office of President, or acted as President, for more than two years of a term to which some other person was elected President shall be elected to the office of President more than once. But this Article shall not apply to any person holding the office of President when this Article was proposed by the Congress, and shall not prevent any person who may be holding the office of President, or acting as President, during the term within which this Article becomes operative from holding the office of President or acting as President during the remainder of such term.

SECTION 2.   This article shall be inoperative unless it shall have been ratified as an amendment to the Constitution by the legislatures of three-fourths of the several States within seven years from the date of its submission to the States by the Congress.

Amendment XXIII [1961]

SECTION 1.   The District constituting the seat of Government of the United States shall appoint in such manner as the Congress may direct:
A number of electors of President and Vice President equal to the whole number of Senators and Representatives in Congress to which the District would be entitled if it were a State, but in no event more than the least populous state; they shall be in addition to those appointed by the states, but they shall be considered, for the purposes of the election of President and Vice President, to be electors appointed by a state; and they shall meet in the District and perform such duties as provided by the twelfth article of amendment.

SECTION 2.   The Congress shall have power to enforce this article by appropriate legislation.

Amendment XXIV [1964]

SECTION 1.   The right of citizens of the United States to vote in any primary or other election for President or Vice President, for electors for President or Vice President, or for Senator or Representative in Congress, shall not be denied or abridged by the United States, or any State by reason of failure to pay any poll tax or other tax.

SECTION 2.   The Congress shall have power to enforce this article by appropriate legislation.

Amendment XXV [1967]

SECTION 1.   In case of the removal of the President from office or of his death or resignation, the Vice President shall become President.

SECTION 2.   Whenever there is a vacancy in the office of the Vice President, the President shall nominate a Vice President who shall take office upon confirmation by a majority vote of both Houses of Congress.

SECTION 3.   Whenever the President transmits to the President pro tempore of the Senate and the Speaker of the House of Representatives his written declaration that he is unable to discharge the powers and duties of his office, and until he transmits to them a written declaration to the contrary, such powers and duties shall be discharged by the Vice President as Acting President.

SECTION 4.   Whenever the Vice President and a majority of either the principal officers of the executive departments or of such other body as Congress may by law provide, transmit to the President pro tempore of the Senate and the Speaker of the House of Representatives their written declaration that the President is unable to discharge the powers and duties of his office, the Vice President shall immediately assume the powers and duties of the office as Acting President.

Thereafter, when the President transmits to the President pro tempore of the Senate and the Speaker of the House of Representatives his written declaration that no inability exists, he shall resume the powers and duties of his office unless the Vice President and a majority of either the principal officers of the executive department or of such other body as Congress may by law provide, transmit within four days to the President pro tempore of the Senate and the Speaker of the House of Representatives their written declaration and the President is unable to discharge the powers and duties of his office. Thereupon Congress shall decide the issue, assembling within forty-eight hours for that purpose if not in session. If the Congress, within twenty-one days after receipt of the latter written declaration, or, if Congress is not in session, within twenty-one days after Congress is required to assemble, determines by two-thirds vote of both Houses that the President is unable to discharge the powers and duties of his office, the Vice President shall continue to discharge the same as Acting President; otherwise, the President shall resume the powers and duties of his office.

Amendment XXVI [1971]

SECTION 1.   The right of citizens of the United States, who are eighteen years of age or older, to vote shall not be denied or abridged by the United States or by any State on account of age.

SECTION 2.   The Congress shall have power to enforce this article by appropriate legislation.

Appendix E *Marbury v. Madison* and *Miranda v. Arizona*

MARBURY V. MADISON
1 Cranch 137, 2 L.Ed. 60 (1803).

[Thomas Jefferson, an Anti-Federalist (or Republican), who defeated John Adams, a Federalist, in the presidential election of 1800, was to take office on March 4, 1801. On January 20, 1801, Adams, the defeated incumbent, nominated John Marshall, Adams' Secretary of State, as fourth Chief Justice of the United States. Marshall assumed office on February 4 but continued to serve as Secretary of State until the end of the Adams administration. During February, the Federalist Congress passed (1) the Circuit Court Act, which, inter alia, doubled the number of federal judges and (2) the Organic Act which authorized appointment of 42 justices-of-the-peace in the District of Columbia. Senate confirmation of Adams' "midnight" appointees, virtually all Federalists, was completed on March 3. Their commissions were signed by Adams and sealed by Acting Secretary of State Marshall, but due to time pressures, several of the justices-of-the-peace (including that of William Marbury) remained undelivered when Jefferson assumed the presidency the next day. Jefferson ordered his new Secretary of State, James Madison, to withhold delivery.

[Late in 1801, Marbury and several others sought a writ of mandamus in the Supreme Court to compel Madison to deliver the commissions. The Court ordered Madison "to show cause why a mandamus should not issue" and the case was set for argument in the 1802 Term.

[While the case was pending, the new Republican Congress—incensed at Adams' efforts to entrench a Federalist judiciary and at the "Federalist" Court's order against a Republican cabinet officer—moved to repeal the Circuit Court Act. Federalist congressmen argued that repeal would be unconstitutional as violative of Art. III's assurance of judicial tenure "during good behavior" and of the Constitution's plan for separation of powers assuring the independence of the Judiciary. It "was in this debate that for the first time since the initiation of the new Government under the Constitution there occurred a serious challenge of the power of the Judiciary to pass upon the constitutionality of Acts of Congress. Hitherto, [it had been the Republicans] who had sustained this power as a desirable curb on Congressional aggression and encroachment on the rights of the States, and they had been loud in their complaints at the failure of the Court to hold the Alien and Sedition laws unconstitutional. Now, however, in 1802, in order to counteract the Federalist argument that the Repeal Bill was unconstitutional and would be so held by the Court, [Republicans] advanced the proposition that the Court did not possess the power."[a]

---

[a]1 Warren, *The Supreme Court in United States History* 215 (1922).

[The Repeal Law passed early in 1802. To forestall its constitutional challenge in the Supreme Court until the political power of the new administration had been strengthened, Congress also eliminated the 1802 Supreme Court Term. Thus, the Court did not meet between December, 1801 and February, 1803.]

[On] 24th February, the following opinion of the court was delivered by Mr. Chief Justice MARSHALL: *   *   *

No cause has been shown, and the present motion is for a mandamus. The peculiar delicacy of this case, the novelty of some of its circumstances, and the real difficulty attending the points which occur in it require a complete exposition of the principles on which the opinion to be given by the court is founded.   *   *   *

1st. Has the applicant a right to the commission he demands?   *   *   *

Mr. Marbury, [since] his commission was signed by the President and sealed by the Secretary of State, was appointed; and as the law creating the office gave the officer a right to hold for five years, independent of the executive, the appointment was not revocable, but vested in the officer legal rights, which are protected by the laws of his country.

To withhold his commission, therefore, is an act deemed by the court not warranted by law, but violative of a vested legal right.[b]   *   *   *

---

[b]Consider Van Alstyne, *A Critical Guide to Marbury v. Madison.* 1969 Duke L.J. 1. 8: "[T]here is clearly an 'issue' of sorts which preceded any of those touched upon in the opinion. Specifically, it would appear that Marshall should have recused himself in view of his substantial involvement in the background of this controversy. * * * Proof of the status of Marbury's commission not only involved circumstances within the Chief Justice's personal knowledge, it was furnished in the Supreme Court by Marshall's own younger brother who had been with him in his office when, as Secretary of State, he had made out the commissions."

2dly. If he has a right, and that right has been violated, do the laws of his country afford him a remedy?

The very essence of civil liberty certainly consists in the right of every individual to claim the protection of the laws, whenever he receives an injury. One of the first duties of government is to afford that protection.   *   *   *

The government of the United States has been emphatically termed a government of laws, and not of men. It will certainly cease to deserve this high appellation, if the laws furnish no remedy for the violation of a vested legal right.   *   *   *

[W]here the heads of departments are the political or confidential agents of the executive, merely to execute the will of the president, or rather to act in cases in which the executive possesses a constitutional or legal discretion, nothing can be more perfectly clear than that their acts are only politically examinable. But where a specific duty is assigned by law, and individual rights depend upon the performance of that duty, it seems equally clear that the individual who considers himself injured, has a right to resort to the laws of his country for a remedy.[c]   *   *   *

---

[c]Consider Redlich, *The Supreme Court—1833 Term*, 40 N.Y.U.L.Rev. 1, 4 (1965): "[T]he Court could have ruled that, since the President had the power to appoint the judges, he also had the power to deliver the commissions which was in a sense the final act of appointment. Viewed as a component of the act of appointment, the delivery of the commissions could have simply been considered as lying within the discretion of the President."

It remains to be inquired whether,

3dly. He is entitled to the remedy for which he applies? This depends on,

1st. The nature of the writ applied for; and,

2dly. The power of this court.

1st. The nature of the writ.   *   *   *

This writ, if awarded, would be directed to an officer of government, and its mandate to him would be, to use the words of Blackstone, "to do a particular thing therein specified, which appertains to his office and duty, and which the court has previously determined, or at least supposes, to be consonant to right and justice." Or, in the words of Lord Mansfield, the applicant, in this case, has a right to execute an office of public concern, and is kept out of possession of that right.

These circumstances certainly concur in this case.

Still, to render the mandamus a proper remedy, the officer to whom it is to be directed, must be one to whom, on legal principles, such writ may be directed; and the person applying for it must be without any other specific and legal remedy.

1st. With respect to the officer to whom it would be directed. The intimate political relation subsisting between the President of the United States and the heads of departments, necessarily renders any legal investigation of the acts of one of those high officers peculiarly irksome, as well as delicate; and excites some hesitation with respect to the propriety of entering into such investigation. Impressions are often received without much reflection or examination, and it is not wonderful that in such a case as this the assertion, by an individual, of his legal claims in a court of justice, to which claims it is the duty of that court to attend, should at first view be considered by some, as an attempt to intrude into the cabinet, and to intermeddle with the prerogatives of the executive.

It is scarcely necessary for the court to disclaim all pretensions to such a jurisdiction. An extravagance, so absurd and excessive, could not have been entertained for a moment. The province of the court is, solely, to decide on the rights of individuals, not to inquire how the executive, or executive officers, perform duties in which they have a discretion. Questions in their nature political, or which are, by the constitution and laws, submitted to the executive, can never be made in this court.

But [what] is there in the exalted station of the officer, which shall bar a citizen from asserting, in a court of justice, his legal rights, or shall forbid a court to listen to the claim, or to issue a mandamus, directing the performance of a duty, not depending on executive discretion, but on particular acts of congress, and the general principles of law?   *   *   *

This, then, is a plain case for a mandamus, either to deliver the commission, or a copy of it from the record; and it only remains to be inquired.

Whether it can issue from this court.

The act to establish the judicial courts of the United States authorizes the supreme court "to issue writs of mandamus, in cases warranted by the principles and usages of law, to any courts appointed, or persons holding office, under the authority of the United States."[d]

---

[d]§ 13 of the Judiciary Act of 1789 provided: "That the Supreme Court shall have exclusive jurisdiction of all controversies of a civil nature, where a state is a party, except between a state and its citizens; and except also between a state and citizens of other states, or aliens, in which latter case it shall have original but not exclusive jurisdiction. And shall have exclusively all such jurisdiction of suits or proceedings against ambassadors or other public ministers, or their domestics, or domestic servants, as a court of law can have or exercise consistently with the law of nations: and original, but not exclusive jurisdiction of all suits brought by ambassadors or other public ministers, or in which a consul, or vice consul, shall be a party. And the trial of issues of fact in the Supreme Court in all actions at law against citizens of the United States shall be by jury. The Supreme Court shall also have appellate jurisdiction from the circuit courts and courts of the several states, in the cases hereinafter specially provided for: and shall have power to issue writs of prohibition to the district courts, when proceeding as courts of admiralty and maritime jurisdiction, and writs of mandamus, in cases warranted by the principles and usages of law, to any courts appointed, or persons holding office under the authority of the United States."

Consider Van Alstyne, supra. at 15: "Textually, the provision regarding mandamus says nothing expressly as to whether it is part of original or appellate jurisdiction or both, and the clause itself does not speak at all of 'conferring jurisdiction' on the court. The grant of 'power' to issue the writ. however, is juxtaposed with the section of appellate jurisdiction and, in fact, follows the general description of appellate jurisdiction in the same sentence, being separated only by a semicolon. No textual mangling is required to confine it to appellate jurisdiction. Moreover, no mangling is required even if it attaches both to original and to appellate jurisdiction, not as an enlargement of either, but simply as a specification of power which the Court is authorized to use in cases which are *otherwise* appropriately under consideration. Since this case is not otherwise within the specified type of original jurisdiction (e.g., it is not a case in which a state is a party or a case against an ambassador), it should be dismissed."

The secretary of state, being a person holding an office under the authority of the United States, is precisely within the letter of the description; and if this court is not authorized to issue a writ of mandamus to such an officer, it must be because the law is unconstitutional, and therefore absolutely incapable of conferring the authority, and assigning the duties which its words purport to confer and assign.   *   *   *

In the distribution of [the judicial power of the United States] it is declared that "the supreme court shall have original jurisdiction in all cases affecting ambassadors, other public ministers and consuls, and those in which a state shall be a party. In all other cases, the supreme court shall have appellate jurisdiction."

It has been insisted, at the bar, that as the original grant of jurisdiction, to the supreme and inferior courts, is general, and the clause, assigning original jurisdiction to the supreme court, contains no negative or restrictive words, the power remains to the legislature, to assign original jurisdiction to that court in other cases than those specified in the article which has been recited; provided those cases belong to the judicial power of the United States.

If it had been intended to leave it in the discretion of the legislature to apportion the judicial power between the supreme and inferior courts according to the will of that body, it would certainly have been useless to have proceeded further than to have defined the judicial power, and the tribunals in which it should be vested. The subsequent part of the section is mere surplusage, is entirely without meaning, if such is to be the construction. If congress remains at liberty to give this court appellate jurisdiction, where the constitution has declared their jurisdiction shall be original; and original jurisdiction where the constitution has declared it shall be appellate; the distribution of jurisdiction, made in the constitution, is form without substance.

Affirmative words are often, in their operation, negative of other objects than those affirmed; and in this case, a negative or exclusive sense must be given to them, or they have no operation at all.

It cannot be presumed that any clause in the constitution is intended to be without effect; and, therefore, such a construction is inadmissible, unless the words require it. *   *   *

The authority, therefore, given to the Supreme Court, by the Act establishing the judicial courts of the United States, to issue writs of mandamus to public officers, appears not to be warranted by the Constitution;[e] and it becomes necessary to inquire whether a jurisdiction so conferred can be exercised.

———

[e]Consider Van Alstyne, supra. at 31: "It can be plausibly argued, however, that the Article III division of judicial power between appellate and original jurisdiction served a useful purpose other than that insisted upon by Marshall. Had Congress *not* adopted the Judiciary Act of 1789 or taken any other action describing Supreme Court jurisdiction, the division itself would have provided a guideline for the Court to follow until Congress was inclined to act." See also id. at 30–33.

By Marshall's interpretation of Art. III. may Congress authorize the Court to exercise appellate jurisdiction in cases involving foreign consuls? See *Börs c. Preston*, 111 U.S. 252, 4 S.Ct. 407, 28 L.Ed. 419 (1884).

The question whether an Act repugnant to the Constitution can become the law of the land, is a question deeply interesting to the United States; but, happily, not of an intricacy proportioned to its interest. It seems only necessary to recognize certain principles, supposed to have been long and well established, to decide it.

That the people have an original right to establish, for their future government, such principles as, in their opinion, shall most conduce to their own happiness, is the basis on which the whole American fabric has been erected. The exercise of this original right is a very great exertion; nor can it nor ought it to be frequently repeated. The principles, therefore, so established, are deemed fundamental. And as the authority from which they proceed is supreme, and can seldom act, they are designed to be permanent.

This original and supreme will organizes the government, and assigns to different departments their respective powers. It may either stop here, or establish certain limits not to be transcended by those departments.

The government of the United States is of the latter description. The powers of the legislature are defined and limited; and that those limits may not be mistaken, or forgotten, the constitution is written. To what purpose are powers limited, and to what purpose is that limitation committed to writing, if these limits may, at any time, be passed by those intended to be restrained? The distinction between a government with limited and unlimited powers is abolished, if those limits do not confine the persons on whom they are imposed, and if acts prohibited and acts allowed, are of equal obligation. It is a proposition too plain to be contested, that the constitution controls any legislative act repugnant to it; or, that the legislature may alter the constitution by an ordinary act.

Between these alternatives there is no middle ground. The constitution is either a superior paramount law, unchangeable by ordinary means, or it is on a level with ordinary legislative acts, and, like other acts, is alterable when the legislature shall please to alter it.

If the former part of the alternative be true, then a legislative act contrary to the constitution is not law: if the latter part be true, then written constitutions are absurd attempts, on the part of the people, to limit a power in its own nature illimitable.

Certainly all those who have framed written constitutions contemplate them as forming the fundamental and paramount law of the nation, and consequently, the theory of every such government must be, that an act of the legislature, repugnant to the constitution, is void.

This theory is essentially attached to a written constitution, and is, consequently, to be considered, by this court, as one of the fundamental principles of our society. It is not therefore to be lost sight of in the further consideration of this subject.

If an act of the legislature, repugnant to the Constitution, is void, does it, notwithstanding its invalidity, bind the courts, and oblige them to give it effect? Or, in other words, though it be not law, does it constitute a rule as operative as if it was a law? This would be to overthrow in fact what was established in theory; and would seem, at first view, an absurdity too gross to be insisted on. It shall, however, receive a more attentive consideration.

It is emphatically the province and duty of the judicial department to say what the law is. Those who apply the rule to particular cases, must of necessity expound and interpret that rule. If two laws conflict with each other, the courts must decide on the operation of each.

So if a law be in opposition to the constitution; if both the law and the Constitution apply to a particular case, so that the court must either decide that case conformably to the law, disregarding the constitution; or conformably to the constitution, disregarding the law; the court must determine which of these conflicting rules governs the case. This is of the very essence of judicial duty.

If, then, the courts are to regard the constitution, and the constitution is superior to any ordinary act of the legislature, the constitution, and not such ordinary act, must govern the case to which they both apply.

Those then who controvert the principle that the constitution is to be considered in court, as a paramount law, are reduced to the necessity of maintaining that courts must close their eyes on the constitution, and see only the law.

This doctrine would subvert the very foundation of all written constitutions. It would declare that an Act which, according to the the principles and theory of our government, is entirely void, is yet, in practice, completely obligatory. It would declare that if the legislature shall do what is expressly forbidden, such Act, notwithstanding the express prohibition, is in reality effectual. It would be giving to the legislature a practical and real omnipotence, with the same breath which professes to restrict their powers within narrow limits. It is prescribing limits, and declaring that those limits may be passed at pleasure.

That it thus reduces to nothing what we have deemed the greatest improvement on political institutions, a written constitution, would of itself be sufficient, in America, where written constitutions have been viewed with so much reverence, for rejecting the construction. But the peculiar expressions of the Constitution of the United States furnish additional arguments in favor of its rejection.

The judicial power of the United States is extended to all cases arising under the Constitution.

Could it be the intention of those who gave this power, to say that in using it the Constitution should not be looked into? That a case arising under the Constitution should be decided without examining the instrument under which it arises?

This is too extravagant to be maintained.

In some cases, then, the Constitution must be looked into by the judges. And if they can open it at all, what part of it are they forbidden to read or to obey?

There are many other parts of the Constitution which serve to illustrate this subject.

It is declared that "no tax or duty shall be laid on articles exported from any State." Suppose a duty on the export of cotton, of tobacco, or of flour; and a suit instituted to recover it. Ought judgment to be rendered in such a case? Ought the judges to close their eyes on the Constitution, and only see the law?

The Constitution declares "that no bill of attainder or ex post facto law shall be passed."

If, however, such a bill should be passed, and a person should be prosecuted under it, must the court condemn to death those victims whom the Constitution endeavors to preserve?

"No person," says the Constitution, "shall be convicted of treason unless on the testimony of two witnesses to the same overt act, or on confession in open court."

Here the language of the Constitution is addressed especially to the courts. It prescribes, directly for them, a rule of evidence not to be departed from. If the legislature should change that rule, and declare one witness, or a confession out of court, sufficient for conviction, must the constitutional principle yield to the legislative act?

From these, and many other selections which might be made, it is apparent, that the framers of the constitution contemplated that instrument as a rule for the government of courts, as well as of the legislature.

Why otherwise does it direct the judges to take an oath to support it? This oath certainly applies in an especial manner, to their conduct in their official character. How immoral to impose it on them, if they were to be used as the instruments, and the knowing instruments, for violating what they swear to support!

The oath of office, too, imposed by the legislature, is completely demonstrative of the legislative opinion on this subject. It is in these words: "I do solemnly swear that I will administer justice without respect to persons, and do equal right to the poor and to the rich; and that I will faithfully and impartially discharge all the duties incumbent on me as _____, according to the best of my abilities and understanding agreeably to the constitution and laws of the United States."

Why does a judge swear to discharge his duties agreeably to the constitution of the United States, if that constitution forms no rule for his government? If it is closed upon him, and cannot be inspected by him?

If such be the real state of things, this is worse than solemn mockery. To prescribe, or to take this oath, becomes equally a crime.

It is also not entirely unworthy of observation, that in declaring what shall be the supreme law of the land, the constitution itself is first mentioned; and not the laws of the United States generally, but those only which shall be made in pursuance of the constitution, have that rank.

Thus, the particular phraseology of the Constitution of the United States confirms and strengthens the principle, supposed to be essential to all written constitutions, that a law repugnant to the constitution is void; and that courts, as well as other departments, are bound by that instrument.

The rule must be discharged.[f]

---

[f] Six days later, the Circuit Court Act Repeal Law was held to be constitutional, *Stuart v. Laird,* 5 U.S. (1 Cranch) 299, 2 L.Ed. 115 (1803). After *Marbury,* the Court did not hold an act of Congress unconstitutional until *Dred Scott v. Sandford,* 60 U.S. (19 How.) 393, 15 L.Ed. 691 (1857).

MIRANDA V. ARIZONA
Supreme Court of the United States, 1964.
384 U.S. 436, 86 S.Ct. 1602, 16 L.Ed.2d 694.

Mr. Chief Justice WARREN delivered the opinion of the Court.

* * *

Our holding will be spelled out with some specificity in the pages which follow but briefly stated it is this: the prosecution may not use statements, whether exculpatory or inculpatory, stemming from custodial interrogation of the defendant unless it demonstrates the use of procedural safeguards effective to secure the privilege against self-incrimination. By custodial interrogation, we mean questioning initiated by law enforcement officers after a person has been taken into custody or otherwise deprived of his freedom of action in any significant way.[4] As for the procedural safeguards to be employed, unless other fully effective means are devised to inform accused persons of their right of silence and to assure a continuous opportunity to exercise it, the following measures are required. Prior to any questioning, the person must be warned that he has a right to remain silent, that any statement he does make may be used as evidence against him, and that he has a right to the presence of an attorney, either retained or appointed. The defendant may waive effectuation of these rights, provided the waiver is made voluntarily, knowingly and intelligently. If, however, he indicates in any manner and at any stage of the process that he wishes to consult with an attorney before speaking there can be no questioning. Likewise, if the individual is alone and indicates in any manner that he does not wish to be interrogated, the police may not question him. The mere fact that he may have answered some questions or volunteered some statements on his own does not deprive him of the right to refrain from answering any further inquiries until he has consulted with an attorney and thereafter consents to be questioned.

[4.]This is what we meant in *Escobedo* when we spoke of an investigation which had focused on an accused.

I

The constitutional issue we decide in each of these cases is the admissibility of statements obtained from a defendant questioned while in custody or otherwise deprived of his freedom of action in any significant way. In each, the defendant was questioned by police officers, detectives, or a prosecuting attorney in a room in which he was cut off from the outside world. In none of these cases was the defendant given a full and effective warning of his rights at the outset of the interrogation process. In all the cases, the questioning elicited oral admissions, and in three of them, signed statements as well which were admitted at their trials. They all thus share salient features—incommunicado interrogation of individuals in a police-dominated atmosphere, resulting in self-incriminating statements without full warnings of constitutional rights.

An understanding of the nature and setting of this in-custody interrogation is essential to our decisions today. The difficulty in depicting what transpires at such interrogations stems from the fact that in this country they have largely taken place incommunicado.

*   *   *

A valuable source of information about present police practices, however, may be found in various police manuals and texts which document procedures employed with success in the past, and which recommend various other effective tactics. These texts are used by law enforcement agencies themselves as guides. It should be noted that these texts professedly present the most enlightened and effective means presently used to obtain statements through custodial interrogation. By considering these texts and other data, it is possible to describe procedures observed and noted around the country.

The officers are told by the manuals that the "principal psychological factor contributing to a successful interrogation is privacy—being alone with the person under interrogation."[10]

[10.]Inbau & Reid. Criminal Interrogation and Confessions (1962), at 1.

* * *

To highlight the isolation and unfamiliar surroundings, the manuals instruct the police to display an air of confidence in the suspect's guilt and from outward appearance to maintain only an interest in confirming certain details. The guilt of the subject is to be posited as a fact. The interrogator should direct his comments toward the reasons why the subject committed the act, rather than court failure by asking the subject whether he did it. Like other men, perhaps the subject has had a bad family life, had an unhappy childhood, had too much to drink, had an unrequited desire for women. The officers are instructed to minimize the moral seriousness of the offense, to cast blame on the victim or on society. These tactics are designed to put the subject in a psychological state where his story is but an elaboration of what the police purport to know already—that he is guilty. Explanations to the contrary are dismissed and discouraged.

* * *

The manuals suggest that the suspect be offered legal excuses for his actions in order to obtain an initial admission of guilt. Where there is a suspected revenge-killing, for example, the interrogator may say:

> "Joe, you probably didn't go out looking for this fellow with the purpose of shooting him. My guess is, however, that you expected something from him and that's why you carried a gun—for your own protection. You knew him for what he was, no good. Then when you met him he probably started using foul, abusive language and he gave some indication that he was about to pull a gun on you, and that's when you had to act to save your own life. That's about it, isn't it, Joe?"[15]

[15.] Inbau & Reid, supra, at 40.

Having then obtained the admission of shooting, the interrogator is advised to refer to circumstantial evidence which negates the self-defense explanation. This should enable him to secure the entire story. One text notes that "Even if he fails to do so, the inconsistency between the subject's original denial of the shooting and his present admission of at least doing the shooting will serve to deprive him of a self-defense 'out' at the time of trial."

When the techniques described above prove unavailing, the texts recommend they be alternated with a show of some hostility. One ploy often used has been termed the "friendly-unfriendly" or the "Mutt and Jeff" act:

> "* * * In this technique, two agents are employed. Mutt, the relentless investigator, who knows the subject is guilty and is not going to waste any time. He's sent a dozen men away for this crime and he's going to send the subject away for the full term. Jeff, on the other hand, is obviously a kindhearted man. He has a family himself. He has a brother who was involved in a little scrape like this. He disapproves of Mutt and his tactics and will arrange to get him off the case if the subject will cooperate. He can't hold Mutt off for very long. The subject would be wise to make a quick decision. The technique is applied by having both investigators present while Mutt acts out his role. Jeff may stand by quietly and demur at some of Mutt's tactics. When Jeff makes his plea for cooperation, Mutt is not present in the room."

The interrogators sometimes are instructed to induce a confession out of trickery. The technique here is quite effective in crimes which require identification or which run in series. In the identification situation, the interrogator may take a break in his questioning to place the subject among a group of men in a line-up. "The witness or complainant (previously coached, if necessary) studies the line-up and confidently points out the subject as the guilty party."[18] Then the questioning resumes "as though there were now no doubt about the guilt of the subject." A variation on this technique is called the "reverse line-up":

[18] O'Hara, Fundamentals of Criminal Investigation (1956) at 105–106.

"The accused is placed in a line-up, but this time he is identified by several fictitious witnesses or victims who associated him with different offenses. It is expected that the subject will become desperate and confess to the offense under investigation in order to escape from the false accusations."[19]

[19] Id., at 106.

The manuals also contain instructions for police on how to handle the individual who refuses to discuss the matter entirely, or who asks for an attorney or relatives. The examiner is to concede him the right to remain silent. "This usually has a very undermining effect. First of all, he is disappointed in his expectation of an unfavorable reaction on the part of the interrogator. Secondly, a concession of this right to remain silent impresses the subject with the apparent fairness of his interrogator."[20] After this psychological conditioning, however, the officer is told to point out the incriminating significance of the suspect's refusal to talk:

[20] Inbau & Reid, supra. at 111.

"Joe, you have a right to remain silent. That's your privilege and I'm the last person in the world who'll try to take it away from you. If that's the way you want to leave this, O. K. But let me ask you this. Suppose you were in my shoes and I were in yours and you called me in to ask me about this and I told you, 'I don't want to answer any of your questions.' You'd think I had something to hide, and you'd probably be right in thinking that. That's exactly what I'll have to think about you, and so will everybody else. So let's sit here and talk this whole thing over."[21]

[21] Ibid.

Few will persist in their initial refusal to talk, it is said, if this monologue is employed correctly.

In the event that the subject wishes to speak to a relative or an attorney, the following advise is tendered:

"[T]he interrogator should respond by suggesting that the subject first tell the truth to the interrogator himself rather than get anyone else involved in the matter. If the request is for an attorney, the interrogator may suggest that the subject save himself or his family the expense of any such professional service, particularly if he is innocent of the offense under investigation. The interrogator may also add, 'Joe, I'm only looking for the truth, and if you're telling the truth, that's it. You can handle this by yourself.'"[22]

[22.]Inbau & Reid, supra, at 112.

* * *

Even without employing brutality, the "third degree" or the specific stratagems described above, the very fact of custodial interrogation exacts a heavy toll on individual liberty and trades on the weakness of individuals.

* * *

In the cases before us today, given this background, we concern ourselves primarily with this interrogation atmosphere and the evils it can bring. In No. 759, *Miranda v. Arizona,* the police arrested the defendant and took him to a special interrogation room where they secured a confession. In No. 760, *Vignera v. New York,* the defendant made oral admissions to the police after interrogation in the afternoon, and then signed an inculpatory statement upon being questioned by an assistant district attorney later the same evening. In No. 761, *Westover v. United States,* the defendant was handed over to the Federal Bureau of Investigation by local authorities after they had detained and interrogated him for a lengthy period, both at night and the following morning. After some two hours of questioning, the federal officers had obtained signed statements from the defendant. Lastly, in No. 584, *California v. Stewart,* the local police held the defendant five days in the station and interrogated him on nine separate occasions before they secured his inculpatory statement.

In these cases, we might not find the defendants' statements to have been involuntary in traditional terms. Our concern for adequate safeguards to protect precious Fifth Amendment rights is, of course, not lessened in the slightest. In each of the cases, the defendant was thrust into an unfamiliar atmosphere and run through menacing police interrogation procedures. The potentiality for compulsion is forcefully apparent, for example, in *Miranda,* where the indigent Mexican defendant was a seriously disturbed individual with pronounced sexual fantasies, and in *Stewart,* in which the defendant was an indigent Los Angeles Negro who had dropped out of school in the sixth grade. To be sure, the records do not evince overt physical coercion or patent psychological ploys. The fact remains that in none of these cases did the officers undertake to afford appropriate safeguards at the outset of the interrogation to insure that the statements were truly the product of free choice.

It is obvious that such an interrogation environment is created for no purpose other than to subjugate the individual to the will of his examiner. This atmosphere carries its own badge of intimidation. To be sure, this is not physical intimidation, but it is equally destructive of human dignity. The current practice of incommunicado interrogation is at odds with one of our Nation's most cherished principles—that the individual may not be compelled to incriminate himself. Unless adequate protective devices are employed to dispel the compulsion inherent in custodial surroundings, no statement obtained from the defendant can truly be the product of his free choice.

From the foregoing, we can readily perceive an intimate connection between the privilege against self-incrimination and police custodial questioning. It is fitting to turn to history and precedent underlying the Self-Incrimination Clause to determine its applicability in this situation.

II

We sometimes forget how long it has taken to establish the privilege against self-incrimination, the sources from which it came and the fervor with which it was defended. Its roots go back into ancient times. Perhaps the critical historical event shedding light on its origins and evolution was the trial of one John Lilburn, a vocal anti-Stuart Leveller, who was made to take the Star Chamber Oath in 1637. The oath would have bound him to answer to all questions posed to him on any subject. The Trial of *John Lilburn and John Wharton*, 3 How.St.Tr. 1315 (1637). He resisted the oath and declaimed the proceedings, stating:

> "Another fundamental right I then contended for, was, that no man's conscience ought to be racked by oaths imposed, to answer to questions concerning himself in matters criminal, or pretended to be so." Haller & Davies, The Leveller Tracts 1647–1653, p. 454 (1944).

On account of the *Lilburn* Trial, Parliament abolished the inquisitorial Court of Star Chamber and went further in giving him generous reparation. The lofty principles to which Lilburn had appealed during his trial gained popular acceptance in England. These sentiments worked their way over to the Colonies and were implanted after great struggle into the Bill of Rights. Those who framed our Constitution and the Bill of Rights were ever aware of subtle encroachments on individual liberty.

*   *   *

The question in these cases is whether the privilege is fully applicable during a period of custodial interrogation.

*   *   *

This question, in fact, could have been taken as settled in federal courts almost 70 years ago, when, in *Bram v. United States*, 168 U.S. 532, 542, 18 S.Ct. 183, 187, 42 L.Ed. 568 (1897), this Court held:

> "In criminal trials, in the courts of the United States, wherever a question arises whether a confession is incompetent because not voluntary, the issue is controlled by that portion of the fifth amendment *   *   * commanding that no person 'shall be compelled in any criminal case to be a witness against himself.'"

*   *   *

Because of the adoption by Congress of Rule 5 (a) of the Federal Rules of Criminal Procedure, and the Court's effectuation of that Rule in *McNabb v.*

United States, 318 U.S. 332, 63 S.Ct. 608, 87 L.Ed. 819 (1943), and *Mallory v. United States,* 354 U.S. 449, 77 S.Ct. 1356, 1 L.Ed.2d 1479 (1957), we have had little occasion in the past quarter century to reach the constitutional issues in dealing with federal interrogations. These supervisory rules, requiring production of an arrested person before a commissioner "without unnecessary delay" and excluding evidence obtained in default of that statutory obligation, were nonetheless responsive to the same considerations of Fifth Amendment policy that unavoidably face us now as to the States.

* * *

Our decision in *Malloy v. Hogan,* 378 U.S. 1, 84 S.Ct. 1489, 12 L.Ed.2d 653 (1964), necessitates an examination of the scope of the privilege in state cases as well. In *Malloy,* we squarely held the privilege applicable to the States, and held that the substantive standards underlying the privilege applied with full force to state court proceedings.

* * *

Aside from the holding itself, the reasoning in *Malloy* made clear what had already become apparent—that the substantive and procedural safeguards surrounding admissibility of confessions in state cases had become exceedingly exacting, reflecting all the policies embedded in the privilege, 378 U.S., at 7–8. The voluntariness doctrine in the state cases, as *Malloy* indicates, encompasses all interrogation practices which are likely to exert such pressure upon an individual as to disable him from making a free and rational choice. The implications of this proposition were elaborated in our decision in *Escobedo v. Illinois,* 378 U.S. 478, decided one week after *Malloy* applied the privilege to the States.

Our holding there stressed the fact that the police had not advised the defendant of his constitutional privilege to remain silent at the outset of the interrogation, and we drew attention to that fact at several points in the decision, 378 U.S., at 483, 485, 491. This was no isolated factor, but an essential ingredient in our decision. The entire thrust of police interrogation there, as in all the cases today, was to put the defendant in such an emotional state as to impair his capacity for rational judgment. The abdication of the constitutional privilege—the choice on his part to speak to the police—was not made knowingly or competently because of the failure to apprise him of his rights; the compelling atmosphere of the in-custody interrogation, and not an independent decision on his part, caused the defendant to speak.

A different phase of the *Escobedo* decision was significant in its attention to the absence of counsel during the questioning. There, as in the cases today, we sought a protective device to dispel the compelling atmosphere of the interrogation. In *Escobedo,* however, the police did not relieve the defendant of the anxieties which they had created in the interrogation rooms. Rather, they denied his request for the assistance of counsel, 378 U.S., at 481, 488, 491. This heightened his dilemma, and made his later statements the product of this compulsion.

* * *

It was in this manner that *Escobedo* explicated another facet of the pretrial privilege, noted in many of the Court's prior decisions: the protection of rights at trial. That counsel is present when statements are taken from an individual during interrogation obviously enhances the integrity of the fact-finding processes in court. The presence of an attorney, and the warnings delivered to the individual, enable the defendant under otherwise compelling circumstances to tell his story without fear, effectively, and in a way that eliminates the evils in the interrogation process.

*   *   *

III

Today, then, there can be no doubt that the Fifth Amendment privilege is available outside of criminal court proceedings and serves to protect persons in all settings in which their freedom of action is curtailed in any significant way from being compelled to incriminate themselves. We have concluded that without proper safeguards the process of in-custody interrogation of persons suspected or accused of crime contains inherently compelling pressures which work to undermine the individual's will to resist and to compel him to speak where he would not otherwise do so freely. In order to combat these pressures and to permit a full opportunity to exercise the privilege against self-incrimination, the accused must be adequately and effectively apprised of his rights and the exercise of those rights must be fully honored.

It is impossible for us to foresee the potential alternatives for protecting the privilege which might be devised by Congress or the States in the exercise of their creative rule-making capacities. Therefore we cannot say that the Constitution necessarily requires adherence to any particular solution for the inherent compulsions of the interrogation process as it is presently conducted. Our decision in no way creates a constitutional strait-jacket which will handicap sound efforts at reform, nor is it intended to have this effect. We encourage Congress and the States to continue their laudable search for increasingly effective ways of protecting the rights of the individual while promoting efficient enforcement of our criminal laws. However, unless we are shown other procedures which are at least as effective in apprising accused persons of their right of silence and in assuring a continuous opportunity to exercise it, the following safeguards must be observed.

At the outset, if a person in custody is to be subjected to interrogation, he must first be informed in clear and unequivocal terms that he has the right to remain silent. For those unaware of the privilege, the warning is needed simply to make them aware of it—the threshold requirement for an intelligent decision as to its exercise. More important, such a warning is an absolute prerequisite in overcoming the inherent pressures of the interrogation atmosphere. It is not just the subnormal or woefully ignorant who succumb to an interrogator's imprecations, whether implied or expressly stated, that the interrogation will continue until a confession is obtained or that silence in the face of accusation is itself damning and will bode ill when presented to a jury. Further, the warning will show the individual that his interrogators are prepared to recognize his privilege should he choose to exercise it.

The Fifth Amendment privilege is so fundamental to our system of constitutional rule and the expedient of giving an adequate warning as to the availability of the privilege so simple, we will not pause to inquire in individual cases whether the defendant was aware of his rights without a warning being given. Assessments of the knowledge the defendant possessed, based on information as to his age, education, intelligence, or prior contact with authorities, can never be more than speculation; a warning is a clearcut fact. More important, whatever the background of the person interrogated, a warning at the time of the interrogation is indispensable to overcome its pressures and to insure that the individual knows he is free to exercise the privilege at that point in time.

The warning of the right to remain silent must be accompanied by the explanation that anything said can and will be used against the individual in court. This warning is needed in order to make him aware not only of the privilege, but also of the consequences of forgoing it. It is only through an awareness of these consequences that there can be any assurance of real understanding and intelligent exercise of the privilege. Moreover, this warning may serve to make the individual more acutely aware that he is faced with a phase of the adversary system—that he is not in the presence of persons acting solely in his interest.

The circumstances surrounding in-custody interrogation can operate very quickly to overbear the will of one merely made aware of his privilege by his interrogators. Therefore the right to have counsel present at the interrogation is indispensable to the protection of the Fifth Amendment privilege under the system we delineate today.

*   *   *

The presence of counsel at the interrogation may serve several significant subsidiary functions as well. If the accused decides to talk to his interrogators, the assistance of counsel can mitigate the dangers of untrustworthiness. With a lawyer present the likelihood that the police will practice coercion is reduced, and if coercion is nevertheless exercised the lawyer can testify to it in court. The presence of a lawyer can also help to guarantee that the accused gives a fully accurate statement to the police and that the statement is rightly reported by the prosecution at trial.

An individual need not make a pre-interrogation request for a lawyer. While such request affirmatively secures his right to have one, his failure to ask for a lawyer does not constitute a waiver. No effective waiver of the right to counsel during interrogation can be recognized unless specifically made after the warnings we here delineate have been given. The accused who does not know his rights and therefore does not make a request may be the person who most needs counsel.

*   *   *

Accordingly we hold that an individual held for interrogation must be clearly informed that he has the right to consult with a lawyer and to have the lawyer with him during interrogation under the system for protecting the privilege we delineate today. As with the warnings of the right to remain silent and that anything stated can be used in evidence against him, this warning is an absolute prerequisite to interrogation. No amount of circumstantial evidence that the person may have been aware of this right will suffice to stand in its stead. Only through such a warning is there ascertainable assurance that the accused was aware of this right.

If an individual indicates that he wishes the assistance of counsel before any interrogation occurs, the authorities cannot rationally ignore or deny his request on the basis that the individual does not have or cannot afford a retained attorney.

* * *

Denial of counsel to the indigent at the time of interrogation while allowing an attorney to those who can afford one would be no more supportable by reason or logic than the similar situation at trial and on appeal struck down in *Gideon v. Wainwright,* 372 U.S. 335, 83 S.Ct. 792, 9 L.Ed.2d 799 (1963), and *Douglas v. People of State of California,* 372 U.S. 353, 83 S.Ct. 814, 9 L.Ed.2d 811 (1963) [See Chapter 21, infra.]

In order fully to apprise a person interrogated of the extent of his rights under this system then, it is necessary to warn him not only that he has the right to consult with an attorney, but also that if he is indigent a lawyer will be appointed to represent him. Without this additional warning, the admonition of the right to consult with counsel would often be understood as meaning only that he can consult with a lawyer if he has one or has the funds to obtain one. The warning of a right to counsel would be hollow if not couched in terms that would convey to the indigent—the person most often subjected to interrogation—the knowledge that he too has a right to have counsel present. As with the warnings of the right to remain silent and of the general right to counsel, only by effective and express explanation to the indigent of this right can there be assurance that he was truly in a position to exercise it.

Once warnings have been given, the subsequent procedure is clear. If the individual indicates in any manner, at any time prior to or during questioning, that he wishes to remain silent, the interrogation must cease. At this point he has shown that he intends to exercise his Fifth Amendment privilege; any statement taken after the person invokes his privilege cannot be other than the product of compulsion, subtle or otherwise. Without the right to cut off questioning, the setting of in-custody interrogation operates on the individual to overcome free choice in producing a statement after the privilege has been once invoked. If the individual states that he wants an attorney, the interrogation must cease until an attorney is present. At that time, the individual must have an opportunity to confer with the attorney and to have him present during any subsequent questioning. If the individual cannot obtain an attorney and he indicates that he wants one before speaking to police, they must respect his decision to remain silent.

This does not mean, as some have suggested, that each police station must have a "station house lawyer" present at all times to advise prisoners. It does mean, however, that if police propose to interrogate a person they must make known to him that he is entitled to a lawyer and that if he cannot afford one, a lawyer will be provided for him prior to any interrogation. If authorities conclude that they will not provide counsel during a reasonable period of time in which investigation in the field is carried out, they may refrain from doing so without violating the person's Fifth Amendment privilege so long as they do not question him during that time.

If the interrogation continues without the presence of an attorney and a statement is taken, a heavy burden rests on the government to demonstrate that the defendant knowingly and intelligently waived his privilege against self-incrimination and his right to retained or appointed counsel. *Escobedo v. State of Illinois,* 378 U.S. 478, 490, n. 14, 84 S.Ct. 1758, 1764, 12 L.Ed.2d 977. This Court has always set high standards of proof for the waiver of constitutional rights, *Johnson v. Zerbst,* 304 U.S. 458, 58 S.Ct. 1019, 82 L.Ed. 1461 (1938), and we reassert these standards as applied to in-custody interrogation. Since the State is responsible for establishing the isolated circumstances under which the interrogation takes place and has the only means of making available corroborated evidence of warnings given during incommunicado interrogation, the burden is rightly on its shoulders.

An express statement that the individual is willing to make a statement and does not want an attorney followed closely by a statement could constitute a waiver. But a valid waiver will not be presumed simply from the silence of the accused after warnings are given or simply from the fact that a confession was in fact eventually obtained. A statement we made in *Carnley v. Cochran,* 369 U.S. 506, 516, 82 S.Ct. 884, 890, 8 L.Ed.2d 70 (1962), is applicable here:

> "Presuming waiver from a silent record is impermissible. The record must show, or there must be an allegation and evidence which show, that an accused was offered counsel but intelligently and understandingly rejected the offer. Anything less is not waiver."

Moreover, where in-custody interrogation is involved, there is no room for the contention that the privilege is waived if the individual answers some questions or gives some information on his own prior to invoking his right to remain silent when interrogated.

Whatever the testimony of the authorities as to waiver of rights by an accused, the fact of lengthy interrogation or incommunicado incarceration before a statement is made is strong evidence that the accused did not validly waive his rights. In these circumstances the fact that the individual eventually made a statement is consistent with the conclusion that the compelling influence of the interrogation finally forced him to do so. It is inconsistent with any notion of a voluntary relinquishment of the privilege. Moreover, any evidence that the accused was threatened, tricked, or cajoled into a waiver will, of course, show that the defendant did not voluntarily waive his privilege. The requirement of warnings and waiver of rights is a fundamental with respect to the Fifth Amendment privilege and not simply a preliminary ritual to existing methods of interrogation.

The warnings required and the waiver necessary in accordance with our opinion today are, in the absence of a fully effective equivalent, prerequisites to the admissibility of any statement made by a defendant. No distinction can be drawn between statements which are direct confessions and statements which amount to "admissions" of part or all of an offense. The privilege against self-incrimination protects the individual from being compelled to incriminate himself in any manner; it does not distinguish degrees of incrimination. Similarly, for precisely the same reason, no distinction may be drawn between inculpatory statements and statements alleged to be merely "exculpatory." If a statement made were in fact truly exculpatory it would, of course, never be used by the prosecution. In fact, statements merely intended to be exculpatory by the defendant are often used to impeach his testimony at trial or to demonstrate untruths in the statement given under interrogation and thus to prove guilt by implication. These statements are incriminating in any meaningful sense of the word and may not be used without the full warnings and effective waiver required for any other statement. In *Escobedo* itself, the defendant fully intended his accusation of another as the slayer to be exculpatory as to himself.

The principles announced today deal with the protection which must be given to the privilege against self-incrimination when the individual is first subjected to police interrogation while in custody at the station or otherwise deprived of his freedom of action in any significant way. It is at this point that our adversary system of criminal proceedings commences, distinguishing itself at the outset from the inquisitorial system recognized in some countries. Under the system of warnings we delineate today or under any other system which may be devised and found effective, the safeguards to be erected about the privilege must come into play at this point.

Our decision is not intended to hamper the traditional function of police officers in investigating crime. See *Escobedo v. State of Illinois*, 378 U.S. 478, 492, 84 S.Ct. 1758, 1765. When an individual is in custody on probable cause, the police may, of course, seek out evidence in the field to be used at trial against him. Such investigation may include inquiry of persons not under restraint. General on-the-scene questioning as to facts surrounding a crime or other general questioning of citizens in the fact-finding process is not affected by our holding. It is an act of responsible citizenship for individuals to give whatever information they may have to aid in law enforcement. In such situations the compelling atmosphere inherent in the process of in-custody interrogation is not necessarily present.

In dealing with statements obtained through interrogation, we do not purport to find all confessions inadmissible. Confessions remain a proper element in law enforcement. Any statement given freely and voluntarily without any compelling influences is, of course, admissible in evidence. The fundamental import of the privilege while an individual is in custody is not whether he is allowed to talk to the police without the benefit of warnings and counsel, but whether he can be interrogated. There is no requirement that police stop a person who enters a police station and states that he wishes to confess to a crime, or a person who calls the police to offer a confession or any other statement he desires to make. Volunteered statements of any kind are not barred by the Fifth Amendment and their admissibility is not affected by our holding today.

* * *

IV

* * *

In announcing these principles, we are not unmindful of the burdens which law enforcement officials must bear, often under trying circumstances. We also fully recognize the obligation of all citizens to aid in enforcing the criminal laws. This Court, while protecting individual rights, has always given ample latitude to law enforcement agencies in the legitimate exercise of their duties. The limits we have placed on the interrogation process should not constitute an undue interference with a proper system of law enforcement. As we have noted, our decision does not in any way preclude police from carrying out their traditional investigatory functions. Although confessions may play an important role in some convictions, the cases before us present graphic examples of the overstatement of the "need" for confessions. In each case authorities conducted interrogations ranging up to five days in duration despite the presence, through standard investigating practices, of considerable evidence against each defendant.

* * *

Over the years the Federal Bureau of Investigation has compiled an exemplary record of effective law enforcement while advising any suspect or arrested person, at the outset of an interview, that he is not required to make a statement, that any statement may be used against him in court, that the individual may obtain the services of an attorney of his own choice and, more recently, that he has a right to free counsel if he is unable to pay. A letter received from the Solicitor General in response to a question from the Bench makes it clear that the present pattern of warnings and respect for the rights of the individual followed as a practice by the FBI is consistent with the procedure which we delineate today. It states:

> "At the oral argument of the above cause, Mr. Justice Fortas asked whether I could provide certain information as to the practices followed by the Federal Bureau of Investigation. I have directed these questions to the attention of the Director of the Federal Bureau of Investigation and am submitting herewith a statement of the questions and of the answers which we have received.
>
> " '(1) When an individual is interviewed by agents of the Bureau, what warning is given to him?
>
> " 'The standard warning long given by Special Agents of the FBI to both suspects and persons under arrest is that the person has a right to say nothing and a right to counsel, and that any statement he does make may be used against him in court. Examples of this warning are to be found in the *Westover* case at 342 F.2d 684 (1965), and *Jackson v. U.S.,* [119 U.S.App.D.C. 100] 337 F.2d 136 (1964), cert. den. 380 U.S. 935, 85 S.Ct. 1353.
>
> " 'After passage of the Criminal Justice Act of 1964, which provides free counsel for Federal defendants unable to pay, we added to our instructions to Special Agents the requirement that any person who is under arrest for an offense under FBI

jurisdiction, or whose arrest is contemplated following the interview, must also be advised of his right to free counsel if he is unable to pay, and the fact that such counsel will be assigned by the Judge. At the same time, we broadened the right to counsel warning to read counsel of his own choice, or anyone else with whom he might wish to speak.

" '(2) When is the warning given?

" 'The FBI warning is given to a suspect at the very outset of the interview * * *, as shown in the *Westover* case, cited above. The warning may be given to a person arrested as soon as practicable after the arrest * * * but in any event it must precede the interview with the person for a confession or admission of his own guilt.

" '(3) What is the Bureau's practice in the event that (a) the individual requests counsel and (b) counsel appears?

" 'When the person who has been warned of his right to counsel decides that he wishes to consult with counsel before making a statement, the interview is terminated at that point, *Shultz v. U. S.*, 351 F.2d 287 ([10 Cir.] 1965). It may be continued, however, as to all matters *other* than the person's own guilt or innocence. If he is indecisive in his request for counsel, there may be some question on whether he did or did not waive counsel. Situations of this kind must necessarily be left to the judgment of the interviewing Agent.

* * *

" '(4) What is the Bureau's practice if the individual requests counsel, but cannot afford to retain an attorney?

" 'If any person being interviewed after warning of counsel decides that he wishes to consult with counsel before proceeding further the interview is terminated, as shown above. FBI Agents do not pass judgment on the ability of the person to pay for counsel. They do, however, advise those who have been arrested for an offense under FBI jurisdiction, or whose arrest is contemplated following the interview, of a right to free counsel *if* they are unable to pay, and the availability of such counsel from the Judge.' "

The practice of the FBI can readily be emulated by state and local enforcement agencies. The argument that the FBI deals with different crimes than are dealt with by state authorities does not mitigate the significance of the FBI experience.

The experience in some other countries also suggests that the danger to law enforcement in curbs on interrogation is overplayed. The English procedure since 1912 under the Judges' Rules is significant. As recently strengthened, the Rules require that a cautionary warning be given an accused by a police officer as soon as he has evidence that affords reasonable grounds for suspicion; they also require that any statement made be given by the accused without questioning by police. The right of the individual to consult with an attorney during this period is expressly recognized.

The safeguards present under Scottish law may be even greater than in England. Scottish judicial decisions bar use in evidence of most confessions obtained through police interrogation. In India, confessions made to police not in the presence of a magistrate have been excluded by rule of evidence since 1872, at a time when it operated under British law. Identical provisions appear in the Evidence Ordinance of Ceylon, enacted in 1895. Similarly, in our country the Uniform Code of Military Justice has long provided that no suspect may be interrogated without first being warned of his right not to make a statement and that any statement he makes may be used against him. Denial of the right to consult counsel during interrogation has also been proscribed by military tribunals. There appears to have been no marked detrimental effect on criminal law enforcement in these jurisdictions as a result of these rules. Conditions of law enforcement in our country are sufficiently similar to permit reference to this experience as assurance that lawlessness will not result from warning an individual of his rights or allowing him to exercise them. Moreover, it is consistent with our legal system that we give at least as much protection to these rights as is given in the jurisdictions described. We deal in our country with rights grounded in a specific requirement of the Fifth Amendment of the Constitution, whereas other jurisdictions arrived at their conclusions on the basis of principles of justice not so specifically defined.

*   *   *

V

*   *   *

Therefore, in accordance with the foregoing, the judgments of the Supreme Court of Arizona in No. 759, of the New York Court of Appeals in No. 760, and of the Court of Appeals for the Ninth Circuit in No. 761 are reversed. The judgment of the Supreme Court of California in No. 584 is affirmed. It is so ordered.

*   *   *

Mr. Justice HARLAN, whom Mr. Justice STEWART and Mr. Justice WHITE join, dissenting.

*   *   *

The earliest confession cases in this Court emerged from federal prosecutions and were settled on a nonconstitutional basis, the Court adopting the common-law rule that the absence of inducements, promises, and threats made a confession voluntary and admissible. *Hopt v. People of Territory of Utah*, 110 U.S. 574, 4 S.Ct. 202, 28 L.Ed. 262; *Pierce v. United States*, 160 U.S. 355, 16 S.Ct. 321, 40 L.Ed. 454. While a later case said the Fifth Amendment privilege controlled admissibility, this proposition was not itself developed in subsequent decisions. The Court did, however, heighten the test of admissibility in federal trials to one of voluntariness "in fact," *Ziang Sung Wan v. United States*, 266 U.S. 1, 14, 45 S.Ct. 1, 3, 69 L.Ed. 131 and then by and large left federal judges to apply the same standards the Court began to derive in a string of state court cases.

This new line of decisions, testing admissibility by the Due Process Clause, began in 1936 with *Brown v. State of Mississippi*, 297 U.S. 278, 56 S.Ct. 461, 80 L.Ed. 682, and must now embrace somewhat more than 30 full opinions of the Court. While the voluntariness rubric was repeated in many instances, the Court never pinned it down to a single meaning but on the contrary infused it with a number of different values. To travel quickly over the main themes, there was an initial emphasis on reliability, e. g., *Ward v. State of Texas,* 316 U.S. 547, 62 S.Ct. 1139, 86 L.Ed. 1663, supplemented by concern over the legality and fairness of the police practices, e. g., *Ashcraft v. State of Tennessee,* 322 U.S. 143, 64 S.Ct. 921, 88 L.Ed. 1192, in an "accusatorial" system of law enforcement, *Watts v. State of Indiana,* 338 U.S. 49, 54, 69 S.Ct. 1347, 1350, 93 L.Ed. 1801, and eventually by close attention to the individual's state of mind and capacity for effective choice, e. g., *Gallegos v. State of Colorado,* 370 U.S. 49, 82 S.Ct. 1209, 8 L.Ed.2d 325. The outcome was a continuing re-evaluation on the facts of each case of *how much* pressure on the suspect was permissible.[4]

[4.]Bator & Vorenberg, Arrest, Detention, Interrogation and the Right to Counsel, 66 Col.L.Rev. 62. 73 (1966): "In fact, the concept of involuntariness seems to be used by the courts as a shorthand to refer to practices which are repellent to civilized standards of decency or which, under the circumstances, are thought to apply a degree of pressure to an individual which unfairly impairs his capacity to make a rational choice."

Among the criteria often taken into account were threats or imminent danger, e. g., *Payne v. State of Arkansas,* 356 U.S. 560, 78 S.Ct. 844, 2 L.Ed.2d 975, physical deprivations such as lack of sleep or food, e. g., *Reck v. Pate,* 367 U.S. 433, 81 S.Ct. 1541, 6 L.Ed. 2d 948, repeated or extended interrogation, e. g., *Chambers v. State of Florida,* 309 U.S. 227, 60 S.Ct. 472, 84 L.Ed. 716, limits on access to counsel or friends, *Crooker v. State of California,* 357 U.S. 433, 78 S.Ct. 1287, 2 L.Ed.2d 1448; *Cicenia v. La Gay,* 357 U.S. 504, 78 S.Ct. 1297, 2 L.Ed.2d 1523, length and illegality of detention under state law, e. g., *Haynes v. State of Washington,* 373 U.S. 503, 83 S. Ct. 1336, 10 L.Ed.2d 513, and individual weakness or incapacities, *Lynumn v. State of Illinois,* 372 U.S. 528, 83 S.Ct. 917, 9 L.Ed.2d 922. Apart from direct physical coercion, however, no single default or fixed combination of defaults guaranteed exclusion, and synopses of the cases would serve little use because the overall gauge has been steadily changing, usually in the direction of restricting admissibility.

* * *

I turn now to the Court's asserted reliance on the Fifth Amendment, an approach which I frankly regard as a *trompe l'oeil.* * * * Historically, the privilege against self-incrimination did not bear at all on the use of extra-legal confessions, for which distinct standards evolved; indeed, "the *history* of the two principles is wide apart, differing by one hundred years in origin, and derived through separate lines of precedents. * * *" 8 Wigmore, Evidence § 2266, at 401 (McNaughton rev. 1961). Practice under the two doctrines has also differed in a number of important respects.

* * *

Having decided that the Fifth Amendment privilege does apply in the police station, the Court reveals that the privilege imposes more exacting restrictions than does the Fourteenth Amendment's voluntariness test. It then emerges from a discussion of *Escobedo* that the Fifth Amendment requires for an admissible confession that it be given by one distinctly aware of his right not to speak and shielded from "the compelling atmosphere" of interrogation. From these key premises, the Court finally develops the safeguards of warning, counsel, and so forth. I do not believe these premises are sustained by precedents under the Fifth Amendment.

The more important premise is that pressure on the suspect must be eliminated though it be only the subtle influence of the atmosphere and surroundings. The Fifth Amendment, however, has never been thought to forbid *all* pressure to incriminate one's self in the situations covered by it. On the contrary, it has been held that failure to incriminate one's self can result in denial of removal of one's case from state to federal court, *State of Maryland v. Soper,* 270 U.S. 9, 46 S.Ct. 185, 70 L.Ed. 449; in refusal of a military commission, *Orloff v. Willoughby,* 345 U.S. 83, 73 S.Ct. 534, 97 L.Ed. 842; in denial of a discharge in bankruptcy, *Kaufman v. Hurwitz,* 4 Cir., 176 F.2d 210; and in numerous other adverse consequences.

*   *   *

The Court appears similarly wrong in thinking that precise knowledge of one's rights is a settled prerequisite under the Fifth Amendment to the loss of its protections. A number of lower federal court cases have held that grand jury witnesses need not always be warned of their privilege, e. g., *United States v. Scully,* 2 Cir., 225 F.2d 113, 116, and Wigmore states this to be the better rule for trial witnesses. See 8 Wigmore, Evidence § 2269 (McNaughton rev. 1961).

*   *   *

A closing word must be said about the Assistance of Counsel Clause of the Sixth Amendment, which is never expressly relied on by the Court but whose judicial precedents turn out to be linchpins of the confession rules announced today.

*   *   *

The only attempt in this Court to carry the right to counsel into the station house occurred in *Escobedo,* the Court repeating several times that that stage was no less "critical" than trial itself. This is hardly persuasive when we consider that a grand jury inquiry, the filing of a certiorari petition, and certainly the purchase of narcotics by an undercover agent from a prospective defendant may all be equally "critical" yet provision of counsel and advice on the score have never been thought compelled by the Constitution in such cases. The sound reason why this right is so freely extended for a criminal trial is the severe injustice risked by confronting an untrained defendant with a range of technical points of law, evidence, and tactics familiar to the prosecutor but not to himself. This danger shrinks markedly in the police station where indeed the lawyer in fulfilling his professional responsibilities of necessity may become an obstacle to truthfinding.

*   *   *

What the Court largely ignores is that its rules impair, if they will not eventually serve wholly to frustrate, an instrument of law enforcement that has long and quite reasonably been thought worth the price paid for it. There can be little doubt that the Court's new code would markedly decrease the number of confessions. To warn the suspect that he may remain silent and remind him that his confession may be used in court are minor obstructions. To require also an express waiver by the suspect and an end to questioning whenever he demurs must heavily handicap questioning. And to suggest or provide counsel for the suspect simply invites the end of the interrogation.

* * *

While passing over the costs and risks of its experiment, the Court portrays the evils of normal police questioning in terms which I think are exaggerated. Albeit stringently confined by the due process standards interrogation is no doubt often inconvenient and unpleasant for the suspect. However, it is no less so for a man to be arrested and jailed, to have his house searched, or to stand trial in court, yet all this may properly happen to the most innocent given probable cause, a warrant, or an indictment. Society has always paid a stiff price for law and order, and peaceful interrogation is not one of the dark moments of the law.

* * *

The Court in closing its general discussion invokes the practice in federal and foreign jurisdictions as lending weight to its new curbs on confessions for all the States. A brief résumé will suffice to show that none of these jurisdictions has struck so one-sided a balance as the Court does today. Heaviest reliance is placed on the FBI practice. Differing circumstances may make this comparison quite untrustworthy,[19] but in any event the FBI falls sensibly short of the Court's formalistic rules. For example, there is no indication that FBI agents must obtain an affirmative "waiver" before they pursue their questioning. Nor is it clear that one invoking his right to silence may not be prevailed upon to change his mind. And the warning as to appointed counsel apparently indicates only that one will be assigned by the judge when the suspect appears before him; the thrust of the Court's rules is to induce the suspect to obtain appointed counsel before continuing the interview. Apparently American military practice, briefly mentioned by the Court, has these same limits and is still less favorable to the suspect than the FBI warning, making no mention of appointed counsel.

[19.]The Court's *obiter dictum* notwithstanding, there is some basis for believing that the staple of FBI criminal work differs importantly from much crime within the ken of local police. The skill and resources of the FBI may also be unusual.

The law of the foreign countries described by the Court also reflects a more moderate conception of the rights of the accused as against those of society when other data are considered. Concededly, the English experience is most relevant. In that country, a caution as to silence but not counsel has long been mandated by the "Judges' Rules," which also place other somewhat imprecise limits on police cross-examination of suspects. However, in the court's discretion confessions can be and apparently quite frequently are admitted in evidence despite disregard of the Judges' Rules, so long as they are found voluntary under the common-law test. Moreover, the check that exists on the use of pretrial statements is counter-balanced by the evident admissibility of fruits of an illegal confession and by the judge's often-used authority to comment adversely on the defendant's failure to testify.

India, Ceylon and Scotland are the other examples chosen by the Court. In India and Ceylon the general ban on police-adduced confessions cited by the Court is subject to a major exception: if evidence is uncovered by police questioning, it is fully admissible at trial along with the confession itself, so far as it relates to the evidence and is not blatantly coerced. Scotland's limits on interrogation do measure up to the Court's; however, restrained comment at trial on the defendant's failure to take the stand is allowed the judge, and in many other respects Scotch law redresses the prosecutor's disadvantage in ways not permitted in this country. The Court ends its survey by imputing added strength to our privilege against self-incrimination since, by contrast to other countries, it is embodied in a written Constitution. Considering the liberties the Court has today taken with constitutional history and precedent, few will find this emphasis persuasive.

In closing this necessarily truncated discussion of policy considerations attending the new confession rules, some reference must be made to their ironic untimeliness. There is now in progress in this country a massive re-examination of criminal law enforcement procedures on a scale never before witnessed. Participants in this undertaking include a Special Committee of the American Bar Association, under the chairmanship of Chief Judge Lumbard of the Court of Appeals for the Second Circuit; a distinguished study group of the American Law Institute, headed by Professors Vorenberg and Bator of the Harvard Law School; and the President's Commission on Law Enforcement and Administration of Justice, under the leadership of the Attorney General of the United States.[22] Studies are also being conducted by the District of Columbia Crime disclaimer, the practical effect of the decision made today must inevitably be to handicap seriously sound efforts at reform, not least by removing options necessary to a just compromise of competing interests. Of course legislative reform is rarely speedy or unanimous, though this Court has been more patient in the past. But the legislative reforms when they come would have the vast advantage of empirical data and comprehensive study, they would allow experimentation and use of solutions not open to the courts, and they would restore the initiative in criminal law reform to those forums where it truly belongs.

---

[22]Of particular relevance is the ALI's drafting of a Model Code of Pre-Arraignment Procedure, now in its first tentative draft. While the ABA and National Commission studies have wider scope, the former is lending its advice to the ALI project and the executive director of the latter is one of the reporters for the Model Code.

[Dissenting opinions of Justice Clark and Justice White, with whom Justices Harlan and Stewart joined, are omitted.]

Glossary

a

acquittal: A legal discharge from guilt for an accused person.

adjudication: A court's decision, or the process of reaching that decision.

administrative warrant: A search warrant issued to check private premises for compliance with local ordinances.

admissible evidence: Evidence that meets the fairness requirements to be considered by the court.

admission: A statement or acknowledgment of facts.

adversarial system: A legal system such as that used in the United States, which places one party against another to resolve a legal issue. Also called *adversary system.*

affiant: A person who signs an affidavit.

affidavit: A sworn statement in writing made under oath.

affirm: A court agreeing with a lower court's decision.

affirmative action: Programs created to spread equal opportunity throughout the diverse American population. Sometimes referred to as *ethnic- and gender-preference programs.*

alibi: A defense asserting that the accused was elsewhere when an act was committed.

amendments: Changes to a constitution or bylaws.

American Dream: Refers to the belief that through hard work anyone can have success and ample material possessions.

amicus curiae: Latin for "friend of the court." A person or organization that is not a party to a legal action, but provides an "amicus brief" to give the court additional facts or arguments regarding a specific case.

Anti-Federalists: Colonists who opposed a strong federal government.

appeal: A review by a higher court.

appearing pro se: Appearing in court without an attorney, representing oneself.

appellant: One who appeals a case.

appellate court: A court that reviews a case appealed from a lower court.

appellate jurisdiction: Describes a court authorized to review cases and to either affirm or reverse the actions of a lower court.

arraignment: Usually the first appearance by a defendant at which time the person is advised of his or her rights, advised of the charges and given the opportunity to enter a plea.

arrest: The detention of an individual; the taking of a person into custody, in the manner authorized by law, for the purpose of presenting that person before a magistrate to answer for the commission of a crime.

b

articulable facts: Actions described in clear, distinct statements.

attenuation: The weakening of the link between illegally obtained evidence and evidence subsequently obtained.

bail: Money or property pledged by a defendant for pretrial release from custody that would be forfeited should the defendant fail to appear at subsequent court proceedings.

balancing test: Striking a balance between individual liberties and the demands of ordering a free society. A manner of decision making.

bifurcated trial: A two-step trial; the first step is determination of innocence or guilt, and the second step is determination of whether to seek the death penalty.

Bill of Rights: The first 10 amendments of the United States Constitution.

booking: The process by which a criminal defendant is officially identified in the arresting agency's records, usually by means of name, photo(s) and fingerprints.

brief: A summary presented to the court that describes the manner in which each side in a legal contest thinks the laws should apply to the facts of the case. To brief a case is to outline the pertinent facts of a case.

bright line approach: Determining the reasonableness of an action according to a specific rule that applies to all cases. In contrast to the case-by-case method.

c

capital crime: A crime punishable by death.

capital punishment: The death penalty.

caption: The title of a case setting forth the parties involved. For example, *Smith v. Jones.*

case law: Common law approach, so named because it is based on previous cases. Law that is decided by precedent set in prior cases brought before the legal system (courts). While constitutional law and statutes provide law that is general in nature, case law describes the results of a specific legal decision that will be used in considering future cases of a similar nature. The decision provides a legal precedent that future cases may rely upon in making decisions on similar facts. Case law may make new law or serve to define or clarify legal questions.

case-by-case method: Determining the reasonableness of an action by considering the totality of circumstances in each case. In contrast to the bright line approach.

certiorari: Latin for "to be informed." The Court uses this term to state which cases it will hear. Legal shorthand might simply state: "cert granted.".

child: *See* **juvenile.**

citation: The way a case is written to tell others where to find it through legal research. For example, *Miranda v. Arizona* is cited as *Miranda v. Arizona*, 384 U.S. 436 (1966), indicating the caption of the case (parties involved) and that the judicial opinion can be found in volume 384 of the U.S. Reports on page 436, and showing the case was decided in 1966. Additional cites might be included to reference other sources as well.

citizen's arrest: The detention of one accused of an illegal act, with such detention being authorized by statutes.

civil liberties: The general concept of rights that provide the freedoms that the framers of the United States Constitution sought to achieve. This is a combination of governmental restrictions and individual guarantees that shape our legal system.

civil rights: The specific rights that the Constitution guarantees so that individuals shall not be discriminated against because of their color, race or religion. The basic liberties that members of a state have, including freedom from excessive interference from the government.

civil wrong: *See* **tort.**

"clear and present danger" test: The test of whether words are so potentially dangerous as to not be protected by the First Amendment.

codified law: Law specifically set forth in organized, structured codes such as the United States criminal code, state statutes of local ordinances. Also called *statutory law.*

commercial bail: Using the services of a bail bondsman.

common law: Early English judge-made law based on custom and tradition. In a broad sense, it is the legal system that, like that of the United States, relies on the general customs and traditions of most English-speaking countries, deciding present cases on past decisions. It also refers to judge-made or case law, as differentiated from statutory or constitutional law.

compensatory damages: Reimbursement of the plaintiff for actual harm done such as medical expenses or lost business.

concur: Agree with a lower court's decision but for different reasons.

concurrent jurisdiction: Two or more courts authorized to hear a specific type of case.

confession: A statement or acknowledgment of facts by a person establishing that person's guilt of all elements of a crime.

constitution: A basic outline of the law of a state or nation. A constitution serves to provide both an outline of the governmental principles and procedures by which that government is to run, as well as to provide a philosophical and political statement as to what that government seeks to accomplish through its organization. A constitution provides a broad framework on which other laws are constructed.

constitutional law: The law developed from the broad and basic framework of a state or county legal system. All applicable law must conform with the basic construct of the constitution. For instance, all state laws must conform with the constitution of that state, and all laws in the United States (including federal, state and common law) must conform with the United States Constitution.

constitutional rights: The rights guaranteed by the Constitution of the United States, including the Bill of Rights.

constitutionalism: A belief in a government in which power is distributed and limited by a system of laws that must be obeyed by those who rule.

contraband: Anything that is illegal for people to own or have in their possession, for example illegal drugs or illegal weapons.

conventional Fourth Amendment approach: Viewing the reasonableness clause and the warrant clause as intertwined, that is, all reasonable searches require a warrant.

corporal punishment: Causing bodily harm, for example, whipping, flogging, beating.

court: A forum having lawful jurisdiction to decide specific disputes. Jurisdiction is granted by federal or state government.

court, federal: A court established by Article 3 of the United States Constitution, including the United States District Courts, United States Courts of Appeals and the United States Supreme Court.

court, inferior: A court from which an appeal is sent or a court with less authority than those above it.

court, state: A court within the states as authorized by the Tenth Amendment of the United States Constitution and state constitutions.

court, superior: The final court that may hear a case.

crime: A wrong against the government and the people it serves. While an individual has been victimized, the real victim is considered to be society itself. An act defined by federal or state statute or local ordinance that is punishable. A crime is a wrong against society, as compared to a tort, which is a wrong against an individual. An act could be both.

criminal law: Law dealing with defining crime and setting forth punishment. Criminal law is primarily statutory in nature. This is said to be substantive law, rather than procedural law.

criminal procedure: The body of law dealing with how criminal law is enforced (procedural rather than substantive). For example, procedural law deals with such areas as search and seizure.

curtilage: The portion of property generally associated with the common use of land, for example, buildings, sheds, fenced-in areas and the like. The property around a home or dwelling that is directly associated with the use of that property. The area protected by the Fourth Amendment.

custody: The detention of someone, which may or may not include actual physical contact.

damages: Financial compensation for injuries sustained by a victim of a crime or civil wrong.

de facto: Latin for "from the fact." De facto law is the law in effect, although not necessarily formally recognized. For example, while the de jure (official) speed limit on a highway may be 55 mph, traffic may be permitted to travel at a de facto speed limit of 60 mph without being stopped.

de jure: Latin for "of right." Refers to what the law is. For example, even if traffic is permitted to travel in excess of the speed limit, the de jure (official) speed limit is that set by law.

decree: Judicial determination and assertion.

defamation: Communication that damages the reputation of another. *See also* **libel** *and* **slander.**

defendant: A person charged by the government of committing a crime or of damaging another in a civil wrong.

defense attorney: The legal representation of the accused. Also called *defense lawyer* or *counsel.*

delegated powers: Powers of the government both enumerated and implied by legal authority.

demurrer: A request that a suit be dismissed because the facts do not sustain the claim against the defendant.

deponent: One who is deposed, or required to be questioned under oath during a deposition.

deposition: A statement made under oath other than in court.

dictum: (plural *dicta*). The statement by a court that may deal with other than the main issue in the case or additional discussion by the court.

discrimination: An action or behavior based on prejudice.

dissent: An opinion by a judge who disagrees with the majority decision of the court.

Doe, John or Jane: A fictitious identification used in legal proceedings involving parties who do not want to be called by name, are unknown or whose identity may not be revealed, e.g. juveniles.

due process of law: The Fifth and Fourteenth Amendment's constitutionally guaranteed right of an accused to hear the charges against him or her and to be heard by the court having jurisdiction over the matter.

entrapment: The act of government officials or agents (usually police) inducing a person to commit a crime that the person would not have otherwise committed.

equity: Equal, fair justice. Also, a system of law in England defining where certain types of cases could be heard.

establishment clause: Clause in the First Amendment that states clearly that "Congress shall make no law respecting an establishment of religion."

evidence: Various types of data that provide a court with information.

exclusive jurisdiction: The only courts that can hear specific cases.

exigent: Emergency.

expunge: Destroy information.

Federalists: Colonists who favored a strong federal government.

felony: The most serious level of criminal offenses as defined by statute.

free exercise clause: Clause in the First Amendment that declares that "Congress shall make no law . . . prohibiting the free exercise [of religion]."

freedom of assembly: A fundamental First Amendment right to gather under circumstances that would not negatively affect the safety of the public.

fresh pursuit: A situation in which police are immediately in pursuit of a suspect.

frisk: A reasonable search for weapons for the protection of the government agent and others. A less intrusive search than a full search, but one that is still regulated by the First Amendment. Generally used by law enforcement agents to "pat down" a subject for safety reasons. Any evidence or contraband may be seized.

fruit of the poisonous tree: Evidence that is tainted because it was obtained from other evidence that came from a constitutionally invalid search or activity.

general jurisdiction: Courts having the ability to hear a wide range of cases.

good faith: Officers are unaware that they are acting in violation of a suspect's constitutional rights. A standard by which one is assumed to have acted honestly in carrying out a legal duty.

Great Compromise: The agreement reached in drafting the Constitution giving each state an equal vote in the Senate and a proportionate vote in the House.

habeas corpus: Latin for "you should have the body." A writ of habeas corpus challenges the legality of custodial detention.

harmless error: Tainted or illegal evidence that is not critical to proving the case against the defendant and so will not cause the case to be dismissed.

hearing: Process in which a judicial body hears assertions regarding a case.

hearsay: Testimony made in court about something heard outside of court offered as proof of the matter asserted.

holding: The rule of law applied to the particular facts of the case and the actual decision.

homicide: The killing of a person by another. There are a number of levels of homicide defined by statute and common law, including justifiable and excusable homicide, etc.

hot pursuit: The period an individual is being immediately chased by law enforcement. A period that influences Fourth Amendment search and seizure concerns; the person to be arrested knows an arrest is about to be made and is actively trying to escape it.

hung jury: A situation in which a jury cannot reach a consensus and the case is ended, but usually tried again.

immunity: Exemption from a legal duty, including diplomatic exemption.

impeach: Discredit or remove from public office. A term used to imply inaccuracy of a witness.

in camera: Latin for "in the chamber." A court hears a case in the presence only of those directly involved.

in dictum: The court's side opinion.

in re: A Latin term that means *concerning*. Often used in juvenile cases to avoid the adult case heading of the government versus the defendant.

inadmissible: Not allowed.

incarcerated: In custody.

inculpatory evidence: Evidence that supports something.

indictment: A formal accusation of a defendant, usually by a grand jury.

indigent: Poor, unable to afford a lawyer.

informant: A person who gives government agencies information on criminal activity.

injunction: A court order for a person to do, or refrain from doing, something.

Jim Crow laws: Laws passed in the American South in the 1800s to discriminate against blacks; the laws strictly segregated blacks from whites in schools, restaurants, street cars, hospitals and cemeteries. Such laws discriminating against blacks by restricting certain liberties were accepted by the Supreme Court until 1954, when separate was no longer considered equal.

judge-made law: Decisions handed down by judges through precedent. Also referred to as *common law*.

judicial activism: Allowing judges to interpret the Constitution and its amendments.

judicial review: The power of a court to analyze decisions of other government entities and lower courts.

jurisdiction: The authority of a particular court to hear certain types of cases, or referencing a geographical area within which particular laws apply.

jury system: A system dating from nineteenth century France in which a group of peers of an accused determine the outcome of the matter.

juvenile: A person determined by the law to not be an adult (usually decided by each state). Most states assert that one under seven years of age is incapable of committing a crime, and that one under twelve or fourteen is incapable of committing a crime unless specific facts indicate the juvenile clearly understood the nature of his or her act(s).

larceny: Theft.

law: A rule of society; a legal rule enforced through consequences that a society establishes to maintain the values of that society.

law enforcement officer: An individual who has legal authority to enforce laws at a particular jurisdictional level, eg. federal, state, county, municipal.

legal opinion: Statement from a court that usually contains (1) a description of the facts, (2) a statement of the legal issues presented for decision, (3) the relevant rules of law, (4) the holding and (5) the policies and reasons that support the holding.

lex: Latin for "law."

libel: Written information that damages the reputation of another.

limited jurisdiction: Restriction of the types of cases that might be heard by a particular court.

litigation: A legal matter that is contested before a legal tribunal. A trail or lawsuit.

living law: The concept that a legal system, such as that in the United States, can change to adapt to the perceived needs of the society it serves; legislative authority can be implemented to change the law as desired.

loyalists: Colonists who did not support the boycott of British goods in the colonies; colonists who still paid allegiance to the British monarchy.

Magna Carta (also spelled *Charta*): The document signed in 1215 granting English citizens certain basic rights that influenced the American Constitution and Bill of Rights.

malfeasance: Misconduct.

malice: The intent to commit a wrongful act that will cause harm to others or make them suffer.

mandate: An order or directive.

mens rea: Criminal intent, the defendant's state of mind.

militia: An armed group of citizens who defend their community as emergencies arise.

minutemen: Colonial soldiers.

misdemeanor: A statutorily defined level of offense that carries a lesser penalty than a felony but still has the potential for jail time and/or a fine as a punishment.

mistrial: A situation in which a trial is discontinued because something jeopardizes the fairness of the trial, which still allows for another trial.

municipal: A locality or local body of government.

natural law: The principles that would govern people if there was no law or before established law, based on reason.

negligence: The legal term that describes a lack of required care that results in injury.

no-knock entry: An unannounced forced entry by government officers authorized by an arrest or search warrant.

notice: Advising one involved in a legal matter that specific action is pending. Adequate notice is a constitutional requirement of due process.

obscenity: Communication that is sufficiently violative of community norms pertaining to sexual matters that it is not considered protected by the First Amendment.

opinion: A written statement by a judge explaining the legal issues and facts involved in a case, the precedents on which the opinion is based and the decision.

ordinances: Laws or codes established at the local level, that is, the municipal or county level.

original jurisdiction: Courts authorized to hear cases first, try them and render such decisions. Often called *trial courts.*

Patriots: Colonists who supported the boycott of British goods in the colonies; colonists who owed allegiance to America rather than to the British monarchy.

penal codes: Criminal codes or laws.

penumbra: A type of shadow in astronomy with the principle extending to the idea that certain constitutional rights are implied within other constitutional rights.

petit jury: A jury made up of fewer members than a grand jury.

petition: A formal request made to a court, or in relation to the First Amendment privilege to petition the government. It is a way to communicate with public officials.

petition for certiorari: A request that the Supreme Court review the decision of a lower court.

petition for the writ of habeas corpus: A federal appeal for release of the defendant or a speedy trial.

plain feel doctrine: Items felt during a stop and frisk may also be retrieved if the officers reasonably believe the items are contraband.

plain view doctrine: Unconcealed evidence that officers see while engaged in a lawful activity is admissible in court.

plaintiff: One who initiates a civil case.

plea: A defendant's assertion to a question of guilt in court.

plea bargaining: An acceptable form of negotiating in criminal court by which the prosecutor and defendant agree to action to be taken by the court so as to avoid a trial.

pleadings: Requests made to the court by those involved with a case.

pluralism: A society in which numerous distinct ethnic, religious or cultural groups coexist within one nation; the idea that a nation is made up of many ethnic, religious and cultural groups.

police: Official law enforcement personnel at a federal, state or local level having powers of arrest and official authority.

police power: The authority of government to pass laws for the protection and welfare of the public, reserved by the states by the Constitution.

popular literature: Publications written for the layperson, for example, *Time* or *Newsweek.*

precedent: An earlier decision by a court that may influence future cases.

preferred freedoms approach: A position that stresses that civil liberties are to take precedence over other constitutional values since they are requisite to a democracy. Under this approach, the burden lies with the government to prove clear and present danger exists when a freedom is limited.

prejudice: A negative attitude regarding a person or thing.

preventive detention: The right of judges to consider the potential criminal conduct of those accused of serious offenses and deny bail on those grounds.

prima facie: That which is obvious, or is, by itself, enough to prove an issue without other argument. For example, in most states, a blood alcohol level of a certain percent constitutes prima facie evidence of intoxication.

primary information sources: Raw data or the original information.

prior restraint: A restriction on publishing certain materials.

private security officers: Security personnel who are not government agents and who are not restrained by the constitutional requirements imposed on public law enforcement personnel.

pro se: Appearing in court without an attorney, representing oneself.

probable cause: Stronger than reasonable suspicion. The sum total of layers of information and the synthesis of what the police have heard, what they know and what they observe as trained officers.

procedural due process: Constitutionally guaranteed rights of fairness in how the law is carried out.

process, service of: A constitutionally acceptable manner of providing information pertaining to a legal controversy. Acceptable notice is a due process requirement.

professional literature: Publications written for the practitioner in the field, for example, *The Police Chief, Police* or *Corrections Today.*

prohibited person: An individual to whom, under the Gun Control Act, it is forbidden to sell firearms.

promulgate: Publish or announce officially a law or rule.

proportionality analysis: In essence, making the punishment fit the crime.

prosecutor: The officer of the court who represents the government in a case.

public safety exception: Allows officers to question suspects without first giving the *Miranda* warning if the information sought sufficiently affects the officers' and the public's safety.

punitive damages: Fines above and beyond the actual economic loss to punish the defendant in a civil trial.

ratify: Approve an amendment.

reasonable: Sensible, rational, justifiable.

reasonable doubt: A situation in which a juror is unable to believe something to a moral certainty.

reasonable force: The amount of force that police or private citizens may be authorized by law to use to protect themselves or others or to take an offender into custody.

reasonableness: A standard sometimes used in court or by law to determine what a "reasonable person" in a similar set of circumstances would be expected to do.

reasonableness Fourth Amendment approach: An interpretation of the Fourth Amendment that sees the reasonableness clause and the warrant clause as separate issues.

reasonableness test: A test of the constitutionality of searches and seizures based on balancing government and individual interests and the objective basis of the searches and seizures. Also referred to as the *balancing approach.*

recesses: Periods when the Supreme Court does not hear cases but rather considers administrative matters and writes opinions. Also, breaks taken during the course of the trial.

redress of grievances: The constitutionally guaranteed right to express concerns, complaints or thoughts to the government.

remand: Return a case to the lower court for further action.

reserve powers: Powers retained by the states.

resolution: A statement by a legislative body holding less authority than an ordinance or law; a referenced proposition of law.

reverse: Overturn the decision of a lower court.

reverse discrimination: Giving preferential treatment in hiring and promoting to women and protected classes to the perceived detriment of white males.

ROR: Released on their own recognizance, meaning that the court trusts defendants to show up in court when required. No bail money is required. (Also called RPR.)

scholarly literature: Publications written for those interested in theory, research and statistical analysis, for example, *Justice Quarterly.*

search and seizure: The examination of a person or property and the seizing of a person or property by government officials, both of which are regulated by the Fourth Amendment.

search warrant: A judicially issued order authorizing the search of a person or property.

secondary information sources: Information based on the raw data or the original information.

sedition: A false, scandalous or malicious assertion against government that is not protected by the First Amendment.

selective incorporation: Holds that only the provisions of the Bill of Rights that are fundamental to the American legal system are applied to the states through the due process clause of the Fourteenth Amendment.

self-incrimination: Testifying against oneself.

shepardizing: Using the resource *Shepard's,* published for each set of official volumes of cases, indicating if a case's status has changed. (Available on CD-ROM.)

sittings: Periods when the Supreme Court hears cases.

slander: Spoken information that damages the reputation of another.

standing: The right to object to the reasonableness of a search or seizure and to claim a violation of other constitutional rights.

stare decisis: Latin for "to stand by decided matters." A legal principle that requires that precedents set in one case be followed in cases having similar circumstances, thus assuring consistency in the law.

statement: Any oral or written declaration or assertion.

statute of limitations: A statutorily determined period after which particular legal actions may not be pursued.

statutory law: Law set forth by legislatures or governing bodies. A written law promulgated by the legislative body having jurisdiction to make such law. Also called *codified law.*

stop: A brief detention of a person, short of an arrest, based on specific and articulable facts for the purpose of investigating suspicious activity.

stop and frisk: A brief investigatory stop of a person by the police and a pat-down of the suspect for weapons.

substantive rights: Rights essential to personal liberty as guaranteed by the Constitution, including freedom of speech and religion.

tort: A civil wrong by one individual against another, with the remedy most often being either an order by the court for particular action or compensation.

trial: A hearing in court to reach a determination on a legal matter.

unenumerated rights: Rights not specifically listed in the Bill of Rights.

venue: The geographical area in which a specific case may come to trial and the area from which the jury is selected.

verdict: The decision reached in a trial.

voluntariness test: A determination as to whether one voluntarily and knowingly relinquished his or her constitutional rights, without pressure to do so.

waiver: A purposeful, voluntary and knowing giving up of a known right.

waiver test: Citizens may waive their rights, but only if they do so voluntarily, knowingly and intentionally. The waiver is what makes the subsequent action reasonable.

wiretapping: The interception of telephone conversations of others.

zones of privacy: Areas into which the government may not intrude.

Author Index

Subject Index